ASIA'S AGING SECURITY

CONTEMPORARY ASIA IN THE WORLD

CONTEMPORARY ASIA IN THE WORLD

David C. Kang and Victor D. Cha, Editors

This series aims to address a gap in the public-policy and scholarly discussion of Asia. It seeks to promote books and studies that are on the cutting edge of their disciplines or promote multidisciplinary or interdisciplinary research but are also accessible to a wider readership. The editors seek to showcase the best scholarly and public-policy arguments on Asia from any field, including politics, history, economics, and cultural studies.

The Black Box: Demystifying the Study of Korean Unification and North Korea, Victor D. Cha, 2024

South Korea's Grand Strategy: Making Its Own Destiny, Ramon Pacheco Pardo, 2023

War and Peace in the Taiwan Strait, Scott L. Kastner, 2022

Power and Restraint in China's Rise, Chin-Hao Huang, 2022

Line of Advantage: Japan's Grand Strategy in the Era of Abe Shinzō, Michael J. Green, 2022

Japan's Aging Peace: Pacifism and Militarism in the Twenty-First Century, Tom Phuong Le, 2021

Japan's New Regional Reality: Geoeconomic Strategy in the Asia-Pacific, Saori N. Katada, 2020

Dying for Rights: Putting North Korea's Human Rights Abuses on the Record, Sandra Fahy, 2019

GMO China: How Global Debates Transformed China's Agricultural Biotechnology Policies, Cong Cao, 2018

Nuclear North Korea: A Debate on Engagement Strategies, revised and updated edition, Victor D. Cha and David C. Kang, 2018

Japan, South Korea, and the United States Nuclear Umbrella: Deterrence After the Cold War, Terrence Roehrig, 2017

Japan's Security Renaissance: New Policies and Politics for the Twenty-First Century, Andrew L. Oros, 2017

The China Boom: Why China Will Not Rule the World, Ho-fung Hung, 2015

Nation at Play: A History of Sport in India, Ronojoy Sen, 2015

The Japan–South Korea Identity Clash: East Asian Security and the United States, Brad Glosserman and Scott A. Snyder, 2015

For a complete list of books in the series, please see the Columbia University Press website.

Asia's Aging Security

HOW DEMOGRAPHIC CHANGE AFFECTS
AMERICA'S ALLIES AND ADVERSARIES

Andrew L. Oros

Columbia University Press
New York

Columbia University Press
Publishers Since 1893
New York   Chichester, West Sussex

Copyright © 2025 Columbia University Press
All rights reserved

Library of Congress Cataloging-in-Publication Data

Names: Oros, Andrew L. author
Title: Asia's aging security : how demographic change affects
America's allies and adversaries / Andrew L. Oros.
Description: New York : Columbia University Press, [2025] | Series: Contemporary
asia in the world | Includes bibliographical references and index.
Identifiers: LCCN 2025001670 (print) | LCCN 2025001671 (ebook) |
ISBN 9780231205603 hardback | ISBN 9780231205610 trade paperback |
ISBN 9780231556088 ebook
Subjects: LCSH: Population aging—Political aspects—Asia | National security—Asia |
United States—Foreign relations
Classification: LCC HQ1064.A78 O76 2025 (print) | LCC HQ1064.A78 (ebook)

Cover design: Chang Jae Lee
Cover image: © Shutterstock

GPSR Authorized Representative: Easy Access System Europe,
Mustamäe tee 50, 10621 Tallinn, Estonia, gpsr.requests@easproject.com

To my graying friends and mentors,
for illuminating the path forward with style and grace

CONTENTS

CONTENTS

FIGURES AND TABLES

NOTE ON ASIAN FAMILY AND PLACE NAMES

Asian family and place names appear differently in English in different publications over time due to different systems of transliterating Asian language scripts, differing social conventions, varying in-house style policies of publications, and politics.

In many Asian countries, family names (often referred to as "last names" or "surnames") precede given names—however, when publishing in English, many Asian authors choose to follow Western convention. In an effort to maintain consistency in English, this book uses the name order most common in English-language publications. Thus, for example, China's and South Korea's leaders appear with their family name first, while Japan's prime minister appears with the family name following the given name.

Where place names are contentious, I endeavor to acknowledge the differing names on first use and then revert to the most common usage throughout the text, except in cases where the disputed name is central to the argument of this book. Also, I employ common colloquial references to countries in the region: China for the People's Republic of China, South Korea for the Republic of Korea, etc. Although the status of Taiwan as a "country" is contested (as opposed to being a part of China), for purposes of linguistic flow, there are places in this book where Taiwan is referred to indirectly as a country.

NOTE ON ASIAN FAMILY AND PLACE NAMES

Finally, I have chosen generally to omit macrons and other markings around foreign-language words, except in rare cases where they are necessary for clarity.

ACKNOWLEDGMENTS

Many individuals and institutions contributed to this book project, more than I can individually acknowledge, but several groups deserve special mention. First, I wish to thank my major financial supporters: Washington College (for providing an extended sabbatical leave and several research grants), the Woodrow Wilson International Center for Scholars (for providing an extended, sixteen-month residential fellowship), and three Asia-based institutions that funded roughly one month each of field work in their respective countries: the Global Taiwan Institute, the Japan Foundation, and the Korea Foundation. The Mike and Maureen Mansfield Foundation—including through its partner, the Luce Foundation—also provided intellectual fellowship and travel support through their inaugural Mansfield-Luce Asia Scholars Network program. In addition, the Wilson Center arranged for several stellar research assistants during my time there: With much gratitude and respect, I thank Bailey Brya, Andrew Gordan, and Meghan Shoop.

Keisuke Nakashima of Kobe City University codeveloped the dataset drawn from UN data that formed the basis of the IP-16/OIP-12 demographic data presented in this project. He also spent many hours with me in person and on Zoom explaining the intricacies of the data, based on his excellent earlier work in this area.

Several individuals helped me to connect with scholars and practitioners related to the demographics–security nexus abroad. I would like to thank, in particular, Yen-hsin Alice Cheng and Chih-Jou Jay Chen of Academia Sinica, Brad Glosserman of Tama University, Hsin-hsin Pan of Soochow University, Cheol-hee Park and Seong-ho Sheen at Seoul National University, and Motohiro Tsuchiya of Keio University. And, in the United States, my sincere thanks especially to Richard Bush, Darcie Draudt, Ian Easton, Kyle Ferrier, Bonnie Glaser, Satu Limaye, Scott Snyder, Troy Stangarone, and Ross Tokola for helping me connect with scholars and institutions in the Indo-Pacific.

Many individuals have commented on draft work and/or recommended me for grants, but special thanks go to John Bradford, Zack Cooper, Ellen Frost, Michael Green, Karl Jackson, Richard Jackson, Nori Katagiri, Eric Langenbacher, Andrew Nathan, Katy Oh, Saadia Pekkanen, Jennifer Sciubba, Amy Searight, JP Singh, Drew Thompson, Hiroshi Yamazoe, Toshi Yoshihara, and James Zumwalt. Tom Le, who himself has written an excellent book on *Japan's Aging Peace*, was especially generous with his time and ideas, reading through multiple draft chapters. I also would like to thank the two anonymous peer reviewers of the draft manuscript for their many helpful suggestions. Finally, many thanks to my editor at Columbia University Press, Caelyn Cobb, for her flexibility and support over the longer-than-expected course of this project that originated during the pandemic; to assistant editor Emily Simon, for answering so many of my questions and offering helpful suggestions throughout the process; and to Anita O'Brien, for her improvements in my prose and usefully flagging numerous other issues in the copy-editing stage.

The Covid-19 pandemic emerged at the start of this project and continued to pose many logistical challenges through its completion. I am especially grateful to the individuals and institutions who worked with me to devise work-arounds, in particular my "Covid Cohort" of visiting fellows at the Wilson Center for their good cheer and companionship in difficult times.

Last, but first in my heart, thank you to my husband and family for their understanding of all of my time away from occasions large and small. I've missed you!

ASIA'S AGING SECURITY

INTRODUCTION

Asia's traditional great powers are together experiencing one of the most consequential challenges of the twenty-first century: the rapid aging of populations that is unprecedented in human history. The median age in China, Japan, Taiwan, South Korea, and Russia, among others, reached into the forties by 2025, and the share of the population of retirement age skyrocketed by up to 50 percent in the 2010s due to declining birth rates and longer life expectancies.[1] Even in territories where population sizes are still growing, median ages and numbers of residents age sixty-five or more are rising—including in the United States, another major Indo-Pacific power. Virtually everywhere in the region is experiencing societal aging and its consequences.

Managing the growing number of security concerns in the Indo-Pacific region is another major challenge facing regional and global security actors. Although major regional powers China, Japan, Russia, and others have managed to maintain a "long peace" for over half a century, in sharp contrast to other world regions, vexing issues such as the divisions of the Korean peninsula and of China–Taiwan as well as new security challenges from a resurgent China, climate change, new technologies, and numerous gray-zone concerns—residing somewhere between war and peace—present a troubling and growing potential for conflict.

What international relations scholars have long referred to as a "security dilemma"—where efforts to increase one's own security can lead to other states increasing their threatening postures in response—appears to be intensifying among Asia's aging powers as new weapons are developed and new methods of conflict devised.[2] There has emerged an "aging security dilemma" in East Asia in two senses of the term: (1) long-standing conflict flashpoints continue and in some ways have intensified in recent years as new weapons are developed and deployed, and (2) as aging states devise and deploy new methods to ensure their security in response to rapid aging, their efforts cause concern among and reactions from neighboring states.

In addition to the "graying" of their populations and continued concerns about numerous conflict flashpoints, regional states face a range of new "gray" conflicts—daily cyberattacks, territorial incursions by nonmilitary actors, and other nefarious actions—that threaten the tenuous military balance. A "dual graying" challenge in the Indo-Pacific today therefore affects not only these states themselves but also a key ally to several of them, the United States, as well as other regional states that rely on Asia's aging powers for commerce, investment, and broader security assistance.[3] This book focuses on how Asia's rapidly aging U.S. allies, U.S. adversaries, and potential partners are responding to these new security challenges, along with the implications of these strategies for the United States and for our understanding of the security conduct of rapidly aging states in general.

Reconsidering Expectations from Rapidly Aging States

Contrary to the predictions of the limited existing scholarly literature on the effect of rapid aging on the likelihood of interstate war, in the region of the world that is experiencing the most severe aging among security rivals— East Asia—tensions are rising and states are increasing their military spending and development of new, more advanced weapons systems.[4] Although this may not lead to war—particularly when other types of conflict are becoming more intense—it still is an area of great concern due to the potential for catastrophic conflict as well as the spillover effects on other regions.

Why are tensions rising and avenues of conflict intensifying if aging states collectively are less likely to go to war, according to statistical analysis and logical deduction presented in previous studies that anticipate the effect of rapid aging on national security? How have regional states—and the United States—addressed these dual aspects of a "graying security" while also continuing to prepare for the seemingly growing potential for the outbreak of traditional military conflict, and how should they?

This book offers answers to these questions based on our early experience with rapidly aging powers in Asia and on demographic projections for the Indo-Pacific region for the next several decades for even more rapid aging. In addition, this book considers the evolving nature of the security challenges facing the Indo-Pacific region, including the proliferation of gray-zone challenges and the planned responses of concerned states to this dual graying. As a country long involved in security matters in what it refers to still as the "Asia-Pacific" region, Russia is included in this study despite the majority of its population residing in its European territory. An explication of the sixteen "Indo-Pacific" countries and territories at the core of this study and the forty-six countries and territories included in the demographic dataset created for this book is provided later in this introduction.

Demographic change is increasingly referenced in discussions of the region's security future, but, in fact, it is already part of the region's security present and recent past. Several rapidly aging states already struggle to meet recruiting targets for their armed forces, even those with mandatory military service, accelerating a shift toward labor-saving technologies and new military strategies that utilize such technologies. Moreover, the major powers of the region all have increased military spending to pay for such new technologies as well as the higher cost of labor and to convey a position of strength despite rapidly aging populations. Tensions are rising after an arms buildup that is partly the result of the region's late-stage rapid aging—what could be seen as the "aging security dilemma" of the twenty-first century.[5]

The Northeast Asian states of Japan, North and South Korea, and China/ Taiwan—as well as Eurasian power Russia—are at the leading edge of rapid aging worldwide. Japan became the world's first "super-aged" global power in 2005, when over 20 percent of its population reached age 65 or over (65+). By comparison, the equivalent figure for the U.S. population in 2005 was 12.4 percent and for the world, 6.3 percent—putting the United States in the "aging" category used by demographers, where 7–14 percent of the population has reached age 65+. In 2023 Japan's aged 65+ population share climbed to 30 percent, and it is projected to rise to nearly 40 percent by 2050. Nine other regional states and territories are projected to become super-aged in this time frame as well, while numerous others will enter the "aging" or "aged" categories—the latter being where 14–20 percent of the population is aged 65 or over, the category that describes the United States in 2024.

Japan and Russia also began to experience a shrinking of their total population sizes around the turn of the twenty-first century, though Russia's population subsequently grew modestly in the 2010s before resuming its shrinking in 2020. The South Korean and Taiwanese populations began to shrink in 2020 (according to their national statistics; 2022 and 2021, respectively, according to UN population data), and China's in 2022. This phase characterized by population shrinkage has been described as a fifth stage of demographic transition that only a few states in the world have yet entered due to rapid aging, but many more will by midcentury.[6] According to a 2020 study by the Organization of Economic Cooperation and Development (OECD), by 2050 ten "Asia-Pacific" countries will be considered an "ageing society" (as compared to eight countries in 2020), five as an "aged society" (six countries in 2020), and eleven as a "super-aged society" (only one country in 2020, Japan).[7]

We now have over a decade of experience witnessing how rapidly aging states, in Asia and elsewhere, act to ensure their security and how they are planning for a future of even more aged populations and smaller workforces and total populations. What we have witnessed—rising defense spending, escalating traditional and gray-zone conflicts, and planning for more sophisticated weaponry, among them—is not what was predicted from older societies in most previous studies. Chapter 1 of this volume reviews many of these previous studies, linking and contrasting their arguments to this book.

The rapid aging of Asia's traditional powers affects national security strategies and readiness through both direct and indirect means. The most direct effect is the shrinking pool of young men to join militaries, which can be addressed by widening recruitment pools (attracting more women, accepting a wider age range, or lowering bars to entry) or relying more on technology to minimize the need for human labor—both of which already are well underway in rapidly aging states in Asia and elsewhere. Indirectly, the effects of a shrinking workforce and competing demands for government spending (such as on pensions and eldercare) challenge defense budgets and, perhaps, more activist military strategies more broadly. In addition, the changing ratio of population size among generations and, in some countries, a growing imbalance in the numbers of males and females are among other demographic factors that affect national and regional security dynamics. In short, the cases illustrated in the following chapters clearly show that rapid aging of the traditional major powers in the Indo-Pacific has contributed to new security policies and priorities that result in new strategies explained in this book.

Important Lessons Already Apparent from Regional Rapid Aging to Date

The Indo-Pacific region more broadly will experience differential demographic change by midcentury, a microcosm of global population shifts underway, where some states will rapidly age and even shrink in population size while others will age more slowly and continue to grow and yet others—all lesser-developed countries—will see continued rapid population growth. Adjusting to these shifts is a near and present necessity, not something far off that governments can wait to address. The aging of Asia matters to regional and global security, in addition to the economic and sociological realms that have been examined in greater detail to date.

The first decades of rapid aging in Asia suggest greater possibilities for conflict than previously imagined, particularly when combined with rising cases of gray-zone security challenges. Changes in technology and advances in health make even aging powers formidable, especially large-population states. These aging powers—which include the United States, to a lesser degree—are highly likely to be the major security actors in the region for decades to come, despite their projected demographic transitions. Thus, understanding new security behaviors as a result of rapid aging—including super-aged status—should be of paramount interest to those seeking to manage and to ensure regional and global stability.

Understanding better the relationship between demographic change and security in the Indo-Pacific also should be of interest beyond just those focused on military security in the Indo-Pacific. Although different countries delineate the boundaries of the region differently, over half of the world's population resides in the Indo-Pacific, which comprises about one-third of world GDP (or well over half, if the United States is included) and about 30 percent of global defense spending (upward of 70 percent if the United States is included).[8] The region also is where the great powers of the world—as well as several rising powers—seek to coexist.

Thus, preventing the outbreak of large-scale war in the Indo-Pacific as well as managing gray-zone conflict are important for global security and prosperity. Moreover, further explicating the linkage between aging populations and security policies in the region should help scholars and analysts better understand this relationship in other regions. Finally, and related to a core audience of this book, the aging of Asia—long-time U.S. allies, principal U.S. adversaries, and current and potential security partners—matters to the United States and its future security policies for the region.

A close examination of the first decades of rapid aging in Asia reveals three important lessons for regional and global security:

1. Even a close grouping of rapidly aging states does not necessarily lead to lessened tensions or fewer perceived threats. The idea of a future "geriatric peace" may be more aspirational than an actual result of rapid aging.[9]
2. Old assumptions about the effect of aging on security need to be revised due to new technologies and new sorts of security threats (including gray-zone conflict), and based on the actual conduct of rapidly aging states to date.
3. Aging and other projected demographic shifts in the Indo-Pacific suggest changes in the security landscape to come, as seen already in rising "middle power" states, new technologies in the process of being implemented, and security planning documents published by multiple actors in the region.

These changes also intersect with efforts by the United States and its partners to reconceptualize and reinvigorate the network of security alliances and partnerships in the region. There are multiple, overlapping logics for why the United States needs to reimagine its network of allies and partners in the Indo-Pacific. Several recent studies have made this case cogently.[10] Each of these studies ignores another important justification: Not only is the system itself showing its age, but many U.S. allies and partners themselves are rapidly aging, in some cases leading to a relative decline in their regional power and to competing future priorities in a broadening conception of their national security.

In sum, this book seeks to explain (1) how the Indo-Pacific region already has experienced important demographic shifts that are affecting security policy outcomes, (2) that security outcomes to date generally have not conformed to predictions in existing scholarly literature about the likely effect of rapid aging on state behavior, and (3) that future projected demographic change will likely have an even greater effect on security policy outcomes than the limited change we have seen to date.

THE SHIFTING GRAVITY OF DEMOGRAPHIC CHANGE GLOBALLY

To admit that demography is not destiny is not to deny its power. Gravity is not destiny either—we have learned to build skyscrapers and airplanes that defy it. Yet we have done so not by ignoring the pervasive effects of gravity but by better measuring and understanding gravity, as well as other forces and how they interact with it.

—JACK A. GOLDSTONE, *POLITICAL DEMOGRAPHY*

Demographic change is a worldwide phenomenon with global implications. This change will not determine the future of security policy of regional governments or regional security overall, but *will* set new parameters for policy choices. Many states outside of the Indo-Pacific also face rapid aging and decreasing total population sizes, primarily in Europe. Of the eight states with populations over ten million that experienced population shrinkage in the 2010s, six were in Europe—in addition to Syria and Japan.[11] By contrast, in Africa and the Middle East, major security concerns stem from quickly *growing* populations and youth bulges. Reversing a major trend of the twentieth century, where populations ballooned around the globe, only Asia and Africa are projected to see substantial population growth in the rest of the twenty-first century, and even that growth will be seen in only parts of each of those regions. By one projection, 98 percent of population growth in the twenty-first century will be in less-developed countries.[12]

Meanwhile, rising median ages and increasing parity between working-age and elderly populations (reflecting a reduction in the number of working-age people supporting the elderly) can be seen on every continent, including in numerous middle-income and lower-income countries, but are especially concentrated at the higher-income end of the spectrum. It was only in 2000 that any country had ever reached a median age above forty (Japan at 41.2 in 2000).[13] In the 2017 UN population data, U.S. ally Japan had the highest median age in the world, followed by U.S. allies Germany and then Italy.[14] By contrast, as compiled by one study, "a majority of the world's people live in poor countries that are very young"—including large youth populations in several countries that are examined in this book, such as India, Indonesia, the Philippines, and Vietnam.[15]

The United Nations Population Division projects that the total global population will peak in the mid-2080s at around 10.3 billion and end the century around 10.2 billion, but other credible studies predict a peak around 2070 under 10 billion with the century ending at around 9 billion.[16] Thus, there are projected to be around 2 billion more people by the end of the century than in the 2020s, and around the same range as soon as 2050. Continued declines in fertility and growing concerns over the long-term effect of the most recent and future pandemics as well as the effects of climate change are the primary reasons for the variance in the projections. According to one study, twenty-three countries could see their current populations halved by the end of the century, including Japan, Thailand, Italy, and Spain.[17] One noted, mass-market book, *Empty Planet*, argues that population growth may slow even more quickly, peaking at around 9 billion between 2040 and 2060, based on trends in the 2010s toward much lower fertility worldwide than projected for midcentury in most other studies.[18] This book, by contrast, limits discussion of demographic implications for policy to 2050—by which time no major country is projected to see such dramatic population shrinkage.

In sum, demographic change projected for the Indo-Pacific region in this century mirrors the global trend of differential growth, but it also differs from the global situation in that there are few remaining fast-growing populations in the Indo-Pacific region—as further explained in chapter 2. The concentration of rapidly aging states in Northeast Asia also mirrors a similar concentration in Europe, another region containing largely economically developed states. Chapter 1 illustrates how many ideas about the effect of changing demographics were based on the twentieth-century booming population growth across the board, and how more recent scholarship has begun to adapt to and reflect this new era of differential growth and rapid aging. This book seeks to build on our understanding of the effects of rapid aging and differential population growth/shrinkage on security policies and behavior.

VIEWING CHANGING DEMOGRAPHICS IN A BROADER INDO-PACIFIC CONTEXT

Regional demographic shifts also have contributed to change in how the region as a whole is viewed. Multiple states in the region, led by U.S. allies Japan and Australia, began to describe the region as the "Indo-Pacific" rather than "Asia-Pacific" or East Asia in the mid-2010s. The United States, India, and the Association of Southeast Asian Nations (ASEAN) regional organization, among others, followed in the late 2010s. China, by contrast, explicitly rejects this conceptualization, in part because it seeks to delegitimize the long-term U.S. presence in the region.[19] Russia similarly rejects the reframing of the region as the Indo-Pacific.[20] This change in conceptualization is not only due to demographic shifts—economic and military growth as well as military strategy also were important factors—but shifting demographics is one factor driving a new conception of the region that now includes what has recently become the world's most populous state, India, as well as numerous other states and territories not traditionally seen as part of the regional security environment.

There are multiple conceptions of which states and territories are included in this new vision of the Indo-Pacific region, but all include the forty-six states and territories that make up the dataset described as "Indo-Pacific 28" (IP28) in numerous tables and figures in this book.[21] Chapter 2 includes a more extended discussion of different conceptions of the region and explains the rationale for the focus of this study on sixteen Indo-Pacific states and territories—the "IP16"—especially important as actors in regional security: the seven Northeast Asian states and territories (China, Japan, Mongolia, North and South Korea, Russia, and Taiwan), six Southeast Asian states (Indonesia, Malaysia, the Philippines, Singapore, Thailand, and Vietnam), plus Australia, India, and New Zealand from the broader Indo-Pacific. In addition, as illustrated in the following chapters, other states—including small-population states like in the Pacific Islands— also can become important in regional security and thus are included in an IP28 dataset.

Differential Demographics in the Broader Indo-Pacific

The Indo-Pacific region faces many long-standing security challenges. As a result of demographic change, approaches to managing these existing challenges have been evolving and will continue to evolve. New security challenges also have emerged and will continue to do so due to demographic change and other reasons. Traditional regional rivals Japan and China will experience further population shrinking and rapid aging in this decade, while other large states in the region—India, Indonesia, and the Philippines among them—will see population growth and remain relatively youthful. Some "middle powers" also will rapidly age and experience population shrinkage (South Korea, for example), while others will struggle to maintain the demographic status quo (Vietnam), and yet others will grow but also rapidly age (Australia).

The United States has been the demographic exception in the developed world and among the existing great powers[22]—with a predicted population *increase* of over forty million people from 2020 to 2050 and less rapid aging—but must adjust to the rapid aging of its traditional allies while also eyeing changes in the security postures of its aging adversaries. All the large states of the developed world (the United Kingdom, France, Germany, Italy, and Japan among them) as well as China and Russia will see more rapid aging and, for most, outright population shrinkage within the next few decades—with most already experiencing these effects. The United States also may need to adjust to less robust population growth than expected just a decade ago, as seen in the latest U.S. census data from 2020, a trend that is likely to deepen due to the longer-term effects of the Covid-19 pandemic and if the restrictions on immigration visible in the past decade continue or intensify. These developments underscore the political choices that lead both to shifting demographics themselves as well as to how states adjust to demographic change.

Demographic change in the Indo-Pacific will challenge each state differently and will interact with technological change to create both new security challenges and new opportunities to enhance security. Overall, the median age in the Indo-Pacific will rise in every state in the region, with substantial rise in many key security actors, including five states/territories projected to reach median ages over 50 by 2050.[23] These include the "leading edge" of aging in Northeast Asia—Japan, South Korea, and

Taiwan—examined in chapter 3 (all of which will reach a median age of 50 or higher in the 2030s) as well as China and Singapore (examined in chapters 4 and 5).

The timing of regional demographic change varies, which affects regional security dynamics, but a commonality among the states of Northeast Asia is rapid aging in the short term. Beyond Northeast Asia, and important for Indo-Pacific security dynamics and the U.S. security posture in the region, the demographic story of the Indo-Pacific is not all about aging and population shrinkage. India's population is expected to grow by 276 million from 2024 to 2050, and Indonesia (by 38 million) and Asia as a whole are expected to grow by over 485 million (including Western Asia), the latter two using the UN Population Division's median-variant projection. What can be expected due to this growing population divergence is a further shift in regional attention away from the traditional powers located in Northeast Asia toward a multipolar security (and economic) environment in the Indo-Pacific as population sizes change and economic growth and total economic sizes also likely shift as a result.

Working-age populations—which are also the military fighting-age populations to a large extent—also are projected to grow in numerous regional states where total populations are still expanding, leading to these states aging much more slowly. Politics and policy will affect how well these states might benefit from a forthcoming "demographic dividend," a term demographers and economists have used to refer to the potential economic growth bonus that may be realized from a temporary youth bulge in a population pyramid. They will not all see the same gains, despite similar age structures, due to variations in such policy decisions as investments in health and education—a topic further considered in chapter 5. Thus, beyond military security, projected population shifts will pose huge economic challenges and opportunities for states, which will affect their overall power resources and ability to pay for military security.

There is a large scholarly and popular literature on economic, social, and environmental implications of changing population size, from the perspective of concerns about both growing populations and shrinking ones.[24] Among the questions raised in this broader literature, several have relevance for this study: Can states with shrinking workforces—or even shrinking total populations—continue to grow economically? Even if they do manage to grow per capita, will the total size of their economies also grow or potentially shrink? Might other values emerge in aging states that focus less on the neoliberal consumption/growth imperative? Finally, and importantly, how well can technology offset some of the negative effects of older, smaller workforces? Might such new technology also affect worker and societal attitudes about the implications of older, smaller workforces? These questions raise a great number of issues, ones that cannot be fully understood in the present day nor fully addressed in this volume, but the following chapters will take on these questions in relation to the military-security focus of this study.

Last, projected demographic shifts ahead also will create new political dynamics as well as challenge existing cultural norms: The ability of governments to respond to new political and cultural imperatives will play a key role in how successfully they adjust to their unique demographic transitions. Demographic change in some states will lead to a transfer of political power across generations with different political beliefs and worldviews. Gender relations and roles of immigrants and migrants in society are two examples of societal factors that may shift due to pressure from new demographic configurations.

The Simultaneous Impact of Technological Change on the Security Landscape and Managing Demographic Change

What about the impact of new technologies on mitigating the effects on societies of rapid aging and population shrinkage? New technologies certainly will help to mitigate the effects of demographic change to some degree, but the use of new technologies in the security realm also presents new security challenges for states to manage. As just one example, uncrewed drones may involve less human labor and protect the lives of pilots, but they also create new security concerns for both military and civilian populations. Examining what promising new technologies are on the horizon as well as those recently employed is thus an important aspect of considering the effect of demographic change on national security moving forward.

Methods of warfare have continually adapted to and employed new technologies available since the beginning of organized human conflicts. This era of renewed great power competition shaped by a growing U.S.–China rivalry, renewed concerns with Russia and North Korea, a proliferation in the number of regional security actors, and a rise of gray-zone conflict is no different in that respect, but it *is* different in that the major global security actors are all rapidly aging states with few more-youthful potential challenger states likely to rise to great-power status by 2050 (with the exception of India, as discussed in chapter 5).

It is difficult—perhaps impossible—to disentangle the contributory incentives for employing new technology due to demographic imperatives versus other security motivations. Of importance to this book is the correlation between many new technologies (both military and civilian) and labor-saving potential. As we imagine great-power military competition in the coming decades, it seems increasingly certain that it will involve fewer "soldiers" in a traditional sense, more machines and artificial intelligence (AI), and a wider range of humans to build and support those machines in terms of military and nonmilitary personnel, gender, age, even nationality. This shift has major implications for technologically advanced aging states, as well as for their rivals and partners.

In the nonmilitary realm, technology has been widely employed to replace human labor—to the extent that there is widespread concern in the advanced industrial world about a future where there is not enough work to employ the existing labor pool.[25] As a result, there is a robust discussion in some advanced industrial democracies about implementing a shorter work week or a "universal basic income" to more fairly distribute remaining human work and to maintain social stability.[26] Other studies, by contrast, have focused on the challenges some states may face from not having a sufficiently large labor pool as a result of rapidly aging and shrinking populations to both sustain the economy and provide needed military security. This concern was especially apparent during the Covid-19 pandemic, when automation was rapidly introduced in many countries and sectors to offset labor shortages.

Looking further out toward 2050, there is a great deal of uncertainty related to the future of labor and technology, both in the civilian and the military sectors. James Feyrer has summed up this uncertainty as part of a broader study of *Demographics and Innovation in the Asia-Pacific*, where he presents research suggesting that "the aging of the higher-income Asian nations will exert a downward pull on productivity over the next thirty years."[27] Still, he concludes that "these predictions are very uncertain" in part "because the older workers of the past were much different from those of today and of the future, due to better healthcare, nutrition, and conditions during childhood," and because "the estimates of the impact of demographics on productivity were performed on data that does not include the sorts of demographic configurations that we will see over the next 30 years." He notes, for example, that in "1975 the highest median age in the world was 35. By 2050 the higher-income nations of Asia will all have median ages above 50."[28] The focus of my study on military-security implications of rapidly aging powers in Asia similarly seeks to illustrate that past data and studies based on a different demographic configuration as well as different security concerns in many cases and different technologies to address those concerns need to be reevaluated in light of the present and future security challenges the Indo-Pacific region faces in an era of dual graying.

In short, the development and use of new technologies in both the civilian and military domains will change the way that countries respond to security concerns in numerous ways and also create new security concerns. Demographic changes projected for the Indo-Pacific through 2050 (and beyond) will incentivize the use of some of these technologies and inspire other sorts of technologies to address anticipated labor shortfalls in Asia's rapidly aging powers. The following chapters offer many examples in relation to the specific demographic and security challenges major states in the region face.

Beyond demographics and changing technologies, there also will be numerous other changes over the course of the twenty-first century that will affect a state's approach to its security. Two, in particular, should be noted at the outset of this study: There is growing talk of "de-globalization" characterizing the coming decades of the century due to a combination of Covid-19 pandemic–related supply chain and disease vector issues. Evolving geopolitics also has put the West on the defensive, which could lead to a significant reframing of existing regional alliances and partnerships, particularly those anchored with the United States.[29] Isolationist and populist trends in domestic politics within the United States and its allies and partners also may cause abrupt shifts in existing regional alliances and partnerships—indeed even the threat of this has spurred new debates and concerns within key regional states. I will return to these issues, and other long-term drivers of change, in the concluding chapter of this volume, after the main focus of this study is developed and supporting evidence presented.

RESEARCH QUESTIONS, METHODS, AND SOURCES

This study was motivated by three questions, which have been researched through an examination of demographic data and projections, review of national security policy decisions and planning documents, and interviews with scholars and policy practitioners across the Indo-Pacific region. These questions are:

1. How has the rapid aging of key U.S. allies, adversaries, and partners either aggravated or ameliorated existing security challenges, and how will it affect the future balance of power in the Indo-Pacific?
2. How have the major states of Northeast Asia—the traditional locus of military power in the region—adjusted their national security practices due to their rapid aging and population shrinkage, and how will they do so in the future?
3. How have the aggregated changes each state enacts to address their demographic transitions altered regional security dynamics, including the U.S. approach to military security in the Indo-Pacific, and how will they do so in the future?

Thus, the focus of this study is on demographic change as a driving force in security policy planning and innovation, what social scientists call an independent variable: one that affects security policy outcomes. In seeking to answer these questions, how and why this demographic change is taking place (demographic change as a *dependent* variable) are not the focus of this study but nevertheless will be explained to some degree in the final section of this introduction, which describes important methods used for demographic calculations and thus seeks to explain why readers should have confidence in these projections for the time frame of this study, looking out to 2035 in the shorter term and 2050 in the longer term.

To some, 2035 and 2050 may seem far away, but they are much closer to us than 2001 and 1989—two years of frequent reference in studies of international politics. Moreover, 2035 is a year where all the military personnel that states seek to employ already have been born: They are young children today, not abstractions based on projected fertility rates. Most weapons systems deployed in 2035 also are already in place or currently under development and thus more easily factored into considerations of military preparedness in 2035; again, they are not abstractions or mere concepts (in most cases).

The year 2050 involves many more contingent variables—demographic (future fertility rates, life expectancies, and possible unexpected events such as a devastating pandemic or manmade biohazard), technological (affecting possible weaponry and/or economic development), and/or geopolitical (wars that might occur, devastating natural disasters). Thus, arguments on the effect of demographic change on the security environment in 2050 are more tentative. Still, demographic projections for 2050 are likely to be fairly resilient—particularly if interpreted with regional expertise—and suggest a "most likely scenario" for security planning today.

The core dataset employed for demographic data in this book is adapted from the 2024 revision of the United Nations Population Division's *World Population Prospects*, which offers historical and projected population statistics—including age and gender breakdowns—for every country and territory in the world (some as part of regional groupings). The data also can be manipulated for a range of future assumptions, as explained in more detail in the final section of this introduction.

Beyond raw demographic data, the analysis presented in this book relies on publicly available government policy documents, supplemented by additional nonclassified materials and interview data. Some of this material relates to national security planning broadly, some to policies to address past and future projected demographic change, and others that explicitly consider the intersection of these two areas. The analysis also is informed by interviews conducted both in person and virtually with scholars and policymakers across the Indo-Pacific region, with special attention given to rapidly aging U.S. allies and partners, Japan, South Korea, and Taiwan (each of which were sites for extended research). In addition, a wide range of secondary literature and media reporting has informed this book. Existing scholarly literature on demographics and its linkage with military security is discussed further in chapter 1. The analysis also draws from a wide range of existing scholarship on national security challenges facing the Indo-Pacific region, with particular attention to concerns from the perspective of the United States and its allies and partners.

What about the "casual mechanisms" on the effect of demographic change on security outcomes, given so many other changing and influential factors? This, of course, we cannot assert with certainty, but we can consider using several methodological techniques, three of which are highlighted here.

First, unlike the bulk of the scholarly literature on this subject to date, this study (1) draws on a decade or more of actual conduct of rapidly aging states—beginning with Japan as the first super-aged military power in 2005—and (2) narrows the focus to sixteen core territories within a single region, to consider broader assumptions about the effect of rapid aging and other demographic change together with regional knowledge and scholarship about a single security ecosystem.

Second, this study considers and discusses numerous other independent—or perhaps intervening—variables in security policy outcomes, such as a shifting balance of power, changing domestic politics, technological innovation, and cultural resistance to change. While social scientists can posit these variables as fully independent, in reality it seems difficult to sustain an argument that demographic change is unrelated to any of these factors: a rapidly aging and shrinking population almost certainly will experience a changing level of objective power resources (a realist concern), shifting domestic politics (a liberalist concern), and challenges to existing conceptions of culture and identity (a constructivist concern). Some may prefer to conceptualize demographic change as an "intervening variable" between these other factors and policy outcomes. Ultimately, however, the core argument of this study would be unchanged: The shifting population demographics of the Indo-Pacific matter to security outcomes and have not been adequately considered to date both in existing scholarship and by policymakers—though both groups are increasingly including demographic change in their discussions of regional security challenges.

Beyond decisions by individual states to address demographic change, and the introduction of new technology, a third important aspect of the impact of demographics on national security is considering demographic change relationally as opposed to examining each country's population shifts individually. As realist international relations theory has long posited, if one country's power is growing and another's is declining, that is a bigger challenge for the declining country than if both countries were declining: Power is a relational variable.[30] This theoretical insight is important for security dynamics in the Indo-Pacific because *all* the current major powers (except India) face a similar demographic future of substantial aging and population shrinking: Asia's great powers are simultaneously its aging powers. However, Northeast Asia's aging democracies are facing this challenge first. One early takeaway from the research presented here is that timing matters: core U.S. allies will face the brunt of demographic challenges before primary U.S. adversaries, making the 2020s a time of unusual demographically driven uncertainty.

That said, some changes in state behavior may occur due to changes in internal demographics apart from the relational component, as suggested by some schools of constructivist and liberalist international relations theories—such as changes in state identity and/or securitization (for constructivists) and/or in the changing relative power of different domestic interest groups due to demographic change (for liberalists).[31] For example, as a larger number of citizens become older, they may express different preferences related to government spending priorities that carry more weight as the size of this age-group grows. The linkage between existing international relations theory and demographic change—and the core arguments central to this study—are presented in greater detail in chapter 1. But first, a short primer on key demographic terms and methods utilized in this book concludes this introduction.

DEMOGRAPHIC METHODS AND TERMINOLOGY EMPLOYED IN THIS STUDY

Informed observers of world politics in the twentieth century will recall many examples of past demographic projections not materializing as expected, with significant impacts on political outcomes. No one in the early 1900s expected a lost generation of young men in Europe after the devastation of what would become the First World War. Many held deep pessimism about China's economic development prospects in the twentieth century given its large and quickly growing population midcentury—a population that later would fuel one of the largest and swiftest sustained economic growth periods in recorded human history and whose future growth is now in question due to unprecedented government policies for population control. Major cataclysmic events can happen that affect a country's demographic profile, but these are very rare. The exact role technology will play in demographic futures also is unknowable but potentially substantial.

This said, with developments in the social sciences and in the field of demography in particular, as well as greater investment in demographic research projections, we can quite confidently predict demographic futures in the short term and, to a large degree, the medium term. What the *effect* of changing demographics will be is a different matter. Demographic pressures must be understood and reacted to by political actors. Herein lies the role for a political scientist.

As a political scientist, I have sought to understand demographic techniques for population projections into the future—including their limitations—in order to better understand political phenomena. Demographic data is very important and widely used in the study of domestic electoral politics, but much less so in the study of international security policy. This book originated in the belief that demographic projections and contingencies should be integrated more into the study of international security. Thus, this section offers a short primer on key aspects of demographic science related to the arguments developed in later chapters. The section is crafted around five main take-away points about how population demographic projections are calculated. It ends with a reminder/caution about the past and potential misuses of a focus on population demographics in human development.

Demographers Offer Researchers a Range of Future Projections

Future population projections are calculated using three factors: life expectancy, fertility, and net migration. Important aspects of these three core factors are explained in the following subsections. The United Nations Population Division offers multiple projections of future population demographics that utilize different assumptions about these three factors, allowing researchers to choose among these assumptions and to contrast different possible futures. For example, researchers can choose among different future fertility rates and levels of immigration scenarios. These projections are updated based on actual developments in the "real world" at regular intervals, typically every three years, though the 2022 revision that was released near the end of Covid-19 pandemic was revised after just two years, in July 2024.

Naturally, the further into the future one seeks to project, the more uncertainty there is. Given the uncertainty about the future—including the greatly changing international security landscape and military technology broadly—this project focuses both on the shorter-term (2035) and the medium-term (2050) security implications of changing population demographics. Only in the conclusion to the book are brief thoughts offered for the Indo-Pacific region beyond 2050—though the United Nations offers demographic projections through 2100 and numerous studies (including several noted in chapter 1) make predictions further out.

Life Expectancy Is Rising Across the Region but Still Varies Substantially

Over the course of the twentieth century, life expectancy increased far beyond what midcentury demographers had imagined, vastly underestimating population growth as a result—as well as the rapid-aging phenomenon that is the focus of this book. Global life expectancy at birth was 46.4 years in 1950; in 2023 it had risen to just over 70 for males and almost 76 for females. There remain, however, significant variations in life expectancy by country, including in the Indo-Pacific, which affects the rate of societal aging. Globally the gap in life expectancy between the most developed regions and least-developed countries was over thirteen years in 2023.

One also must consider this insight from demographers: Life expectancy rises when calculated beyond one's year of birth. As Sciubba illustrates: "On average across the OECD, if someone makes it to age 65 today, they're expected to live another 21 years."[32] Thus, when calculated from the age of 65, life expectancy within the OECD rises to 86 years old. United Nations projections of life expectancy at birth for Japan in 2015–2020 were 84 years, while in India it was only 69, a difference of 15 years. In that same time frame, the life expectancy at birth for strategic rivals Russia, China, and the United States was 72, 76, and 79, respectively (though in the case of Russia there is a very large male-female gap).

It is possible that life expectancy will dramatically change globally or in specific countries by 2050—either in the life-extending direction due to advances in medical technology or in the life-shortening direction due to the spread of illness, a major war, or chemical/nuclear/biological accident. This does not seem especially likely in the next three decades—considering that even the Covid-19 global pandemic has only modestly affected life expectancies to date—but is a wildcard that is considered in the conclusion of this book.[33] Life expectancy in the United States was adjusted downward due to the effects of the opioid epidemic as well as the Covid-19 pandemic in 2020 and 2021, but only very modestly (a small fraction of one year). From 2050 to 2100 it is much more probable that there will be an unexpected demographic disruption due to future possible technological advances and other uncertainties about the world in general (including growing concerns about the effects of climate change), which, in part, is why the arguments developed in this study conclude at 2050.

Different Scenarios for Total Fertility Rates Greatly Affect the Speed of Aging

Also over the course of the twentieth century, fertility—specifically, the "total fertility rate" (TFR)—decreased to far below what midcentury demographers imagined, leading to the countervailing trend (in contrast to increased life expectancy) of slowed population growth in much of the world and even outright shrinking of national populations in a small number of states in the early twenty-first century, primarily in Europe, though also in Japan. This trend of decreased fertility has continued in much of the world, though some places that had suffered low fertility have experienced modest rebounds in fertility rates (including in Russia in the 2010s)—a topic written about at great length by demographers, but not a trend generally expected to continue. A "replacement birth rate" is generally seen as 2.1 TFR, though statistically it is likely to be a bit less in developed countries where more females live through childbearing age. Few countries in the developed world have TFRs of 2.1 or higher, which leads to population shrinkage in the medium term, unless immigration (a third factor considered below) offsets the decline.

Related to the different future scenarios that UN demographers consider and model, this book adopts the position that the standard "medium variant" scenario in UN population projections for low-fertility Indo-Pacific states—which models gradually *increasing* fertility rates in places like China and South Korea—is overly optimistic. As such, the dataset created for this project utilizes the "constant fertility rates" for countries with a current TFR below 2.0, which includes most of the IP16 countries that are the focus of the chapters that follow (all but Indonesia and Mongolia). By contrast, this book follows the view of the mainstream of UN demographers that current high-fertility countries are likely to see declining fertility over time, and so the dataset developed for this study utilizes the "medium variant" projection for those countries with current TFRs of 2.0 or higher.[34]

The difference between these two projections is especially striking for the countries of Northeast Asia with very low birth rates. For example, in Sciubba's 2022 study of the likely impact of future population trends, she writes: "By 2050, those ages 20 to 69 will shrink by 16.2 percent in South Korea, 14.9 percent in Taiwan, and 8.9 percent in China."[35] Sciubba uses the UN Population Division's 2019 medium-variant projection that assumes (as does the 2024 UN revised projection) increasing birth rates in these countries in the coming decades. By contrast, the percentage decrease of the size of the twenty-sixty-nine age-group if one assumes a constant TFR from 2020 is 28.9, 26.4, and 14.6, respectively. This is a huge difference in terms of actual numbers of human beings—in the case of China, about 57.3 million fewer people in that age-group if calculated using the 2022 constant fertility rate over this period.

Moreover, some expect fertility rates in these low-fertility countries to *further* decline. Indeed, the 2024 revision of *World Population Prospects* lowered fertility projections for the region (while maintaining the underlying assumption that they would gradually rise toward 2050). Thus, to underscore the point, scholars must interpret demographic data based on judgments of the future based on informed expertise—it is not simply a matter of rote application of one magic set of numbers that can be expected to accurately predict the future. Indeed, the UN Population Division itself updates its dataset regularly (roughly every three years) to adjust to the latest trends observed—which, as noted, lowered projected TFR in the medium-variant scenario for East Asian countries in both the 2022 and 2024 revisions. For example, the projected 2024 TFR in the 2024 revision was lowered from 2.73 to 1.92 in the case of the Philippines (and thus from projected population growth to one of future shrinkage) and from 1.13 to 0.87 for Taiwan (a level that will hasten population shrinkage and aging). In total, the 2024 revision lowered the TFR estimate for fifteen of the sixteen IP16 countries that are the focus of this study (all but Australia), from an average TRF among of the IP16 of 1.68 in 2022 to 1.55 in 2024. (TFRs for each of the IP16 countries are provided in table 2.1 in chapter 2.)

Immigration Keeps Some Indo-Pacific States from
Population Shrinkage but Not Aging

UN Population Division demographic projections also factor in the population impact of net migration (i.e., the difference between emigration and immigration in a particular state). Since this factor is the result of more immediate policy decisions than the other two components of population projections discussed earlier, it is more likely to change unexpectedly—and, indeed, recent years have seen unexpected and sharp shifts in acceptance of immigrants in many advanced industrial states due to the Covid-19 pandemic as well as growing nativism and nationalism in the domestic politics of many advanced industrial states. Several countries within this study have projected population increases through 2050 entirely due to net migration (including Australia, New Zealand, and Singapore), which is a political factor that will be examined at the country level in later chapters. The United States also is such a country—where population growth in recent years has been entirely due to immigration, which also has reduced the rate of societal aging.

The percentage of the Earth's inhabitants who live outside their country of birth is quite small overall: ranging from 2.8 percent at the start of the twenty-first century to 3.6 percent in 2020.[36] Moreover, immigrants also are concentrated in a relatively small number of states: More than half of the total in 2019 were in just ten countries, including three in the scope of this study: the United States (#1 at around 51 million), Russia (#4 at 12 million), and Australia (around 8 million).[37] Note, however, that Russians also were the fourth-largest group residing outside of their home country (about 11 million), so Russian population growth due to immigration was only modestly positive in the late 2010s—and these numbers are from before the 2022 escalation of the Russia–Ukraine War, which is widely reported to have increased out-migration. Indian and Chinese nationals were the largest and third-largest groups of nationals living outside of their country of birth, at around eighteen million and eleven million, respectively; they both host far fewer immigrants than they lose to outward migration. Given this concentration of net migration in a relatively small number of states, several of which are in the Indo-Pacific, immigration is an especially important factor to states within the IP16 focus of this study—more so than in states worldwide.

By contrast, four of the top-ten immigrant-hosting countries are in Europe (apart from Russia), which explains why the European Union grew by almost one million people in 2019 despite roughly half a million more deaths than births.[38] As a 2017 Pew Research Center study has noted: "Without future immigration, Europe's population would shrink from about 521 million to about 482 million by mid-century, but with steady levels of regular immigration, the population size will remain fairly stable."[39] Immigration also can lead to other internal population shifts. For example, Sweden is projected to see growth in its Muslim population to between 11 and 31 percent of the *total* population by 2050, versus 8 percent in 2016, depending on whether immigration is totally halted (unlikely) or continues at the high rate seen in 2014–2016 (also unlikely).[40] The root cause of this rise in the percentage of the Muslim population in Sweden is immigration, but it becomes an internal demographic change as children of immigrants are born as native residents and citizens. Such a large internal demographic shift is not projected within any of the IP16 countries of this study, but some other internal demographic changes on the horizon nevertheless should be considered in relation to the demographics–national security focus of this study, as noted in the following subsection.

Other Demographic Measures Beyond Aging of Relevance to National Security

Internal population shifts beyond aging and overall shrinking of the population also may affect national security and certainly affect human security. In particular, rural to urban migration, changing ethnic and religious population ratios, and changing male-female ratios are relevant to both external and internal security concerns and thus are discussed in the following chapters, though not the focus of this study. For example, internal migration may relate to national security through effects such as depopulation of rural and remote areas and shifting ethnic distributions within the national population that can exacerbate existing ethnic tensions.

Globally, the percentage of the world's population living in urban areas crossed 50 percent in 2007, reaching 55 percent in 2018—a number expected to increase to 68 percent in 2050.[41] The Indo-Pacific region similarly is projected to experience substantial growing urbanization broadly, meaning that rural areas will see fewer residents, and cities may face stresses to handle growing populations despite possibly shrinking total national populations overall. Northeast Asia's presently shrinking populations—China/Taiwan, Japan, and South Korea—all are experiencing substantial growth in the populations of their largest cities despite a shrinking total population.

A Reminder and Caution on Past and
Current Misuses of Demographic Science

Before concluding this chapter and in transition to considering twenty-first century challenges in chapter 1, it is important to acknowledge the past abuses of demographics-focused government policies on human beings, in particular related to the eugenics movements of the twentieth century, the legacy of forced abortions and sterilizations, and policies of ethnic cleansing, and on the oppression of women especially and people in developing countries more broadly. Such atrocities sadly have not been left behind in the twentieth century but rather continue around the globe, including in numerous places within the Indo-Pacific region.

Policies designed to reduce the size or even eliminate unfavored ethnic or religious groups remain features of the twenty-first century Indo-Pacific demographic landscape, such as against the Uyghurs and other ethnic minorities in China and the Rohingya Muslims in Myanmar. Moreover, while China's infamous One-Child Policy, initiated in 1979 shortly after the death of Mao Zedong, was largely ended by 2020, the legacy of two generations of mostly one-child families and millions of adults emotionally and often physically scarred by this policy remain. The opposite sort of government-sponsored manipulation of reproduction, where governments actively encourage large families in order to shift demographics for security reasons—what some scholars refer to as "wombfare"—also should be acknowledged.[42] As one scholar has cautioned: "Painting demography as a threat to national security risks legitimizing oppression in the name of defending the state."[43]

Population-related abuses not only were—and are—committed by governments, but also can spring from individual choices. The scale of sex-selective abortions and other forms of family planning are shockingly apparent in skewed sex ratios at birth (SRB) in numerous countries in the world, including several in the Indo-Pacific (particularly in China, India, and Vietnam)—what media reporting often describes as the "missing girls" phenomenon.[44] China's SRB was 107.2 in the 1982 census (soon after the start of the One-Child Policy) but grew to 116.9 in the 2000 census, and 117.9 in the 2010 census, numbers significantly greater than the roughly 105 boy:girl ratio that demographers view as a biologically natural level.[45] Numerous studies have shown that this unnatural imbalance is even more pronounced if one examines only births beyond a first child. For example, one study found that the ratios in South Korea in 1990 were 113.44 for a first child but 192.22 for a third child.[46] Fortunately, South Korea's SRB had returned to near-natural levels by 2008, but that is roughly when Vietnam's imbalance began to climb.[47] Sex imbalances in a state's population pyramid also can occur due to immigration, as seen in the guest worker–heavy Persian Gulf states.[48] Internal migration also can create large sex imbalances in certain regions of countries, typically urban areas.

Although this study does not focus on the *causes* of low TFRs or the proposed policy solutions to address the perceived problem of a low TFR, the effect of this demographic trend is that population size continues to be securitized by government leaders of all of the countries examined in the following chapters. Demographic change is a security concern for Asia's rapidly aging states; we all have a responsibility to guard against women or other underrepresented populations being scapegoated or unduly burdened in proposed solutions to the challenges ahead.

Chapter Structure

This introduction has set out the main research questions for this study, some initial answers to those questions, and a primer on key terms and concepts related to population demographics. Chapter 1 broadens the discussion by explaining the principal ways that rapid aging affects military security outcomes by drawing on existing scholarly literature, including identifying where this study seeks to make significant contributions. Chapter 2 returns to the core research questions of this study, providing a more detailed presentation of demographic data for the Indo-Pacific region that underscores the *relational* impacts of regional demographic change, an analysis of the primary security challenges the region faces today and is projected to face in the medium term, and the linkages between the two where demographic change is most likely to affect the regional security balance.

Chapters 3–5 provide more detailed analysis of country-level demographic change and the national security implications of this change, including discussion of policy responses to date. Chapter 3 focuses on the rapid aging of Northeast Asia's democracies—Japan, South Korea, and Taiwan—which are at the leading edge of this unprecedented demographic transition worldwide. Chapter 4 looks at Northeast Asia's rapidly aging autocracies—Russia, North Korea, and China—which will experience a similar transition but with delayed timing and some important differences due to their autocratic governments and unique internal demographic compositions. Chapter 5 expands the analysis to the broader Indo-Pacific, considering both rapidly aging and also still-growing and comparatively youthful states with a focus on potential security partners of the United States and its allies. The chapter also considers in more depth the growing range of security challenges regional actors seek to manage beyond those related narrowly to military security. The concluding chapter returns to the primary research questions and a summary of major lessons learned, policy prescriptions for different regional security actors as well as the United States, and consideration of some alternative scenarios for the region's demographic and security future.

Chapter One

RECONSIDERING THE DEMOGRAPHICS-NATIONAL SECURITY NEXUS THROUGH A TWENTY-FIRST-CENTURY INDO-PACIFIC LENS

The ways that population demographics affect national security planning and practices of states are changing as patterns of worldwide demographic shifts themselves have changed. Several excellent studies that focus on the global security implications of twenty-first-century demographic change complement the central arguments of this book, but a close examination of how rapid aging has affected the security landscape of the Indo-Pacific reveals a number of developments that are contrary to predictions in existing scholarly literature and popular media reporting. Importantly, despite a growing awareness among government policy planners and lawmakers of the rapid aging taking place and its societal and economic consequences, security policy planning and practices have not shifted as predicted away from escalating military tensions toward policies that focus on expected different demands from a larger number of older citizens. This chapter highlights the divergence between past predictions and current realities. In addition, the chapter situates the arguments of this book within the broader literature on the effect of population size and age on national security—both historical and contemporary—as it relates to Asia's graying security challenges in the twenty-first century.

The new, twenty-first century wave of differential demographic change seen in the rapid aging of Asia's traditional military powers and in the population growth of numerous middle-power states in the Indo-Pacific resembles the differential growth seen in other regions of the world, but with important differences. For one, there are no longer any high-fertility countries in the Indo-Pacific region. As a result, some of the lessons drawn from the global experience with population change are not as relevant to Indo-Pacific security concerns and demographic realities.

Existing scholarship that considers "the graying of the great powers" argues that the resulting challenges to global security will be profound, affecting not just military manpower and budgets but ideology, political stability, technological innovation, and economic growth.[1] As the world enters its third decade of super-aged states, there are a growing diversity and number of rapidly aging states: A first wave involved nearly all highly developed democracies (such as Japan, South Korea, and Taiwan, as discussed in chapter 3), whereas the second wave includes several less-developed states as well as nondemocracies like China, North Korea, and Russia (chapter 4). A third wave also can be projected to emerge in the 2050s worldwide (as illustrated further in chapter 5).

This chapter also summarizes historical data that contrast the huge global population growth of nearly all states in the twentieth century with the differential growth pattern of the twenty-first century, drawing implications for earlier studies that examined the demographics–national security nexus based on twentieth-century growth trends and technology. The chapter additionally reviews the body of recent literature that has sought to consider twenty-first-century demographic trends from a military-security angle, drawing out potential lessons for—and deviations to—the country cases presented in later chapters.

Contrary to the predictions of the small but growing literature on the effect of rapid aging on the likelihood of interstate war, in the region of the world that is experiencing the most severe aging among security rivals—Northeast Asia—tensions are growing, and states are increasing their military spending and development of new, more advanced weapons. They also are engaging in new "gray" forms of conflict that both increase the potential for escalation into more traditional forms of warfare and pose serious challenges in their own right. Why are tensions rising and avenues of conflict intensifying if aging states collectively are less likely to go to war, according to statistical analysis and logical deduction presented in previous studies of the effect of rapid aging on national security?

One potential answer to this apparent puzzle is that it is problematic to hold the nature of warfare constant by using datasets of twentieth-century conflicts in a region where new technologies and grayer forms of conflict are proliferating. The evolving nature of warfare due to technological change and proliferating gray-zone conflicts assists rapidly aging states to stay on top. Moreover, the nature of conflicts these states face has evolved, though numerous twentieth-century conflict flashpoints remain, as further explained in chapter 2.[2] In an impressive large-n study, Brooks et al. acknowledge the uncertainty of Asia's graying security landscape in the conclusion to their globally focused study, writing: "The world has never experienced a situation in which countries with very powerful militaries undergo a rapid, dramatic aging process, and there are reasons to worry that security dynamics could get worse before they get better."[3] In short, to follow a metaphor from noted demographer Jack Goldstone mentioned in the introduction, there is a shifting "gravity" pull of demographics on military security in the twenty-first-century graying Indo-Pacific: How demographics affected potential for twentieth-century and earlier conflict is not as relevant to potential twenty-first-century conflict in the Indo-Pacific, at least among the aging powers. The next section elaborates on the contrasts.

THE DEMOGRAPHICS-NATIONAL SECURITY NEXUS HISTORICALLY AND IN INTERNATIONAL RELATIONS THEORY

The incredible population growth in the twentieth century was one of that century's defining hallmarks. Total world population nearly quadrupled, far exceeding the growth projected for the twenty-first century. It took all human history to reach the then–high mark of an estimated 1.6 billion people on the planet in 1900, but only one hundred years to add 4.6 billion more by the end of that century. Both popular writing and academic scholarship expressed widespread alarm at twentieth-century population growth, which was widely viewed as contributing to interstate conflict, threatening economic development of especially poorer countries, and perhaps even leading to a worldwide resource shortfall that would result in mass starvation.[4] Many predictions both about how population demographics would shift and about the effects of these shifts on human security turned out to be incorrect.

While this study focuses on the demographic challenges posed by twenty-first-century population trends in the Indo-Pacific (which, as explained, are quite different from twentieth-century demographic shifts), it is important to understand how demographic change was understood to affect national security at that time, as insights and memories from the period still inform (sometimes mistakenly) policy decisions and scholarship in this century. Moreover, instances of international conflict in the twentieth century have shaped existing international relations theory and, in several cases, remain conflict flashpoints in the Indo-Pacific in the twenty-first century (as discussed further in chapter 2).

Five Stages of Global Demographic Transition: Toward Late-Stage Rapid Aging

Brooks and her coauthors provide a useful summary of the world's overall demographic transition beginning even before the twentieth century that underscores the scale of recent change and implications for global security, drawing especially on Ronald Lee's "The Demographic Transition: Three Centuries of Fundamental Change."[5] The first stage, they summarize, is the one that described all countries prior to around 1800, which "displayed three characteristics: (1) very short lifespans (life expectancy was around twenty-seven years on average in all centuries prior to 1800); (2) very high birth rates (approximately six births per woman on average prior to 1800); and (3) relatively stable population sizes (as death rates more or less offset high fertility levels, with occasional short-term spikes in mortality caused by pandemics, famines, or wars)."[6]

This first stage sets the demographic context for military-security strategies and experience for most of recorded human history and is one that is not at all relevant to the Indo-Pacific security environment today, where demographics across the entire region differ from this early stage.

A second stage of demographic transition began in the Northern Hemisphere early in the nineteenth century, where mortality rates declined and thus average life expectancy increased due to numerous factors that Lee's summary explains. The third stage is when fertility rates decline in response to longer life expectancies (due especially to decreased infant mortality), but populations continue to grow due to longer life expectancies and still above-replacement birthrates. It was this stage that resulted in the ballooning of populations worldwide in the twentieth century and continues in some regions of the world in the twenty-first century (especially South and Western Asia and Sub-Saharan Africa).

Late-stage rapid aging—the focus of this study—characterizes the fourth and fifth stages of the worldwide demographic transition underway. The fourth phase began to emerge particularly in advanced industrial countries in the 1970s, with several Asian countries on the leading edge of this change, where there is decline of fertility below the replacement level combined with long life expectancies, resulting in significant aging of generally stable population sizes. This stage occurred naturally as a result of personal decisions in Japan and elsewhere in the early 1970s as well as through China's One-Child Policy government mandate (officially from 1979 but less systematically prior to that as well).

In the fifth stage of demographic transition theory, which only a few states have yet experienced (including China, Japan, Russia, South Korea, and Taiwan), fertility rates are so low that total population sizes begin to shrink, combined with even faster aging of the total population due to further increasing life expectancies. This new stage is projected to result in a proliferation of "super-aged" societies worldwide by the mid-twenty-first century, including all the Northeast Asian region apart from Mongolia and others in the southern Indo-Pacific region as well. It also is projected to lead to a large number of states around the world experiencing total population shrinkage.

To underscore the growing shift into this fifth stage of the global demographic transition, consider these 2024 statistics from the UN Population Division: In 63 countries and territories, containing 28 percent of the world's population in 2024, the size of the population peaked before 2024. In an additional 48 countries and territories, accounting for 10 percent of the world's population in 2054, population size is projected to peak between 2025 and 2054.[7] Thus, worldwide, 111 countries and territories are projected to experience population shrinkage by 2024. This is the new demographic reality for the twenty-first century and one impetus for this study: to consider the security implications of this important shift in human development.

The next section focuses on the first three stages of worldwide demographic transition, considering how international relations theory and security planners understood the impact of changing population characteristics through the ballooning population phase. The following section then contrasts theories based on twentieth-century experience with the new demographic realities of the twenty-first century Indo-Pacific, where nearly all traditional regional powers have entered the fourth and fifth stages of demographic transition, including the late-stage rapid-aging phenomenon.

The Demographics–National Security Nexus in International Relations Theory Historically: Key Lines of Argument

Population size, in particular a large number of young men historically, can enhance state power though military personnel as well as economic production. Yet, history shows that a large and growing population also can be a burden, and that expanding populations can create conflict through territorial aspirations and competition over limited resources.[8] Such competition continued well into the twentieth century, Goldstone notes, citing work by Choucri and North (among others) that points to "the critical role of rising populations in the European powers provoking the tensions and competition for resources that led to World War I."[9] In short, human experience with national security—at least with leading powers (an important qualification)—is that more people is better and fewer worse. This experience sets the stage for concern about rapid aging and shrinking populations currently underway in Asia and elsewhere.

At the same time, the need to balance the size of a nation's population with available resources also has long been seen as a primary concern of a country's leaders. As the third stage of global demographic change got underway in Europe near the end of the nineteen century, Thomas Malthus's influential essay cautioning leaders that population growth was far exceeding the limited resources of the planet generated widespread concern.[10] Scholars from many different theoretical traditions as well as mainstream international relations textbooks explain rising European (and other) colonialism and tensions leading to the outbreak of the Second World War at least in part due to growing population pressures—in particular the need to balance population and resources, lest nature do the balancing for them.

Although Malthus's predictions about a near-term population catastrophe being on the horizon proved incorrect, largely due to technological innovation, neo-Malthusians continue to raise concerns about the ability of the planet to sustain an ever-increasing population. There is today a vocal strand of such thought related to concerns about the human-created components of global climate change. Even though global population growth is projected to end around midcentury—only a few decades from now—concerns about potentially rising consumption patterns of the next several billion inhabitants of the planet, as well as economic development of the current population, keep Malthus's nineteenth-century concerns alive. In the security realm, this growth fuels fears about rising interstate violence as a result of a growing competition for resources and/or growing instability due to lack of sufficient resources that could lead to state failure. Thus, in some ways, past arguments about the effect of population size on national security remain relevant today.

The characteristics of a country's population—whether it be total size, ethnic or religious composition, or age structure, among other variables— have been of interest to all major schools of international relations theory historically, though each stresses different aspects of a country's population attributes. The realist school sees population size and characteristics as one aspect of state power and is concerned especially with relative power vis-à-vis other states, which can be related to population growth or decline. A state with a growing population that is *well harnessed*—a critical caveat discussed shortly—is seen as a growing threat by offensive realists, who see rising powers as more likely to lead to interstate conflict.[11] Defensive realist theory, by contrast, could be understood to predict a growing potential for conflict as the demographics of powerful states become more challenging to manage, especially if in relation to states with more youthful and growing population profiles. Sciubba describes this body of theory as positing that, for example, "those states, particularly aging ones, that have a decreased ability to fund defense may have a higher likelihood of going to war with an adversary."[12] Thus, one might predict greater risks of conflict among states projecting future demographic challenges, such as in East Asia today—a troubling prospect in the short term.

One could consider the aging security dilemma idea advanced in this study as another facet of this predicted future insecurity—that as an aging state seeks to reinforce its security capabilities for new demographic realities, neighboring states can perceive these new capabilities as threatening and respond with their own security enhancements. This prediction would make the 2020s in the Indo-Pacific a period especially likely for instability and potential miscalculation due to the demographic transitions underway in so many powerful and rising states simultaneously. Indeed, Sciubba's prediction in 2012 along these lines related to Russia looks prescient after Russia's multistage invasion of Ukraine, initially through gray-zone tactics in Crimea and Eastern Ukraine in 2014 and later with a hard-power-backed military invasion in 2022.[13]

Looking beyond the realist school, as noted in the introduction of this book, one strand of liberalist international relations theory is focused on the relative power of different interest groups and actors *within* a state, which also can be related to changes in population composition over time. One example of such internal shifts that is examined in the following case chapters is the possibility that as a population ages, there may be increased political power for older-age cohorts as they grow to outnumber younger cohorts. The idea that an aging block of political power will emerge is an empirical question, though—not something that should be assumed. The case chapters that follow call into question this idea. A shift in the political balance of power between urban and rural areas also could be precipitated by internal demographic change—but, again, this is an empirical question, and one that assumes that political structures would adapt to this demographic shift, which is not a trend evident in Asia's rapidly aging democracies to date.

Constructivists' interest in state identities and in how certain issues become "securitized" by policymakers also can relate to demographic characteristics of a state's population. Moreover, perceptions of aging states— both internally and externally held—might be best understood through constructivist conceptions of identity. Ultimately, though, whether or how perceptions of aging states matter also is an empirical question, one investigated further in the subsequent chapters.

Despite these many potential linkages between demographic change and existing international relations theory, it has not been common for analysts of international security to include discussion of regional or global demographic trends explicitly in their analyses. More often, with one major exception, future or past demographic change is stated as a black box or future concern that is considered ad hoc.

Organski et al.'s "power transition theory" is an exception to this general trend, providing one example of a school of international relations

Size	Productivity	Political Capacity
• Total population size • Working-age population size • # of males of military age • # of utilized population (females, elderly, marginalized) + • Inward migrants • Mercenaries • Formal military allies • Security partnerships	• Economic productivity per capita • Level of military training • Technological resources • Military strategy	• Government ability to utilize resources • Strategy for adapting to change • Government ability to implement change • Societal willingness to adapt

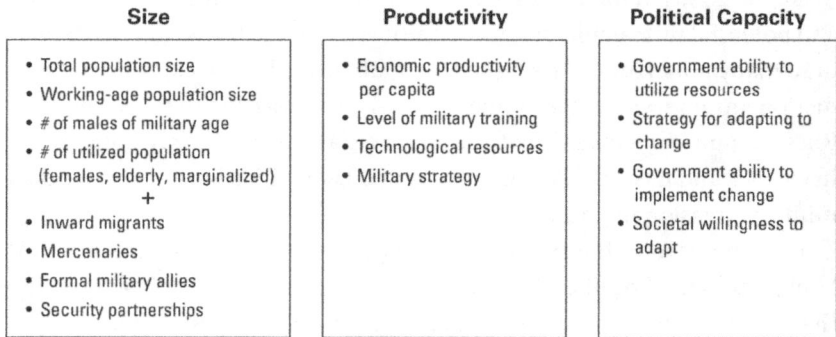

FIGURE 1.1. Population variables affecting military security. *Source*: Author.

scholarship that explicitly considers the impact of demographics on national security.[14] Numerous studies in this school advance a three-pronged model that starts with population size but add *productivity* and *political capacity* as important factors affecting the value of population size. Moreover, this work expands on the variable of "size" itself, noting that population size can be supplemented by alliances, foreign legions, and mercenaries, and through immigration. Better utilizing the existing population is another way to affect size—such as the incorporation of older workers, women, and marginalized populations (ethnic, religious, sexuality, etc.) into the workforce. Figure 1.1 expresses these ideas visually.

These insights have great relevance for the case studies that constitute the later chapters of this book. As one example, numerous militaries of aging Asian states are widening their pool of potential recruits by expanding the acceptable age range, considering dual nationals, and making greater efforts to recruit and retain females into military service. Another example relates to one of the core findings of this study: that demographic pressures of America's aging allies reinforce a trend toward deepening alliances and partnerships with other like-minded states. A similar pattern can be seen by Russia's recent efforts at partnership-building with states like China and North Korea as it seeks to address its military-age population shortages due to its war with Ukraine.

The two additional categories to consider related to the value of population size—productivity and political capacity—also have great relevance for the case chapters that follow. Although it seems intuitive, it is worth under-scoring that there is a substantial difference between states with large, pro-ductive populations and those with large, unproductive populations. Indeed, in looking to the principal threat in the Indo-Pacific as seen by the United States and its allies, China's increasing military capability is due, in part, to it *decreasing* the number of its military forces in favor of produc-tivity increases per soldier. China's total military size was reduced from around 4.5 million soldiers in the 1980s to around 2.3 million in the 2010s, but no one would argue that its military capabilities decreased as a result.[15]

This insight applies in the nonmilitary arena as well. As Sciubba writes on the importance of the productivity category: "Absolute labor strength is only one driver of economic growth. Technology, efficiency, and capital are also essential. ... There is no reason that today's workers cannot be more productive than their parents."[16] Indeed, as illustrated in later chapters, studies of the likely economic growth trajectories of Northeast Asia's aging powers overwhelmingly predict continued increases in total GDP for these states despite dramatically shrinking workforces and total population sizes.

Thus, in both areas of population advantage subscribed to for centuries—military manpower and economic production—there is not a perfect cor-relation between size and capabilities. The contrast between the economic size and military might of Taiwan during the early Cold War period (despite its small population size) versus population Goliath China at that time offers one such example. In addition, as Sciubba argues: "Population aging can be a positive force that drives innovation because societies have to compen-sate for the changes aging brings." Relating directly to this study, she notes: "Aging states are quite different from aging individuals, whose cognitive capacity may dwindle over time. Japan and Germany are leaders in inno-vative technology at the same time that they lead the world in aging."[17] This is one area where technology may at least partly fill a gap created by popu-lation shrinkage, again as illustrated in the case chapters that follow.

The role of government in managing demographic transitions—the vari-able of political capacity—is another critical factor. Case studies later in this volume repeatedly illustrate Sciubba's observation that "the literature underestimates the role of the state in mediating the effects of population aging."[18] One area of political capacity that becomes apparent across the breadth of Indo-Pacific cases is the different potential in principle between democracies and nondemocracies to enact change based on demographic pressures. Related to political capacity is also the issue of cultural or societal willingness to adopt new norms based on shifting demographic pressures. One could ultimately view this as a matter of political capacity—an ability for politicians and policymakers to overcome cultural or societal obstacles to change—but it may be more useful to examine this type of change (or resistance to change) separately (or additionally), as a societal variable.

Returning to the regional focus of this volume, innovations in productivity—both military and nonmilitary—and political entrepreneurship both are widely apparent in how Asia's aging powers have sought to adjust to rapid aging and shrinking of their working-age populations. As one example, the very idea of a "working-age population" itself should be understood as a cultural construct. OECD data show a wide variation of both government-encouraged retirement ages as well as actual average retirement ages chosen by individuals in OECD countries.[19] South Korea, Japan, and the United States all have longer effective working lives than "normal retirement" set by government policy; in many European countries, it is the opposite: Many workers retire *before* normal retirement age. This variation is not due to significant differences in life expectancy across these states, but rather to cultural preferences and norms.

In sum, existing scholarly literature identifies at least four hypothesized effects of late-stage rapid aging on military security (see figure 1.2). Two of these effects—indicated by black arrows—are essentially empirical facts, though the *implications* of these effects are not as certain as often portrayed. Two others—indicated by gray arrows—are possible, and generally portrayed as likely, effects.

On the empirically more certain side (indicated by the black arrows in figure 1.2), late-stage rapid aging results in shrinking working-age populations and a shifting balance of political power among age groups and/or generational cohorts. These effects are indeed evident in the cases detailed later in this book, as, in general, previous studies anticipated. The effects of these shifts are a different matter, but the direction is not the same in every case. Cross-nationally, as illustrated in chapter 3 (figure 3.1), elderly populations in the Northeast Asian democracies do not express consistent attitudes about military security that differ from younger age-groups. Even within states, whether the elderly hold different views related to military security varies by country.

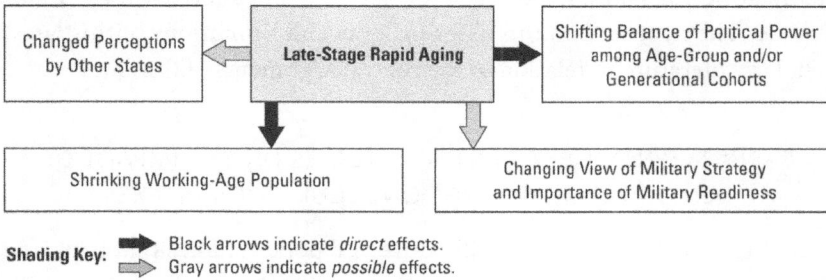

FIGURE 1.2. Hypothesized effects of late-stage rapid aging on military security. *Source:* Author.

On the more tentative predicted effects of late-stage rapid aging on military security (indicated by the gray arrows of figure 1.2), numerous existing studies predict that rapid aging will lead to changed perceptions of aging states by other states, altering the relational security dynamics as a result and also leading to changing views of military strategy and the importance of military readiness among rapidly aging populations. The case studies that follow in this volume, however, do not confirm these predictions based on the first decades of rapid aging in Asia. Whether these predictions will come to pass in the medium term should continue to be considered in future research.

In sum, and to return to a core argument introduced in the introductory chapter, the hypothesized effects of rapid aging on military security should be understood to be about *domestic* attitudes and decisions in addition to being *relational* among states within a shared security ecosystem. For this reason, this study closely examines attitudes and decisions within several country cases as well as considering the dynamics among states within a single security ecosystem, the Indo-Pacific region. The research presented in the chapters that follow shows that to date the effect of rapid aging is not as predicted by the general scholarly literature. Aging powers are not necessarily viewed and treated as weaker, more vulnerable powers. And older citizens of aging powers are not, as a group, prioritizing their personal security—i.e., health or retirement contributions—over national security.

Several recent studies have begun to examine the security implications of this new demographic reality of differential growth and rapid aging of many powerful states, including a few focused on countries in the Indo-Pacific. The next section discusses insights and limitations of this latest scholarly literature in relation to the central arguments of this book.

EARLY TWENTY-FIRST-CENTURY STUDIES ON THE IMPACT OF DEMOGRAPHIC CHANGE ON SECURITY OUTCOMES

A first round of new scholarly literature and policy studies that appeared early in the twenty-first century and that argued that rapid aging of military powers would have important security consequences highlighted the unprecedented nature of demographic change on the horizon but could draw on only limited anecdotal evidence bolstered by hypotheses based on demographic projections.[20] Mark Haas notably predicted a "geriatric peace" that might emerge as states focused more on the domestic consequences of aging and spent less on military defense as a result.[21] Jennifer Sciubba's early work considered both aging states as well as states with still-growing populations and, like others at the time, set out numerous hypotheses based on logical deduction that could not yet be illustrated with more than anecdotal evidence about how the conduct of aging states would change based on their future demographics.[22] Among her claims, she suggested that such states would experience both resource constraints (due to shrinking working-age populations) as well as attitudinal change about security as a result of aging (including due to generational change).

In the early 2010s, studies began to appear that applied new twenty-first-century demographic concerns specifically to countries in the Indo-Pacific.[23] Seongho Sheen notably applied Haas's earlier argument on the "geriatric peace" to suggest a coming "demographic peace" for Northeast Asia based on the shared demographic trends of otherwise rivals China, Japan, and South Korea.[24] An edited volume by Susan Yoshihara and Douglas Sylva also includes several chapters that consider the implications of changing demographics on the security challenges of specific countries in the Indo-Pacific.[25] Numerous contributors to that volume suggest that external perceptions of aging states may alter the regional balance of power, a phenomenon not yet seen by the mid-2020s but perhaps a concern that is motivating aging states currently to maintain and even increase their defense spending and capabilities.

Two extended studies that address the security implications of Japan's rapid aging draw on that country's actual experience and security conduct over the course of its first decade of super-aged status and population shrinkage—the first major power in Asia to experience this demographic stage.[26] One central argument both make is that Japanese attitudes about security will change as Japan ages further. Tom Phuong Le focuses on the impact of generational change that will see a generation of peace activists pass and thus could lead to different security attitudes among the population.[27] Brad Glosserman posits a future where Japan looks further inward, adjusting its regional security posture commensurately. Neither study, however, incorporates the relational dynamic of changing demographics of other states in the region nor examines the changing regional security environment as central to its analysis. As a result, as I argue in chapter 3, both studies underestimate the degree of Japan's military response to its changing security environment that would emerge in the 2020s despite intensifying demographic pressures.

The most comprehensive study to date to consider the effect of rapid aging on security globally is by Brooks et al., who use numerous large datasets to test several hypotheses on the effects of both rapid aging and youth bulges on the outbreak of war. Their main finding is that states with high fertility and/or low median ages are more prone to conflict, while states with low fertility and/or high median ages are less likely to be involved in interstate conflict. More specifically, they write: "According to our analysis, the likelihood of interstate conflict drops sharply (to around one-quarter or one-third below the peak values) once countries reach the following thresholds: (1) a median age above 30 years, (2) a youth-bulge ratio below 20 percent of the adult population, (3) a fertility level below two births per woman, and (4) a life expectancy above 75 years."[28] This is using a *global* dataset—but should we expect these findings to apply equally to potential future conflict in the Indo-Pacific? Several lines of argument suggest that we should not, supported by evidence presented in the following chapters.

By Brooks et al.'s combined measures, the following states in the Indo-Pacific would be less likely than most other states to engage in interstate conflict, using demographic data for the year 2024 as the baseline: Japan, South Korea, Taiwan, China, and the United States—but not Russia or North Korea due to their below-threshold lower life expectancies.[29] (Subsequent chapters of this volume present more detailed demographic data about these seven territories.) On why "old societies" are likely to be more peaceful, Brooks et al. write: "Old societies at the advanced stages of the demographic transition are likely to have a reduced capacity for conflict for two core reasons: The first reason pertains to the effects of societal aging on the ability of these states to secure funds for military spending, what we term the 'crowding out' effect. The second concerns ... the high per unit costs of military personnel in old societies." They continue, "The more that governments spend on elderly care, the less money they can spend in other areas."[30]

These are both reasonable arguments and predictions. Empirically speaking, however, as discussed in the following chapters, the aging powers of Northeast Asia have not to date shifted military spending to address other needs of an aged population; to the contrary, defense spending has risen in the first decade of rapid aging regionwide, 2010–2020 (as illustrated in table 3.2 in chapter 3)—though in some cases this has been achieved through deficit spending that does not appear to be sustainable in the long-term. In terms of the second concern, rising costs per soldier, the implications of this for overall security are more nuanced than they appear on the surface. Empirically-speaking, fewer but more expensive soldiers may provide more robust security than greater numbers of less expensive soldiers. Note, in addition, that this concern relates to whether there will in fact be a shortage of labor in the marketplace that drives up labor costs, which may not be the case given the effect of technological innovation broadly, as noted in the introduction to this volume and discussed in more detail here and in the chapters that follow. In short, however, early experience with rapid aging in South Korea and China shows that youth employment nevertheless remains stubbornly high, in part due a mismatch of skills versus market demand and in part due to conflicting preferences between young job-seekers and the market. In addition, in the United States and Australia, two states with still-growing population sizes and younger median ages, their militaries also face persistent recruiting challenges that in many ways look similar to those of super-aged Japan.

Apart from simple numbers of potential military recruits, the cost of employing soldiers in the context of a shrinking labor pool is another factor that Brooks et al. emphasize. Again, this concern relates to future uncertainty about whether there will in fact be a shortage of labor in the marketplace, given the effect of technological innovation broadly. In the present and near-term future, however, it is clear that Northeast Asia's aging democracies in particular face difficulties in recruiting adequate numbers of soldiers, and they are paying more for the ones they do recruit. This problem is not confined to all-volunteer militaries. In the Indo-Pacific, where many countries require military service from most young men (none require military service from women), governments face pressure to pay conscripted soldiers a reasonable wage (if not exactly a market-level wage). Indeed, as will be discussed in chapter 3, elected governments in both South Korea and Taiwan have faced substantial pressure to modify conscription and have done so despite countervailing demographic pressures.

On the surface, at least, the increasing cost of maintaining military personnel appears directly related to the shrinking pool of potential recruits. Brooks et al. note that over the period where the number of eligible young men for military service declined, "the North Atlantic Treaty Organization (NATO) powers in Europe and North America averaged a 58 percent increase, in real terms, in the unit costs of their military personnel between 1975 and 1999. Japan, Australia, and New Zealand experienced even more dramatic increases in costs per soldier, with the amounts rising by more than 150 percent from 1981 to 1995." Moreover, they continue, "countries with expanding prime military-age cohorts in the second half of the twentieth century, in contrast, frequently experienced sharp declines in the unit costs of military personnel."[31]

However, when we consider both the evolving demographic profiles of aging states and evolving threats and military technology, an alternative—or at least complementary—explanation for rising costs of military personnel arises: that soldiers in the advanced militaries of aging states in the early twenty-first century may possess better skills due to more intensive training and new technologies and thus be able to do the work of a larger number of soldiers than in the past. In essence, increased individual capabilities may enable fewer of them to provide for the same level (or an even greater level) of security. The previous example of China's shrinking military personnel size but increased capabilities offers one such case. A similar phenomenon is likely to be seen as South Korea shrinks its total military personnel size due to a dramatically reduced number of young men in their society.

Even still, this does not deny that there are rising labor costs; rather, it is meant to illustrate that the number of military personnel alone is only one measure of capability. Indeed, in the Indo-Pacific context, where the largest standing armies in the world are based, this point is especially stark: The million plus soldiers maintained by China and North Korea have historically been countered by far smaller but more technologically advanced militaries of neighboring Japan, South Korea, and Taiwan—as well as a much smaller number of U.S. military forces in the area. (Table 3.2 illustrates this point.) Thus, while the logic of Brooks et al.'s argument that "unless military budgets are expanding, increasing personnel costs as a percentage of these budgets will necessitate cuts in other areas, which will diminish the capacity to project power, all other things being equal," is certainly sound and an important consideration, in the actual security environment of the Indo-Pacific, all other things are *not* equal.[32] The following chapters develop this argument further in relation to specific country cases.

This critique is not meant to discard the contribution that studies such as Brooks et al. make by demonstrating with data the broad pressures aging states face to maintain their military security. Rather, what this book argues is that the impact of demographic change on aging (and other) states will be determined by a wider number of factors, including the specific military threats each country faces, the technologies available to address these threats, and the political will and policy savvy of these individual states. As a rejoinder to the technology- and training-based argument advanced here, Brooks et al. rightly note that "even if states are able to substitute capital for labor while maintaining or even enhancing combat power, military missions such as counterinsurgency, nation-building, and militarized humanitarian operations will continue to be labor intensive."[33] However, these examples of specific military missions are only a small subset of potential military-use scenarios, with none of them being primary military ambitions for Asia's aging powers—with the notable exception of Russia's apparent ambitions in the European theater of its operations vis-à-vis Ukraine and border regions of other neighboring states. This exception, though, is a good illustration of how rapid aging and the resultant demographic pressures it creates may shape future military ambitions. This issue will be further discussed in the country-specific sections of the chapters that follow.

RECONSIDERING THE EFFECTS OF RAPID AGING ON NATIONAL SECURITY: A PREVIEW

Two decades into our twenty-first-century experience of late-stage rapid aging, it is now possible to examine in greater detail how aging states—especially aging powers—are adjusting their security policies and military readiness for their projected futures of much higher median ages and smaller working-age and total populations. We can examine the conduct of the few major powers who already have crossed into their fifth-stage demographic transition—which in 2025 Asia are China, Japan, Russia, South Korea, and Taiwan—and we also can examine the military and broader security planning of other states that are just entering or about to enter their next stage of demographic transition. We also can contrast this conduct and policy planning by rapidly aging states with conduct and planning of still-growing and less rapidly aging states in the same region, something that was not possible until the first "super-aged" states in world history emerged early this century.

To return to a conceptual framework for considering the effects of rapid aging on national security, in addition to four primary first-order hypothesized effects of rapid aging on military security common in existing scholarly literature as illustrated in figure 1.2, eight second-order effects also are commonly argued to result from rapid aging, as visualized in figure 1.3. In the following chapters, these first- and second-order predicted effects of late-stage rapid aging on military security are examined in the six Northeast Asian territories currently experiencing or on the cusp of their rapid-aging transition, as well as in others in the broader Indo-Pacific region.

Figure 1.3 illustrates eight second-order effects of rapid aging posited in existing scholarly literature that derive from the four first-order effects explained earlier (and shown in figure 1.2). Of these second-order predicted effects, only one—a smaller recruiting pool for militaries—is a virtual certainty, but even this factor is not an absolute certainty because states could virtually double the pool of potential recruits by including women, as Israel and some Northern European countries do. None of the states in this study seem willing to follow that path, however—instead planning only modest increases in female military service.

The other seven second-order predictions summarized in figure 1.3 also generally have not emerged as expected. For example, a smaller recruiting

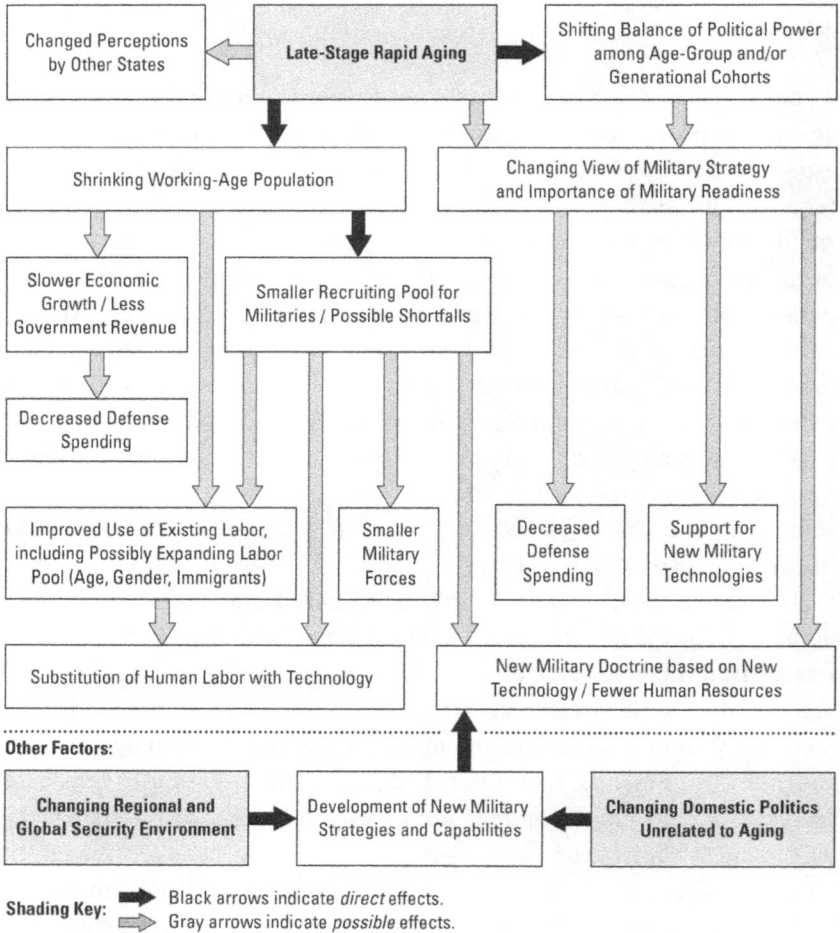

FIGURE 1.3. Second-order effects of late-stage rapid aging on military security. *Source*: Author.

pool for militaries has not necessarily resulted in a smaller military: States might expand the pool of eligible recruits to address the shortfall or increase incentives to retain troops for a longer period. As another example, decreased defense spending has not necessarily resulted from less government revenue or changing views of the importance of military readiness (themselves contingent first-order predictions); indeed, less government revenue itself is not seen in the case chapters that follow in these first decades of rapid aging. Rather, these states have continued to grow economically despite a smaller working-age population, and government revenue has increased as a result. Moreover, as will be discussed in chapters 3 and 4, all six of the rapidly aging states of Northeast Asia have *increased* their defense spending as they begin to experience rapid aging.

In addition to these eight predicted second-order demographic consequences, figure 1.3 illustrates that other factors apart from demographics in the changing security environment of the Indo-Pacific also may lead to an outcome similar to that predicted from rapid aging. Including the categories of "changing regional and global security environment" and "changing domestic politics unrelated to aging" is meant to acknowledge other variables contributing to security policy change.

New technologies such as robotics and other unmanned systems, including AI, surely will offer some offsets for shrinking working-age populations, as indicated in several boxes of figure 1.3. At the same time, however, such new technologies themselves are also altering the nature of the regional—and global—security landscape, including the emergence of new security domains in cyberspace and outer space as well as new dimensions of traditional security domains. For example, in the United States, the U.S. Space Force (USSF) was established December 2019, creating the first new branch of the U.S. armed services in over seventy years. By contrast, protection from cyber threats is a responsibility shared across military services and other government institutions, but it has garnered increased attention in recent years beyond traditional military security concerns to include a range of so-called soft infrastructure targets, such as municipal or private power plants and commercial chemical facilities. As these two examples of new security domains illustrate, responding to the new threat aspects of these technologies will require a large number of personnel, even if in other ways these new domains and technologies offer labor-saving possibilities.

New military technologies that are designed more explicitly to involve fewer human beings also can result in new military concerns that then generate an increased need for human labor. Though there may perhaps be a net savings of labor overall, or at least an increased flexibility of the type and location of that labor, the ability to reduce personnel due to the use of new technologies is likely much less than it may appear on the surface—at least in the short to medium term. One example of such apparently labor-saving technology is "uncrewed" aerial drones, many of which are piloted by human beings remotely. A second-order example would be to consider smaller aerial "swarm" drones that are envisioned in the medium term to be controlled largely by AI. On the surface, this technological development and its implementation reduce the need for human pilots (whether in an actual plane or in a trailer controlling a drone remotely), but at a deeper level this sort of new weapons system introduces an entirely new type of military threat for which human labor must develop and deploy solutions—and pay for. Thus, the true extent to which this new technology is labor-saving is unclear.

Finally, in considering how evolving military and civilian technologies may offset or exacerbate demographic challenges of rapidly aging states, other technologies also are being introduced into conflict scenarios that do not have an obvious connection to demographics nor to new security domains but nevertheless are forcing military strategists to adapt their planning for future conflict. This latter category of important technological change affecting military security planning in the Indo-Pacific would include improvements in missile technology (both hypersonic and conventional), proliferation of nuclear weapons (though there is potentially a demographic aspect to explore there), and the spread of the most advanced weapons platforms to more countries in an economically booming region. These and other examples are elaborated on in chapter 2 and later chapters.

In sum, this book—in the chapters that follow—illustrates four broad points about the potential mitigating influence of technology on the coming demographic changes, especially for the world's aging powers. First, there are a surprising number of non-high-tech potential solutions to shrinking workforces and aging that also could be employed by military forces, such as outsourcing and enhancing efficiencies using existing technologies. Second, different sorts of threats utilize technology differently: There is no universal answer to whether technology can offset the need for military personnel in conflict in the abstract. For example, invading and occupying a country require different technology than protecting against an invasion. Third, there often still is a need for people to operate many uncrewed systems, and to design, build, and pay for them. Fourth, the rise of gray-zone conflicts and other new military concerns is shifting the nature of warfare in ways that affect the type of human labor required for military security.

This study does not seek to assign relative causal weight to which factors are contributing more or less to the direction of security policy evolution in the Indo-Pacific. Rather, the goal is to illustrate how the unprecedented demographic transition underway creates new pressures for action and accommodation—in short, that demographic pressures, too, are a "variable," and one underappreciated in studies of the evolving security landscape of the Indo-Pacific to date. Unlike some earlier studies that argue that a new "demographic peace" is likely to emerge from these new pressures, the case studies that follow illustrate how the effect of demographic transition on each state varies based on a large number of factors, including domestic politics, cultural resistance, available technology, and the specific nature of the security threats each state faces (even within a single regional security ecosystem). Still, the pressures exerted by the variable of population change are evident across the board and lead to recognizable patterns and stages of state-level policy responses to this change.

There is a consensus in existing scholarship that changing worldwide demographics will exert an important impact on security globally, but insights from this literature are only partially applicable to the specific security challenges of the contemporary Indo-Pacific, particularly when the impact of new and emerging technologies is factored in. Some predictions based on other regions are not directly relevant, such as those based on states with very high fertility rates, of which there are none in the Indo-Pacific at present. Other predictions are based on an intensive study of only one country, not factoring in the relational aspect of security concerns. And yet other predictions were made before the actual rapid aging in Asia was well underway and without an updated consideration of how the contemporary regional security environment had evolved.

Chapter 2 seeks to address these gaps in the existing literature by illustrating the differences in population changes in the Indo-Pacific region compared to the world as a whole, considering how the variation in population shifts among countries in the region will affect regional security dynamics and explaining the primary security challenges facing the region, which include growing gray-zone as well as traditional and nontraditional security concerns.

Chapter Two

INDO-PACIFIC SECURITY CHALLENGES AND RAPID AGING

Pressures for New Security Architecture

> For centuries, the United States and much of the world have viewed Asia too narrowly—as an arena of geopolitical competition. Today, Indo-Pacific nations are helping to define the very nature of the international order, and U.S. allies and partners around the world have a stake in its outcomes.
>
> —*INDO-PACIFIC STRATEGY OF THE UNITED STATES*, FEBRUARY 2022

Understanding the effect of demographic change on national security in the Indo-Pacific requires both data on the differential demographic change projected for the region as well as an awareness of what sorts of security challenges the region and its states face. Unlike the aging powers of Northeast Asia, the states and territories of the broader Indo-Pacific region are projected to experience widely varying population changes. In addition, the range of perceived national security challenges in the broader Indo-Pacific region also is much greater, and identifying them more contested, than in Northeast Asia. This chapter provides an overview of both demographic trends in the Indo-Pacific and major security challenges faced by the region. It begins with a discussion of regional demographic change projected over the next several decades through a series of figures and tables and then links this change to the primary regional security challenges facing Indo-Pacific states and territories. Next, the impact of these changing demographics and evolving security challenges on U.S.-led security architecture in the region is discussed. Overall, the chapter seeks to emphasize the relational nature of the impact of demographic change on both the region and individual states before moving to the country-based case discussions presented in the next three chapters. Moreover, the overview discussion of major regional security challenges is designed to provide background and context about these challenges that can be drawn on and elaborated on in subsequent chapters that consider these challenges from the perspective of an individual state or territory.

Two points emphasized earlier should be repeated at the outset. First, every regional state and territory is aging, as measured by rising median ages and rising percentage of their aged 65+ populations. Second, the security challenges themselves increasingly reside in the gray zone between full-scale war and peace or even areas not directly rooted in military security, such as pandemic responses and climate change. There is a dual-graying of security in the Indo-Pacific, even as concerns about conventional military conflict continue over numerous long-standing conflict flashpoints.

At the same time, the Indo-Pacific region today presents a security paradox: It is a region that has not experienced major interstate war for two generations, yet also one that generates many headlines and research studies over existential security threats, including great power competition, nuclear and other weapons proliferation, transnational terrorism and piracy, numerous pandemics, the impacts from climate change, and rising gray-zone challenges such as endemic cyberattacks and rampant cognitive warfare. While highlighting the great diversity of the region—comprising roughly fifty states and territories, tiny to mammoth in population, with varied geographies and levels of development—this chapter focuses on regional security challenges from the perspective of the United States and its allies, though it also will introduce interstate military security challenges as perceived by other states.

What is *not* the focus of this chapter are many of the nonmilitary conceptualizations and concerns related to national security, which nevertheless might be concerns that have more immediacy to many residents of the region, such as access to clean water, adequate housing, or protection from local criminal gangs—all of which also are affected by the region's changing demographics. Almost any issue can be "securitized"—employing a word from the constructivist lexicon—such as immigration or protection of core cultural values. Some of these broader security concerns will be discussed in later chapters that focus on specific countries since they are widely perceived concerns for a specific country only. In this chapter, however, even this reduced scope limited primarily to interstate military concerns still encompasses a very wide range of often conflicting perspectives on regional security challenges that inhibits cooperation and could lead to outright military conflict. Shifting demographics could exacerbate such tensions if policymakers are not attuned to the varied nature and implications of the coming changes.

As quoted in the epigraph to this chapter, U.S. national security documents and policy statements identify the Indo-Pacific region as one of critical importance to future U.S. prosperity and security.[1] It is also the region where the U.S. military has experienced substantial casualties in war in the past century, including in the Pacific theater of the Second World War, the Korean War, and the Vietnam War.[2] U.S. Cold War rival Russia (then the Soviet Union) also has identified what it still refers to as the Asia-Pacific as important to its security.[3] Together now with China's and India's (re)emergence into the regional and global security landscape, the region provides an unparalleled intersection for great power rivalry. In addition, numerous "middle-power" states have articulated Indo-Pacific strategies in the past decade, including the Northeast Asian states of Japan, South Korea, and Taiwan; Australia and New Zealand in Oceania; and the ASEAN regional organization.[4]

The name and conceptualization of the region has evolved from the Far East/East Asia to Asia-Pacific to Indo-Pacific over the lifetime of the U.S. regional treaty ally system.[5] Multiple states in the region, led by U.S. allies Japan and Australia, now operationalize the region as the "Indo-Pacific" rather than "Asia-Pacific" or East Asia, with the United States following that development in recent strategy documents and the renaming of the U.S. Pacific Command (PACOM)—itself the successor of the "Far East Command" in 1957—to Indo-Pacific Command (INDOPACOM) in 2018.[6]

Since the conclusion of the Vietnam wars, the region has experienced a notable lack of major interstate war and, not unrelatedly, a growing prosperity across its states. Nevertheless, in part due to growing economies, military spending also has increased notably in the twenty-first century, creating concerns about how to manage growing military capabilities across the region. In the first decade of rapid aging across the Indo-Pacific, 2010–2020, U.S. allies/partners Japan, Taiwan, and South Korea increased defense spending 14 percent, 23 percent, and a whopping 67 percent, respectively.[7] Countries in Southeast and South Asia increased defense spending 41 percent and 39 percent, respectively.[8] And China, North Korea, and Russia increased their defense spending by the highest percentages, 249 percent, 262 percent, and 250 percent, respectively.[9]

The region's complex and noncomprehensive institutional architecture to manage security challenges is also a source of concern. The aging U.S. alliance system conceived as "spokes" radiating from the U.S. center is not well-suited to address the range of actors and security challenges of the mid-twenty-first century. Like the region itself, this Cold War–era security system is aging. As Abraham Denmark has argued, "Sustaining the old order is insufficient; [the United States] must find a way to also evolve that order to reflect geopolitical realities."[10]

While long-standing conflict flashpoints of the traditional "East Asia" or "Asia-Pacific" regions continue as principal security concerns of the United States and its core allies in the Indo-Pacific—including the growth of China's military ambitions and capabilities, the divided Korean peninsula and North Korea's nuclear ambitions, and the status of Taiwan—new security concerns, emerging technologies, and emergent networks with new security partners necessitate changes to overall U.S. strategy for peace and stability in the region for itself and its allies and partners. Thus, the need for change is not rooted solely—or even primarily—in demographic change, but demographic change is one important factor for both U.S. and regional policymakers to consider as they conceptualize the region's security approach and architecture.

New security challenges perceived by the United States as well as allies and partners—such as the new security domains of cyber and outer space, the recent and past pandemics, and climate change—also must be addressed within the context of an expanded region and its changing demographics. Even beyond the center of rapid aging in Northeast Asia, the Indo-Pacific region as a whole must adjust to aging populations and graying security challenges, since the populations of every territory in the region are aging, just at differential rates.

INDO-PACIFIC SECURITY ACTORS AND DEMOGRAPHIC TRENDS: THE IP16, THE OIP12, AND BEYOND

The contemporary Indo-Pacific comprises over half of the world's total population and includes three of the nine countries projected to constitute half of world population growth through 2050.[11] The region includes a minimum of fifty states and territories, though that could expand to dozens more depending on the conceptualization (in particular, how many Western Asian and East African states are included). There is tremendous variation in size, wealth, and security concerns within this region—from Pacific Island states like Tuvalu (population just over 10,000) and small ASEAN states like Brunei (population just over 400,000), to middle powers such as Australia (2023 population 26 million) and Vietnam (2023 population 97.8 million), to continental powers China and India (populations around 1.4 billion each). Some of the richest and poorest states in the world coexist in the Indo-Pacific. There are large continental powers with advanced militaries and nuclear weapons and tiny island states that have formally delegated the management of their external security to other states.[12] Overall, many states in the region conceptualize security primarily as internal security or through broader notions of human security or comprehensive security and thus maintain only very limited military forces directed toward external military-security concerns.

To focus on the primary security actors and security concerns of this vast region from the viewpoint of the United States and its allies and partners, this study employs a framework that groups states and territories in the region into a core "Indo-Pacific 16" (IP16) and a secondary "Other Indo-Pacific 12" (OIP12). These two groups together comprise forty-six states and territories, since the OIP12 includes three groupings of Pacific islands that are themselves made up of twenty-one states and territories.[13] Figure 2.1 shows the IP16 and OIP12 geographically, where it should be visually apparent that the IP16 covers the vast majority of territory in the Indo-Pacific region.

Drawing out the IP16 from the greater region underscores how a small subset of the total number of countries and territories in the Indo-Pacific have dominated regional—and even global—security concerns and challenges, including great power rivalries and hot conflicts from the Cold War era. IP16 states and territories include all six U.S. treaty allies in the region (Australia, Japan, New Zealand, the Philippines, South Korea, Thailand), the three principal regional U.S. adversaries (China, North Korea, Russia), six additional regional security partners of the United States and many of its allies (India, Indonesia, Malaysia, Singapore,

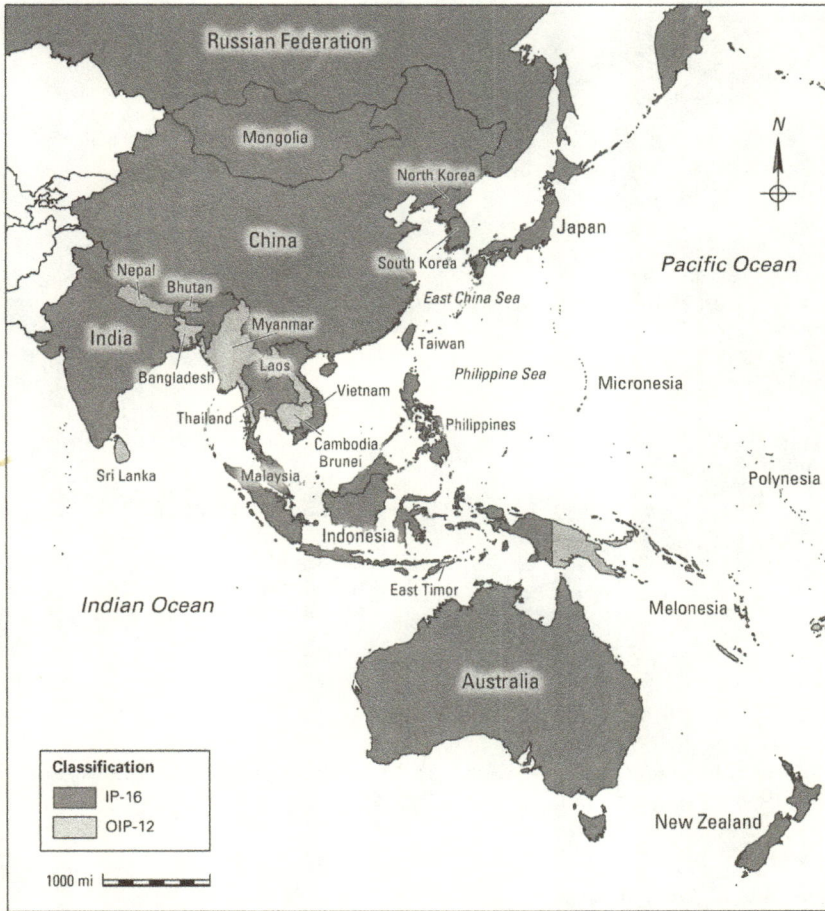

FIGURE 2.1. The IP16 and OIP12 in the Indo-Pacific region. *Credit*: Network Graphics.

Taiwan, Vietnam), plus the one remaining state in Northeast Asia not included in these other categories (Mongolia).

These sixteen states and territories are core to regional security interactions and thus provide important illustrations of the effects of rapid aging and population shifts on regional security to date and looking forward to 2050. As seen in figures 2.2 to 2.4, representing data from 2023/2024, the IP16 alone constitutes nearly half of the world's population, 48 percent,

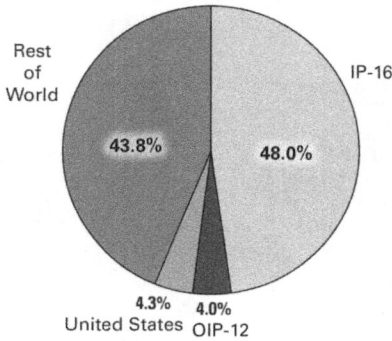

FIGURE 2.2. Indo-Pacific share of world population, 2023. *Source*: UN Population Division, 2024 revision.

Region	Population
IP-16	3.87 billion
OIP-12	318.37 million
United States	342.48 million
Rest of World	3.53 billion

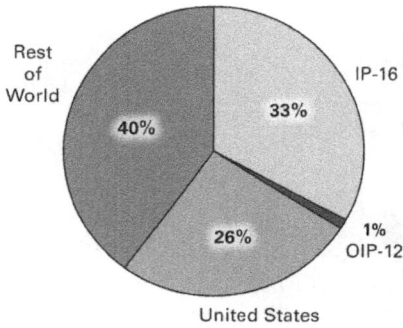

FIGURE 2.3. Indo-Pacific share of world GDP, 2023. *Source*: IMF, World Economic Outlook database (April 2024).

Region	GDP (US$ trillions)
IP-16	34.81
OIP-12	0.81
United States	27.36
Rest of World	41.80

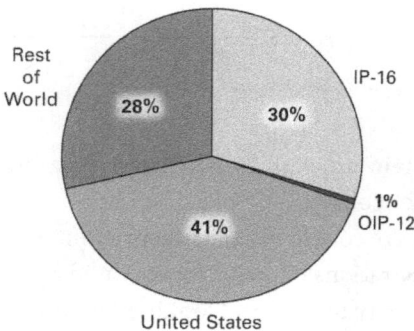

FIGURE 2.4. Indo-Pacific share of world defense spending, 2023. *Source*: *Military Balance* (2024).

Region	Defense Spending (US$ billions)
IP-16	659.47
OIP-12	10.66
United States	905.46
Rest of World	624.33

compared to about 4 percent each for the OIP12 and the United States. The IP16 comprises 33 percent of the world economy (much higher if calculated using purchasing power parity, PPP)—versus less than 1 percent for the OIP12 and 26 percent for the United States. Further, the IP16 comprises 30 percent of global military spending—less than the United States on its own, at 41 percent, but more than the rest of the world combined.

Table 2.1 provides an overview of projected population changes among the IP16 together with corresponding data on the United States. Of particular note for this study, all seventeen states are projected to see an increase in the share of their aged 65+ population (in many cases by double digits), and eight of the seventeen are projected to experience total population shrinkage by 2050 (in most cases well before 2050).[14]

The OIP12 also includes states and territories that are or may become important to the regional security landscape but are at present less central

TABLE 2.1
U.S. + IP16 estimated population change, 2020 v. 2050

Country / territory	TFR 2024	Population 2020 (millions)	Population 2050 (millions)	Change in population 2020 v. 2050	% Population 65+ 2020	% Population 65+ 2050	Change in % population 65+ 2020 vs. 2050
United States	1.62	339.14	379.16	11.8%	16.1	23.2	7.1
Russia	1.45	146.56	130.1	−11.2%	15.5	24.1	8.6
Mongolia	2.69	3.27	4.48	37.0%	4.3	11.6	7.3
China*	1.0	1,425.44	1,240.78	−13.0%	12.6	31.6	19.0
Taiwan	0.87	23.68	19.25	−18.7%	15.9	39.3	23.4
North Korea	1.78	26.09	26.14	—	11.1	21.2	10.1
South Korea	0.72	51.83	44.26	−14.6%	15.8	40.7	24.9
Japan	1.21	126.58	104.12	−17.7%	28.9	38.0	9.1
Philippines	1.92	111.48	137.36	23.2%	4.7	10.9	6.2
Indonesia	2.13	273.75	320.46	17.1%	6.6	14.7	8.1
Malaysia	1.55	33.7	44.18	31.1%	6.7	16.7	10.0
Singapore	0.94	5.68	5.99	5.5%	11.6	27.2	15.6
Thailand	1.21	71.58	66.15	-7.6%	12.9	29.8	16.9
Vietnam	1.91	97.62	112.21	15.0%	7.6	19.6	12.0
Australia	1.64	25.66	32.39	26.2%	16.3	23.9	7.6
New Zealand	1.67	5.04	5.79	14.9%	15.6	23.9	8.3
India	1.98	1,395.97	1,716.14	22.9%	6.4	14.3	7.9
Total/average	1.55	4,163.07	4,388.96	7.17%	12.27	24.16	11.9

Source: UN Population Division, 2024 revision.

Notes: TFR stands for total fertility rate. Countries with below 2.0 TFR projected with constant TFR; those above 2.0 (Mongolia and Indonesia) use UN "Medium Variant."
* Data on China excludes Hong Kong, Macao, and Taiwan, which are listed separately in UN demographic projections.

actors. It includes a few large-population states but mostly smaller-population states, territories, and island groupings (with the latter indicated in italics)—in alphabetical order: Bangladesh, Bhutan, Brunei, Cambodia, Laos, *Melanesia*, *Micronesia*, Myanmar, Nepal, *Polynesia*, Sri Lanka, and Timor-Leste. Disaggregating the three UN groupings of Pacific Islands brings the OIP12 total to twenty-eight territories, with a total population of 309.1 million in 2020—less than 8 percent of the IP16 total of 4.16 *billion* in 2020. Even states small in population can play important roles in regional security, however, as illustrated by the case of the Pacific Islands in chapter 5—or the cases of New Zealand and Singapore as part of the IP16, also discussed in chapter 5.

All the OIP12 are projected to experience total population growth by 2050, five by 30 percent or higher (as shown in table 2.2). For some of these states, rapid population growth could become a security concern, both for internal governance and by neighboring states. However—and closely related—all these states and territories also will experience aging, though with a notably slower increase in the percentage of the population aged 65+ between 2020 and 2050 than seen in the IP16 (a 7.4-point increase for the former, 11.9 for the latter). This increase in aging is due to a large degree to greater life expectancy in these places that still are experiencing

TABLE 2.2
OIP12 estimated population change, 2020 v. 2050

Country / territories	TFR 2024	Population 2020	Population 2050	Change in population 2020 v. 2050	% Population 65+ 2020	% Population 65+ 2050	Change in % population 65+ 2020 v. 2050
Laos	2.42	7.3m	9.7m	33.3%	3.8	9.9	6.1
Cambodia	2.58	16.6m	21.9m	31.9%	5.4	11.6	6.2
Brunei	1.75	445,077	527,715	18.6%	5.6	19.0	13.4
Myanmar	2.12	52.8m	58.6m	11.0%	5.2	13.5	8.3
Bhutan	1.46	767,294	844,412	10.0%	6.0	15.9	9.9
Nepal	1.98	28.7m	34.6m	20.6%	6.1	11.1	5.0
Bangladesh	2.16	165.6m	233.6m	41.1%	5.8	13.0	7.2
Sri Lanka	1.97	22.5m	25.4m	12.9%	10.7	19.8	9.1
Timor-Leste	2.71	1.3m	1.9m	46.2%	5.5	7.0	1.5
Micronesia	2.85	517,059	598,347	15.7%	5.0	12.9	7.9
Melanesia	3.06	11.9m	18.0m	51.3%	3.6	7.8	4.2
Polynesia	2.54	687,130	734,500	6.9%	7.4	17.5	10.1
Total/average	*2.3*	*309.1m*	*406.4m*	*25.0%*	*5.8*	*13.3*	*7.4*

Source: UN Population Division (2024).
Note: Countries with below 2.0 TFR projected with constant TFR; those above use UN "Medium Variant."

population growth, consistent with the fourth stage of demographic transition discussed in chapter 1.

More expansive notions of the region would encompass numerous additional states, large and small—including those to the west of India as far as the African east coast and on the western side of the Pacific Ocean, such as Canada, the United States, and other states of the Americas. Core U.S. ally Japan—one of the first states to articulate an Indo-Pacific vision—generally includes the eastern side of Africa in its conceptualization of the region, seeing one hallmark of the region being the joining of two great oceans, the Pacific and Indian. India also articulates a vision of the Indo-Pacific that focuses more on maritime space, including what it refers to as the Indian Ocean Region (IOR). As just one illustration, only eight of the twenty-three member states of the Indian Ocean Rim Association are part of this study (those east of India).[15] Expanding the regional definition of this study to incorporate those states would generate even greater demographic variation and range of security concerns, undermining one of the core aims of this study—to generate greater insights into the implications of demographic change for military security by narrowing the scope of previous studies that focus on worldwide security concerns. For example, piracy concerns off the coast of East Africa have provoked a coordinated response by numerous Indo-Pacific states. In addition, the territorial dispute between India and Pakistan over Kashmir certainly could be argued to constitute a central Indo-Pacific concern (and one where changing demographics is playing a role). Numerous other security concerns within an expanded definition of the region could be considered vis-à-vis demographics in future scholarship, such as an examination of the generally faster population growth rates on the East Africa side of an expanded notion of the Indo-Pacific.

Important Demographic Commonalities and Differences Between IP16 and OIP12

The Indo-Pacific region already has experienced tremendous demographic change since the end of the Second World War, as indeed the world has, with ballooning populations across the region and a well-utilized "demographic dividend" of large working-age populations with small elderly populations to support in many states. Regionwide and worldwide, we are now experiencing another, differently unprecedented stage of demographic developments, including the new phenomenon of late-stage rapid aging. Many of the roughly fifty states and territories of the Indo-Pacific region are projected to experience dramatic population changes over the next twenty-five years, and indeed notable changes already are underway, as illustrated in this section.

Every state or territory in the Indo-Pacific already is experiencing growth in the percentage of their elderly populations (aged 65+), and this percentage is projected to increase in every state/island grouping in the region in the coming three decades (as previously illustrated in tables 2.1 and 2.2). Ten of the twenty-eight states/island groupings—including nearly all the most powerful states today militarily—will see their proportions of aged 65+ populations rise by more than 10 percentage points, with key U.S. security partners South Korea and Taiwan seeing rises of over 20 percentage points, leading to over one-third of their total populations projected to be 65+ by 2050.

To put this in a broader context of the new demographic phenomenon of rapid aging, in 2020 only one of the twenty-eight states and territories/ groupings that are the focus of this study was categorized as "super-aged" (Japan)—meaning over 20 percent of the population was aged 65+. By 2050, ten of the IP16 are projected to be super-aged (with two of the OIP12 close behind), in addition to the United States and numerous other countries around the world.

This growth in elderly populations in the region, and the unprecedented nature of it, is one reason why it is so important to study the security implications of rapid aging. Among the IP16, the average percentage of the population aged 65+ is projected to nearly double from 2020 to 2050, from 12.27 percent to 24.18 percent; in the OIP12, the average will more than double, from 5.8 percent to 13.3 percent.[16] The median age of every state/island grouping in the Indo-Pacific also is rising. Five places in the region are projected to reach median ages over fifty years old by 2050: China plus U.S. allies or partners Japan, Singapore, South Korea, and Taiwan. (See table 2.3 for a listing of median ages for the full IP16 plus the United States.)

It is not just rapid aging that has security implications, but also the total population sizes that must both support an expanding aging population as well as provide for military security. Although all the Indo-Pacific states/ island groupings are experiencing aging (at differential rates), the region shows great variation in other demographic projections. For example, eight are projected to experience total population shrinkage by 2050, with five of these already experiencing it (China, Japan, Russia, South Korea, and Taiwan). Meanwhile, four countries and the island grouping of Melanesia are projected to see total population increases of over 30 percent from 2020 to 2050 (as indicated in tables 2.1 and 2.2).

Demographic Variation Within the IP16 Will Make New Security Partners More Attractive

Among the IP16, eight face rapid aging *and* population shrinkage by 2050 (and in most cases much earlier): China, Japan, North Korea, Russia, Singapore, South Korea, Taiwan, and Thailand. Notice that seven of these eight states are widely considered ones with major security concerns and/or regional security roles. By contrast, the IP16 grouping also includes five large and growing populations that also remain comparatively youthful: India, Indonesia, Malaysia, the Philippines, Vietnam—plus one smaller-population state with a growing and youthful population, Mongolia. Each of these six states has present and projected median ages under forty through 2050, and none is projected to enter the super-aged category by 2050. (See tables 2.1 and 2.3 for data on these states.) These six, considered individually in chapter 5, thus present particularly positive demographic profiles as deepened security partners in the future, and, indeed, they already have been pursued actively for deepened security cooperation by numerous regional states. India, in particular, has been courted to join multiple institutionalized trilateral security forums as well as the so-called Quad grouping of Australia, India, Japan, and the United States.

The IP16 also includes two other states that fall in between the two groups just described, where super-aged status is on the horizon but population growth continues due to immigration: Australia and New Zealand. These two states are projected to become super-aged in 2031 but also to experience substantial population growth through 2050 (and likely beyond)—over 26 percent for Australia and nearly 15 percent for New Zealand compared to 2020 population sizes. The United States also falls in this category, projected to reach super-aged status in 2029 and with projected population growth of nearly 12 percent from 2020 to 2050. That this projected growth is due to immigration underscores how government policies affect demographic outcomes so directly (and also how demographic projections can be inaccurate if something changes in the world—such as the recent Covid-19 pandemic—or in local policy that affects immigration).

The OIP12: Fast-Growing Pacific Islands and Youthful Large-Population States with Potential Demographic Dividends or Rising Tensions

The OIP12 includes a wider range of actors, from the micro-states of the Pacific Islands to large but less-developed states such as Myanmar and Bangladesh. None were super-aged in 2020 nor even projected to be by 2050, and all are projected to experience growth in their total populations through at least 2050, many by a substantial amount. Timor-Leste as well as the island grouping of Melanesia are each projected to experience population growth of around 50 percent of their 2020 populations by 2050, a particular security concern for areas where climate change is expected to reduce space for living and farming. On the positive side of the demographic spectrum, their elderly populations (aged 65+) are projected to remain under 8 percent through 2050 (and likely much later).

Thus, with this broader regional grouping of the OIP12, it is necessary to consider both sides of the regional demographic picture: aging states (the focus of this book) as well as growing and youthful populations that face demographics-related security challenges of a different sort. Such challenges as potential domestic instability and migration-related conflict are widely apparent in regions outside of the Indo-Pacific, especially in the Middle East and Africa, as noted in the review of the existing scholarly literature on the nexus of demographic change and national security presented in chapter 1. Such a development should not be dismissed out of hand as future possible challenges to the Indo-Pacific region as well, if the growing states of the Indo-Pacific do not manage their potential demographic dividends as well as the Northeast Asian states did during their population-growth years.

Thus, aging states in the region may have to contend with new security challenges that result from challenges facing their younger and growing regional neighbors. For example, the Pacific Islands are coveted both by the United States and its allies as well as by China's growing network of cooperative states, as will be discussed in chapter 5.[17] Political instability in Sri Lanka, exacerbated by climate- and pandemic-related insecurity, opens pathways for domestic-originated insecurity as well as manipulation by nefarious foreign actors.

TABLE 2.3
Median age of U.S. allies, adversaries, and select partners in Asia, 2005–2050

Country/territory	Median age 2005	Median age 2020	Median age 2035	Median age 2050	% Increase 2020–2050
United States	35.2	37.2	40.5	42	12.9%
U.S. allies					
Japan	42.6	47.7	52.6	53.4	11.9%
South Korea	33.6	42.8	51.4	57.5	34.3%
Philippines	19.9	24.1	29.9	35.2	46.1%
Thailand	31.2	38.2	44.3	48.8	27.8%
Australia	35.5	36.9	40.7	42	13.8%
New Zealand	34.5	36.5	40.6	42.4	16.2%
U.S. adversaries					
Russia	36.4	38.7	43.9	42.1	8.8%
North Korea	31.4	35.3	39.5	42.4	20.1%
China	31.8	37.5	45.9	52.9	41%
U.S. partners					
Taiwan	33.8	41.7	50.7	56.8	36.2%
Malaysia	23.2	28.6	34.9	39.9	39.5%
Indonesia	25.2	29.1	32.8	35.8	23%
Vietnam	24.8	31.0	37.1	39.5	27.4%
Singapore	32.4	34.5	42	51.4	49%
India	22.2	27.0	32.5	37.4	38.5%
Total average median age	*30.9*	*35.4*	*41.2*	*45*	*27.91%*

Source: UN Population Division, 2024 revision, constant fertility projection.

An Aging of the IP16 and Its Security Concerns

To conclude this broad overview of projected demographic change in the Indo-Pacific to 2050, we return to this study's focus on aging in the sixteen major security actors in the region at present (the IP16 minus Mongolia but including the United States). Table 2.3 shows their projected change in median age categorized by U.S. treaty ally, U.S. adversary, or select U.S. security partner. Of the U.S. treaty allies, the Philippines is a clear outlier for its relative youth—the only one with a median age in the twenties in 2005 and 2020. Among select U.S. partners, numerous states have median ages below the U.S. treaty allies and below the three U.S. adversary states. By contrast, U.S. Northeast Asian allies and partners Japan, South Korea, and Taiwan stand out for their high and still-growing median ages, all projected to climb into the fifties by 2035 and to the mid-fifties by 2050.

Since this is an unprecedented situation, we cannot say with certainty how the coming demographic change in the Indo-Pacific will alter the security environment and the challenges for the United States in managing its alliance system, but initial moves by aging states, increased participation in regional security by rising states, and scholarly research on past international conflict suggest a number of challenges and trends that should be better understood and addressed. Thus, this chapter will now shift focus to consider the principal security challenges faced by region and, in particular, by America's aging allies and partners in the region.

INDO-PACIFIC SECURITY CHALLENGES AND DEMOGRAPHIC CHANGE

The overview of major security concerns in the region presented in this section underscores the many challenges ahead as well as the long-term nature of many of these enduring areas of conflict. Although the impact of demographic change also is experienced primarily through a long-term time frame, the intensification of rapid aging in the past decade and increased pace looking forward already are affecting the way individual states seek to manage some of the region's most significant security challenges—seen both in evolving strategies as well as in new weapons systems procured or envisioned (as discussed further in the following case chapters).

A core argument of this book is that the effect of demographic change on national security is both internal to each country as well as relational among states facing or initiating a security concern. Thus, this book examines changing demographics both relationally at the regional level (in the earlier sections of this chapter) and within individual states and territories (in the following three chapters).

Although all states and territories in the region are projected to experience population aging in the coming decades, and some states and territories will experience dramatic changes to their total population size, these demographic factors will not necessarily play a major role in some of the security challenges individual states and the region face. In many cases, however, demographic change has altered and will likely further alter existing regional security dynamics and potentially introduce new regional security challenges. This section illustrates how demographic change may differently affect specific regional security concerns. Subsequent chapters will expand on the nature of the security concern from the perspective of major security actors facing substantial demographic change and discuss other security concerns perceived by individual states.

Security challenges in this large and diverse region are many, with differing priorities and concerns emphasized by individual states (and often subactors within states). Moreover, there is also reason to believe—as will be discussed in the next chapters—that individual states' perception of security challenges may shift as a result of changing demographics within their populations. For the United States and its allies, China has become the overwhelming primary security concern. North Korea's belligerent conduct continues to pose existential threats to numerous regional states as well. Russia also has reemerged as a disruptive regional security concern.

Beyond these state-focused concerns, traditional security threats such as territorial disputes and piracy continue to be pervasive in the Indo-Pacific, though generally localized and contained, while gray-zone concerns are on the rise (including related to territorial disputes). There also is greatly increased focus on so-called new security challenges in the region, including on the new security domains of cyberspace and outer space. New military and civilian technologies have introduced numerous other new security concerns as well, including in more traditional military areas such as expanded missile capabilities (including hypersonic missiles) and upgraded ships and planes. Looking beyond a narrower focus on military-security concerns, two broader security concerns that have greatly risen in priority among regional states are pandemic and climate change responses and preparedness. The following subsections outline the demographic dimensions of these primary regional security concerns.

The China Challenge

The primary national security concern for the United States and its allies is China. China has been a growing challenge for several decades—intensifying in the first decade of rapid aging in Asia—but has come to dominate security planning documents, dialogues, and policies. The security challenges posed by China are numerous and diverse, with different regional states more concerned with some aspects than others, which complicates coordinated responses to China's growing assertiveness and power. Some states are experiencing escalating territorial disputes with China, others threatened by its growing military assertiveness, and yet others more concerned with other security-related aspects of its behavior, including its cyber activities and policies that may spur another global pandemic and exacerbate climate change. China's economic, trade, and industrial policies also increasingly are viewed through a security lens by regional states. This trend of the country's growing assertiveness is reshaping regional security dynamics, causing every state in the region to reevaluate its practices and how to plan for the future.

Territorial disputes with China could lead to a major interstate war if not managed adequately. The lack of a long-term resolution of China's civil war that ended with the communist takeover of the mainland and the establishment of the fleeing Nationalist government on Taiwan in 1949 is the most prominent and dangerous of the many regional territorial disputes.[18] Tensions over Taiwan have flared up numerous times in the past seventy-five years but are widely seen as at a boiling point in the mid-2020s. Demographic change among the principal actors in this security challenge factors into military strategies, particularly for Taiwan (which is seeing a smaller recruiting pool for its military forces, as discussed in chapter 3), but also may factor into the timing of China's response to the long-standing stalemate (as discussed in chapter 4).

The differential timing of demographic change within Taiwan and China contributes to rising tensions over this long-standing conflict, which will likely increase later in the 2020s as both Taiwan and China grapple further with their challenging demographic futures. Taiwan's birth rate fell much earlier than China's, plummeting to just 1.33 in 2000 and hitting a record low of 1.07 in 2021 (which was also considered the worldwide low that year).[19] Societal attention to this problem within Taiwan focused early-on on economic and social challenges posed by the resultant and projected change to the population pyramid in Taiwan, but more recently, in Taiwan's second decade of rapid aging, the national security challenges posed by demographic change have risen in the consciousness of security planners. In particular, the challenges of recruiting an adequate number of military personnel and longer-term budgetary implications have risen to the forefront of discussion. By contrast, China's declining birth rate began to gain greater popular attention early in the past decade, with the 2030s projected to be the first where a rapidly aging society poses more widespread challenges for China. Moreover, China's enormous population size compared to Taiwan's means that shifting demographics in either state will merely accentuate the long-standing population asymmetry between the two territories. Chapters 3 and 4 examine these dynamics in greater depth.

China is involved in territorial disputes with numerous neighboring states, including a regionwide concern over islands and maritime space in the South China Sea that involves multiple parties, as examined further in chapter 5. China is indirectly involved in other territorial issues on the edges of the Indo-Pacific (as defined in this study), such as the India-Pakistan dispute over Kashmir (which includes the Chinese-claimed and controlled territory of Aksai Chin) and territorial control among rival factions in Afghanistan. The two territorial disputes where demographic factors are most apparent are with the two other major military powers in the region, Japan and India.

Japan's dramatically shifting population demographics—as the world's first super-aged society—poses significant challenges for its future military posture, as examined in greater depth in chapter 3. However, in Japan's first decade of population shrinkage, it rigorously checked China's escalation over the Senkaku-Diaoyu islands—which Japanese official policy states is not disputed territory, despite plainly being a major regional conflict flashpoint. (Technically the dispute also involves Taiwan as a third claimant, but in terms of militarized escalation, the core challenge is between Japan and China.) Both states have significantly expanded their coast guard and naval forces in the first decade of the region's rapid aging, which has stretched Japan's resources both financially and in terms of personnel. As with the Taiwan conflict, however, since China's demographic challenges will not materialize greatly until the late 2020s at the earliest, and its population size in any case hugely exceeds Japan's, the early demographic effects on this conflict focus on Japan's challenges (as examined in chapter 3).

The China-India territorial dispute is one of few cases of active interstate military conflict in the Indo-Pacific in recent decades, having resulted in twenty-four deaths of soldiers on both sides in the June 2020 clash.[20] As a localized and carefully contained conflict among the two largest-population states in the world, demographic change has to date played essentially no direct role in this conflict. In the short term, India has surpassed China as the world's most populous country, and in the medium term India's still-growing labor force (along with that of other nearby growing states) will likely acquire jobs currently filled by China's now-shrinking labor force, but the military security implications of this projected demographic change are decades away, as further discussed in chapters 4 and 5.

In the South China Sea territorial disputes—most apparent with Vietnam and the Philippines, but simmering with Indonesia, Malaysia, and Brunei as well—demographic change to date has played essentially no role in how these conflicts have developed. Looking forward, according to findings from existing literature on the security effects of youth bulges and growing populations, demographics could potentially play a bigger role in the coming years as southern Indo-Pacific states continue to expand in population size and remain more youthful while China's population shrinks and ages. The escalation of the territorial dispute between population-growing Philippines and population-shrinking China may be partly related to these contrasting demographics, though by no means would this book argue that demographics are the *primary* driving factor of rising tensions.

As a regional security challenge, China's unilateral construction and militarization of artificial islands in disputed maritime space should be considered one of the largest military-security challenges that the region faces.[21] China's own projected demographic transition also may alter the regional security environment, as examined in greater depth in chapter 4. China's population size already has begun to shrink. Moreover, the median age of China's population is projected to rise rapidly beginning in the late 2020s as the One-Child Policy generation reaches retirement age. In addition, China's internal demographics have changed in other ways that affect broader conceptions of security, such as the gender imbalance in births in recent decades (also known as the "missing girls" phenomenon) and dramatic declines in birth rates among persecuted ethnic groups such as the Uyghur minority in China's western province of Xinjiang.[22]

China's demographic transition also may affect some of the broader regional security concerns, particularly climate change policy and preparedness. Moreover, the China Challenge, like demographics, is inextricably linked to challenges and opportunities afforded by new technologies, including new military technologies and cyber threats, as discussed in the next section and explored more deeply in chapter 4.

North Korean Weapons Development and Military Provocations

Another long-standing and potentially existential set of regional security concerns emanates from North Korea, which exists as another Cold War–era unresolved security conundrum, the divided Korean peninsula. For U.S. ally South Korea, North Korea poses both an existential security threat as well as the preeminent security-related ambition: unification of the divided country in some form. Beyond this peninsular ambition, the third-generation communist leader, Kim Jong Un, acts as a major destabilizer of the security status quo, primarily threatening neighboring South Korea and Japan, but also increasingly posing a hard security challenge to the United States through its long-range missiles and limited nuclear weapons capabilities, which also are raising concerns in other countries in the Indo-Pacific. China and Russia maintain more ambiguous relationships with their former patron, North Korea—alternately seeming to cooperate with other regional states in containing some of Kim Jong Un's most belligerent threats and actions, but also benefitting from (and at times even fomenting) the distraction and resource-drain North Korean actions inflict on the United States and its regional allies. The start of the third year of the Russia–Ukraine war in 2024 saw closer relations between North Korea and Russia emerge, with North Korea providing weapons to Russia and even some front-line soldiers.

North Korea maintains one of the world's largest standing armies, a force of over 1.2 million personnel.[23] South Korea and the United States devote significant planning and resources to deter against a large-scale invasion of South Korea by North Korea, while other security concerns of the United States and its allies are North Korea's nuclear weapons and advanced missile development. Pyongyang tested six nuclear devices from 2006 to 2024 and was thought to possess approximately sixty nuclear weapons by late 2020.[24] In addition, Kim Jong Un has been expanding conventional missile capabilities as well as the number of missiles that can reach anywhere in Japanese and South Korean territory and now can target the entire Indo-Pacific region as well as the U.S. mainland with a much smaller number of long-range missiles. Moreover, Pyongyang is an active malicious cyberspace actor, as discussed further in the next subsection.

Given the declared urgency of addressing these threats, the longer-term trends of demographic change matter less to present North Korea security challenges, though they still are important to consider related to North Korea's medium-term place in the region, as discussed in chapter 4. North Korea's demographic transition comes later than that of its democratic neighbors, but it is still aging and facing total population shrinkage around 2035.[25] It has had the youngest median age of the three U.S. regional adversaries throughout the twenty-first century (though is projected to exceed Russia's median age by 2050). The primary demographic challenges posed by North Korea are not its own demographics but rather the demographics of the surrounding U.S. allies, particularly Japan and South Korea (discussed further in chapter 3).

Other Traditional Security Concerns in the Region

Rounding out the primary traditional security concerns of the region from a U.S. and allies' perspective are other territorial disputes as well as waxing and waning concerns over piracy in a region dependent on maritime trade. Russia's destabilizing actions worldwide also affect security dynamics in the Indo-Pacific, with Russia deepening security cooperation with other principal security concerns China and North Korea as its isolation from other states is perpetuated by its war with Ukraine. Russia's belligerent behavior and outright aggression in Ukraine and in other territories along its European borders serve to underscore a central argument of this book—that demographic pressures do not determine state policy choices. That said, and as further discussed in chapter 4, Russia's recent policy choices related to its war with Ukraine are seriously taxing its population resources and will limit future policy choices in the Indo-Pacific region.

Numerous territorial disputes in the region beyond those involving China continue to engage regional security actors and expend military resources and to limit security cooperation in other areas, leading to suboptimal regional security cooperation. U.S. allies Japan and South Korea dispute uninhabited islets between the two countries, which contributes to the deep (though perhaps lessening) animosity between two otherwise similarly positioned states in terms of security concerns and demographic challenges. Japan and Russia also dispute islands between them, which has inhibited a formal peace treaty between the two states at the conclusion of the Second World War. Despite all three of these states facing future population shrinkage and rapid aging, demographic change is not likely to affect resolution of these issues—except perhaps in the long term if there is generational attitudinal change related to the conflicts.

In South and Southeast Asia there are both some minor territorial disputes between states plus a major one in the case of India–Pakistan. Internal territorial disputes by way of regional separatists are a security concern in several South and Southeast Asian states, however, where changing demographics may exacerbate tensions as internal demographics of those countries change, including differential growth or decline among different ethnic/religious/regional populations. This aspect of the demographic-national security linkage is discussed further in chapter 5.

Piracy in the Indo-Pacific is another traditional security concern that affects nearly all states in the region and where some link to shifting demographics can be seen. Incidents of piracy spiked in the post–Cold War 1990s, leading to a coordinated response by numerous security actors, including some of Japan's first major regional forays as a regional security provider in the postwar period.[26] Youth bulges predicted for some Southeast Asian states may exacerbate existing challenges in this area in the coming decades, combined with possibly reduced human resources to counter this threat by the more developed and more rapidly aging states. The Regional Cooperation Agreement on Combating Piracy and Armed Robbery Against Ships in Asia (ReCAAP) group of twenty-one states (as of 2024) has sought to coordinate a regional response to this shared concern since its creation in 2006. This issue will be considered further in chapter 5.

Shared Regional Challenges and New Security Concerns

Looking to 2035 and 2050, new security threats and domains will likely play a greater role in the security agenda for states in the Indo-Pacific—such as new threats from advanced weapons technologies like uncrewed aerial vehicles (UAVs), swarm technologies, artificial intelligence, and hypersonic missiles and issues emanating from the current and possible future pandemics as well as climate change. Demographic change may affect these various threats in numerous ways, but it will depend on the specific threat and the demographics of the countries involved. Thus, these new issues will be considered in greater depth in relation to specific countries in the following chapters. Two broad predictions about the interaction of these new security challenges and demographic change, however, should be considered in a regional context, as follows.

First, new weapons and civilian technologies may allow states with expertise and financial resources to operate with fewer human soldiers. The technological replacement of human labor, such as AI making more decisions on behalf of humans, also may save economic resources. At the same time, however, these technologies have led to and will continue to drive the development of new security challenges that will require human resources to address, as we already have seen in the increasingly alarming cybersecurity domain.

Second, shifting population demographics will affect the nature of threats from future pandemics and from man-made climate change. Societies with growing populations require additional resources that can lead to overtaxing of resources, which can exacerbate climate change—particularly in the energy arena but also in other areas such as deforestation caused by overlogging for construction. By contrast, future shrinking populations in some states may allow for more ambitious carbon-reduction targets, among other possible benefits. These dual threats—pandemics and climate change—also can affect population demographics directly, as seen with reduced life expectancies society-wide due to the Covid-19 pandemic or with population relocations necessitated by climate change due to extreme heat or cold, or too little or too much water, among other factors.

At a regional level, as the definition of the region has broadened to the "Indo-Pacific" and the number of regional actors thus increased, perceived security challenges illustrate a much higher degree of variation, including beyond the primary challenges stressed in U.S. strategic planning documents for the region. This expansion and varying degree of priority of issues present a growing challenge to the United States in engaging with an increasingly diverse set of security partners on an expanding range of issues. For some states, climate change will pose a more immediate and urgent threat. Many developing states use their militaries as much (or even more) for internal security or nation-building. Ethnic tensions within states also may be exacerbated by shifting demographics, which in some cases will lead to some ethnic groups growing proportionally and others shrinking. With these evolving threats and changing actors, the U.S. security approach to the region also has had to evolve—and will need to continue to evolve—as discussed in the next section.

AN AGING U.S. SECURITY ARCHITECTURE FACING
GEOPOLITICAL AND DEMOGRAPHIC CHANGE

U.S. approaches to managing its security interests in the Indo-Pacific have evolved with shifting geopolitics, but not as much with shifting demographics. The United States has been engaged with the Indo-Pacific since its founding but became deeply embroiled in Indo-Pacific security-related issues only in the mid-twentieth century.[27] Still in the twenty-first century, however, five of America's seven formal military alliances are in the Indo-Pacific.[28] The practice of forward-positioning U.S. military forces at bases hosted by formal treaty allies has continued since the establishment of this "hub-and-spoke" system in the 1950s.[29]

The core approach of maintaining a small number of formal alliances that are supplemented with ad hoc security partnerships and multilateral institutions has continued for over seventy years across many different security challenges and demographic changes, a system that many see as also showing its age and ripe for revitalization. Mira Rapp-Hooper writes, for instance, in *Shields of the Republic*: "This remarkable alliance system, however, does not meet the trials of our time. Detached from its original goals, the system and its logics have not been updated for the contemporary world."[30] Former deputy assistant secretary of defense Abraham Denmark cast a positive spin on this challenge, writing in 2020: "The United States has an opportunity to revitalize its alliances and partnerships across the region, to harness their growing capabilities, and to empower them to play a more significant role in sustaining the liberal regional order."[31] Undergirding this call to action, however, is a reality that the aging alliance network needs this revitalization, both to address new security concerns and to create efficiencies that can withstand the demographic pressures many U.S. allies will face in the years to come.

The creation of the seven U.S. alliance "spokes" as visualized in figure 2.5—Japan, South Korea, Taiwan (now not a formal ally), the Philippines, Thailand, Australia, and New Zealand—took place within the context of growing populations worldwide and of the Cold War, evolving over the years into the current era of strategic competition with China and differential demographic shifts, though with several important Cold War–era legacies remaining, such as the divided Korean peninsula and standoff over China-Taiwan.

FIGURE 2.5. U.S. treaty allies in the early Cold War period. *Credit*: Network Graphics.

Security challenges to the United States and its allies and partners in the Indo-Pacific have evolved since the end of the Second World War in part in response to a changing distribution of power related to population demographics and differential economic growth rates regionally. Like worldwide population growth in this postwar period, the United States and its allies saw large population growth from 1950 to 2000, with the U.S. population nearly doubling and America's Indo-Pacific allies well over doubling on average (Japan being the notable exception, growing its population by only about 50 percent). As a result, the ratio of population between the United States and its Indo-Pacific allies shifted over the latter half of the twentieth century, starting at an almost even 50-50 split in 1950 to U.S. allies comprising about 56 percent of the combined population of the alliances by 2000.

This level of population growth of America's Asian allies is not projected to continue in the first half of the twenty-first century, however, as indicated by the greatly declining total fertility rates (TFR) shown in table 2.4. The average TFR of the United States and its allies in the Indo-Pacific fell from 4.88 in 1950 to 2.85 in 1975 to the below-replacement level of 1.86 in 2000. Among these Indo-Pacific allies, none now possesses a replacement-level TFR (with the Philippines the last to drop below this level in the early 2020s), and only Australia and New Zealand are anticipated to make up the replacement shortfall caused by low TFR with robust immigration (as seen in table 2.1), though the Philippines will continue to see population growth well beyond 2050 due to its above-replacement TFR until recently.

Important differences in how the six alliances were established and maintained over time have continued resonating today. Most notably, Taiwan is no longer a formal ally as a result of the U.S. shift of diplomatic recognition to the People's Republic of China in 1979, though Taiwan remains an important regional security partner and Washington has repeatedly

TABLE 2.4
Population demographics of seven U.S. treaty allies, 1950–2000

	1950		1975		2000	
	Population	TFR	Population	TFR	Population	TFR
United States	158.8	3.31	219.08	1.77	281.71	2.04
Japan	82.8	2.96	112.41	1.83	127.52	1.30
S. Korea	19.21	5.65	35.38	2.92	48	1.21
Taiwan*	7.6	6.72	16.47	2.74	21.97	1.33
Philippines	18.58	7.42	41.29	5.46	77.99	3.70
Thailand	20.71	6.14	42.33	3.92	62.95	1.60
Australia	8.18	3.18	13.77	1.99	18.99	1.77
New Zealand	1.91	3.69	3.04	2.18	3.86	1.95
Total/average	317.79	4.88	483.77	2.85	642.99	1.86

Source: UN Population Division (2019).

Note: Population in millions.
* Taiwan ceased being a U.S. treaty ally in 1979, though it remains a close security partner.

emphasized U.S. resolve to protect it in an unprovoked military crisis. In addition, U.S. bases in the Philippines—which had provided a crucial logistical hub for military operations in the Vietnam War—closed in the early 1990s: Clark Air Base was the largest overseas U.S. military installation until the U.S. withdrawal in 1991, and Subic Bay Naval Base held that title of largest overseas U.S. military installation until the withdrawal there in 1992. Some of the repair facilities from Subic Bay were moved to security partner Singapore, others to treaty ally Japan. The U.S.-Thailand alliance lost prominence at the conclusion of the U.S. war with Vietnam and further weakened after a military coup in Thailand in 2006, though Thailand and the United States continue to cohost Cobra Gold, the Indo-Pacific region's largest annual multinational military exercise. Finally, on an alliance-weakening front, the United States declared a suspension in its obligations to New Zealand under the ANZUS treaty in 1985 over New Zealand's unilateral declaration of its "nuclear-free zone" policies. The two countries continue to cooperate militarily, however, and in 1997 the United States designated New Zealand as a "major non-NATO ally" (MNNA), a status conferred to eighteen non-NATO allies as of June 2021.[32]

By contrast, the alliance relationship with the region's two population-shrinking and rapidly aging U.S. allies—Japan and South Korea—has deepened over time. The security guarantee to Japan provided under Article 5 of the U.S.-Japan security treaty of 1960 has been repeatedly restated and the regional aspect of the alliance substantially deepened. While the alliance may initially have been as much about containing a former enemy state as it rebuilt in the postwar era, in recent decades Japanese military forces—not just bases located on Japan's territory—have grown to become an essential component of U.S. regional military strategy.[33] The U.S. alliance relationship with South Korea also has deepened in recent decades, with Seoul substantially building up its own military capabilities and taking steps toward more regional security engagement.[34] In sum, U.S. military strategy in the region clearly has been rooted in these deepening alliances, and thus the challenging demographic futures of these two core allies are cause for concern. In addition, these two states themselves have begun to consider in much greater depth how to adjust their security strategies for their graying security futures—a topic further addressed in chapter 3.

Since the beginning of the post–Cold War period, and especially more recently in the context of China's resurgence regionally and globally, the

United States and its now six treaty allies have come to recognize that the U.S. regional alliance system itself is showing its age, having been born into a regional environment over a half-century ago, when most regional states were poor and lacked regional security engagement and only a few states largely determined the course of events. Although several of the principal security challenges from that time continue today, these challenges need to be approached differently due to the different regional balance of power, which in part is a result of changed demographics. In addition, many new security challenges have emerged, including many gray-zone concerns, to the extent that one could argue, as Rapp-Hooper has, that "the nature of competition itself has evolved. Adversaries are developing sophisticated military approaches to erode security guarantees and bypassing those guarantees altogether by acting in 'subconventional' and nonmilitary domains. Information warfare, maritime assertiveness, hacking, and economic coercion are the terms of modern competition."[35]

The regional distribution of power also is affected by an expanded notion of the region away from "East Asia" or the "Asia-Pacific" to the larger "Indo-Pacific" conception that includes a much wider range of demographic trends among its territories. The United States and its allies and partners have been making renewed efforts to adapt the "hub-and-spoke plus security partners" alliance system that was established under different demographic and geopolitical realities. These efforts began decades ago but have taken on new urgency in this current era of proliferating security concerns combined with growing concerns about the credibility of the United States and its security architecture to deliver security to U.S. allies and partners, particularly after Donald Trump returned to the presidency of the United States in January 2025.

A first round of regional security architecture building in the post–Cold War era created several large multilateral institutions that provided forums for a wide range of states to interact and express security concerns, forums that continue to fill the annual calendars of government officials, such as the ASEAN Regional Forum (ARF), the East Asian Summit (EAS), and the Shangri-la Dialogue.[36] More recently, the United States and its major security allies and partners have developed smaller "minilateral" forms of cooperation to supplement the long-standing hub-and-spoke alliance network, such as institutionalized trilaterals (United States–Japan–Australia, United States–Japan–South Korea, and the AUKUS grouping of Australia–United

Kingdom–United States), as well as one prominent quadrilateral grouping, the so-called Quad of Australia, India, Japan, and the United States.[37]

What characterizes this more recent round of institutionalized cooperation are its ad hoc nature, breadth of issues, and smaller number of actors (in each grouping). This sort of minilateral cooperation also can be networked into cooperation among a larger number of actors in a specific issue area, such as supply chain resilience or cybersecurity. As described by one prominent U.S. security analyst, Richard Fontaine: "The result is an emerging regional security structure that, at its best, can be adaptable and inclusive in order to tackle modern threats." Moreover, stressing the continued centrality of the hub-and-spoke U.S. alliances, Fontaine continues: "This growing security network is set to augment, rather than replace, the United States' traditional 'hub and spokes' system of bilateral alliances in Asia."[38] Notably, this is a strategy being employed not only by the United States but by U.S. allies and partners as well, who create their own minilateral forums. Australia, Japan, and South Korea all have pursued such supplements to their "core alliance" with the United States.[39]

Through this evolution of regional security architecture, a small number of non-U.S. allies have emerged as especially important security partners, though not as "allies" in a traditional sense. The United States and numerous other regional states have formal "security partnerships" with a large number of states, but not all these partnerships signal deep or significantly expanding security cooperation. In the Indo-Pacific, five states in particular have deepened their security partnerships not just with the United States but also with other U.S. allies in the region: India, Indonesia, Malaysia, Singapore, and Vietnam. Together with Taiwan, a former U.S. ally and continued important security partner, these six states merit special attention when considering the evolving security environment of the expanded Indo-Pacific region. The substantially different demographic profiles of these states compared to U.S. treaty allies also deserves additional attention and thus are examined in greater depth in chapter 5.

Figure 2.6 illustrates Indo-Pacific security alignments vis-à-vis the United States in 2024. The three principal security adversaries of the United States—Russia, North Korea, and China—are shaded in black. The six U.S. treaty allies—Japan, South Korea, the Philippines, Thailand, Australia, and New Zealand—are shaded in light gray. Six important and deepening U.S. security partners—India, Indonesia, Malaysia, Singapore, Vietnam, and

FIGURE 2.6. Indo-Pacific security alignments with the United States in 2024. *Credit*: Network Graphics.

Taiwan—are shaded in dark gray. These fifteen states, together with the United States—and increasingly other outside-of-region actors like the major European powers—will together most define the security challenges and strategic approaches to managing them in the coming several decades, though over time and based on unexpected developments other states also may rise in prominence.

Population shifts projected for the coming three decades (and beyond) in the Indo-Pacific will exert new pressures on the United States and its allies and partners vis-à-vis regional security architecture and approaches. The region will experience unprecedented population change over the next twenty-five years, and indeed dramatic change already is underway, as detailed earlier in this chapter. Table 2.5 summarizes projected population trends for the United States and fifteen important regional security actors related to aging and total population size (the IP16 minus Mongolia), contrasting the situation in 2020 with projections for 2035 and 2050. Especially notable is projected demographic change among the six U.S. treaty allies. Only one of the six was super-aged in 2020 (Japan), but five will be super-aged by 2035 (all but the Philippines). Japan and South Korea are currently experiencing population shrinkage, but three of the six will be in 2025, when Thailand is projected to reach that demographic milestone.

Underscoring the relational component of regional demographic change, it is also important to emphasize projections for the three principal regional U.S. adversaries. None was super-aged in 2020, but two of three are projected to be by 2035 (China and Russia)—and likely much before then, with North Korea expected to follow in 2040. Moreover, China and Russia also are currently experiencing a decreasing total population size, as North Korea is projected to by 2035.

These demographic shifts will affect how the United States and its allies and partners will address military security concerns in the region moving forward. Some U.S. allies and partners already struggle to fill military recruiting targets and to pay for new weapons systems as government debt mounts and demands for greater spending on the elderly grow louder. This struggle will intensify in the 2020s for important U.S. allies Japan and South Korea. Chinese relative military power vis-à-vis the United States and its allies in the region will almost certainly increase over this decade, in part due to demographic challenges of key U.S. allies, but then China will fall off a "demographic cliff" much steeper than experienced by U.S. allies and partners (which aged more slowly over decades).[40] That said, China's very large total population size and authoritarian system of government will likely enable it to manage the security implications of its demographic transition differently than regional U.S. allies do—a topic considered further in chapter 4.

Among these Northeast Asian states, demographic change will further push militaries to embrace high-tech solutions to offset the effects of costlier labor and, in many cases, recruiting shortfalls. By contrast, further

TABLE 2.5
Demographic change of U.S. allies, adversaries, and select partners, 2020–2050

	Total population decreasing			Population Age 20–64 decreasing			Super-aged*		
	2020	2035	2050	2020	2035	2050	2020	2035	2050
United States	—	—	—	—	—	—	—	✓	✓
U.S. allies									
Japan	✓	✓	✓	✓	✓	✓	✓	✓	✓
South Korea	(2021)	✓	✓	✓	✓	✓	—	✓	✓
Philippines	—	—	—	—	—	—	—	—	—
Thailand	—	✓	✓	(2021)	✓	✓	—	✓	✓
Australia	—	—	—	—	—	—	—	✓	✓
New Zealand	—	—	—	—	—	—	—	✓	✓
U.S. adversaries									
Russia	✓	✓	✓	✓	✓	✓	—	✓	✓
North Korea	—	✓	✓	(2023)	✓	✓	—	(2040)	✓
China	(2022)	✓	✓	✓	✓	✓	—	✓	✓
U.S. partners									
Taiwan	✓	✓	✓	✓	✓	✓	—	✓	✓
Malaysia	—	—	—	—	—	—	—	—	—
Indonesia	—	—	—	—	—	—	—	—	—
Vietnam	—	—	(2055)	—	—	✓	—	—	(2051)
Singapore	—	—	✓	—	✓	✓	—	✓	✓
India	—	—	—	—	—	—	—	—	—

Source: UN Population Division (2024), "constant fertility" scenario.

* "Super-aged" is defined as over 20 percent of the population 65 or older.

south in the Indo-Pacific, already large-population states like India, Indonesia, and the Philippines will experience youth bulges in the coming decades that will offer wider military options for these states and potentially make them even more attractive security partners, as will be discussed further in chapter 5. Already there has been a notable post–Cold War shift to additional security partners and more "networking" among allies and partners. Demographic shifts already underway—which will intensify—add urgency to this shift in strategy.

The overviews of regional demographic change projected through 2050 and of principal security challenges facing the Indo-Pacific discussed in this chapter are intended to provide important background and context for the following three chapters, which examine the impact of demographic change on security concerns of specific regional countries and territories as well as of the growing network of regional alliances and security partnerships.

Beyond the central focus of this study on the demographic aspects of aging and population size, these chapters also will note other demographic changes underway and on the horizon that may have second-order security implications, such as a growing gender imbalance in some states (China, India, and Vietnam, in particular) and differential growth rates among different ethnic groups within states.

Chapter Three

NORTHEAST ASIA'S RAPIDLY AGING DEMOCRACIES

The Leading Edge of Super-Aging in Asia

COMPARING NORTHEAST ASIA'S RAPIDLY AGING DEMOCRACIES AND AUTOCRACIES

The locus of rapid aging, population shrinkage, and security concerns in the world is Northeast Asia. In this region, three rapidly aging democracies and security partners of the United States face three rapidly aging autocracies that regularly signal nefarious intentions through their military activities and bellicose statements, including through rising gray-zone actions and provocative use of their potent military forces—and, in the case of Russia, outright invasion of one of its European neighbors, Ukraine.

On the surface, there is a rough parallel of demographic direction among these security partners and rivals, but the later aging of China, North Korea, and Russia is one important difference—perhaps explaining differences in behavior in the past decade as aging has intensified but not yet reached super-aged status for the aging autocracies. Moreover, when examined in the greater depth presented in this and the following chapter, beyond differences in the timing of each demographic transition, levels of economic development, total population size, and ability to shape the actions of populations through government control result in significant variation across these six core cases in how rapid aging affects military readiness and broader security strategies of these aging powers. This variation underscores both a central argument of this book—that population demographics are indeed a variable in Asia's aging security landscape, not a constant—and helps to elucidate the many ways that demographic change is changing each state's approach to military security as well as where it is not.

The three traditional U.S. allies in Northeast Asia—Japan, South Korea, and Taiwan—face the most dramatic aging and shrinking populations in the Indo-Pacific in the 2020s. Yet, to date, none have moved in the direction of reducing their military capabilities or readiness due to their rapid aging. To the contrary, each has begun to implement strategies to adjust to actual and projected demographic change while strengthening military capabilities in response to rising perceptions of threats.

Still, many challenges remain that are specific to the unique demographic and security challenges each faces—with two common threads being intensified aging and population shrinking and a growing concern about the military actions of Northeast Asia's aging autocracies, despite those states' own population shifts underway. Another common thread seen among these rapidly aging democracies is a growing engagement with security partners, especially a deepening of their security relationships with the United States.

American allies and partners in the Indo-Pacific region are all aging, but the Northeast Asian democracies face particularly challenging future demographics, as noted in earlier chapters—more intensified aging, especially low fertility rates, and little immigration, resulting in total population shrinkage. Japan, South Korea, and Taiwan form the leading edge of rapid aging in Asia. They all have median ages of over 40, and all are projected to be super-aged in the 2020s (which Japan reached in 2005) and to climb to median ages over 50 years old in the 2030s.

Northeast Asia's rapidly aging autocracies—security rivals to the United States and the Northeast Asian democracies—face a similar demographic future but on a later timetable, as illustrated in table 3.1. While Japan, South Korea, and Taiwan all will have reached super-aged status by the 2020s, this milestone is projected to be reached by China and Russia in the mid-2030s, and North Korea only in 2040. China and North Korea also reached the earlier "aged" status later than Northeast Asia's democracies.

This later timing matters in the security arena for several reasons. First, the later agers can potentially learn from approaches taken and technologies

TABLE 3.1
Speed and milestones of aging in Northeast Asia

	Reached aging status	Reached aged status	Years to aged status	Reached super-aged status	Years to super-aged status	Reach(ed) 30% 65+	Years to 30% 65+
Japan	1969	1994	25	2005	11	2025	20
South Korea	2000	2018	18	2025	7	2036	11
Taiwan	1994	2018	24	2025	7	2042	15
China	2000	2023	23	2032	9	2049	16
Russia	1967	2017	50	2031	14	Post-2050	n/a
North Korea	2002	2029	27	2040	11	Post-2050	n/a

Source: UN Population Division (2024), constant fertility projection

Notes: "Aging" status is 7–14 percent of a population 65 years or older; "aged" is 14–20 percent of a population 65+; "super-aged" is from 20 percent of a population 65+.

developed to manage the aging transition by earlier-aging states. Second, to the extent that aging is a disadvantage in terms of military power—which is not a foregone conclusion in twenty-first-century conflict scenarios—the later-aging states would benefit from this delayed transition. Finally, related to the discussion of relevant scholarly literature in chapter 1, some argue that states may seek to lock in advantages of youth prior to predicted aging on the horizon, making the period of aging transition in the 2020s especially dangerous—the so-called power transition theory, which can lead to an aging security dilemma.[1]

In addition to the different year each state reaches its aging milestones, the speed at which it reaches each milestone varies among these Northeast Asian territories, also with important implications. South Korea, notably, has progressed from "aging" to "aged" status more quickly and is projected to similarly reach the super-aged and 30 percent milestones much more quickly as well. Looking further ahead, South Korea also is projected to overtake Japan as the region's most-aged state by 2050, when over 40 percent of its population is expected to be aged 65+. It is also worth underscoring that these next milestones for all the region's territories could happen even faster than projected and likely will, given further-declining birth rates and Russia's additional population losses as a result of its war with Ukraine (through both increased deaths and emigration).

Beyond the rapid aging of societies in Northeast Asia, one could also view the Northeast Asian political regimes and their militaries as undergoing changes related to their advancing age. However, contrary to the societal movement toward super-aged status and the connotation of weakness and vulnerability that implies (rightly or wrongly), the military forces of all these states have entered a sort of "middle age" that could be characterized as showing growing confidence and more mature capabilities. China, Taiwan, North Korea, and South Korea all effectively became new states and created new militaries in the late 1940s/early 1950s, roughly seventy years ago. Moreover, each of these places apart from North Korea experienced significant internal changes in the late 1980s/1990s that led to considerable economic growth. As a result of both political and economic change, the militaries of these states embarked on significant modernization campaigns beginning in the 2000s that continue today. Japan's military also could be viewed as on a similar postwar trajectory, though initially for the different reason of its defeat in the Second World War. In Japan's case, its postwar military force, the Japan Self Defense Force (JSDF), was created in 1954. Similar to China, Taiwan, and South Korea, the JSDF has embarked on a significant modernization campaign (though starting somewhat earlier, in the late 1980s) that has culminated more recently in new military roles and ambitions. The elevation of the Japan Defense Agency (JDA) to the Ministry of Defense (MOD) in 2008 and the crafting of its first formal national security strategy document in 2013 are two milestones in Japan's military middle age.[2]

The relatively recent development of the contemporary political, economic, and military structures of these territories can be seen in generational attitudes related to military security discussed later in this chapter. More than age-period (the numerical age of those in different generations), the age-cohort effect is quite robust around generational groups within several of the territories examined in this chapter, which further dilutes scholarly predictions on the effect of aging on security outcomes, since those predictions generally, though not exclusively, are based on numerical age. For example, the generation that fought in wars to establish the current political regimes have identifiable traits versus the latest adult generation that grew up under greater economic prosperity. What are not apparent from the cases in this chapter are consistent attitudes about military security based on numerical age cross-nationally. As one example illustrated later in this chapter, those of the same numerical age-groups in Japan, South Korea, and Taiwan illustrate different attitudes

TABLE 3.2

First decade of rapid aging in Northeast Asia, 2010-2020

	% change total population[i]	% change 65+[ii]	TFR 2020 (Δ TFR)[iii]	Change in defense spending[iv] Local currency / US$	Δ Military size[v]	Δ Debt/ GDP ratio[vi]	Average annual GDP growth[vii]
Japan	−1.36	+25.1	1.30 (−0.06pts)	+14.37% / +3.75%	−0.24%	+14.18%	1.26%
South Korea	+6.53[a]	+43.6	0.81 (−0.42pts)	+67.03% / +43.13%	−8.55%	+43.27%	3.31%
Taiwan	+0.21[b]	+47.2	0.99 (+0.07pts)	+23.16% / +13.37%	−43.8%	−11.39%	3.60%
China	+5.82	+44.8	1.24 (−0.45pts)	+249.23% / +89.34%	−10.94%	+68.19%	7.67%
Russia	+1.83	+15.5	1.82 (+0.36pts)	+250.23% / +34.12%	−13.96%	+36.63%	2.10%
North Korea	+0.47	+11.1	1.82 (−0.07pts)	+262.23% / n/a	+7.56%	n/a	n/a

i / ii / iii UN Population Division (2024).

iv SIPRI (2021), US$ figure is 2019 constant USD, North Korea comparison is through 2018.

v International Institute for Strategic Studies (IISS) (2021).

vi /vii 2010–2019, IMF (April 2021).

a South Korean sources report a population drop of 23,700 drop from 2019 to 2020 (*Nikkei Weekly*, 3/21); UN data shows the drop a year later.

b Taiwan sources report a population drop of 41,885 from 2019 to 2020 (*Taipei Times*, 1/21); UN data shows the drop a year later.

about security. Across these societies, there are numerous examples of older age-groups expressing a preference for greater military spending and engagement than younger age-groups, again contrary to what is predicted in existing scholarly literature.

In everyday portrayals, aging is often perceived as leading to weakness, frailty, and vulnerability—as well as to wisdom, wealth, and experience.[3] In the case of Northeast Asia's population-aging states, the developments in security policies after a decade of rapid aging lean toward the latter characteristics: All have increased their defense spending and military capabilities with no signs that this trend will lessen in the next decade of rapid aging and projected population shrinkage. (See table 3.2 for the specific spending increases.) They have achieved this change in part due to increased wealth and experience.

At the same time as the aging democracies began to experience increased effects of rapid aging, their regional security environment significantly worsened—as introduced in chapter 2—leading to a much grayer set of security challenges in addition to an escalation of conventional military threats. For example, North Korea test-fired more than sixty missiles in 2022, the most ever in a single year, and forty in 2024.[4] Many of the tests were of nuclear-capable missiles designed to strike the U.S. mainland and

South Korea, with Japan also a viable target. As another concern, from 2010 to 2020 China increased its defense spending by 249.23 percent (89.34 percent in constant 2019 USD), far higher than any U.S. ally or partner in the region. Japan's December 2022 national security strategy warns that Japan faces "the most severe and complex security environment since the end of WWII" and concludes with these ominous words: "In no way can we be optimistic about what the future of the international community will bring."[5] South Korea's and Taiwan's national security documents express similar stark concerns, as discussed in later sections of this chapter.

Given growing security challenges, it may not seem surprising that in the period 2010 to 2020, Japan, Taiwan, and South Korea increased defense spending 14.37 percent, 23.16 percent, and a whopping 67 percent, respectively (calculated in local currency)—and that Japan soon after put into place a plan to increase its defense spending by around 65 percent over a five-year period from 2022 to 2027, with South Korea and Taiwan announcing plans to significantly increase their defense spending as well. Each also embarked on notable campaigns to increase military capabilities, including offensive capabilities. None of these reactions seems surprising through a realist balance-of-power lens, but they run contrary to predictions of numerous scholars and media analysts about the likely effect of rapid aging on military readiness. For example, as noted in chapter 1, Japan, South Korea, and Taiwan—and China as well—all have reached demographic milestones that make them statistically far less likely to engage in war than other, "younger" states.[6]

Other factors beyond demographic change and the changing regional and global security environment additionally contribute to changes in security policies seen in Asia's aging states. The dramatic proliferation of gray-zone conflicts is one factor. Change in military technologies is another, which has resulted in entirely new security domains for competition—such as cyber and outer space. New patterns in domestic politics, including the role of new political leaders, are yet another factor. But within the mix, the rapid aging of the region and intensifying population shrinkage are also affecting the specific trajectories of military preparedness. Shrinking populations and expanding tensions are an apparent paradox of Northeast Asia in the 2020s, leading to growing concerns that an aging security dilemma has emerged.

Comparative Indicators from the First Decade of
Rapid Aging Across Northeast Asia

At the outset of this chapter examining the effect of rapid aging and population shrinkage in Northeast Asia specifically, it is useful to consider several comparative indicators from the first decade that all of Northeast Asia
(apart from Mongolia) experienced rapid aging, from 2010 to 2020, as illustrated in table 3.2. This decade is Japan's second decade of super-aged status, which explains its lower rise in the percent of its population aged 65+,
while in contrast South Korea, Taiwan, and China all experienced over
40 percent increases in their aged 65+ population sizes, with Russia and
North Korea aging considerably more slowly. Table 3.2 also shows that
Japan's total population shrank in this ten-year period (a trend that started
in 2011), while the others grew only modestly.

Although the scale of aging and population shrinkage will intensify in
the coming decades as each state reaches super-aged status, the experience
of this first decade indicates that security policy outcomes often did not
move in the direction anticipated by previous scholarship related to the
effect of rapid aging on security outcomes. For example, all these states
increased defense spending in this first decade of rapid aging, contrary to
expectations advanced in the demographics–security literature. By contrast,
all the states except North Korea followed expectations by reducing the
number of total military forces. Moreover, all but Taiwan saw an increase
in their debt-to-GDP ratio as they increased their military spending, indicating, as the literature predicts, that aging populations may not be willing
to devote additional tax dollars to military spending instead of social spending and thus instead do both through deficit spending.

Table 3.2 also indicates how all these places have total fertility rates below
replacement level and that have declined from 2010 to 2020 in all but Taiwan and Russia (which nonetheless both saw declines in the final years of
the decade that intensified in the early 2020s). Each place also managed
annualized economic growth over this period, though at quite anemic levels in the cases of Japan and Russia.

Table 3.3 offers a snapshot of important demographics–security indicators for each of the major Northeast Asian states and Russia at the start of
the second decade of rapid aging in these states in 2020. This table illustrates the wide variation in defense spending and military size relative to

population size and total GDP, a facet of Northeast Asian security through-out the postwar period. Note in particular that the number of military personnel is not closely correlated to total population size, with North Korea's military size the second largest, despite having the second smallest total population size, and Japan having a military size less than one-third the size of Russia's, despite a similar total population size. Variations in levels of defense spending also are remarkable, such as South Korea's and Japan's near parity despite Japan's economic size being over three times larger. (Defense spending as a percentage of GDP is provided in later tables summarizing key demographics–security data for each country case.) Table 3.3 also clearly shows Japan to be the leader of aging in Northeast Asia in 2020, with the number of people aged 65+ nearing 30 percent of its total population (which it reached in 2023). Japan also shows a very large debt-to-GDP ratio, which is in part due to increased spending on the elderly, and not yet due to big increases in defense spending that only began in the 2020s.

In sum, in terms of broad statistics, what we see at the start of Northeast Asia's second decade of rapid aging are a number of large and formidable militaries with growing economies increasing their military spending and developing new, more advanced weapons systems. Although this may not lead to war—particularly when other methods of conflict, including gray-zone conflicts, are becoming more intense—it still is an area of great concern, particularly given the formidable concentration of military power in this one region. However, as illustrated in the tables and further discussed in subsequent case sections, most of these countries are only on the cusp of—or even a decade or more away from—super-aged status, so some of the predictions related to the effect of rapid aging on their national security approaches may still be on the horizon.

The following sections of this chapter and the next chapter examine in greater depth each of the six rapidly aging territories in Northeast Asia, with more attention to the earlier-aging democracies. As introduced in chapter 1, unlike some previous studies that argue that a new "demographic peace" is likely to emerge from the new pressure of rapid aging, the case studies illustrate how the effect of demographic transition on each state varies based on a large number of factors, including domestic politics, cultural resistance, available technology, and the specific nature of the security threats each state faces (even within a single regional security ecosystem). Still, the pressures exerted by the variable of population

TABLE 3.3
Northeast Asia security snapshot, 2020

	Total population[i]	65+ population[ii]	Defense spending[iii] (billion US\$)	Military personnel[iv]	GDP[v] (billion US\$)	Debt/GDP ratio[vi]
Japan	125.54	28.9%	\$48.16	247,150	\$5,048.79	258.71%
South Korea	51.53	15.8%	\$45.735	599,000	\$1,644.68	48.70%
Taiwan	23.68	15.9%	\$12.155	163,000	\$673.18	32.14%
China	1,425.44	12.6%	\$244.934	2,035,000	\$14,862.56	70.14%
Russia	146.56	15.5%	\$66.838	900,000	\$1,488.12	19.16%
North Korea	26.09	11.1%	\$4.31*	1,280,000	\$16.3*	n/a

[i/ii] UN Population Division (2024). [iii] SIPRI (2021). [iv] IISS (2021). [v/vi] IMF (April 2023).
* U.S. State Department, World Military Expenditures and Arms Transfers 2021 for 2019 spending.

change are evident across the board and lead to recognizable patterns and stages of policy responses to this change that will be summarized in later sections of this chapter and in chapter 4. The first section examines the region's first super-aged military power, Japan, followed by sections devoted to Northeast Asia's other two rapidly aging democracies, South Korea and Taiwan. The chapter then discusses some shared threads of these early agers, drawing implications for other states, including shared threads among Asia's aging autocracies that are considered in chapter 4.

JAPAN: ASIA'S FIRST SUPER-AGED MILITARY POWER

The strategy that Japan's leaders have developed to address their deteriorating regional security environment goes against what many expected of a rapidly aging society with a shrinking population and serious fiscal challenges as well as against its long-standing antimilitarist strategic culture. Rather than looking inward, Japan is in the midst of increasing its military spending and capabilities substantially and is expanding the number and depth of security partnerships with other states. Japan has pursued this course not only because of rising concerns over traditional military threats but also because security concerns that it perceives also have "grayed" together with its population. Multiple gray-zone challenges have contributed to a robust plan to devote more resources to military security broadly defined. Geopolitically speaking, as arguably the most important military ally to the United States in the region, Japan's defense moves also must be understood within the broader context of intensifying U.S.-China rivalry and the resultant push by successive U.S. presidents for Japan and other military allies and partners to do more to balance against China's increasingly assertive military posture.

Japan has, to date, also defied expectations from its so-called pacifist past as well as its aging future. As the first major military power to experience rapid aging, beginning around two decades ago, it provides an important empirical case to reconsider earlier theories that predicted how rapidly aging states would act—particularly as a super-aged military power. Looking into the 2030s and beyond, however, Japan faces bigger hurdles as its aging intensifies, its population shrinkage accelerates, and its fiscal situation likely worsens. By that time, though, new technologies, deepening security partnerships and alliances with other states, and the rising demographic challenges of Japan's principal adversaries may create a more favorable security environment from what Japan faces today—but also it may not, given rivals China, North Korea, and Russia's rapid development of new military capabilities and China's projected higher economic growth vis-à-vis Japan's (as discussed in chapter 4).

There is cause for concern—from Japanese for their own security and from Japan's security ally and partners—but also signs of hope that a powerful actor that champions nonmilitary approaches to conflict resolution will continue to actively be engaged in regional (and global) security. On the cautionary side, Japan's defense-planning documents stress a worsening security environment due to rising threats in the traditional military realm—larger numbers of more accurate missiles within range of Japan, more frequent threatening incursions into Japan's air-defense zone and areas close to (and sometimes into) its maritime space, and greater military capabilities in general from hostile states—as well as growing gray-zone challenges to its territorial sovereignty. As noted earlier, the introduction to Japan's December 2022 national security strategy—only the second such document in Japan's postwar history—warns that Japan faces "the most severe and complex security environment since the end of WWII."[7] In addition, Japan's economy, while still growing in absolute size despite a shrinking total population, has markedly declined as a share of the global economy—from 14 percent in 1990 to 8.7 percent in 2010 to 3.5 percent in 2022,[8] and in 2023 it fell to the fourth-largest economy in the world from the number three position it held for decades.

TABLE 3.4
Japan's demographics–security nexus

Total fertility rate (2024)[a]	1.31		
Total population (millions)[a]	**2024**	**2035 (est.)**	**2050 (est.)**
	124.07	116.0	104.12 (–16.1% from 2024; 19.95m)
Percentage of population 65+ ("super-aged")[a]	**2024**	**2035 (est.)**	**2050 (est.)**
	29.9%	32.8%	38.0%
U.S. treaty ally?[b]	Yes		
Active military forces (2023)[b]	247,000		
Defense spending (2023)[b]	$49.04 (in US$billion), 1.16% of GDP		
Total GDP in US$ (2015) trillion[d]	**2023**[c]	**2030 (est.)**	**2050 (est)**
	$4.213	$4.889	$5.739 (+36% from 2023)

[a] UN Population Division (2024), constant fertility projection
[b] IISS, *Military Balance* (2024)
[c] IMF, *World Economic Outlook Database* (April 2024)
[d] Institute of Energy Economics Japan, *IIEJ Outlook* (2023)

On the more hopeful side, despite intensifying aging and other challenges, Japan's leaders have implemented ambitious plans to modernize and streamline many long-known obstacles to more proactive military strategies. Moreover, economic forecasting predicts total Japanese GDP to grow for decades to come (albeit at lower percentage increases than in the past). As one Japanese defense analyst recently argued, "Japan remains a formidable neighbor despite its relative decline, and one with which even a vastly superior China must coexist."[9]

The Paradox of Aging yet Strengthening

Japan became the world's first super-aged global power in 2005. In 2023 over 30 percent of its population crossed the aged 65+ threshold. Japan's median age also is the highest in the world (apart from city-state Monaco). It was the first country to have a median age of 40 years old, back in 1998; in 2023 the median age exceeded 49 (compared to the global median age of 30.6 and U.S. median age 38.3) that year. Being at the leading edge of global aging has led to substantial research and theorizing about how this would affect Japan's economic, social, and security future—most of it rather bleak.[10] For example, Brad Glosserman predicted in 2019 that "an aging population will squeeze pension systems, cut productivity, drain innovation and energy, and sharpen conflicts among constituencies over dwindling government revenues. There's likely to be an intergenerational fighting for government services—guns versus butter or, more accurately, guns versus wheelchairs."[11] Pension systems are indeed squeezed in Japan today (and more broadly deficit spending is among the highest in the industrial world), and productivity growth is lower as Japanese society has aged, but intergenerational fighting and the implication that Japan's military posture and spending would suffer as a result is not evident in the first two decades since Japan became the world's first super-aged state.

Japan underwent what I described in an earlier work as a "security renaissance" in the decade that followed its entrance to super-aged status from 2006 to 2016, defying then-common expectations that a rapidly aging state would look inward and reduce its external defense commitments, falling back to its postwar antimilitarist cultural roots.[12] During that period, a series of six different prime ministers from opposing political parties altered bureaucratic and administrative obstacles to a coordinated defense strategy and built up Japan's military capabilities through new acquisitions as well as alliance deepening with the United States and creation of new regional security partnerships. Japan's first postwar national security strategy document was published in December 2013, announcing a more "proactive" approach to security for Japan and a more coordinated approach within government, as seen in the establishment of a new National Security Council and National Security Secretariat.[13]

Even after this period of robust enhancement of military capabilities in Japan's first decade of rapid aging, prominent experts cautioned that the expected effects of rapid aging on defense posture would kick in. Glosserman argued, for example, that "the Abe era [December 2012–September 2020] is the apogee of Japanese power and that a combination of structural and attitudinal constraints will limit Japan's ability to adapt to current and future challenges. This is 'Peak Japan.'"[14] Glosserman also notes, correctly, that Japanese spending on its military did not match Abe's rhetoric on defense, growing only about 2 percent a year on average during Abe's roughly eight-year tenure—and this after defense spending had hit a twenty-year low point in 2012 after reaching an all-time high in 2001.[15] Tom Phuong Le argued at that time that due to a combination of rapid aging and Japan's antimilitarist culture, it was not imaginable that Japanese leaders could raise defense spending above the long-standing de facto limit of 1 percent of GDP.[16]

He also notes, correctly in terms of relative spending and capabilities, that "despite a universal acknowledgement among security experts...that China and North Korea have substantially augmented their power projection capabilities, Japan has been unwilling and unable to keep pace."[17]

Yet, in Japan's December 2022 national security strategy document, even more robust approaches to military security were announced, including the planned development of offensive "counter-strike capabilities" to respond to increasing concerns about missile threats, especially from North Korea and China, and the near-doubling of defense spending to reach the NATO standard of 2 percent of GDP by 2027.[18] In constant USD (2021), Japanese defense spending hit an all-time high in 2022, and with planned increases in defense spending over the following four years, this peak is slated to continue to grow. It should be noted, however, that in current U.S. dollars, Japanese defense spending looks to have declined in both 2021 and 2022 due to the weakening value of the yen.[19] Although most of Japanese defense spending is on domestic items (labor is number one),[20] the weakening yen does have implications for Japan's planned purchases of U.S. defense equipment and may broadly be linked to Japan's challenging demographic situation.

Questioning Attitudinal Change as
Japanese Society Further Ages

In addition to Japan's unprecedented demographic transition, its postwar antimilitarist culture also is unique. Despite long having one of the world's most capable militaries and being a top-ten world defense spender, Japan has enjoyed seventy-nine years of peace from 1945 to 2024. No JSDF member has ever died fighting a war (i.e., since those forces were created in 1954). Thus, it is no surprise that there is disagreement among Japanese people about Japan's future security policies. In addition, despite Japan's actions since reaching super-aged status defying many expectations based on demography alone, its demographics clearly do affect its security planning and constrain its actions. As Le correctly argues in his extended study *Japan's Aging Peace*, Japan's antimilitarist culture and its aging population trend reinforce a limited defense role. The argument of my book, though, is that these two important constraints nonetheless do not determine Japan's actions, nor do they ensure a more peaceful future with similarly aging neighbors: rapid aging—even if in a region of rapid aging—will not directly lead to a less robust military posture, even combined with Japan's long-standing antimilitarist culture.

One example of the importance of recognizing these dual forces—antimilitarist norms as well as rapid aging—is to point out that the JSDF has been challenged in meeting its recruiting targets from the time of its creation in 1954, when the Japanese population was still growing (and, indeed, experiencing a baby boom). Tomoyuki Sasaki explains how standards for JSDF admission had to be lowered and accepting fewer total numbers was necessary even in—perhaps especially in—the early years of Japan's fledging military when skepticism about this new military force was high.[21] Le illustrates this point visually in later years, from 1975 to 2019, showing shortfalls in total planned force size as high as 14 percent in the early 1980s and an average of around 8 percent since 2008.[22] Thus, there were actually greater shortfalls in JSDF force posture when Japan's demographic challenges were less intense and, as emphasized further below, a three-year reduction in the shortfall in the early 2020s.

Another example of the potential interplay between antimilitarist norms and rapid aging is the hypothesis that as the generation that experienced the Second World War as well as the generation that followed (which largely created Japan's postwar antimilitarist norms) age into retirement and eventually pass on, perhaps new generations of Japanese will no longer subscribe to these norms—a frequently heard concern expressed by some analysts at the time of Prime Minister Abe's many simultaneous changes to Japan's security practices from 2012 to 2020. Polling data from the 2010s as well as more recently does not show any large divergence or growing disjuncture between generations, however. Corey Wallace compares attitudes of three generations of postwar Japanese across a range of topical security questions such as views on constitutional revision, JSDF participation in United Nations Peacekeeping Operations (UNPKO), and proposed JSDF development of missile strike capabilities. He finds differing levels of support by age on some indicators but not on others, and some surprising generational variation among questions rather than a consistent propeace or prodefense stance by any single generation. One core question posed in his study was whether the youngest generation (aged 25–49 at the time of his study) were showing markedly different attitudes toward military security; he finds that they generally did not.[23]

More recent public opinion polling conducted by Japan's Cabinet Office also shows fairly modest variation by age cohorts in responses to regular questions asked related to national defense (many of the same questions as in Wallace's study). The variation was much less than the fairly substantial variation based on gender (a large factor also in the South Korean case examined later in this chapter). In the November 2022 survey, for example, respondents under 30 and 70 or over had more positive impressions about the JSDF than those of middle age—but in every age group those with positive or fairly positive impressions were the vast majority (90.8 percent). Similarly, support for the Japan-U.S. alliance ranged only from 89.7 percent "strongly positive" for those aged 70+ to 92.4 percent among those under 30. Over 86 percent of respondents across all age-groups thought there was real "risk of Japan becoming involved in a war," though those aged 70+ perceived this somewhat less strongly while 40-somethings perceived "no risk" by about 2 percentage points above the average of 12.8 percent.[24]

Interestingly, a larger variation among age-groups on a national security-related question in the 2022 Cabinet Office survey is in the opposite direction of what much of the general literature on elderly views of defense predicts, with more people in their sixties and aged 70+ expressing a view that the size of the JSDF should be increased (48.4 percent of those in their sixties versus only 34.2 percent of those in their forties). This finding contradicts a common argument in the general demographics–national security literature that the elderly will favor less spending on defense and rather emphasize social welfare programs that would benefit their age cohort. Moreover, as discussed further in a comparative perspective later in this chapter, figure 3.1 shows the self-reported "willingness to fight" of three different age cohorts in Japan (as well as South Korea and Taiwan) where, in Japan's case, those aged 65+ express twice the level of willingness to fight as the younger-age cohorts. (Methodologically speaking, however, one might question whether elderly respondents have essentially less to lose in saying this given that they have aged out of years for military service.)

These examples of age-group-based polling are not meant to suggest that there will not be change in attitudes about Japanese security practices as Japan continues to rapidly age, but rather to emphasize that the evolution of Japanese security views since Japan's start of rapid aging does not show signs of substantial aging-based change of views. The different generations do not show substantial disagreement about military security in the way more evident in the South Korea and Taiwan cases discussed later in this chapter. Still, as Japan further ages and a generational transition is completed, is it worth monitoring who, for example, will staff and visit Japan's many peace museums built by an earlier generation (as Le catalogues in *Japan's Aging Peace*) and whether big security decisions from the past—such as whether Japan should possess nuclear weapons—are revisited by a new generation facing a different security environment and a shrinking population. To date, though, predictions from the general literature on the effect of rapid aging on attitudes toward military security have not appeared in Japan's case—despite the many challenges Japan is facing related to its rapid aging, as discussed in the next section.

One recent policy move, however, which directly relates to the general literature on aging—a proposal to increase defense spending substantially—may indicate such an impending change as society-wide aging intensifies in Japan. Public opinion polling that includes a breakdown by age about the Japanese government's December 2022 decision to seek to increase defense spending to 2 percent of GDP is limited, but one poll by the right-of-center *Sankei* newspaper found that support for the move by those aged 70 or older was about 10 percentage points lower (in the 30 percent support range) than for those aged 40–60 (in the 40 percent support range).[25] Overall opposition in polling not broken down by age also is high—particularly if raising taxes is involved—which would seem to support the common view in the literature on aging that older societies would oppose such moves, but at this point the causality is unclear given limited data.[26]

Challenges of Staffing and Funding
Expanded Security Roles in an Aging Japan

Prime Minister Fumio Kishida warned in his 2023 opening speech to Japan's parliament that Japan's low birth rate puts the country "on the brink of being unable to maintain social functions"—noting with alarm that the number of new births in 2022 dropped below 800,000 for the first time since modern record-keeping began.[27] The trend of a substantial drop in the number of young people eligible to serve in the JSDF is not new, however. Japan's largest-ever birth year was in 1949, with almost 2.7 million births; the replacement-level birth rate ended in 1972, twenty-four years later. The number of 20-year-old men, those of prime interest for military service, peaked in 1968 at over 1.2 million, falling below one million for over two decades before peaking again at just over one million in 1993—over three decades ago. By 2023 that number had fallen to 611,000, a nearly 40 percent drop. In 2042 the number of 20-year-old men is projected by the United Nations Population Division to be 441,000, but given that actual births in 2022 dropped below 800,000, the number in 2042 will surely be lower. In terms of total population size, as visualized in table 4.2, it is projected to fall to just over 104 million by 2050 (and below that level soon after). By contrast, the percentage of elderly residents aged 65+ is projected to soar, to 38 percent by 2050.

Japan's MOD has developed numerous policies to address the persistent shortfall in the number of planned forces that has plagued the country's military for decades, in part due to Japan's postwar antimilitarist culture but more recently also due to the declining number of eligible recruits (as well as very low unemployment rates). It is interesting to note, though perhaps transitory, that the three highest-recruiting/retaining years for the JSDF in the ten years from 2013 to 2022 were the most recent three, with 2020 as the peak.[28] Nonetheless, the shortfall of total troops remained in the fifteen- to twenty-thousand-person range of a target of just over 247,000. There is reason to believe, moreover, that shortfalls may worsen due to the declining number of people of military-service age. Media reporting that the recruiting shortfall in 2023 spiked to almost 50 percent of the target made headlines in Japan. This number should be contextualized by noting that the recruiting target was increased in FY2022 and FY2023 in an effort to make up for overall personnel shortages, but even still the number of JSDF personnel recruited from FY2019 to FY2023 dropped each of those five years—from 15,548 to 9,959.[29]

Recent years have seen new MOD policies to maintain existing force levels, but whether it is enough to offset the declining number of eligible recruits in the pipeline is questionable. The maximum age for new JSDF recruits was raised from 26 to 32 in 2018, the first increase since 1990. The retirement age for senior officers started rising gradually in 2020. Japan's 2022 *National Defense Strategy* sets out a plan to raise the retirement age even further to expand the pool of those able to serve.[30]

The MOD also has set a goal to increase the share of women in the JSDF to 9 percent by 2030. Women made up just 7.4 percent of JSDF members in

2020, compared with an average of 13 percent among NATO countries at that time—but Japan's rate had risen to 8.7 percent in 2022, and the ratio of women among new recruits in the past decade has soared, from only 7.5 percent in 2010 to 20.1 percent in FY2022 and 18.0 percent in FY2023.[31] Note, however, that in terms of absolute numbers, this achievement is rather small given the comparatively small size of Japan's military and its annual recruiting: 1,796 women were recruited in FY2023 of 9,959 total recruits that year, down from 2,500 in FY2019 of 15,548 total recruits. By contrast, in the United States, women made up 17.3 percent of the active-duty force in 2022, totaling 231,741 members—a number greater than Japan's total military forces.[32]

The 2022 *Defense Buildup Program* document devotes five pages to additional measures to recruit and to retain JSDF members.[33] In sum, as described by one contributor to the development of Japan's latest national security strategy, Japan has followed a "*yonjin* [four persons] strategy" for managing its shrinking working-age population. As summarized by Le: "The four persons included, (1) *mujin* (literally 'unattended' but implies automation or autonomous systems), (2) *shojin* (implies saving manpower), (3) *rojin* (old people, which implies reemploying retired people), and (4) *fujin* (women, which implies increasing the recruitment of women)."[34]

Given persistent JSDF shortfalls in recruiting and retention and the future demographic pinch ahead, despite the plan to roughly double defense spending from 2022 to 2027, there is no planned increase in the total number of military personnel. Instead, a wider range of civilians and technological offsets are envisioned while new measures to maintain even the current force posture are put in place. Even with an ambitious list of new initiatives to maintain current military personnel levels, this will be a challenge given the declining number of young people projected in the coming decades. Moreover, beyond the total number of desired personnel, a separate challenge is to recruit in fields where shortfalls have been high in the past—such as cyber-defense and sailors for ship-based deployments.[35]

Beyond the JSDF, potential shortages of skilled workers in the defense sector (and in the economy as a whole) are also a concern as Japan seeks to enhance domestic production of military equipment as it substantially increases defense spending. Japan's unemployment rate was at 3 percent or lower from September 2016 to August 2024 (the date when latest figures are available for this study). In Japan's first decade of super-aged status

(2005–2014) the unemployment rate average was 4.3 percent; in the second decade to date (2015–August 2024) the average had fallen to 2.7 percent.[36]

The 2022 *National Defense Strategy* devotes several pages to reinforcing Japan's defense production base but does not highlight possible labor shortages as a challenge in that area.[37] Notably, the total size of Japan's labor market has actually increased in the first decades of Japan's rapid aging due the nature of the population pyramid that initially saw the biggest age-cohort shortfall at those aged 15 and younger but also due to a wider range of workers employed, including more women, older workers, and guest workers/immigrants. The total size of the labor force in 2010 (the year of Japan's peak population) was 66.2 million, while in 2021 it was 69.07 million.[38] In other words, there were about 2.7 million more workers despite the working-age population shrinking by thirty thousand people over those twelve years.

However, as the total size of Japan's working-age population shrinks even more rapidly, the ability to offset the shrinking number of prime working-age men will become more limited—apart from the option of greatly increasing the number of guest workers/immigrants. In December 2022 there were just over three million registered foreign residents in Japan, about 2.4 percent of the total population.[39] The total size of this population has grown as Japan has aged, but from a very low starting point. Most experts agree that an increase in the scale of immigration into Japan needed to stabilize the current size of the workforce is not socially supported nor politically feasible—nor perhaps even possible if desired given that many other advanced industrial states are seeking immigrant labor and may offer a more welcoming environment (such as the Australia, New Zealand, and Singapore cases discussed in chapter 5).[40]

Beyond staffing Japan's military-security needs—both in the military and the civilian workforces—another primary challenge Japan will face in the coming decades is how to pay for these workers and/or for the new technologies that may enable fewer workers to achieve the same (or more) output. Japan has suffered declining productivity growth per worker in its first decades of rapid aging, but productivity is predicted to continue to grow enough to achieve total GDP growth of about 25 percent through 2050 compared to a 2020 baseline—even with accelerated population shrinkage. By contrast, China's total GDP is expected to grow threefold in that same period—creating an intensified security challenge.[41] Moreover, Japan currently runs the largest budget deficit of any developed country by far (over 6 percent of GDP), with total debt projected at 258 percent of GDP for 2023.[42] Thus, serious economic and fiscal challenges lie ahead.

The difficulty of achieving the goal stated in Japan's *2022 National Security Strategy* of a militarily stronger Japan will challenge political leaders in the coming years. In the short term, the Kishida government envisioned reaching the 2 percent of GDP defense spend-rate by 2027 through substantial annual increases in defense spending. Faced with very low approval ratings, however, he chose not to stand for reelection as head of his party and thus handed over this goal to a new prime minister, Shigeru Ishiba (a noted defense hawk) on October 1, 2024.

Whether there will be political support for reaching this level of spending is not certain—and even if there is, whether this level of spending can be maintained over time, as Japan's super-aging continues and total population further shrinks, also is unclear. As noted in table 4.2, Japan's total population is projected to shrink by almost twenty million from 2024 to 2050, and the percentage of those aged 65+ to rise 8 more percentage points from the 2024 level.

The emergence of gray security challenges in addition to an intensification of traditional military concerns is one explanation for Japan's more robust military strategy. As Japan's *2022 National Security Strategy* notes, "gray zone situations over territories, cross-border cyberattacks on critical civilian infrastructures, and information warfare through spread of disinformation are constantly taking place, thereby further blurring the boundary between contingency and peacetime." The document continues: "Furthermore, the scope of national security has expanded to include those fields previously considered non-military such as economic, technological and others, and thus the boundary between military and non-military fields is no longer clear-cut either."[43]

Rising gray-zone challenges can be linked to existing rivalries or threats perceived from other states such as North Korea and China and also from nonstate actors. In Japan's National Institute for Defense Studies 2023 edition of its annual *China Security Report*, there is a focus on China's aim to control the cognitive domain and gray-zone events. The report notes that it is not only Japan that is devoting increased attention and resources to address gray-zone situations but also the Philippines, South Korea, Taiwan, and Vietnam, among others.[44] Intensifying and expanding security concerns—both gray and traditional—create urgency to adapt regional security cooperation and strategies for maintaining peace and stability, which is another goal of Japan's 2022 *National Security Strategy.*

These two graying challenges—aging populations and the rise of gray-zone conflicts—are connected through the increased labor and resources that addressing rising gray-zone conflicts requires, exactly at a time when rapidly aging states like Japan are experiencing labor and resource shortages. Indeed, another challenge set out in the introduction to the 2022 *National Security Strategy* is Japan's "declining and aging population."[45] On the one hand, gray-zone concerns include a wider range of actors than traditional militaries—such as cyber- and supply-chain defenses within other government departments as well as the corporate sector—which could in principle reduce burdens on military forces alone. On the other hand, such an expansion in the range of security actors also poses challenges to coordinated responses from government departments and the private sector and ultimately involves *more* people, not fewer (again, at a time when Japan faces a shrinking total labor pool).

Fortunately for Japan, it does not need to address these challenges alone. It can coordinate with its formal military ally, the United States, as well with a growing number of other security partners—some of which face similar challenges of rapid aging and others of which boast still-growing and more youthful populations. Moreover, these states together can pool resources and capabilities to counter shared security threats collectively. Thus, while Japan's own population is shrinking in number, the total number of people devoted to Japan's defense is effectively growing.

Building Strength Through Expanded Security Partnerships and New Technologies

The U.S.-Japan security alliance has deepened and broadened considerably since Japan became the world's first super-aged society. On the surface, this may appear puzzling, but it can partly be explained by Japan's perceived need to strengthen its military posture in the face of growing threats but being hindered by the challenges of going it alone—challenges exacerbated by a rapidly aging and shrinking population.[46] The U.S. forward-positioning of roughly fifty thousand military personnel in Japan greatly enhances Japan's military deterrence. The geopolitical context of increased U.S.

demands for allies to bear a larger burden within the alliance framework also should be noted—affecting not only Japan but U.S. allies worldwide and having a similar result of increased defense spending as a share of GDP for many such allies. The first months of the Trump administration in the United States in 2025 saw a further advance of such demands for more contributions from U.S. allies, also potentially leading to increased spending to hedge against future potential U.S. diminishment of such partnerships.

This movement by Japan toward deeper and broader security cooperation with the United States also illustrates how alliances and security partnerships are not only about formal solider-to-soldier cooperation but also about shared facilities, technologies, and diplomatic objectives—all of which also are important aspects of Japan-U.S. security cooperation. Indeed, in the long history of the Japan-U.S. military alliance, the ability to forward-deploy U.S. forces at bases in Japan was seen as one of the principal contributions of Japan to the alliance, which in itself did not require substantial coordination with Japan's military forces (though such coordination did happen in some areas, especially with Japan's Maritime Self-Defense Forces).

Thus, it is another apparent paradox of Japan's rapid aging and now shrinking population that compared to earlier periods when the number of younger working-age men was higher, the JSDF personnel contribution to the U.S.-Japan alliance is larger in this recent period of a shrinking working-age population as the two militaries work more closely together in preparing for a wider range of joint action, such as countering an amphibious assault and fighting together in a Taiwan contingency.[47] At the solider-to-soldier level, in recent decades the JSDF has deepened integration into shared roles and missions with U.S. forces at unprecedented levels to address shared Japan-U.S. regional security concerns, creating greater efficiencies and a more robust posture for both states.[48]

Japan's 2022 *National Security Strategy* and related documents identified numerous additional areas to further deepen alliance coordination and capabilities in the coming years, laying out an agenda to "work in coordinating with the United States to strengthen the Japan-US alliance in all areas, including diplomacy, defense, and economy."[49] In the military sphere, deeper cooperation on integration of force operations could reduce personnel needs in some areas by reducing areas of duplication. Similarly, in the economic and cyber areas, more technology sharing and joint production could reduce labor needs—though, it should be noted, a key part of Japan's plan to greatly increase defense spending is to redouble efforts at domestic production of military assets.

Japan's movement toward alliance deepening with the United States is clear. The extent to which Japan actually would become involved in a fighting war with the United States—beyond gray-zone competition—is not clear and at times is likely overstated or overestimated in the popular media. Japan's possible reluctance in such a contingency does not appear to be informed much by its rapid aging, however, but rather is a result of broader strategic questions as well as the continued resilience of its antimilitarist traditions.[50]

Beyond the Japan-U.S. alliance, several newer security partners for Japan will grow in population size and also remain more youthful in the coming decades. Fellow Quad member India's population is projected to grow by 276 million from 2024 to 2050; Australia by nearly 6 million. Fellow U.S. ally the Philippines—which also is deepening its security cooperation with the United States, as discussed in chapter 5—is expected to grow by 22 million from 2024 to 2050. These states are among those with which Japan has sought to deepen security ties.[51] Demography alone does not drive Japan toward these relationships but rather adds to other factors such as shared concerns about China, geographic location, and convergence over maritime interests to push Japan in this direction—as previously discussed in chapter 2.

Looking beyond the Indo-Pacific region, numerous aging powers in Europe have shown interest in bolstering their own security profiles through new partnerships with Japan.[52] Recent developments in conjunction with Japan's December 2022 national security strategy include the enhanced security relationship between Japan and the United Kingdom agreed to in January 2023, as well as a new joint fighter development plan among Japan, the UK, and Italy in December 2022.[53] Japan is also one of four partners of NATO in Asia. (The others are Australia, New Zealand, and South Korea.) In July 2023 Japan and NATO announced an "Individually Tailored Partnership Programme" to further deepen institutionalized security cooperation.[54] The idea of establishing in Tokyo NATO's first liaison office in Asia also was discussed at the annual NATO summer in June 2023, though no action has yet been taken in that regard, and the conversation of NATO's future moved in a different direction in the early months of the second Trump administration in the United States in 2025.[55]

Despite these proactive and positive developments for better providing for Japan's security in an increasingly difficult environment, several sets of challenges lie ahead as Japan's aging intensifies and its population shrinkage accelerates. Moreover, one unknown factor in Japan's response is whether new technologies will emerge to fill gaps caused by Japan's demographic shifts before the situation becomes too severe.

New technologies will play an important role in how Japan and other states manage the effects of demographic change on their security strategies. Part of Japan's expanded security cooperation with the United States and other partners is focused on jointly developing these military technologies of the future. Robotics and other uncrewed systems, including AI, will likely provide offsets for shrinking populations for states like Japan. At the same time, however, such new technologies themselves will further alter the nature of the regional security landscape beyond what already is apparent as regional states have adopted newer technologies. With the expected transformation in the nature of warfare among major powers by midcentury, we should view new technologies not solely as offsets for demographic change, but also as posing new challenges.

Conclusion: Significant Challenges Ahead

The dual graying of Japan's security landscape already has led to major changes in Japan's military posture and planning, with additional major changes sure to come as both trends deepen. The modern world has never experienced such a demographic transition nor an expansion of security competition across so many security domains (air, ground, sea, cyberspace, outer space, gray-zone, etc.). Japan's security documents of December 2022 acknowledge this, but still many political, logistical, and technological challenges remain that will require creative approaches and a willingness to adapt at a level not yet seen in Japan's first two postwar national security strategies.

Yet, despite many challenges that arise from the rapid aging phenomenon, Japan has shown a notable range of innovative approaches to address these challenges, including increased automation, outsourcing of some defense roles, improving efficiency and streamlining procedures, and increasing/deepening international partnerships. Moreover, despite static academic studies that assume that shrinking populations will lead to shrinking economies, the Japanese economy has continued to grow and is projected to increase in total size through 2050 (and likely beyond) despite a shrinkage in total population projected at around 16 percent (about 20 million people) from 2024 to 2050.

Japan's experience to date, moreover, provides a useful template for how other states in the region and worldwide also could maintain a strong defense posture despite the challenges posed by rapid aging. In many ways, South Korea's initial responses to rapid aging and working-age population shrinkage show similar approaches, though South Korea's starting point—a much larger military per capita staffed by conscripted forces and facing a land border with a hostile, million-person army—is quite different. These similarities and contrasts are the subject of the following section.

SOUTH KOREA'S TRANSITION FROM LOW-COST LABOR TO HIGH-TECH DEFENSE

South Korea is the only U.S. ally in the world with active-duty forces numbering over 400,000—and one of only ten other countries in 2020 with this level of forces.[56] This will likely no longer be the case by the 2030s due to South Korea's rapid aging and shrinkage of its military-aged male population. Thus, unlike the Japanese case—the first case of a super-aged military power—the South Korean case looks quite different given South Korea's different economic development trajectory and different existing military posture, including a system of universal male conscription. Still, while on the surface the South Korean case may look to conform more closely to predictions from previous literature on the effect of rapid aging on military security, South Korea also has been increasing its military spending as it prepares for further aging and population shrinkage while seeking to maintain a robust deterrence posture together with its close military ally, the United States. This alliance relationship has been essential to South Korean security and useful to the United States regionally and globally, which is one reason why the effect of South Korea's rapid aging is such an important concern to the United States and to the region.

South Korea is projected to become Northeast Asia's second super-aged military power in 2025. As indicated at the start of this chapter, it will reach this demographic milestone much faster than Japan did and with a lower per capita income. It also faces the additional hurdles of sharing a land border with a hostile state that boasts a military of over one million soldiers and of attempting to maintain a total force size over twice the per capita level of Japan's with a smaller number of U.S. forces based on its soil. On the more positive side, South Korea can draw on a long tradition of mandatory military service (for men) and thus a much higher number of trained soldiers among its population, a strong domestic defense production base, and its recent status as a top-ten economy in the world that is poised to still benefit economically from the generational transition underway in its workforce, likely resulting in higher future economic growth than Japan.

As a divided country technically still in a state of war with its northern neighbor, South Korea faces a more immediate traditional military threat than does Japan; one more similar to its neighbor off its eastern coast, Taiwan. As with Japan vis-à-vis China, North Korea's provocative military actions and weapons development have pushed South Korea to improve its military capabilities and maintain readiness, including from constant cyberattacks and other gray-zone challenges. China's military modernization and provocative actions toward South Korea, in addition to its support for North Korea, also motivate South Korea's increased military spending and capability enhancements despite its intensifying challenges from its rapid aging. Like Japan, South Korea also has been playing an increasing security role regionally and globally as well as building up its military capabilities in response to growing capabilities of neighboring states.

Rapid Aging and Persistent Generational Differences

South Korea became an "aging" state only in 2000 (over 7 percent of its population aged 65+) and an aged one (over 14 percent 65+) in 2018. And yet by 2050 it is projected to exceed Japan in the percentage of its population 65+ (at 40.7%) and with a higher median age (of 57.5 versus Japan's 53.4). South Korea experienced a record-low fertility rate of 0.72 in 2024, a further drop below the 1.0 threshold first breached in 2018, despite the efforts since 2005 of the Presidential Committee for the Aging Society and Population Policy (PCASPP). From 2006 to 2018, the South Korean government spent over US$135 billion on incentives for families and subsidies for children, an annual rate equal to over half of the country's total defense budget in 2018.[57] Under President Yoon Suk Yeol (2022–2025), the committee worked on its

Table 3.5
South Korea's demographics–security nexus

Total fertility rate (2024)[a]	0.72		
Total population (millions)[a]	**2024** 51.74	**2035 (est.)** 50.14	**2050 (est.)** 44.26 (−14.5% from 2024; 7.48 million)
Percentage of population 65+[a]	**2024** 19.3% ("aged")	**2035 (est.)** 29.8% ("super-aged")	**2050 (est.)** 40.7%
U.S. treaty ally?[b]	Yes		
Active military forces (2023)[b]	500,000		
Defense spending (2023)[b]	$43.84 (in US$billion), 2.57% of GDP		
Total GDP in US$ (2015) trillion[d]	**2023**[c] $1.712	**2030 (est.)** $2.091	**2050 (est.)** $2.796 (+64% from 2023)

[a] UN Population Division (2024), constant fertility projection
[b] IISS, *Military Balance* (2024)
[c] IMF, *World Economic Outlook Database* (April 2024)
[d] Institute of Energy Economics Japan, *IIEJ Outlook* (2023)

sixth plan for addressing growing population challenges, hoping not only to halt the consistently falling fertility rate but to see it rise, though during his period in office it continued to fall, resulting in the declaration of a "demographic national emergency" in June 2024.[58]

South Korea's fertility rate has not been at the 2.1 replacement level since 1983—over four decades ago—which is why the number of young men of conscription age continues to decline year on year. South Korea's largest-ever birth year was in 1971, with just over one million births; the replacement-level birth rate ended just twelve years later. The result of this reduced time frame between the highest number of births and below-replacement fertility is a much more rapidly aging society than most other places. The year 2023 saw the lowest number of births to that point in South Korea since statistics were collected in the postwar period, with just 236,394. In fifty years, the total number of births per year has dropped by over 664,000 (over 70 percent). With roughly half of these births being male, this represents a decline in the pool of military conscripts of 332,000 potential new soldiers each year.

South Korean life expectancy also has increased substantially in the past several decades, greatly contributing to rapid aging—from about 62 years of age in 1970 to over 84 in 2024. The rapid growth in an elderly population that came of age before South Korea's remarkable economic development—and before a national pension system had been established—leads the elderly to be the poorest generational group in South Korea today, unlike the Japan case. According to the OECD, the poverty rate of South Koreans over age 65 in 2021 was 39.3 percent—the second-highest in the OECD, and far higher than Japan's rate of 20 percent; 15.5 percent was the OECD average that year.[59] Only two other OECD states had rates above 30 percent that year (Estonia and Latvia). While South Korea's overall poverty rate is also on the high side of the OECD spectrum at 14.8 percent, it is not nearly the same level of exception as the elderly rate is. The more marked difference between generations in contemporary South Korea versus Japan also is illustrated in numerous differences in political attitudes, including over military security.

Unlike in Japan, South Korean generational differences are more evident in public opinion polling, with three generational groupings widely reported on in the media and political analysis: those in their mid-seventies or higher who came of age during the Korean War and immediate postwar years; the so-called 386 Generation born in the 1960s, and thus in their sixties presently, who experienced the democratization movement; and the "younger generation" who grew up in an affluent and democratic South Korea, which also could be subdivided into two distinct groups of middle-aged and 20-somethings.[60]

As noted previously, the elderly generation in South Korea today is the poorest generation. They also have levels of education far lower than the youngest generation. As Elizabeth Stephen notes, illiteracy rates at the end of the Japanese occupation period in 1945 have been estimated at 78 percent, describing the situation South Korea's oldest residents would have experienced.[61] In addition to a poverty rate at the second-highest level in the OECD in 2021 (the latest year comparative statistics were available in 2024), this generation developed shockingly high rates of suicide from the early 2000s—rising to as much eight times the OECD average, despite no other OECD country having a rate even twice the average.[62] Attitudes of this generation are more concerned with North Korea (against which they fought a war and experienced family separation) and more willing to sacrifice for civic duty, shaped by experience of their working lives spent under authoritarian rule.

By contrast, the 386 Generation tends to be politically progressive, with many student activists of this generation having continued into professional careers in politics or political advocacy. Having experienced the anticommunist rhetoric and scapegoating of authoritarian rule, they hold more liberal attitudes toward North Korea and more suspicion of the military, including the practice of mandatory male conscription. Finally, the youngest generations have traditionally been viewed as swing voters, having grown up under relative affluence and removed from the fighting of the Korean War and for democracy, but are beginning to exercise greater power in South Korean politics by expressing dissatisfaction with high youth unemployment (despite the shrinking labor force) and sky-high housing prices.[63] In June 2021 a 36-year-old man was elected head of the main conservative party, though he did not become its presidential candidate due to not meeting the minimum age requirement of 40 to become president.[64] In that election, young males voted overwhelmingly for the conservative candidate and ultimate victor, President Yoon Suk Yeol, pushing him over the finish in a close race. This generation expresses the least threat perception from North Korea and expresses a higher level of disdain for the conscription system partly as a result, and also since they are the ones forced to serve in the military through conscription.

An additional generational difference related to demographics in South Korea is the rise in the number of immigrants in the twenty-first century as South Korea began its aging phase and more so-called multicultural Koreans (those of mixed ethnic heritage) emerged. According to Erin Chung, "South Korea's total foreign population has grown around fourteen-fold from less than 180,000 in 1995 to over 2.5 million in 2019." Part of this growth is due to liberalization of marriage regulations which led marriage to foreign spouses to soar, reaching 13.5 percent of all marriages in 2005, rising to one in three in some rural areas.[55] Numerous social problems emerged from this influx, however, including domestic violence against these so-called marriage migrants. Still, successive presidential administrations from both left and right have pursued policies related to creating a more multicultural South Korea[66]—with the continued declines in fertility rate and intensified population shrinkage likely to lead to more immigrant workers and marriage migrants, though also likely with similar levels of pushback from native Koreans concerned about the effect of increased migrants especially on lower-wage and less-educated Korean workers, concerns also widely apparent in other advanced industrial democracies. In 2012 the compulsory military service law was changed to require all male citizens of South Korea, regardless of ethnic background, to satisfy the national military service requirement.[67]

South Korea's shifting demographics on multiple fronts—rapid aging, population shrinking, generational attitudinal differences, and increased immigration—affect South Korea's security policies in numerous ways, but the most immediately noticeable is in the shrinking military size despite growing threat perceptions in both the traditional and gray areas.

Growing Security Challenges, Shrinking Military Forces

South Korea's military capabilities have increased substantially, especially in the twenty-first century, and the country maintains the largest active-duty force of any U.S. ally.[68] However, though South Korean capabilities have increased, so have North Korea's—in addition to more threatening behavior by the North. Bennett offers a useful, if disturbing, catalogue of North Korean offensive weaponry that threatens the South, including over seven thousand artillery pieces within range of Seoul, thousands of tons of chemical weapons, and nuclear weapons that threaten both U.S. and South Korean military forces and the South Korean civilian population, as well as cohesion of the two allies at a time of crisis.[69]

In addition to growth in conventional military threats, gray-zone security concerns are also on the rise. South Korea established a cyber command in 2010 to counter North Korean activities in that area, which itself was reported to have been hacked by North Korea in December 2016.[70] China also has engaged in multiple gray-zone provocations, including regular intrusion of Chinese fishing vessels into South Korea waters (sometimes with Chinese naval or coast guard vessels as well), violation of the South Korean air defense identification zone (ADIZ), and economic warfare in response to the U.S. deployment of the Terminal High Altitude Area Defense (THAAD) missile defense system.[71]

While deterrence of expanded North Korean provocations and of outright invasion has been successful, North Korean leader Kim Jong Un continues his long-standing goal of breaking up the U.S.-South Korea alliance and in particular the forward deployment of U.S. personnel and equipment in South Korea. The substantial projected shrinking number of South

Korean army members raises concerns among many experts about future deterrence, in addition to numerous weaknesses of South Korean military forces, including much old equipment, insufficient numbers of equipment, and inadequate training of reserve forces.[72]

One area where the effect of a shrinking youth population already is seen is in the declining numbers available for the mandatory conscription of young men into the military, but even in this area the effect of the demographic pressure is not as one would predict, as the length of conscription was reduced as the number of men of conscription age declined. As a result, the size of South Korean army has been reduced by 40 percent from 2000 to 2021, though as with China (discussed in chapter 4), this is not entirely due to demographics but also due to efforts at military modernization.

The political aspects of the conscription issue should be considered in relation to South Korea's approaches to its future demographic challenges. A return to a two-year conscription period would yield a substantial boost to the number of forces but seems politically impossible in the present climate. Should South Korea's security situation dramatically worsen, however, it is one option—as seen, under very different circumstances, with Russia's decision to greatly ramp up conscription in its war with Ukraine. This contrast also underscores a major difference between policy options of democracies and those available to autocratic leaders, as discussed further in chapter 4.

In 2018, under President Moon Jae-in (2017–2022), a new "Defense 2.0" strategy document was released that once again addressed the challenge of the country's coming demographic transition for maintaining existing force levels, envisioning a drop to 500,000 troops by 2022 from 618,000 at that time. In December 2022, under the succeeding President Yoon Suk Yeol, South Korea's demographic transition strategy was further articulated, including—like Japan—a goal of maintaining the current force size for at least the next five-year period, in part through an additional 6.8 percent annual boost in spending over that five-year period, much of it directed at increasing pay for military personnel in an effort to bolster retention.[73] As in Japan, however, the Korean Army has failed to meet its recruiting and retention goals even before the latest exacerbating of South Korea's demographic challenges.[74] Defense spending has increased by 35 percent (in USD) from 2016 through 2021 to implement the combined vision of these two administrations, with a similar level of increase annually planned for 2022–2027.[75]

Even with these significant reductions in South Korea's number of troops to date, experts project that South Korea once again will not meet its more modest recruitment target in 2025 and that the new shortfalls will lead to a reduction in the target number again by another 60,000 troops. This would reduce the target size from the current 360,000 to 300,000 by around 2038, according to defense planners—but this slow timeline for further reduction will likely mean that the lower target of 300,000 also cannot be met, given the dramatic decline of potential conscripts of the target age and gender.

The alarming rate of decline in fertility will have even greater implications for South Korea's military in the 2040s, when those recently born reach military-service age. Even the present drop in number of young men of conscription age is serious—based on the nonreplacement fertility rate in 2003 of 1.17. The number of twenty-year-old men peaked in 1989 at just over half a million, falling to below 340,000 in 2009 and below 262,000 in 2023. This number is projected to fall below 144,000 in 2043, illustrating the stark reality that motivates South Korea's recent defense-planning moves.

As with the Japanese, one potential offset for the shrinking number of young men available for military service is to recruit more women—or even to require women to serve in the military, as Israel and some Northern European countries do. This issue has been litigated several times in South Korean courts, with a 2023 ruling reaffirming that gender equality provisions in the Korean constitution do not prohibit conscription being limited to men in the legislative Military Service Act. A legislative change is still possible, but with the public more or less evenly divided on the issue, female conscription does not seem likely anytime soon. However, President Moon sought to raise the rate of female voluntary service from the 2018 level of 6.6 percent of the military to 8.8 percent in 2022—a target not reached.[76] Given the size of the South Korean military, a higher target could make a notable difference given South Korea's challenging demographics. As Troy Strangarone calculated in 2021: "If South Korea were to maintain the current plan to reduce its military to 500,000 troops but match NATO's current 10.9 percent of female troops, it would require 54,500 fewer male troops and reduce the burden on the shrinking male population."[77] Beyond mere numbers, there also has been expansion in the roles where women can serve.

Looking beyond the 2020s, South Korea's demographic challenges will become much more severe. The ballooning of social spending that will be necessary to cover additional costs associated with a much larger elderly population as well as labor shortfalls that will result are two major concerns. On the security front, however, the demographic profiles of the South Korea's major security rivals, North Korea and China (as well as Russia), also will become more challenged in the 2030s, as further discussed in chapter 4. North Korea's total population is projected to begin to shrink around 2035, and already the country faces the hurdle of maintaining a force more than twice the size of South Korea's with just over half of South Korea's population size. With both states experiencing shrinking populations, demographers expect their population size ratio will remain roughly the same as now—which is at least a better situation than if North Korea were projected to continue to grow its population.

It also should be noted that in addition to concern about a future war with North Korea, there is an alternate scenario of reunification of the Korean peninsula—either by peace negotiations or as a result of success in a war or due to regime collapse in the North. While none of these scenarios at present looks especially likely, in terms of the time frame of this study up to 2050, they should not be ruled out. A sudden unification scenario, as a result of a war or regime collapse in the North, could have severe demographic consequences for both Koreas. As Kathryn Botto notes, millions died in the 1950–1953 Korean War, including an estimated 20 percent of the total North Korean population.[78]

In principle, a negotiated peace could have some positive impact for South Korea demographically, given North Korea's younger population, but, as discussed in chapter 4, the North is also on a later path toward rapid aging and total population shrinkage, with rapid aging exacerbated by longer life expectancies likely to emerge among the former North Korean population in a unification scenario. That said, less-skilled North Korean labor could, in principle, fill gaps in the South Korean labor market, and increased productivity over time of former North Korean workers could also possibly create more of a demographic boost in the workforce than initially apparent.

Building New Capabilities While Shrinking Force Size

The South Korean government has greatly increased defense spending and capabilities as it enters a new phase of aging. Substantial capability enhancements are planned for the coming decade, despite a dramatic drop in the number of fighting-age citizens—and indeed probably because of this drop.[79] Due to the plain reality that there simply are 30 percent fewer young men than a generation ago and will be even fewer in the next generation, senior leaders have no choice but to address long-known limitations of a roughly two-year universal male conscription system that was created under very different circumstances than present-day South Korea faces.

South Korea's military's transformation-in-progress is necessitated by a demographic imperative, but it parallels similar transformations underway in the most advanced militaries worldwide. China's military transformation over the past two decades shows many similarities in investing in the development and deployment of better military technology and shrinking of the size of its total military forces in order to pay them better and retain them longer for the purpose of having a more effective force—despite the country not needing to shrink its force size due to demographic challenges (at least not yet). In addition, as previously noted, China's military transformation itself contributes to South Korea's moves—as do North Korea's growing capabilities and provocative behavior. South Korea faces and is itself a contributor to the aging security dilemma apparent in 2020s Northeast Asia.

Despite the demographically unprecedented challenges South Korea will face in the coming decades, paradoxically its military forces stand to benefit from changes implemented due to demographic pressures in three important ways, at least in the shorter term. First, although the total number of South Korean forces have declined, the ratio of volunteer-to-conscripted forces is in the process of a substantial shift toward more volunteer forces, likely resulting in a better-trained military. (Note that the South Korean government does not publicly release figures on the ratio of its forces who are conscripted versus volunteers.) It is also likely in the more distant future that the country's lackluster reserve forces will be reformed in a way that utilizes the largely untapped resource of the vast majority of middle-aged Korean men who received a first round of military training through conscription.[80]

Second, a wide array of new technology is being developed and introduced to handle many functions that underpaid young men previously were forced to perform—as well as new technologies that will vastly exceed previous capabilities, despite the smaller total force size. High-tech sensors and robots already are being utilized on a large scale to monitor the demilitarized zone between the North and South, a task previously handled by military conscripts with limited training and experience. The army established an AI Research Center in 2018 to further improve such capabilities; at the time, the top commander of the army advocated for the use of advanced technologies for training as well as enhanced drones for ISR and munitions transportation.[81] It certainly helps that South Korea is a global frontrunner in digital technologies.[82]

This leads to a third area of change in South Korea's defense planning that is incentivized by its demographic transition: a deepening and broadening of its security partnership with the United States both in traditional areas of alliance cooperation between the two states as well as in new areas such as joint technology development and coordinated economic security initiatives. The economic security aspect was stressed in the March 2021 Biden-Moon joint statement as well as the April 2023 Biden-Yoon joint statement during Yoon's state visit to the United States. In combination with these two factors—better/longer training and better/more technology—the two militaries have more areas for collaboration, including a potential for greater interoperability of military forces and equipment. Moreover, the declining number of South Korean military personnel expected in the coming decades underscores the benefit of additional forces provided by security partners such as the United States. This pressure also may partly explain the South Korea's growing rapprochement with Japan, another U.S. ally facing significant population shrinkage in the next several decades.

Challenges of Funding Expanded Security Commitments: A Second Demographic Dividend?

Beyond staffing South Korea's military security needs—in both the military and civilian workforces—another primary challenge South Korea will face in the coming decades is how to pay for these workers and/or for the new technologies that may enable fewer workers to achieve the same output. South Korea's working-age population (20–64) is projected to fall by

36 percent, or over twelve million people, from 2020 to 2050 based on a constant fertility rate of 0.72. On the surface, then, maintaining even the current level of economic output would seem challenging—but, in fact, economists expect that South Korean GDP will continue to grow through 2050 (and likely beyond) and per capita income will exceed that of Japan's in the early 2030s.

This perhaps surprising prediction of continued total GDP growth for South Korea is linked to South Korea's more recent rise in economic development status. It was only two generations ago that South Korea was considered a developing country, rather than the roughly tenth-largest economy in the world it more recently has risen to. In part due to a generation of aging workers who were less educated and less healthy now retiring, economic forecasters expect the South Korean economy to grow in total economic size by about 70 percent from 2020 to 2050 despite the dramatically shrinking working-age population that is South Korea's medium-term demographic destiny.[83] This projected economic growth will help South Korea to manage the challenge of maintaining defense spending while also increasing social welfare spending to provide for a larger retired population.

In addition, South Korea's public spending on pensions as a percentage of GDP has been far below the OECD average.[84] The country's public debt level is also comparatively low—less than 20 percent of Japan's level—as noted in table 3.3 for 2020. In large part, this is due to the late development of a public pension scheme, which was only partly developed in the 1990s and only covered around 60 percent of workers in 2000.[85]

As demographers and economists come to better understand the new challenges of rapid aging for economic growth and sustainable retirements for larger proportions of the population, the idea of a "second demographic dividend" has been floated, which parallels the original demographic dividend concept through emphasizing the importance of targeted government policies to realize the dividend.[86] This second dividend is possible if workers are encouraged to save for retirement in ways that diminish their reliance on unfunded public earnings support. Not only would such a practice lessen a strain on future government finances, but such a high level of savings during working years would create substantial accumulated capital to potentially generate economic growth—as was seen to some extent in the Japanese case, where the latest generation of elderly were able to save at a high rate before retirement due to Japan's earlier economic development.

As Lee and Mason explain, "If workers are encouraged to save and accumulate pension funds, population aging can boost capital per worker, productivity growth, and per capita income."[87] As summarized in Stephen's application of the concept to South Korea, the theory is that "higher levels of education will increase productivity in the labor force, thereby offsetting the decrease in the number of working-age people. This combined with increased assets invested domestically will assist in tempering the falling support ratio."[88] Stephen offers a useful summary of five categories of policy recommendations for how South Korea can realize a second demographic dividend that includes ways to increase fertility, immigrant and female workforce participation rates, and productivity and length of working lives.[89]

Stephen also describes additional cross-national research that finds that decreasing labor growth resulted in increasing labor productivity through additional investments in more-scarce human capital.[90] Indeed, in the first year after South Korea's total population began to shrink in 2020, economic growth surged to 4 percent, an eleven-year high[91]—although that was only the first year of South Korea's population shrinkage, and the future projected drop is much steeper. That more recent South Korean citizen entries into the aged 65+ category are wealthier as a group than the previous generation also will offer more opportunity for reconsidering government support for the growing elderly population—though, on the other hand, due to the increased life expectancy, current retirees are expected to live longer as well.

South Korea has enjoyed the last stages of its well-executed demographic dividend as a more recently developed economy, where retiring workers are being replaced with much better-educated and healthier workers. This stage has ended, however, due to South Korea's new aging demographics—with productivity growth expected to decline from an average of 4.8 percent per year in the 1990–2020 period to 2.6 percent per year from 2020 to 2030, 1.8 percent from 2030 to 2040, and 1.1 percent from 2040 to 2050.[92] Still, although productivity growth is expected to slow as its population further ages, this level of projected growth is enough to achieve total GDP growth through at least 2050—even with a dramatically shrinking working-age population. By contrast, China's total GDP is expected to grow over threefold in that same period versus South Korea's roughly 70 percent growth, leading to continued relational security concerns.[93]

Conclusion: Extending the "Global Korea" Vision to Defense?

South Korea faces significant challenges ahead—in terms of both its demographics and its military security. Despite the coming rapid aging of its principal security rivals North Korea and China, there does not seem on the horizon to be a coming period of de-escalation of security tensions and reduction in military capabilities and spending. There is, however, a substantial change in South Korea's military strategy and tactics on the horizon as a result of its shrinking population and resulting decreasing size of its military forces, which contrasts with the Japanese case examined earlier. There is also reason to believe that South Korean attitudes about military security will continue to shift as a result of generational change ahead, with evolving attitudes of the youngest generation likely to play an important role. The impact of the so-called New Koreans—ethnically mixed Koreans, largely with ethnicities from nearby East Asian countries—also may shift in a positive way South Korea's relations with other Indo-Pacific States, building on South Korea's deepening economic and social connections with especially the Southeast Asian region.[94] This subregion has, in many ways, complementary demographics to South Korea's and has received increasing attention over two presidential administrations though their New Southern Policy and Indo-Pacific/Global Pivotal State strategies, respectively.

Chung Min Lee has called for a much bolder agenda for next steps of defense reform in response to increasingly challenging demographics, calling for South Korea to "modernize and revamp military training, education, and doctrines; maximize interoperability with US forces; ensure greater joint warfighting capabilities; and lay the foundation for intensified US-South Korea defense technology cooperation."[95] To a large extent, this is indeed the path being followed at present, though there is more to be done. Lee notes that in addition to North Korea's large ground force located close to the South Korean border,

with North Korea now armed with nuclear warheads and wide-ranging ballistic missiles, including sea-launched ballistic missiles, South Korea's armed forces must be reconfigured to meet a growing array of asymmetrical threats. Meanwhile, China's anti-access area-denial capabilities—including sophisticated anti-ship missiles and growing air and naval power—could significantly constrain, deter, or even deny the possibility of coordinated US-South Korean and/or US-Japan military operations in acute crises or wars.[96]

Thus, as seen in the Japan case as well, increasing security threats—in both traditional and new security domains—will likely continue to play a key role in South Korea's evolving security preparedness, even despite serious demographics-related challenges.

The recent deepening of the South Korea–U.S. security alliance may partly be explained by South Korea's perceived need to strengthen its military posture in the face of growing threats but being hindered by the challenges of going it alone—challenges exacerbated by a rapidly aging population. Early signs in 2023 and 2024 of a rapprochement between Japan and South Korea, including plans for annual dialogues in the area of military security as well as diplomacy, also may be partly related to demographic challenges both countries face and expect to intensify in the coming years.[97] The political leadership transition currently underway in South Korea after the impeachment of President Yoon in December 2024 and the suspension of his presidential powers may further solidify a generational shift in that country's political leadership that may lead to new approaches to the ever-declining birth rate and to national security broadly.

TAIWAN'S INTENSIFYING DUAL-GRAYING CHALLENGE

Taiwan's security situation is quite different from Japan's and South Korea's, despite it also facing similar demographic challenges to South Korea. Taiwan faces a much larger adversary in China in terms of population and economy, and a state that regularly emphasizes its ultimate goal of (re)integrating Taiwan's full territory into China's governing structure and regularly engages in threatening conventional as well as gray-zone hostile actions.[98] In an additional contrast to the previous cases of Japan and South Korea, Taiwan has not been a formal U.S. ally since January 1, 1980, when the Mutual Defense Treaty signed in 1955 was ended after the United States established diplomatic relations with China—though the Taiwan Relations

Act of 1979 specifically directs the United States "to provide Taiwan with arms of a defensive character; and to maintain the capacity of the United States to resist any resort to force or other forms of coercion that would jeopardize the security, or the social or economic system, of the people on Taiwan."[99] U.S. leaders, including members of Congress, also regularly state their intention to protect Taiwan in the event of an unprovoked attack from China, and the Taiwanese military is deeply connected to U.S. military structures and training. At a minimum, therefore, Taiwan should be viewed as a special security partner of the United States, even if no longer a formal ally.

All the Northeast Asian democracies examined in this chapter have designed their defensive strategies together with U.S. military forces, but the case of Taiwan is the most extreme case of dependence on the United States given the pressing existential threat Taiwan faces. At the same time, the very specific nature of this threat allows both the United States and Taiwan to plan and to focus on specific defensive scenarios. In essence, the main objectives are to deter a Chinese military invasion of Taiwanese territory, to defeat an invasion force if overt hostilities are initiated, and more broadly to deny the Chinese military the ability to achieve its political objectives vis-à-vis Taiwan.

One key tension in Taiwan's defense planning is the balance of resources divided between these two distinct missions—deterrence of an invasion and defeating an invasion if one is initiated—which increasingly involves different equipment and technology as the tools of warfare evolve. Beyond the population-aging challenges facing Taiwan's society and its military, there is another aging-related challenge that Taiwan, Japan, and South Korea all face that relates to the tension between these two core missions: the internal battle among military services and policy planners between old-school ideas about how to protect their territories through expensive, large-scale weapons/weapon systems versus newer, smaller-scale asymmetric weapons and technologies.

Taiwan's evolving security challenges and readiness also underscore how population size alone does not determine military strength, since the territory that in 2024 is over sixty times smaller in population than China's maintained military superiority for decades after 1949 in the feared invasion scenario and also enjoyed a robust missile defense/deterrent advantage (putting aside China's nuclear capabilities). Taiwan's security situation has declined precariously due to China's intense military modernization of the twenty-first century, however, with a consensus among experts that Taiwan no longer enjoys technological or overall military superiority in its defensive operations. Moreover, Taiwan's population faces intensified aging and shrinkage in the coming decades as well as intensifying gray-zone provocations from China.

Taiwan also faces challenges similar to Japan's related to remote islands that are largely uninhabited apart from military and coast guard personnel, such as Pratas Island in Taiwan's case as well as lightly populated Kinmen and Matsu, two islands within visual distance of the Chinese mainland. Similar to China's apparent strategy with the Senkaku Islands, claimed and administered by Japan, regular incursions into Taiwan's remote islands' air and maritime space help to establish China's long-term presence in territory it claims as its own. The increased frequency of such activities puts new strain on Taiwan's aging naval and air forces, the latter of which saw three fatal crashes in 2020–2021 alone. As a result, the Taiwanese Air Force announced in March 2021 that it expected to spend US$76 million more in 2021 to counter PLA operations.[100]

Taiwanese defense-planning documents acknowledge the deterioration of Taiwan's defensive capabilities vis-à-vis China, including a recognition of their demographic challenges ahead. For example, Taiwan's 2019 *National Defense Report* includes the following concern: "For the past few years, the PRC has been procuring weapons and conducting combat training and drills specifically aiming for a Taiwan scenario. Now, it is capable of initiating joint blockades and point firepower strikes against Taiwan, and is posing severe challenges to our defense preparations and defensive operations."[101] Alluding both to growing concerns about gray-zone threats as well as the effect of Taiwan's declining population, the 2017 *Quadrennial Defense Review* includes this concern: "In recent years, our country has faced constraints in defense financial resources and manpower, difficulty in acquiring advanced weapons systems, increasing threats to cyber security, decreasing defense awareness in the public, and increasing incidents of complex emergencies, all of which require a serious and careful response."[102] Thus, concerns about manpower (or, more broadly, personnel, since Taiwan has the highest percentage of women in its military of the territories examined in this chapter) are only one of several pressing concerns in Taiwan's changing security environment, but it is an important one, as illustrated in the following discussion.

Like South Korea, Taiwan also followed an early path to address its shrinking military-age population in a counterintuitive way—when President Ma Ying-jeou, a member of the Nationalist Party (KMT), yielded to popular antipathy toward universal male conscription in 2008 by promising to transition the military to an all-volunteer force over a roughly ten-year period. His successor, President Tsai Ing-Wen from the Democratic Progressive Party (DPP), however, maintained a four-month conscription period that took effect in 2013.[103] She declared a plan in December 2022 to reinstitute one-year mandatory male conscription in 2024, after the result of the January 2024 presidential election (which she was not running in due to term limits). The candidate from Tsai's party, Lai Ching-te (also known as William Lai), won that election and allowed Tsai's plan for an increase of conscription to one year to stand.

In addition to a reversal related to Taiwan's aging population, the combination of China's growing military capabilities and increasing gray-zone coercion has pushed Taiwan to put into motion additional important changes in its defense posture away from one grounded in direct military competition using comparable (and expensive) weapons toward an asymmetric strategy to repel the feared Chinese invasion if one were initiated. Planning for such a shift has been articulated in Taiwan's Quadrennial Defense Reviews since 2009, but implementation has been difficult and slow. Taiwan's increasingly severe demographic challenges further underscore the benefits of such a shift in strategy, however—as noted in the Taiwan's latest defense-planning documents.

As with the Japanese and South Korea cases, Taiwan's increasingly severe decline in the number of young men—and young people in general—combined with innovations in defense technologies have created strong pressures for the adoption of new military strategies for the next era of Taiwan's defense. Like Japan and South Korea, Taiwan implemented large defense-spending increases in the 2020s—up 46 percent in Taiwan dollars from 2020 to 2023, to US$16.6 billion.[104] This increase in spending once again illustrates that rapidly aging societies are capable and willing to respond to rising security challenges.

While the military challenge facing Taiwan appears quite severe and dire—and perhaps it indeed is, depending on how one judges Chinese intentions—it is also important to note that Taiwan has faced an existential threat from China since the fleeing of the Republic of China's Nationalist government to Taiwan in 1949. Moreover, Taiwan's de facto sovereign status has relied on expected U.S. support in the event of military hostilities initiated by China since that time. Newer challenges of a so-called Taiwan contingency have the potential to draw other regional states into the conflict—particularly Japan—as well as for the conflict to escalate into a nuclear conflict between the United States and China, making the stakes at this time quite high.

The issues of how Taiwan can best protect itself from an aggressive China and how other concerned states can help in this—including by deterring Chinese action—are the subject of countless books and articles, particularly after Russia's full-scale invasion attempt on Ukraine in February 2022. This book cannot provide such depth of analysis but rather seeks to illuminate the demographics-related aspects of war planning and how military strategy over the defense of Taiwan is evolving due to both changing demographics and the broader evolution of military technologies.

Demographic Challenges to Taiwan's Military Security

In Taiwan's early days as a de facto sovereign territory free from Japanese colonization and PRC control, its population size soared. Taiwan's total fertility rate hit a high of 6.68 in 1952, but with a rising population size, the number of annual births increased until 1966. As primarily an agrarian society, it was common for women to bear six or seven children. Annual births in the 1950s and 1960s were generally in the 400,000s, peaking at 462,000 from 1964 to 1966.

Taiwan has changed in countless ways since those early days, including a stark drop in the number of annual births. In 2010, when that number hit a then-record low of 166,866, then-president Ma Ying-jeou treated the matter as a national security crisis, leading to policies that saw a modest rebound in the birth rate before starting the present path of decline.[105]

In the first decade of Taiwan's rapid aging, from 2010 to 2020 (as illustrated in table 3.2), Taiwan's population aged 65+ increased by 42.7 percent, a huge jump, and while its total population grew 0.21 percent over the course

TABLE 3.6
Taiwan's demographics–security nexus

Total fertility rate (2024)[a]	0.87		
Total population (millions)[a]	2024 23.26	2035 (est.) 22.01	2050 (est.) 19.25 (–17.2% from 2024; 4.01 million)
Percentage of population 65+[a]	2024 19.2% ("aged")	2035 (est.) 28.4% ("super-aged")	2050 (est.) 39.3%
U.S. treaty ally?[b]	No		
Active military forces (2023)[b]	169,000		
Defense spending (2023)[b]	$18.89 (in US$billion), 2.51% of GDP		
Total GDP in US$ (2015) trillion[d]	2023[c] $0.7566	2030 (est.) $0.781	2050 (est.) $1.092 (+44% from 2023)

[a] UN Population Division (2024), constant fertility projection
[b] IISS, *Military Balance* (2024)
[c] IMF, *World Economic Outlook Database* (April 2024)
[d] Institute of Energy Economics Japan, *IIEJ Outlook* (2023)

of the decade, total population shrinkage would begin the following year. As existing theories of the importance of aging on national security generally predict, Taiwan followed expectations by reducing the size of its military forces by almost 44 percent in that first decade of rapid aging. Moreover, while defense spending did increase by just above 23 percent over that ten-year period, this was less than one-tenth of the increase of its principal adversary and only a tiny fraction of China's increase in total spending. Taiwan's spending also was only about half the level of spending as a percent of GDP as its de facto ally and protector, the United States. The next decade, as Taiwan further ages, looks to be different in this regard, as explained further below, and as seen in Taiwan's 2023 defense spending level (table 3.6).

Taiwan has followed a similar pace of aging as Japan, but on a much later timeline (as illustrated in table 3.1). While it took both places about twenty-five years to transition from the beginning of the "aging" process to "aged" status, Japan started that journey in 1969, Taiwan in 1994. While it took Japan eleven years to subsequently reach super-aged status in 2005, Taiwan is projected to reach that demographic milestone in just seven years, in 2025.

Taiwan's 2024 TFR is reported comparatively as the second-lowest in Northeast Asia, after South Korea. Using that rate of 0.87 as a future projection, Taiwan's total population is projected to shrink by 17.2 percent from 2024 to 2050, about four million people—as indicated in table 3.6. At that point, upward of 39 percent of Taiwan's population will be aged 65+. In the shorter term, however, while Taiwan's total population size has begun to shrink, Taiwan's National Development Council projection from August 2020 calculates that "the country will not experience negative growth in the labor force until 2031, thanks to a rising labor participation rate in the run-up to that year."[106] Partly due to this, and to increasing worker productivity expected, Taiwan's total GDP is projected to grow by over 43 percent from 2020 to 2050. Thus, as with Japan and South Korea—and as we will see with China in chapter 4—a common assumption that a shrinking population size necessarily means a shrinking GDP is not what economists predict.

After a decade of experiencing near-annual declines in the number of young people, the need for more decisive action to address the challenge to Taiwan's military forces has become apparent. As noted by researchers at the International Institute for Strategic Studies (IISS): "Demographic pressure has influenced plans for force reductions and a shift towards an all-volunteer force, which the 2021 *Quadrennial Defense Review* credited for helping the armed forces reach its staffing goals. Nonetheless, issues with recruitment and retention have reportedly created personnel challenges for combat units, and an extension of the current four-month military conscription requirement under consideration."[107] This plan of instituting a return to one-year universal male conscription was implemented in 2024, with the first one-year conscripts reporting for training on January 25, 2024, and the equivalent of around US$130 million allocated for upgrades to training facilities and barracks.[108]

In line with the decline in the number of young people available to serve in the military in the 2010s, Taiwan's Ministry of National Defense (MND) announced in 2014 that it would reduce military personnel from 275,000 to 215,000, and later it announced further reductions to around 175,000—actually overshooting that planned reduction due to shortfalls in recruiting the target number of professional versus volunteer forces.[109] As a result, Taiwan's active-duty military shrunk to 165,000 in 2020 from 275,000 just three years prior.[110] Drew Thompson provides this useful comparison to U.S. recruiting challenges based on more favorable 2019 demographic data for Taiwan: "Taiwan's annual military recruitment targets range between 18,000 and 28,000 per year, but the total annual number of births is between 180,000–200,000 per year (and declining steadily). Taking low figures of each, Taiwan's military must attempt to recruit roughly 10 percent of the 18-year-olds entering the workforce each year to maintain its current force size."[111]

It is important to emphasize, however, that the transition to an all-volunteer force was not only—or even primarily—a result of demographic challenges. Initially, under President Ma Ying-jeou, it was largely a populist move that also comported with Ma's general lack of prioritization of Taiwan's military readiness. Later, in the implementation phase under President Tsai Ing-wen, the shift was also used as a way to address the perceived need for longer training periods for new personnel to effectively handle more advanced weapons technology and systems.

More reliance on advanced technology requires additional training, requiring either longer conscription times or more reliance on professional forces (or both). As Dee Wu writes in her analysis of Taiwan's then-planned transition of an all-volunteer force, "professional forces have the service time needed to become capable of operating command and control (C2) systems, or to become experts in repair and logistics, which requires expertise in handling both hardware and software. As Taiwan is looking to build its own Aegis ships, the need for an elite force to operate such advanced technology will only grow stronger."[112] The 2019 *National Defense Report* reports positively of the training experience of the professional forces, writing: "Recent field training and drills have revealed that voluntary service members have several positive traits, such as serving longer, being more experienced, adaptive, and skillful in operational settings, and being psychologically stable."[113]

Another demographic-related concern apparent in the 2010–2020 aging decade, also predicted by the general literature on the effect of rapid aging on national security, is that personnel costs rose substantially as Taiwan sought to maintain even the smaller number of military forces. As McNamara observes: "Personnel costs … already constitute a meaningful part of Taiwan's defense allocations, representing 46 percent of the FY18 budget, crowding out other necessary expenditures such as procurement and operations and maintenance."[114] As noted in a different study, the cost savings from manpower reductions provided some margin to improve individual pay and benefits, housing, and incentive pay;[115] however, these savings were insufficient to cover the full increase in manpower-related costs needed to attract and retain personnel under the new system. As with McNamara, this second study also notes that the "unanticipated magnitude of transition costs has led Taiwan to divert funds from foreign and indigenous defense acquisition programs, as well as near-term training and readiness."[116] Thus, like the earlier cases of Japan and South Korea, there was a clear need for greater defense spending due to the combination of higher personnel costs (despite fewer personnel in total) and more technology to offset the fewer personnel.

Beyond more spending, the MND also implemented new approaches to recruitment targets in several other ways. It increased goals for the number of women serving and expanded the roles they could fill. It even collaborated with a television production company to portray military life in a more romantic fashion.[117] The *2017 Quadrennial Defense Review* provides this additional list of efforts: "The ROC Armed Forces have been improving recruiting efforts by enhancing forces training, providing well-rounded care to dependents, realizing career plans for service members after retirement, offering complete supporting measures for recruitment and policy incentives to enhance personnel quality and organizational efficiency and creating an elite defense force."[118]

Most broadly, and as seen in cases of Japan and South Korea as well, Taiwan's recent defense-planning documents include multiple other examples of new lower-tech labor-saving practices common in the commercial sector. In addition, as discussed in the next section, a number of higher-tech weapons systems are planned in part to reduce the need for human labor, in addition to adapting to newer weapons being developed by China as well as the United States. Finally, as with South Korea, new attention has been given to Taiwan's reserve forces as a result of the experiment with lessening the conscription period.[119] With the return to a one-year conscription period in 2024, a more robust reserve force may supplement Taiwan's defenses despite Taiwan's shrinking overall force posture.

New Strategic Approaches to Address Intensified Dual Graying

"Maintaining cross-strait stability in the face of an increasingly well-resourced and modernizing PLA requires continual innovation and adaptation, including the updating of defense concepts"[120]—this is the moving target Taiwan faces in its next stage of strategic competition with China as both militaries plan for a new era of shrinking and rapidly aging populations (though from a much larger population baseline in the case of China).

In the coming decade, Taiwan plans to adapt its defense strategy and general readiness to address the intensified dual graying challenges it expects to face. The *2021 Quadrennial Defense Review* for the first time explicitly mentions the need to counter the PLA's "gray-zone" threat, devoting a full section to the wide range of gray-zone threats Taiwan faces (primarily from China).[121] As an introduction to that new section, it states: "In recent years, the PRC has been frequently using gray zone tactics, such as cognitive warfare, IW [information warfare], and incursion by aircraft and vessels, aiming at weakening morale, depleting the resources of the ROC Armed Forces, and eroding the national security, which urgently require precautions and responds [*sic*]."[122] Specific actions are set out to address each type of gray-zone concern, which differ in many ways from the gray-zone challenges faced by Japan and South Korea due to Taiwan's unique status in relation to China. In the conclusion of the report, the number one point includes addressing gray-zone challenges together with the prior goals of building asymmetric capabilities as well as maintaining forces for traditional deterrence.[123]

Since the publication of the *2021 Quadrennial Defense Review*, China's provocative gray-zone actions have only intensified, including now regular incursions into Taiwan's ADIZ and maritime space that had previously been respected. In August 2022 China conducted its largest military drills to that point around Taiwan after House Speaker Nancy Pelosi's visit to Taipei. Since then, such large-scale drills have become common. The *2023 National Defense Report* refers to this new reality under a section titled, "Normalization of Grey Zone Harassment and Incursions."[124]

In addition to a new focus on rising gray-zone challenges, key elements of a new "Overall Defense Concept" (ODC) proposed in 2017 by Taiwan's then-chief of General Staff, Admiral Lee Hsi-min, also appear in the *2019 National Defense Report* as well as in the subsequent *2021 National Defense Report*.[125] As summarized by Thompson,

> The ODC describes an asymmetric defense approach where Taiwan maximizes its defense advantages and targets an invading force when it is at its

weakest: in Taiwan's littoral. While Taiwan's previous strategy focused on fighting across the entire Taiwan Strait and defeating the enemy through attrition, the new concept divides Taiwan's defense operations into three phases: force preservation, decisive battle in the littoral zone, and destruction of the enemy at the landing beach.[126]

The ODC's calls for additional investments in mobility, deception, camouflage, concealment, jamming, redundancy, rapid repair, and reconstitution are apparent in the 2019 and 2021 defense-planning documents. Notable for linkages to systems that require less direct human labor, the ODC envisions fleets of future UAVs bolstering Taiwan's defense with strategic early-warning, tactical reconnaissance, target acquisition, and coastal fires.[127] In addition, a "new fleet of automated, fast minelaying ships are being built ..., with the first vessel of the class launched in August 2020." Building on this labor-saving automation, it is envisioned that "while invading ships are slowed by mine fields, swarms of small fast attack boats and truck-launched antiship cruise missiles will target key PLA ships."[128]

In June 2024 Admiral Samuel Paparo, U.S. INDO-PACOM commander, described in an interview with the *Washington Post* U.S. preparations and planning to engage in a similar asymmetric defense approach in support of Taiwan called "Hellscape."[129] The U.S. DOD had announced in March 2024 that it would spend $1 billion on a program called "Replicator" to build swarms of unmanned surface ships and aerial drones for this strategy.[130] As described in the *Post* interview: "The idea is that as soon as China's invasion fleet begins moving across the 100-mile waterway that separates China and Taiwan, the U.S. military would deploy thousands of unmanned submarines, unmanned surface ships and aerial drones to flood the area and give Taiwanese, U.S. and partner forces time to mount a full response."[131] Developing this capability and speaking about it publicly is presumably intended to strengthen deterrence and to convey that even aging powers can possess and employ formidable military assets.

By contrast, it is widely thought that Taiwan's expensive fixed-wing aircraft would not survive initial Chinese bombardments in an actual invasion scenario, and even if they did, maintaining functional runways would be an additional challenge. Taiwan's large naval assets, such as its destroyers, also are not expected to survive in an actual invasion scenario. Still, there is a perceived need to modernize older aircraft and ships in Taiwan's air force and navy in order to provide peacetime deterrence and to counter growing gray-zone pressures.

Thus, at least in the current state of military technology competition, most agree that Taiwan should invest in both types of military hardware. Indeed, this is seen as one objective of an adversary related to gray-zone conflict: to force an opponent to expend resources and to calculate a level of response that will not risk an all-out war but still protect national interests. For example, according to reporting by Bloomberg, Chinese warplanes made more incursions into the southern part of Taiwan's ADIZ in 2020 than in the previous five years combined, forcing a response by Taiwan's Air Force.[132] Such incursions have continued at a rapid rate since.

Taiwan's geography lends itself to the newer asymmetric approach, which Thompson notes is a complex landscape that includes seawalls, paddy fields, bridges, tunnels, and ports with thousands of shipping containers, all of which could be used to conceal smaller weapons such as missiles. By contrast, China's demographic/personnel challenges are much greater as the potential invader. As Thompson summarizes: "Beijing can use blockades, coercion, hybrid warfare, or gray zone pressure, but the only thing that guarantees that Beijing can achieve its political objective of Taiwan's surrender is putting PLA boots on the ground and physically seizing control of the island."[133] Thus, although Taiwan suffers from a severe imbalance in military forces compared to its cross-strait adversary, arguably the number of forces needed for its defensive mission are considerably fewer, particularly with new technologies and the asymmetric strategy envisioned.

Further adding to Taiwan's defensive advantage, as noted earlier, Taiwan's broader defense strategy is not imagined to be operating solo: Taiwan's defense posture is designed for the Taiwanese military to survive long enough as an effective fighting force to provide the United States (and potentially other security partners, like Japan) the time to be able to assist. Thus, unlike the war between Russia and Ukraine, Taiwan has always known it faced an invasion threat from its much larger-population neighbor and long has planned how to protect against this—working closely with the United States on these plans. One lesson from Russia's large-scale invasion of Ukraine in 2022 is that an invaded state is likely to need to fight invading forces on its own while waiting for allies to engage, underscoring this defensive strategy of Taiwan.

As with the earlier cases of Japan and South Korea examined in this chapter, Taiwan also has deepened its security ties with the United States as it begins its demographic transition to a population-shrinking, super-aged territory. As Chinese escalation and military modernization further progresses, the United States has agreed to provide longer-range missiles to Taiwan to allow for more accurate and impactful strikes on the Chinese mainland if need be—both to enhance deterrence and to contribute to degrading Chinese military superiority in the event of an actual fighting war.[134] U.S. military assistance to Taiwan also has increased greatly in response to China's more aggressive military posture. The December 2022 U.S. National Defense Authorization Act, setting defense spending for FY2023, included up to $10 billion in assistance to modernize Taiwan's defensive capabilities over five years—a sum equal to around 15 percent of Taiwan's annual defense spending.[135] In addition, Congress passed legislation in 2023 to grant so-called presidential drawdown authority (PDA) to the U.S. president to transfer U.S. military equipment to Taiwan (which is then replaced with new equipment later to U.S. forces); President Biden subsequently announced that he would exercise this authority to transfer US$345 million of defense equipment to Taiwan in 2023.[136] In addition, it was reported that an even larger military equipment transfer was planned for late 2024—as much as $567 million.[137] Through this military assistance, interoperability between U.S. and Taiwanese military forces also will improve, with benefits for both militaries—though anticipated changes to U.S. policy in the new Trump administration may modify the trajectory of the Biden administration.

Beyond investment in new sorts of weapons and recapitalizing older conventional weapons, another more recent initiative that has garnered increased urgency as a result of the Russia-Ukraine conflict is the need for sufficient stockpiles of munitions and other weapons. Even before the escalation of the Ukraine conflict underscored this point, Taiwan had sought to increase the domestic production of weapons (as South Korea long has done and Japan more recently has sought to further emphasize—despite their respective rapid aging). Here, too, as Thompson notes: "The ODC is particularly well aligned with President Tsai's industrial strategy to develop Taiwan's indigenous defense industry. The numerous, small, maneuverable, affordable platforms called for in the ODC can generally be made by domestic firms." Moreover, he adds, "increasing spending on domestic defense contractors benefits Taiwan's economy and increases domestic support for more defense spending, while also reducing reliance on the United States as Taiwan's sole supplier of weapons."[138] As one notable example, the Taiwanese military was expected to take possession of over one thousand domestically produced cruise missiles in 2024 to contribute to the next stage of Taiwan's defense.[139] Thus, here again we see that an aging power is not necessarily a weaker one but rather can possess additional capabilities due to greater experience and (manufacturing) prowess.

Significant Challenges Ahead Despite Positive Changes

Despite multiple initiatives to bolster Taiwan's defense in response to increasing threats from China in a way that complements Taiwan's industrial and technology base as well as its rapidly aging and shrinking population, significant challenges and questions remain. Beyond defense policy, other costs will rise as Taiwanese society rapidly ages—though, as noted earlier, a shrinking workforce is a decade away, and productivity growth will create additional resources. Another concern in the case of Taiwan's politically divided society facing aggressive gray-zone disinformation operations by China is the potential evolution of attitudes about and support for military security.

Looking further ahead, an increasing security threat from China coming from new types of weapons, including cyber, remains a serious concern. At the same time, Taiwan's own cyber-capabilities are quite advanced, given its experience with China's regular cyber-attacks on both military and civilian targets in Taiwan. It is expected that Taiwan also would deploy significant offensive cyber-operations in an actual shooting war with China that would degrade China's conventional military operations, particularly when combined with U.S. cyberwarfare.

Taiwan's shrinking diplomatic space is another concern. Taiwan continues to lose more of the few states that recognize it diplomatically and to be isolated in international forums. Still, the Taiwanese government's New Southbound Policy, announced in November 2016, seeks to build on the broader framing of the Indo-Pacific region that other leading states have adopted and to develop closer economic and cultural ties with multiple states in the region.[140]

There are also some signs of increased military cooperation with countries beyond the United States. For example, in 2021 *Newsweek* reported that the Taiwanese navy and JSDF seemingly engaged in a joint surveillance operation of a Chinese warship passing through the Miyako Strait, a narrow path between Taiwan's main island and Japan's westernmost inhabited island, Yonaguni, which lies less than seventy miles from Taiwan's east coast.[141] That said, neither Japanese nor Taiwanese officials would confirm the *Newsweek* report, indicating the continued sensitivity of the matter. Similarly, Reuters has reported modestly deepening Taiwanese security ties with Singapore and India, though the report also noted that Indian military officers regularly visit Taiwan on ordinary rather than official passports.[142]

Maintaining the U.S. security commitment in the face of U.S.-China competition and also procuring and deploying appropriate defensive technologies despite a growing divergence between Taiwan's defensive needs and U.S. military equipment and expertise are two additional challenges ahead that are not directly related to Taiwan's dual graying concerns. For example, Taiwan is developing an indigenous diesel-powered submarine since the U.S. submarine force is now exclusively nuclear and other potential suppliers such as Japan, Australia, and several European manufactures were not willing to risk sanctions from China if they supplied such equipment to Taiwan.[143]

In summary, as Dee Wu has argued, although personnel shortages are currently an issue in Taiwan's military, a more positive spin on the challenges ahead is to see them as an opportunity for the Taiwanese military "to correct its organizational inertia" and make more efficient use of its forces.[144] For the United States there is also a benefit in Taiwan's moves toward implementation of its new defense approach. As Thompson writes, "cooperation with Taiwan is a laboratory for developing innovative future warfare concepts." Moreover, he continues, "Taiwan's proximity to China is an advantage which could benefit networked US forces operating at greater stand-off distances if those forces are networked with their Taiwanese counterparts."[145] In these ways, it is imaginable to see Taiwan's aging as reinforcing positive attributes of aging such as maturity, experience, and even strength.

Taiwan's strategic posture transformation is a result of a large confluence of factors. Taiwan's declining number of young people to staff its military is one factor that directly led to a number of important policy changes in the 2010s and now 2020s. The shape of the changes implemented also were greatly affected by China's more aggressive military actions, changing military technologies available and being developed, and also domestic

political considerations such as concern for the welfare of professional soldiers and conscripts. In this third aging Northeast Asian democracy case, a
number of commonalities with the earlier cases are evident, but several
unique aspects are also present. The next section will compare and contrast the policy responses seen from Northeast Asia's aging democracies to
date before transitioning to a consideration of Northeast Asia's rapidly aging
autocracies in chapter 4.

TRENDS AND SURPRISES FROM NORTHEAST
ASIA'S AGING DEMOCRACIES TO DATE

Three shared trends are apparent from the aging frontier of Northeast
Asia in how these three rapidly aging democracies have begun to adjust
their national security strategies and practices in anticipation of intensifying demographic pressures to come. First, even rapid aging across
rival states has not led to lessened tensions or less-perceived threats. An
aging peace does not appear to be on the horizon. Second, existing
assumptions about the effect of aging on security must be revised due to
new technologies and observation of how aging states have responded to
the new security challenges of aging itself and other new security challenges, including the proliferation of gray-zone conflicts. Third, aging
and other demographic change in the Indo-Pacific will nevertheless
likely contribute to further changes in the security landscape to come,
based on policy changes to date and policy planning documents published by actors across the region. By contrast, divergent approaches,
despite similar demographic trends, also are apparent due to their different security challenges, political and cultural contexts, and timing and
stages of economic development—findings further illustrated in the set of
cases presented in chapter 4.

Reconsidering First-Order Predictions of the
Demographics–National Security Linkage

Chapter 1 summarized four first-order effects anticipated by scholars and
analysts related to the effects of rapid aging on security outcomes (visualized in figure 1.2). This section reconsiders those assumptions based on the
actual experience of Northeast Asia's rapidly aging democracies.

Of the four anticipated effects, three are apparent in the cases of Northeast Asia's rapidly aging democracies, though the implied results of these effects are not as they were predicted to be. A fourth first-order effect is not evident: There is no indication that external actors view Japan, South Korea, or Taiwan as less powerful due to their rapid aging. Indeed, rival states such as China and North Korea regularly decry what they describe as rising militarism and unnecessary development of weapons that they blame for a regional arms race among the aging powers. In essence, the most aged powers are blamed for the apparent aging security dilemma that has emerged. The United States also describes recent enhancements in defense capabilities and increases in defense spending of these rapidly aging democracies as important to countering intensifying regional security concerns.

On the economic front, there have been expressed concerns about Japan's at times anemic level of economic growth since its "bubble economy" burst in 1989—what was once referred to as a "lost decade" and then "lost decades"—which has more recently evoked the trope of aging being related to decline. However, stories that focus on Japan as a rising military power also are common: strength in older age. There is, in addition, a growing collection of media stories about the region's low fertility and anticipated population shrinking that often paint quite dire portraits of the future, but these portrayals do not seem to be shaping how rival states view and treat each other—quite the contrary, tensions are rising. In sum, based on Northeast Asia's early experiences with rapid aging, aging states are seemingly not treated or viewed differently due to their higher median ages or rising elderly populations.

Three other predicted first-order effects of rapid aging on security are apparent in the cases of Japan, South Korea, and Taiwan, but the second-order effects are not necessarily as predicted. First, each has experienced total population shrinkage as a result of its late-stage rapid aging. At the same time, each has implemented a number of policies to bolster the actual size of their workforces despite the shrinking size of that population age-range. There is clearly room for improvement in this area, however, which on the positive side means that there is potentially still a latent workforce waiting to be utilized—particularly working-age women, as will be discussed shortly. There is more cause for concern looking into the 2030s and 2040s, however, as population shrinkage accelerates in each of these places.

A second first-order effect that is apparent within Northeast Asia's rapidly aging democracies is a shift underway in the balance of political power among age groups and their related generational cohorts. All three democracies see a larger number of older voters as well as the emergence of a new generation of younger voters who are seen as possessing a distinctive set of values and preferences that could potentially swing elections. This shift, however, does not show a consistent cross-national pattern related to the aging–security policy nexus as predicted in existing scholarly literature, which also relates to a third predicted first-order effect that posits that older voters would prioritize social spending over more robust managing of security affairs. Instead, what seems more apparent is that the transition in generational cohorts underway is altering democratic politics in each democracy, but the effect of age itself is less clear, particularly when one looks across time and place, as visualized in figure 3.1.

The general assertion in existing scholarly literature is that older populations will be more conflict-adverse and less supportive of military action due to the economic costs of such action. However, data from two rounds of World Values Survey polling conducted in the 2010s shows that actual age-group preferences on two important security questions vary across countries and over time: There is not a consistent effect of age.[146] Figure 3.1 depicts the effect of age on attitudes toward security expressed in two questions polled across Japan, South Korea, and Taiwan (and elsewhere in Asia) in two time periods, 2010–2014 and 2017–2019. (The exact dates of the survey in each country varied within those year-ranges.) These surveys asked respondents to express their general concern for war as well as their "willingness to fight" for their country. As is visually apparent in the figure, at least among the three rapidly aging democracies in Northeast Asia, age cohorts (below 44, 41–65, 65+) are *not* a consistent predictor of the security attitudes across these different territorial populations. What is more notable is the grouping of attitudes by territory more than by age across territories—meaning that there is much more noticeable clustering of the Japanese, South Korean, and Taiwanese attitudes than there is clustering around the age cohorts.

Given how one might objectively view security threats facing each territory, it is surprising that Japanese concern for war is the highest among the three territories, though Taiwanese concern grew notably between the first and second time periods of the survey as tensions with China rose. Also,

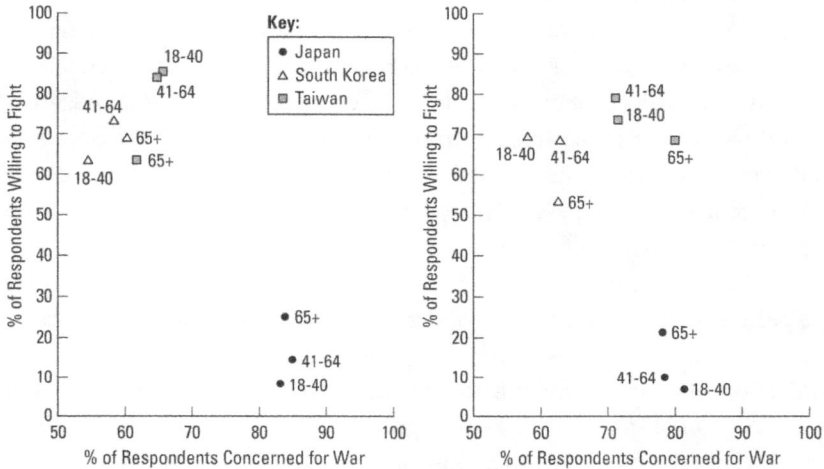

Source: World Values Survey: Wave Six (2010-2014)   Source: World Values Survey: Wave Seven (2017-2022)

Note: *This figure was created together with Prof. Hsin-hsin Pan of Soochow University (Taiwan) as part of a joint research project.*

FIGURE 3.1. Age cohorts/security attitudes in Japan, South Korea, and Taiwan, 2010–2014 and 2017–2022.

perhaps paradoxically given their heightened concern for war, the Japanese were also by far the least willing to fight for their country—though this number did increase in another, related survey in polling conducted in April 2022, but still not even rising to 20 percent on average across age-groups.[147]

By contrast, there is very little difference by age cohort within each territory about "concern for war," with the one exception of the Taiwanese 65+ age cohort in the 2017–2019 round, who were notably more concerned about war (by about 10 percentage points, 80 percent versus about 70 percent for the other age-groups). There is a notable difference by age cohort about "willingness to fight," but it varies by territory as to which age-group is more/less willing and also varies by time period within each territory.

In Japan, the 65+ group is most willing and the 18–40 group least willing to fight in both time periods, and at a similar level for each—with the 65+ group more than twice as willing, though still at low levels (under 10 percent versus just over 20 percent). In Taiwan, the 65+ group is least willing across time periods (by over 20 percentage points) and the 41–64 group most willing (at around 80 percent), with the 18–40 group declining across the two periods to a percentage in the low seventies. In South Korea, the willingness-to-fight level decreased in all age-groups across the two time periods, but which cohort was most or least willing changed over that period, with the 65+ age-group dropping almost 20 percentage points to just over 50 percent. Thus, to underscore the point, there is no consistent relationship between age-group and willingness to fight, contrary to what is predicted in the general literature.

In all democracies—the three considered in this chapter included—there are periods of robust discussion of the so-called guns-versus-butter trade-off. In the case of Northeast Asia's rapidly aging democracies, there is no indication that rapid aging is leading to increased frequency or intensity of consideration of this trade-off—though certainly in each democracy there is active disagreement about the appropriate level of defense spending and defense capability enhancements, as there has been in earlier periods. In this first decade of rapid aging cross-nationally, however, we see a common decision across countries to increase defense spending in response to increased threat perception.

Reconsidering Second-Order Predictions of the Demographics–National Security Linkage

The aging experience to date of the Northeast Asian democracies shows more consistency with the eight predicted second-order predictions from the general literature set out in chapter 1 (visualized in figure 1.3). Here we see evidence of these predicted second-order effects in six of the eight categories—all but decreased defense spending and slower economic growth/less government revenue. Related to the latter, however, there has been a decrease in economic productivity growth that may be due to an aging workforce. Due to continued overall economic growth, however, there has not been less total government revenue, though spending has increased both on defense and on social spending related to older people that is leading to higher deficit spending in some cases.

In terms of the other six predicted second-order effects, in line with general predictions, the Northeast Asian democracies did experience (1) smaller recruiting pools for their militaries, with increased planning to address further anticipated shortfalls, (2) smaller military forces in total, (3) improved use of the existing labor, including expanding the labor pool via greater inclusivity related to age, gender, and migrant workers (though still at quite low levels for the latter), (4) greater support for new military technologies, including explicitly in areas where new technology is seen as addressing a related labor shortage, (5) more substitution of human labor with technology, and (6) new military doctrine based on new technologies and fewer human resources.

At this juncture, before a transition to consider early signs of demographics-related policy shifts in Northeast Asia's aging autocracies, it is an opportunity to emphasize that this study does not seek to assign relative causal weight to how much it is rapid aging versus other factors, such as available technology, shifting domestic politics for nonaging reasons, or changes in threat perception, that are more or less contributing to the direction of security policy evolution in Northeast Asia. Rather, the goal is to illustrate how the unprecedented demographic transition underway creates new pressures for action and accommodation—that demographic pressures, too, are a variable, and one underappreciated in studies of the evolving security landscape of the Indo-Pacific to date. What is clear in the cases of Northeast Asia's rapidly aging democracies is that there is greater reference to demographic challenges each face and increasing numbers of policies that specifically reference this challenge and securitize it.

One way that each of these democracies has sought to address workforce shortage challenges is to make better use of its existing population while also taking very limited steps toward increasing work-force size through additional immigration and/or use of temporary workers from abroad. As discussed in chapter 1 and visualized in figure 1.1, while total population size may be more or less fixed in the short term as a result of the prevailing level of fertility (TFR), there are numerous ways that a utilized population can be expanded in size as well as ways that the productivity of the utilized population can be increased.[148] Both of these factors can be affected by what some scholars refer to as "political capacity," which also or alternatively can be considered a "cultural" context.

One way the next decade of rapid aging of Northeast Asia's democracies will be different is that they will be joined in their super-aged status by their primary security rivals, Russia, North Korea, and China. The regional "arms race" that many observe today is in part a result of many aging territories in the region spending more to shift the composition of their armed forces due in part to challenging demographics, particularly countries that previously had relied on cheap, conscripted military forces like South Korea and Taiwan (and, to some extent, China). An aging security dilemma is apparent. Chapter 4 considers early indications of how the likely experiences of Asia's rapidly aging autocracies will differ from the experiences to date of Japan, South Korea, and Taiwan.

Chapter Four

NORTHEAST ASIA'S RAPIDLY AGING AUTOCRACIES

Later Timing, Greater Control

Northeast Asia's aging autocracies will experience rapid aging later than Northeast Asia's democracies and in different ways due to their different political regimes, economic strategies, and other differing population demographics. Still, though the full impact of demographic change will come later, its impact already is being felt. Moreover, as the United States and its Northeast Asian security partners craft their security strategies for maintaining peace into midcentury, the coming demographic challenges their principal adversaries will face also should be closely studied, though conclusions at this point will be more tentative since the aging process is not yet as advanced.

China has become the overwhelming primary security concern for the United States and its allies, as noted in chapter 2, though North Korea's belligerent conduct continues to pose existential threats to numerous regional states as well. Russia also is viewed as an increasing regional security threat, despite—and in part because of—the quagmire it faces with its European border state, Ukraine. Overall, the primary regional military concerns and rivalries in the Indo-Pacific are between its aging democracies and aging autocracies: This is the present reality and is highly likely to be the security reality of the coming decades as well, based on demographic projections and a consideration of the limited potential challenger states on the horizon (beyond India's notable rise, as discussed in chapter 5).

Apart from later aging of their populations, Northeast Asia's autocracies also share the commonality of long-serving leaders who appear likely to continue governing during the demographic transition ahead, though, of course, it is possible that their autocratic resilience is less robust than generally thought. Governing actions in other policy areas—for example, Putin's handling of the Ukraine war and Xi Jinping's and Kim Jong Un's strict Covid-related policies—illustrate how autocratic leaders possess the ability to implement policy more quickly and forcefully than Northeast Asia's aging democracies, suggesting in some ways that they may be better equipped to manage the demographic challenges ahead. Thus, it is worth stressing at the outset of this chapter that "choices" made by individuals in these states is a relative term. "Volunteer" military forces may in fact have been highly coerced, and technical rules about conscription are often adapted to the needs of the moment of the ruling autocrats.

Another reason to carefully consider Northeast Asia's aging autocracies is that there is a growing diversity among the increasing number of rapidly aging states worldwide, as noted in chapter 1—moving beyond the "first wave" that were nearly all highly developed democracies to now a "second wave" that includes less-developed states and nondemocracies like China, Russia, and North Korea. Insights from the consideration of how Northeast Asia's autocracies will be affected by their coming demographic transitions—and how they have managed them to date—thus offer an additional perspective on challenges facing rapidly aging states in the broader Indo-Pacific and in other regions, including other states aging on later timelines.

This chapter first reviews Russia's and North Korea's demographics–national security nexus and then examines in greater depth China's role in shaping the security environment in the Indo-Pacific and the challenges it is projected to experience as its demographic transitions intensify later in this decade and deepen further in the 2030s and beyond. Finally, and in transition to considering the security implications of the greater demographic diversity of the broader Indo-Pacific region in chapter 5, the conclusion to this chapter will draw some summary points from Northeast Asia, the locus of rapid aging in the Indo-Pacific today, including comparisons across the Northeast Asian 6 considered in this and the previous chapter.

RUSSIA'S MILITARY RESURGENCE AND
RENEWED REGIONAL ENGAGEMENT

Russia offers a surprising case for proponents of the theory that aging societies are less likely to support offensive wars. In 1967 Russia was the first state in this IP16 study to reach "aging" status (where 7–14 percent of the population has reached age 65+)—even before Japan—and also faced population shrinkage earlier than any others in this study (from 1995 to 2008). Its ability in the 2010s to raise its fertility rate significantly (though temporarily), reverse population shrinkage (again, temporarily), and become involved in several active shooting wars makes it an essential case to consider in a study of the effect of rapid aging on military security policies, even if it is only partly an Asian country. It is notable in this context to point out that Russia is in fact Asia's largest country in terms of landmass, and that about three-quarters of its territory is east of the Urals (the traditional demarcation of Asia as a continent). Moreover, slightly over 25 percent of its total population lived in its Asian regions as of January 2023, and two of its four military districts include its Asian territory, with sizable portions of its military equipment and personnel deployed there.[1] Russia also maintains a military presence on the disputed "Northern Territories" islands north of Japan's main islands off the coast of the Northeast Asian mainland.

Russia's significant increase in the size of its military forces and spending from 2020 to 2023—roughly 300,000 additional forces (larger than Japan's *total* military forces, despite a similar total population size) and a roughly one-third increase in spending (US$20 billion), as seen in tables 3.3 and 4.1—shows once again that demographics alone do not dictate security policies, particularly when states are moved to respond to perceived threats. In addition, substantial further increases in military spending are reported to be planned as the Russia-Ukraine war continues. The Russian Defense Ministry released documents saying defense spending could rise by more than 68 percent in 2024, to $111.15 billion. Spending at that level would amount to about 6 percent of Russia's GDP and represents more than the total spent on social programs.[2]

This contrast between increasing challenges with its population demographics and more activist security policies also was seen in the early 2010s, though Russia's fertility rate increased during that period, and population shrinkage also was halted from 2006 to 2020. Deborah Brooks and colleagues also note this apparent anomaly in their large-*n* statistical study of the effect of age on likelihood a state will go to war, writing: "Despite its severe aging problem, Russia has undertaken a number of assertive foreign policy actions since 2010. ... Beginning in that year, Moscow committed to a decade-long, large-scale increase in military spending that has significantly improved the country's arsenal. And recently, its leaders have displayed a growing willingness to use force."[3]

Thus, Russia's actions to date as an aging power suggest that it is willing to make sacrifices in other areas to maintain a robust international presence and protect its perceived security interests. For example, it spends roughly twice the percentage of GDP on defense than does China: higher than the United States, the world's largest-total military spender, as well. Since Russia is not projected to reach super-aged status until 2031, its recent conduct combined with its more favorable population demographics compared to Northeast Asia's democracies suggest a continuing of the status quo in its regional policies—though the next steps of its war with Ukraine could shift Russian policies in unexpected ways, as seen in 2024 with

TABLE 4.1
Russia's demographics–security nexus

Total fertility rate (2024)[a]	1.45		
Total population (millions)[a]	2024 146.56	2035 (est.) 138.37	2050 (est.) 130.10 (−11.12% from 2024; 16.46 million)
Percentage of population 65+[a]	2024 17.2% ("aged")	2035 (est.) 20.5% ("super-aged")	2050 (est.) 24.1%
U.S. treaty ally?[b]	No		
Active military forces (2023)[b]	1.1 million		
Defense spending (2023)[b]	$74.76 (in US$billion), 4.01% of GDP		
Total GDP in US$ (2015) trillion[d]	2023[c] $1.1997	2030 (est.) n/a	2050 (est.) n/a

[a] UN Population Division (2024), constant fertility projection
[b] IISS, *Military Balance* (2024)
[c] IMF, *World Economic Outlook Database* (April 2024)
[d] Institute of Energy Economics Japan, *IIEJ Outlook* (2023)

President Vladimir Putin's summit meetings with the leaders of China, India, and North Korea and the addition of North Korean forces on the front lines of the war with Ukraine.

Russia's intensifying demographic transition and its challenging war with Ukraine may exert further pressure on Russia to limit its engagement with the Indo-Pacific region in some ways, but they also have led to deepened outreach and relationship efforts with fellow autocracies China and North Korea. In addition, Russia continues to be a robust supplier of low-cost yet advanced weapons to numerous Indo-Pacific states, including Quad-member India, as well as an exporter of primary products region-wide. Russia also had deepened its relationship with China since the start of its military operations in Ukraine in 2013 as its diplomatic isolation from the West intensified. In 2023 and 2024 Russia engaged in summit diplomacy with North Korea, reportedly providing that country with advanced weapons technologies in exchange for assistance with weapons production related to its war with Ukraine (as well as the aforementioned dispatch of North Korean troops to the front lines).

Given this array of reasons for Russia's regional security engagement with the Indo-Pacific, Russia's projected aging and shrinking population should be of interest to those considering the region's future security environment and Russia's role in it. As the first major power to experience population shrinkage in the modern era (in the aftermath of the collapse of the Soviet Union) and the first of the Northeast Asian 6 to reach "aging" status (in 1967), there is an unusually long window of opportunity to study Russia's security conduct as an aging state.

As introduced in chapter 3 and illustrated in table 3.1, Russia's unusual demographics date to the Soviet period and also are related to the breakup of the Soviet Union. Russia in the Soviet period initially reached aging status in 1967 but did not reach "aged" status until 2017. Its total fertility rate fell from a replacement-level 2.03 in 1989 to a low of 1.18 in 1999, its first decade apart from the Soviet Union. As a result of a national campaign to address this decline, however, rates started to rise incrementally more or less every year until 2015 to 1.79 but then began to decline again. Russian total population also experienced an early period of shrinkage after the Soviet Union breakup, from 1995 to 2008, of about 4.57 million people (from 148.38 million to 143.81 million) before a rebound back up to 146.56 million in 2020. (Note that this includes a population boost from the 2014 annexation of Crimea, which added more than two million people to Russia's reported population.)

Russia's early population shrinkage—unprecedented among majors powers until that time—was due both to declining birth rates and to higher emigration after the breakup of the Soviet Union, drawing attention from a number of scholars and policymakers as an early case study of the likely effect of population change on security policies, particularly given Russia's status as one of the world's largest military powers.[4] A decade or more after these early studies, we can see that Russia's overall military conduct has not been moderated by its early demographic challenges. Indeed, both its demographic trends and its military activities surged in the 2010s—with its population decline halted, birth rate increased, and military actions undertaken in Syria and Ukraine as well as gray-zone activities elsewhere along its borders and beyond.

In terms of demographic trends, however, the Russian fertility rate has again declined and population shrinkage resumed in 2020. As illustrated in table 4.1, unless Russia's TFR increases above 2.0 or significant immigration into Russia takes place, both unlikely, total population shrinkage will continue for the foreseeable future—estimated at a drop of over 11 percent (over sixteen million people) from 2020 to 2050, and this before the full population effects of its war with Ukraine are known.

A report by Stratfor in 2020, drawing on Russian national statistics, discusses the likelihood of even greater population shrinkage due to deaths outpacing births and higher than expected emigration, suggesting in its most negative of three scenarios a population drop of twelve million by 2036.[5] Again, this is before the effect of the escalating war with Ukraine initiated in 2022 is factored in, which is widely reported to have contributed to additional emigration and the deaths of tens of thousands of young men, perhaps more. On a more positive demographic note, and illustrating the advantages of an autocratic regime, in 2018 the Russian government put into place a plan to extend retirement ages by four years in the 2020s (up to 65 for men, 60 for women), which is projected to increase the size of the labor force despite the total population shrinkage, as well as to raise revenue for increased social programs (or, in the recent context, for its ongoing war with Ukraine).

Russia has undergone a much slower process of aging in part due to the higher birth rate it achieved in the rebound period in the 2010s and in part because of much lower life expectancy than the other Northeast Asian 6, as seen in table 4.2. Russian life expectancy in 2024 was estimated to be more than ten years lower than Japan's and South Korea's and even slightly lower than North Korea's. With a 2024 life expectancy only about eight years beyond the aged 65+ threshold versus nearly twenty years for Japan in 2022, Russia's total aged population is much smaller, and thus its median age is also lower than Northeast Asia's democracies (as illustrated in table 2.3). As a result, a number of the concerns about the rapid aging–national security nexus expressed by scholars and pundits—such as ballooning spending on healthcare and pensions—apply less to Russia. Moreover, and again indicative of greater policy options of autocratic states, the Russian legislature delinked pensions from inflation rates in October 2016, in part to devote additional resources to military spending.[6]

However, as indicated on table 4.2, life expectancy is predicted to rise notably by midcentury—though, again, this estimate was conducted before the full effects of the war with Ukraine are known, which will likely lead to downward adjustments. For one, it is estimated that around half a million Russians have left Russia since the outbreak of the full-scale war with Ukraine in 2022, with it reasonable to assume that such emigres are likely to be on the younger end of the demographic spectrum, which would result in the more-rapid aging of the remaining population. Moreover, though death and injury rates from the Russia-Ukraine war to date span a wide range, it seems likely that another half a million Russians have been killed or injured so far, with a growing number virtually certain as fighting continues, which also is likely to lead to higher statistics on Russian median age as these causalities will largely be on the younger end of the spectrum.

TABLE 4.2
Russian vs. other Northeast Asian (predicted) life expectancy, 1990–2050

	1990		2005		2022/24		2035		2050	
	Total	M / F	Total	M / F	Total	M / F	Total	M / F	Total	M / F
Russia	69.3	63.8 / 74.5	65.2	58.8 / 72.4	73.3	67.5 / 79.2	75.3	69.9 / 80.7	77.9	73.2 / 82.6
Japan	79.0	75.9 / 81.9	82.0	78.5 / 85.4	84.8	81.8 / 87.8	86.5	83.5 / 89.5	88.3	85.3 / 91.4
South Korea	71.9	67.5 / 76.4	78.5	74.9 / 81.9	84.0	80.7 /87.1	85.6	82.4 / 88.7	87.4	84.2 / 90.6
Taiwan	74.0	71.6 / 76.9	77.2	74.2 / 80.8	81.3	78.1 / 84.5	83.6	80.8 / 86.3	85.6	83.0 / 88.3
China	68.0	65.7 / 70.4	74.1	71.6 / 76.8	78.6	76.0 / 81.3	81.1	78.9 / 83.5	83.8	82.0 / 85.6
North Korea	70.2	65.4 / 73.8	69.3	65.0 / 72.7	73.6	71.0 / 76.1	75.3	72.7 / 78.0	77.5	75.0 / 80.1

Source: Russia: UN Population Division (2024), constant fertility projection; other states: UN Population Division (2022), constant fertility projection

Russia's gap between male and female life expectancy also is notable—over 10 years in 2024, which is actually less than the 13.6-year gap in 2005, but also likely to be adjusted as a result of the Russia-Ukraine war. In nearly all countries of the world, male life expectancy is lower than that of females, but the Russian case is extreme.[7] Unhealthy levels of alcohol consumption among men are seen as the main reason for the gender disparity, which has implications for Russia's military recruiting and retention as well as broader workforce productivity.[8]

One security-related effect of Russia's decreasing population size was seen before total population shrinkage began in 2020 with the lower yield of the semi-annual draft of young men in 2018, which was reported to have yielded the lowest number since 2006. The Russian government explained the shortfall as in part due to the planned transition to a greater reliance on volunteer forces, but there was a shortfall in volunteer enlistment and retention as well.[9] As with the Northeast Asian democracies, future demographics will pose even greater challenges to the conscription system. As reported in a 2023 study, "a decade ago, [Russia] could draft 130,000 men two times a year out of an eligible cohort of 1.2 million men. Now, the size of that cohort has fallen to 700,000, making efforts to pull that many men into the army much more difficult and simultaneously much more consequential demographically, economically and politically."[10]

Nevertheless, in response to the war with Ukraine, the Russian government expressed plans to further increase the size of the Russian military by 350,000 from 2023 to 2026 by raising the maximum draft age from 27 to 30 and increasing the numbers signing up for volunteer service as well as retaining volunteers longer—a tall order in the middle of a war.[11] The increase in the number of one-child families as Russia's birth rate has declined, combined with the recent decision to end the draft exemption for only-child families, has further contributed to recruiting challenges for the Russian military, which had already seen a decline in the number of total forces by almost 14 percent from 2010 to 2020 (as indicated in table 3.2).[12]

The new challenges that Russia faces in recruiting undercut a military modernization plan that was underway before the 2022 escalation of the Ukraine conflict and that mirrors policies put in place in South Korea and Taiwan to rely less on conscripted soldiers by increasing the proportion of volunteer forces and modernizing weapons and logistics technologies to need fewer soldiers. This shift, however, faced challenges in implementation, due both to further declines in the working-age population and to opposition within military ranks.[13] This is similar to challenges faced in South Korea and Taiwan in the early stages of their planned force transitions. Russian policy shared another similarity with Taiwan in that before the escalation of the war with Ukraine, Putin had pledged to abolish conscription entirely and rely instead on a fully volunteer force.[14] As with Taiwan's case, though, subsequent security and demographic realities forced a change in course. Moreover, as with the Northeast Asian democracies, the shift to reliance on a higher proportion of volunteers costs significantly more, eroding some of the impact from Russia's boost in defense spending by 250.23 percent (in Russian currency) from 2010 to 2020 (as indicated in table 3.2).[15]

Russia's military modernization of the past decade as well as its actual combat experiences with Ukraine and earlier in Syria and elsewhere have shown the uneven nature of the Russian threat to concerned states within the Indo-Pacific and beyond. On the one hand, Russia's naval investments have shifted to ships better suited for defending Russian littoral waters (in addition to its submarine-based deterrent), and its only remaining blue-water aircraft carrier is not operational.[16] Moreover, as a result of its Ukraine operations, its forces and equipment have been severely depleted. On the other hand, Russia remains a formidable competitor in the development of next-generation weapons such as hypersonic missiles and drone technologies. It also has shown, at least to the point of three years into its full-scale war with Ukraine in 2025, that it is able to mobilize a large fighting force despite its demographic challenges—an "advantage" of its autocratic system to at least some degree, as it is widely reported to selectively conscript ethnic minorities and to spare White elites in its politically important European cities of Moscow and St. Petersburg. As discussed further in later sections of this chapter, a similar ability can be assumed to be possible in North Korea and China as well, if the number of military forces were to be perceived as falling short in a perceived crisis. By contrast, as noted in chapter 3, Japan's constitution is understood to ban conscription as part of its post–World War II legacy, while South Korea and Taiwan already conscript nearly all young men in their populations for mandatory military service, though they have reduced the length of service due to strong popular pressures expressed more openly in a democracy.

Russia's deepening security cooperation with China also potentially enables collaboration and further advancement in the development of next-generation weapons. Moreover, even in more conventional military activities, Russia continues to make its presence known in the Indo-Pacific region, especially Northeast Asia. For example, it enhanced both air and sea power based in the disputed Northern Territories with Japan in the early 2020s, territory that it has occupied since the conclusion of the Second World War.[17] It regularly flies military planes at the edge of Japanese airspace, causing Japanese fighter planes to scramble in response.[18] Russia also has increased its joint training exercises with China in the Asian region.[19] In June 2023 it sent two warships through a narrow strait between Japan and Taiwan, leading both militaries to send naval vessels in response.[20] In short, Russian military activities in the Indo-Pacific—both traditional and gray—continue despite its first stages of population aging and engagement in a protracted war on its European border.

Russia's demographic challenges combined with its current preoccupation with its war with Ukraine make it unlikely that it will undertake significant new initiatives in the Indo-Pacific in the near term—and indeed its diplomatic reputation in major international fora has suffered as a result of its actions in Ukraine and elsewhere. However, Russia's diplomatic isolation from the West could lead to deeper relations with some Indo-Pacific countries of the Global South, beyond its deepened engagement with China—as seen via summitry with North Korea and India. At the same time, Russia's long history with the region also suggests that its regional presence and influence will not evaporate despite challenges on its European side and more challenging demographics ahead. Moreover, Russia's conduct in Europe and elsewhere shows that it is willing to devote significant resources and endure substantial hardships in order to continue robust military activities, as with fellow autocracy North Korea, discussed in the next section. Given Russia's historical pattern of cyclical bursts of engagement with the Indo-Pacific region, often linked to new initiatives of particular leaders, it can be expected that there will be further surprises with Russian military activity in the Indo-Pacific region despite Russia's current challenges and its more challenging demographic future ahead.[21] Even a grayer Russia will remain a formidable Indo-Pacific power and potentially a rising concern despite its future projected aging.

NORTH KOREA'S LATER AGING AND
GREATER POPULATION CONTROL

North Korea's pace of aging is the slowest in Northeast Asia (apart from Mongolia). Of the Northeast Asian 6, North Korea is the only one that is not yet experiencing population shrinkage—which is not projected to occur until 2035. However, as noted in table 3.1, North Korea too is projected to reach super-aged status by 2040—after only reaching aged status in 2029, and after the Northeast Asian democracies already are all super-aged.

North Korea is an outlier in the demographic–security nexus in other ways as well, which serves to underscore that demographics are not deterministic of security policies. It maintains the second-largest standing army in East Asia, over one million, despite a total population of just over twenty-six million—compared to China's standing army of about double the size with a fifty-times greater population size; as noted earlier, South Korea's standing army is less than half the size of North Korea's, despite South Korea having about twice the population size. Moreover, North Korea is estimated to spend over one-quarter of its total GDP on the military, including on its

TABLE 4.3
North Korea's demographics–security nexus

Total fertility rate (2024)[a]	1.78		
Total population (millions)[a]	2024 26.46	2035 (est.) 26.85	2050 (est.) 26.14 (−2.7% [0.72 million] from 2034 peak of 26.86 million)
Percentage of population 65+[a]	2024 11.7% ("aging")	2035 (est.) 17.7% ("aged")	2050 (est.) 21.2% ("super-aged")
U.S. treaty ally?[b]	No		
Active military forces (2022)[b]	1.28 million		
Defense spending (2019)[c]	$4.31 (in US$billion), 26.4% of GDP		
Total GDP in US$ (2015) trillion[c]	2019[c] $0.0163	2030 (est.) n/a	2050 (est) n/a

[a] UN Population Division (2024), constant fertility projection
[b] IISS, *Military Balance* (2024)
[c] U.S. State Dept, *World Military Expenditures and Arms Transfers 2021*

rogue nuclear weapons program and ambitious missile development program. It manages this level of spending and size of military through intense and brutal control of its population and an intensive propaganda campaign that stresses the military as a key pillar of society, which suggests that even when its demographics become less favorable through its more gradual aging, it will be able to continue to fill its military ranks.[22]

The primary security concern of the United States and its allies is North Korea's nuclear weapons and advanced missile development, not its large standing army—though South Korea and the United States together devote significant planning and resources to deter against a large-scale invasion of the South by North Korea. Despite North Korea's delayed population shrinking and rapid aging, it is projected to maintain a roughly similar population ratio to the South over time—an important relative concern for South Korea, that while the South's population shrinking starts earlier, the North also will begin to shrink. By 2050 it is projected that the North's population will be slightly smaller than its 2024 size as well as its peak in 2034—at 26.86 million, versus South Korea's roughly 44.3 million (down from nearly 52 million in 2024).

It should be noted that collecting reliable statistics on North Korea is challenging, and that as a poor, resource-starved country, it is especially vulnerable to unpredictable demographic shifts. A famine in the 1990s, which North Koreans are forced to refer to as "the march of hardship" or "Arduous March," is estimated to have led to the premature deaths of over a half-million people in addition to malnutrition and lower birth rates in millions more.[23] The long-term effect of that period continues to be evident in the country's population pyramid.

As South Korea's technological capabilities continue to increase and to be utilized to offset its shrinking working-age population and number of troops, North Korea may continue to rely on brute numbers to balance against an inter-Korean conflict—supplemented most likely by a continued nuclear deterrent against any attempt at regime change from the South and/or the United States. In addition, China has repeatedly shown a willingness to support its quasi-ally North Korea in hard times, and though China will begin to suffer from much more challenging demographics in the coming decades (as discussed in the next section), it certainly will be capable of supporting a small state and economy such as North Korea if it chooses to do so.

It is difficult to see how changing demographics of either North or South Korea, or surrounding states as well as the United States, will affect the many conflict dynamics with North Korea. In the past, even at times when North Korea was severely challenged by famine—or more recently with Covid—it did not alter its aggressive and suspicious security posture. Thus, demographically speaking, there is no reason to expect that North Korea will moderate its many nefarious activities that run the gamut from its nuclear weapons and missile development to gray-zone cyber and other organized criminal operations due to its projected aging in the coming decades.

THE CHINA CHALLENGE AND CHINA'S VARIED DEMOGRAPHIC CHALLENGES

As the largest-population country in the world until 2022, China's population demographics have been the subject of frequent fascination and attention for many years—often with exaggerated claims that overemphasize the latest population trend or projections. A recent batch of stories that predict dire consequences for China's economy and social stability as it enters a period of rapid aging follow this familiar script. With a population of around 1.4 billion, China operates at a scale unique to itself and rival power and neighbor India (which became the world's largest-population country in 2023). To be sure, China does face daunting challenges related to its future economic development and social stability that will be affected by its changing demographics, particularly the speed and extent of its rapid aging, as discussed later in this section.

In the security realm, however, China's scale often means that demographic changes in percentage terms that seriously hamper smaller-population countries have a more nuanced impact on China. China also faces a wide range of demographic changes and challenges that are not apparent in the Northeast Asian democracies, such as concerns about a large (but narrowing) sex ratio imbalance between males and females, differential birth rates among different ethnic groups and regions, and a growing economic and social divide between an increasingly urban population and a shrinking rural one. China's evolving population demographics will certainly affect future government policy decisions on a wide range of policy issues, but the direct effect on China's military readiness and future military strategy will likely be much less than in other areas due to a much larger potential pool of military recruits compared to almost any other state (even if the number is declining in absolute terms), China's decades-long push to reduce the number of personnel in its military in favor of a more technologically advanced force, and its continued economic growth potential as a still-developing economy in many areas.

China's strategic competition with the United States is highly likely to be the principal shaper of the security environment in the Indo-Pacific for the foreseeable future, as initially discussed in chapter 2. China's coming demographic challenges are unlikely to change this within the timeframe of this study (through 2050) but may affect how China exerts its power in the region in the coming decades that could have important consequences for China's neighbors and the broader regional security environment. Technology competition is at the center of the strategic balance, which connects with shifting demographic pressures in surprising ways—including the incentive this creates for more cross-national collaborations discussed in chapter 3, a trend that disadvantages China as its rivals seek to limit its access to leading-edge technologies and to create more resilient supply chains. Nevertheless, China's inexorable moves to develop greater military capabilities now and for the foreseeable future are widely predicted to continue. For example, the U.S. Department of Defense assessed in 2020 that, "in spite of forecast difficulties for China's economic growth in the 2020s, the Party has the political will and fiscal strength to sustain a steady increase in defense spending over the next decade," though the rate of growth may slow.[24]

Comparative data and case illustrations from the other Northeast Asian 6 offer clues to how China will seek to manage its demographic transition ahead and how this might affect its broader security posture. For example, all the Northeast Asian 6, apart from Japan, utilize conscription—and all those except North Korea are altering their conscription practices based on newer military challenges that are only partly demographically driven. All six are increasing their defense spending to pursue new technologies that include labor-saving implications. All six—except, perhaps, North Korea—face challenges to fill their military ranks with adequate numbers of personnel who possess the desired skills to capitalize on increasingly technologically sophisticated weapons and systems. China also has implemented policy changes in all these areas and likely will implement more as its demographic pressures mount.

China's military faces similar recruiting challenges to the more demo-graphically challenged Northeast Asian democracies (as well as many states elsewhere) in seeking to attract talented college graduates and others to a job that can be physically demanding, with potentially long periods away from family and friends and potentially facing physical danger.[25] Moreover, like the Northeast Asian democracies, China's military also is hampered by a large and politically powerful army while naval and air forces increas-ingly are areas China seeks to develop to create a stronger overall force.[26] Unlike Japan and Taiwan, however, though similar to South Korea, the high unemployment seen among recent college graduates in China may benefit efforts to recruit more college graduates with desirable skills such as in tech-nology and engineering, particularly if more efforts are made to improve military pay and conditions to make that career path more attractive.

The idea that China may face a future of inadequate numbers of work-ers contrasts sharply with concerns in the past century but is an important new reality to prepare for based on future demographic projections. Chi-na's demographic challenge for centuries was too *many* people, though its population also was seen as an asset at various points in its history. China's powerful postwar leader, Mao Zedong, saw power in numbers. He used a numerical advantage in military personnel to create a stalemate in the Korean War in early 1950s and pushed back on suggestions from party offi-cials to limit births beyond an expansion of birth control options.[27] After Mao's death, however, China's population size and growth trajectory became viewed as a cause for concern, leading to the draconian One-Child Policy (OCP) that became nationwide government policy—with notable exceptions—from 1980 to 2016. Note, however, that even with often brutal enforcement measures, China's total fertility rate never fell to 1.0, in part because certain ethnic minorities and regions were exempted and in part due to steadfast resistance by some Chinese.[28] Ironically, the fertility rate fell sooner and more substantially in Taiwan, where no strict government policies to reduce birth rates were implemented.

China's population growth in the twentieth century also was due to dra-matic increases in life expectancy, as in most of the world in the twentieth century—as discussed in the introduction to this book. Global life expec-tancy in 1950 was under 46.4 years, compared to 73.2 years in 2023. In China, life expectancy was under 44 years in 1950, exceeding 65 in 1982, and far exceeding the global average in 2023 at 78. This laudable achievement for human welfare will lead to mounting pressures within China to devote more resources to elder-related care, a greater burden for China in some ways due to its less-developed policy infrastructure in this area—though this also is a potential benefit compared to Northeast Asia's democracies in terms of greater ability to control costs as new policies are implemented.

The government policy dictate of China's One-Child Policy is what created the steep "demographic cliff" that the country faces around 2030. As illustrated in table 3.1, China has followed a similar pace of aging as Japan and Taiwan, but on a much later timeline. It took Japan and Taiwan twenty-four and twenty-five years, respectively, to transition from the beginning of the "aging" process to "aged" status, with China taking twenty-three years, but Japan started that journey in 1969, Taiwan in 1994, and China only in 2000. China is projected to reach super-aged status in 2032, though current low birth rates suggest that it will likely be several years earlier. China's population aged 15–64 peaked at just over one billion in 2015, with a steady decline projected through the time frame of this study and beyond. In 2050 this age-group is projected to total just under 740 billion—a drop of about 260 million people; within that same time frame, 2015–2050, China's total population is projected to shrink by 185 million.

The Impact of China's Population Shifts on Military Security to Date

China faces a delayed onset of demographic pressures and fewer domestic political constraints in the short term due to its autocratic regime but will face more severe pressures in the 2030s. Thus, unlike the Northeast Asian democracies examined in chapter 3, China's more delayed aging and much larger total population size means that how its changing future demographics will affect its military security strategy and readiness is much less clear. As seen in table 3.2, China's aged 65+ population rose by over 44 percent from 2010 to 2020, and its TFR fell by 0.45 to 1.24 (despite first relaxing and then entirely eliminating the OCP in this period). However, China's defense spending grew 249.23 percent (in Chinese yuan terms) during this ten-year period. In this period, however, China was only in the first stage of aging (under 14 percent aged 65+), and population shrinkage had not yet begun. The 2020s, and especially the 2030s, will see much greater movement in aging and population shrinkage—but even still, most experts expect China's defense spending to continue to rise.

The 2019 to 2024 U.S. Defense Department reports to the Congress on China's military, the so-called China Military Power Reports, do not emphasize military recruiting as a concern for China's military, though they do note this challenge for Taiwan, and the 2023 edition includes a "special topic" section on the PLA's changing recruitment practices that makes some reference to China's growing demographic challenges.[29] This brief mention underscores that China also has begun to face demographic pressures that will greatly intensify in the 2030s and beyond, due in part to its extremely low TFR in 2024 of just 1.10 (see table 4.4). Also notable is its projected population shrinkage of 13 percent by 2050, a process that began in 2023. Perhaps most concerning for China's future social stability and its policymakers is the projected more than doubling of its aged 65+ population from 2020 to 2050, when over 30 percent of its total population is expected to reach that threshold, well beyond mere super-aged status. The direct military-security implications of this transition are less clear, however.

Despite these projected future population challenges, China's defense spending climbed to US$219.46 billion in 2023 according to the International Institute for Strategic Studies—though estimates of China's actual military spending vary widely and almost certainly is higher than this IISS

TABLE 4.4
China's demographics–security nexus

Total fertility rate (2024)[a]	1.10		
Total population (millions)[a]	2024 1,420.91	2035 (est.) 1,370.97	2050 (est.) 1,240.78 (−12.7% from 2024; 180.13m)
Percentage of population 65+[a]	2024 14.7% ("aged")	2035 (est.) 22.9% ("super-aged")	2050 (est.) 31.6%
U.S. treaty ally?[b]	No		
Active military forces (2023)[b]	2.035 million		
Defense spending (2023)[c]	$219.46 (in US$billion), 1.24% of GDP		
Total GDP in US$ (2015) trillion[c]	2023[c] $17.66	2030 (est.) $23.979	2050 (est.) $44.383 (+251% from 2023)

[a] UN Population Division (2024), constant fertility projection
[b] IISS, *Military Balance* (2024)
[c] IMF, World Economic Outlook Database (April 2024)
[d] Institute of Energy Economics Japan, IIEJ Outlook (2023)

figure; SIPRI calculates China's 2023 spending at $296.44 billion, and the 2024 DOD China Military Power Report estimates Chinese defense spending at US$330 to $450 billion.[30] Either way, this level of spending puts China in a class of its own in the Indo-Pacific, second only to the United States globally (though a distant second, with U.S. defense spending in 2023 totaling $905.46 billion, 41 percent of world defense spending and far more than total IP16 defense spending, without adjusting for purchasing power parity, as noted in chapter 2). It is notable that this total amount was still less than half the U.S. percentage of GDP devoted to defense (3.45 vs. 1.24 percent) in 2023, indicating a potential for future growth.[31] (Note Russia's 4 percent and North Korea's 26.4 percent of GDP in this context.) Moreover, while the total amount that China spends on its military is not fully transparent, and in addition there are challenges in comparison with the Northeast Asian democracies and the United States due to issues of purchasing power parity, it is notable that China continued to increase defense spending in excess of its economic growth rate even with the outbreak of the Covid-19 pandemic, and even as its rapid aging intensifies (though, as noted, it is not yet a super-aged state and is not projected to be one until the early 2030s).[32]

A state's ability to continue robust defense spending despite challenges of rapid aging is another concern raised in existing scholarly literature on the demographics–national security nexus, as discussed in chapter 1. Compared to the Northeast Asian democracies examined in chapter 3, China is at an earlier stage in its development arc, with positive implications for its economic future as a result. Thus, it has greater economic growth potential with its workforce transition ahead as very poorly educated 50-something workers retire and are replaced by much better-educated (and often healthier) 20-somethings. As a result, economic forecasters predict GDP growth by as much as 245 percent from 2020 to 2050—though, it should be emphasized, numerous "Peak China" pessimists offer a much more dismal economic outlook for China (which is only partly related to its challenging future demographics).[33] This issue, of the economic impact of China's rapid aging and population shrinkage, will be returned to in the conclusion of this section. Overall, however, despite challenging demographic projections and some notable disagreement about its economic future, China is widely expected to enjoy substantial economic growth ahead, though at a slower pace than when its population was younger. China was predicted in 2021 to overtake U.S. economic size by 2028, several years earlier than previously predicted, though continued challenges of thriving in the post-Covid era will likely push that estimate back again, as discussed later in this section.[34]

A core difference between China and the Northeast Asian democracies and Russia is that demographic pressures are not currently forcing changes in China's military strategy and planning. Nevertheless, China has been reducing its force size over several decades to better train and maintain a more capable force. Even in the mid-2010s, as military spending surged and China still had plentiful numbers of young men, it made six-figure cuts in its military size (a figure higher than the *total* number of Japanese military forces)—but not because of demographic concerns.[35] In some ways, this shift parallels efforts by the Northeast Asian democracies—especially South Korea and Taiwan—to transition from larger numbers of troops toward greater technological and networked strength. The U.S. Congressional Research Service summarized China's military transition circa 2016 as follows:

China has engaged in a sustained and broad effort over more than 25 years to transform its military, the People's Liberation Army (PLA), from an infantry-heavy, low-technology military into a high-technology, networked force with an increasing emphasis on joint operations and naval and air power. China has emphasized quality over quantity during this modernization: the number of military personnel and certain platforms (e.g., aircraft, tanks, certain vessels) has declined even as overall capabilities have improved.[36]

Although dated in terms of the latest numbers, the study of China's "incomplete military transformation" by Michael Chase and colleagues usefully draws attention to a number of the continued challenges China's military faces in the 2020s. In particular, it highlights that many analysts believe that the Chinese military is too large personnel-wise, noting the substantial resources required to maintain such a large standing force.[37] More recently, a 2020 report by the U.S.-based Council on Foreign Relations expressed a similar view, writing that while "the Chinese government believes it must invest more in new technologies and improve logistics …

many analysts say the military's main challenge is personnel, in that it has struggled to recruit, train, and retain a professional fighting force."[38] Thus, again, China's scale and unique demographics–security configuration differ from the Northeast Asian democracies and Russia that are currently struggling to maintain their force sizes due to present demographic challenges (and, in Russia's case, its war with Ukraine).

While it is correct that unlike earlier rising powers such as Germany, the United States, or Japan, China is ascending as a global power at a time when its population has begun to rapidly age and shrink, its large population size and ascent in a different technological period may enable this rise in ways not possible in a previous era—despite many challenges ahead, as discussed in a later section. Still, as Brooks et al. argue, "because China will become old before it can become a global peer of the United States, the likelihood of a dangerous power transition involving China and the United States is much lower than analysts often assert."[39] "Nevertheless," they also note, "there is still cause for concern given the effect of closing window-of-opportunity dynamics. As the costs of China's rapidly aging population begin to surge, China's leaders may feel that they confront a shrinking demographic window of opportunity to achieve international objectives that are likely to require the use or threat of force."[40] This latter logic is, in part, what leads some to expect China to act militarily to reunify with Taiwan in the 2020s, before the more serious uncertainties of China's rapid aging emerge in the 2030s.

China's not-yet-materialized labor shortages demographically mean that its conscription system and its challenges also differ from the other territories discussed in chapter 3 and earlier in this chapter that are implementing changes to their conscription systems due to population shortfalls. Although Chinese law requires all Chinese to serve in the military for two years, in fact it is a largely voluntary system and acts as a pathway to longer-term professional service in the military. John Pike offers this comparative illustration based on 2019 demographic data: "Annual quota numbers for both the PLA [People's Liberation Army] and PAP [People's Armed Police] were estimated by the US DOD to be 500,000. Conscription in China with over 10,000,000 men reaching militarily significant age annually, of whom perhaps 8,000,000 are fit for service, would produce an army of at least 16,000,000 men. In fact, conscripts in the PLA Ground Force appear to number about 800,000, only about five percent of the total potential number."[41] Note, however, that like the United States, the PLA also finds that increasing numbers of potential recruits do not meet basic physical and emotional fitness standards.[42]

In South Korea and Taiwan, by contrast, nearly all young men must serve in the military for the mandated period. Like these other systems, however, China's military is a mix of professional military officers, conscripted forces, and noncommissioned officers (NCOs), though China does not report the ratio of its forces among these categories. One estimate is that roughly 35 percent of the total force, or about 700,000 people, are "conscripted" (in quotes because most in fact volunteered), with about 23 percent officers and civil cadres and 42 percent NCOs.[43]

China's military also is seeking more educationally advanced military personnel given its ambitious force modernization goals. The educational background of PLA forces began to improve in 2001 with the recruiting of those with college backgrounds. The Military Service Law was reformed in 2011 to remove the deferment of college students, and by 2014 nearly 150,000 of the PLA's 400,000 annual recruits were college students and graduates. Physical requirements for enlistment changed in June 2014, relaxing height, weight, and eyesight requirements, also targeted to attract additional college graduates.[44] In 2022 the PLA increased the maximum recruitment age for college graduates to 24, and for those holding postgraduate degrees to 26.[45] As a result of this combination of changes, the number of college graduates in the PLA has been steadily rising.

China's growing technological capabilities also will help to offset future demographic challenges, as has also occurred in the Northeast Asian democracies. In addition, however, China is developing new military capabilities in other areas unrelated to demographic challenges that will create a more lethal force. As noted in the U.S. Defense Department's 2020 annual report on China's military: "The PRC is pursuing a number of advanced military capabilities with disruptive potential such as hypersonic weapons, electromagnetic railguns, directed energy weapons, and counterspace capabilities." The 2024 report noted that the "PRC has the world's leading hypersonic missile arsenal and has dramatically advanced its development of conventional and nuclear-armed hypersonic missile technologies during the past 20 years."[46] In addition, as summarized in another study: "The Chinese military and China's defense industry have been pursuing significant investments in robotics, swarming, and other applications of artificial intelligence (AI) and machine learning (ML)."[47] The U.S. DOD 2020 China Military Power Report also stresses these developments, including noting "AI-enabled unmanned surface vessels, which China plans to use to patrol and bolster its territorial claims in the South China Sea," and adding in the 2024 report that the "PRC aims to overtake the West in AI R&D by 2025 to become the world leader in AI by 2030. The PRC has designated AI as a priority, national-level S&T development area and assesses that advances in AI and autonomy are central to intelligentized warfare, the PRC's concept of future warfare."[48]

Thus, and important to this study, China's pursuit of the most advanced military technologies, including autonomous weapons, is not principally driven by demographics. It is being aggressively pursued by the United States first and foremost, the state that has the most favorable demographics of the major world powers (apart from India, perhaps)— and then by China in its attempt to reach peer-competitor status with the United States.[49] However, this direction in military technologies does have major implications for states that do have more challenging demographics. Moreover, both the United States and China also face challenges in their efforts to recruit and retain appropriate personnel despite their more positive demographics, suggesting that a future with more autonomous weapons and other labor-saving technology will be a boon for their militaries as well.

To conclude this section's focus on the present and near-future impact of China's projected aging and population shrinkage on its military approach, it is worth emphasizing that even with advanced technologies, for the foreseeable future at least, people are what make militaries work. Even with the next-envisioned steps with AI, people will have to make judgments based on new data/analysis available.[50] The U.S. military has the advantage in this area with its favorable demographics and extensive combat experience versus the PLA's limited combat experience and challenges in drawing from its large population appropriate human resources, and with a shrinking human resource base ahead.[51] Moreover, more defense spending does not necessarily mean that such spending will address core weaknesses and/or improve human resources.[52]

All of the Northeast Asian 6 have challenges with recruiting the right people into their militaries, except perhaps North Korea, where the military is framed as a core pillar of its society and where members of the military enjoy extensive social and economic privileges.[53] As a state that is seen to be planning offensive military operations—as opposed to the avowedly defensive postures of Northeast Asia's aging democracies— China's changing demographics pose additional potential challenges. And yet, to date, these challenges seem to be manageable for China. Moreover, as Toshi Yoshihara and Jack Bianchi noted in 2021, "the tangible effects of a graying population on military affairs are likely to take place well beyond this decade, by which point the PLA may have achieved many, if not most, of its modernization goals."[54] Additional demographic hurdles need to considered in China's case, however, as well as medium-term challenges China will face as it approaches and proceeds past the so-called demographic cliff and into the 2030s.

Additional Demographic Pressures Beyond Rapid Aging with Security Implications

China's demographic future also presents other challenges related to security not seen to the same degree in the other Northeast Asian 6. Although these additional demographic categories depart from this book's focus on the effects of rapid aging on military security, they pose important challenges for China that already are eliciting policy responses and also relate to security concerns perceived in the broader Indo-Pacific discussed in the next chapter. Thus, they will be introduced briefly in this section. Four areas beyond China's aging that have been securitized to some degree are of particular note in its coming demographic transition: (1) the impacts of a society where being an only child is the new normal, (2) the male-female sex ratio imbalance, (3) differential birth rates of China's ethnic minorities and efforts to control that, and (4) increased urbanization and inequality.

China has the largest percentage of only-child families in the region; lower TFRs elsewhere are primarily due to a greater number of women having no children rather than only one. Moreover, given its large population size in total, China has an unprecedented total number of one-child families, which is a massive departure from its historical traditions and generally not expected to rebound. More than reported in Japan, South Korea, and Taiwan, China's only children are described as having significant socialization issues, and its parents are described as much more protective of these children than past generations were.[55] This links to a broader literature worldwide about the attitudinal differences of parents of only children versus multichild families.[56]

There is not robust data on this phenomenon, in part due to the sensitive nature of the implications, but one study in 2007 estimated that only-children would make up half of the PLA officer corps between 2010 and 2020.[57] That study suggests no significant differences among only-children and those from multichild families, but further research on this possibility is warranted. Another potential impact of the rise of only-child families relates to casualty aversion, and thus the decision to join the military at all, including the support (or lack thereof) from family members. Concerns of family members about only-sons joining the military are not necessarily only about emotional ties but also about financial support in a country and culture where children are expected to assist their elderly parents and where state-provided pension systems for parents may be lacking. Beyond the financial, there also is a strong and persistent cultural attachment to the need for a son to carry on the family lineage, which, when limited to only one son, could result in additional casualty aversion. This final point links to a broader argument of this study, introduced in chapter 1, that the ability of states to adjust cultural and societal norms to new demographic realities is one essential component of a successful policy response to demographic pressures.

A second demographic challenge that may affect China's future social stability and security approach is its sex imbalance between males and females. China's once-a-decade census reported 34.9 million more males than females in 2020.[58] One 2019 estimate suggests that, as a result, "by 2020, China will have 24 million single men of marrying age unable to find wives."[59] Some fear security concerns as a result, with one reporter asking rhetorically: "Imagine the combined male populations of Texas and New York State were perpetually lonely, depressed and sexually unfulfilled."[60] By contrast, one also might consider these "bare branches" (as they have been referred to in some scholarly literature) as ripe for military service.[61] Various security implications of this demographic factor have been posited, though, as with other unusual aspects of China's demographic transition, there is little systemic historical or comparative data on the security effects of this phenomenon that allows for sustained analysis. That said, Beardson notes in his overview study of China's efforts to manage its population size that sex imbalances were widely reported in earlier centuries of

Chinese history, well before the OCP, mainly due to female infanticide—arguably with noticeable military-security implications.[62]

China's male-female gender ratio has skewed male for decades due to selective abortions and infanticide motivated by a preference for male children under the OCP, so if there were a strong impact of this sex ratio on security conduct, early signs should have become apparent. Sex-selective abortions were only officially banned in 2016, though with a new government emphasis on increasing the overall birth rate, they can be expected to be enforced with at least some degree of vigilance.[63] In the Indo-Pacific, India and Vietnam also are experiencing this phenomenon despite not having had a harsh one-child policy, which will be discussed in chapter 5. South Korea also went through a period where it saw a rising and then falling skewed sex ratio, illustrating that policy as well as cultural responses to this tragedy can be effective.

These first two trends—of one-child families and fewer women in the general population—also pose serious strains on women who marry and also often are working outside of the home. The so-called 4-2-1 phenomenon for one-child families, where each young Chinese faces supporting four grandparents, two parents, plus their one child, poses stark implications for China's younger generation, especially women. As one reporter has noted, "this is a generation of women who will be spending a big chunk of their lives caring for others."[64]

A third concern with security implications of China's demographic transition relates to China's internal ethnic composition. Unlike Japan, North/South Korea, and Taiwan, but similar to Russia and numerous states in the southern Indo-Pacific, China is a state composed of substantial concentrations of multiple ethnicities that the government perceives as a potential internal security problem. *Han* is the Chinese term for China's majority ethnicity, which constituted 91.11 percent of the total Chinese population in the 2020 census. From the 2010–2020 period, the census reports a slightly higher increase in the share of the collective ethnic minority population, totaling 0.4 percentage point. While that increased share is quite small, it does also reflect a growth rate over twice that of the Han population in that ten-year period, 10.26 percent vs. 4.94 percent. Officially, the 2020 Chinese census data summary casts a positive light on this differential, writing: "The steady increase of the population of the ethnic groups fully reflected the comprehensive development and progress of all ethnic groups under the leadership of the Communist Party of China."[65] In reality, however, official concerns about differential growth are widely known.

In recent years, the economic development of the far western region of Xinjiang has become especially securitized, but in an earlier era, similar concerns were seen over the regions where the Tibetan ethnicity is concentrated. As with the Tibetan population in the twentieth century, extreme measures have been instituted to control non-Han populations in the Xinjiang region in the twenty-first century, including forced sterilizations and IUD insertions. The BBC News reported in 2021, "Chinese birth-control policies could reduce the ethnic minority population in southern Xinjiang by up to a third over the next 20 years, according to new analysis by a German researcher"—a range of 2.6 to 4.5 million fewer births in total over this period.[66] According to a study by the Australian Strategic Policy Institute, there was a 48.7 percent decline in birth rates in ethnic minority areas of Xinjiang between 2017 and 2019.[67] The result of this different type of population policy, that study notes, could be an increase in the percentage of the ethnic Han population from its 2020 level of 8.4 percent to about 25 percent by 2040. Such a development—as well as the sex ratio imbalance issue noted earlier—underscores a point made in the introduction to this book about the moral dangers of securitizing demographic concerns.

Finally, rising inequality in an increasingly urban China is frequently mentioned as an internal security and social stability concern, which includes unequal aging across China's regions. The 2020 China census reports an urban population of nearly 902 million people, 63.9 percent of the population—up from 49.7 percent in 2010.[68] Managing internal security challenges, including those stemming from persistent inequality generally as well as regionally, is a growing concern. As summarized by one post-2020 census study: "The Northeast rustbelt population is shrinking and getting older, while coastal provinces are experiencing population growth and getting younger." The study offers the contrast between northeastern Liaoning's population of 42.9 million, where 25.7 percent of residents are aged 60+, versus Guangdong's 126.01 million, where only 12.4 percent of residents are aged 60+.[69] The study also refers to other scholarship that warns that no country with the level of inequality that China currently is experiencing has ever successfully escaped the middle-income trap that China is actively seeking to achieve by 2050.[70]

Even with China's autocratic governance and additional moves to quash dissent reported as Chinese president Xi Jinping has consolidated his political power as China's non-term-limited president, protests still are widespread in China—with those from the military and elderly related to pensions and other benefits especially notable for this study. As Chase et al. write: "Retired soldiers have repeatedly been at the center of protests and calls for better veterans' benefits and pensions, a development that is almost certainly noted by and worrisome to currently serving PLA soldiers and officers still looking ahead to their own demobilizations."[71] Another report noted that "according to China Labor Bulletin's Strike Map, in 2018 there were 172 instances of workers protesting or striking over social security and pension-related concerns. Notably, in summer 2018, thousands of veterans across several cities staged protests over inadequate healthcare and pensions."[72] That report also illustrates the wide disparity in pension benefits between urban and rural recipients.

In sum, China faces a range of intensifying demographic challenges that will almost certainly affect its future development trajectory, including in the area of military security. Unlike the Northeast Asian democracies examined in chapter 3, however, these effects are only beginning to be widely felt in China. Still, they offer clues to the medium-term challenges China faces related to its demographic transition, as discussed in the next and final section on the Chinese case.

China's Many Medium-Term Challenges and Its "Demographic Cliff": Security Aspects?

China faces many future challenges across a wide range of areas, most of which intersect with its changing demographics but—as with the demographics–national security nexus—will not be determined solely by its changing demographics. The pace and scale of China's economic growth and military rise over the past several decades are unprecedented. Maintaining the momentum and successfully transitioning to the next stage of economic development (i.e., escaping the so-called middle-income trap) and building a world-class military that is a peer-competitor to the United States also would be unprecedented, especially doing so without sparking a major regional or global military confrontation.[73] China's more challenging future demographics add to the complexity of the transitions ahead, but these population pressures will affect China differently from the other Northeast Asian 6 examined earlier.

As with Northeast Asia's aging democracies, in the medium-term China will face new pressures from a rapidly aging society and shrinking workforce. But unlike in the democracies, Chinese leaders do not necessarily need to be responsive to new demands to the same degree, and China does not currently have in place universal healthcare and nationwide pension schemes that will automatically balloon spending as the percentage of elderly grow—though despite that, many existing local pension schemes are severely underfunded and in some cases being guaranteed by the national government.[74]

To date, the pressures of the early stages of rapid aging have been mitigated by the cultural expectation that children—not government—will provide for care of the elderly and by lower expectations of many older people whose life experience was with a much less economically developed China with fewer material comforts. Still, China's aged 65+ population is projected to more than double from about 180 million in 2020 to almost 390 million in 2050, and many troubling signs related to China's much less severe aging to date are concerning. The liquidity of pension systems is widely believed to be vastly underfunded.[75] As one source noted in 2020: "Already, nearly half of China's provinces are slated to report operating shortfalls in their basic pension funds by 2022, compared to six in 2015, according to a report by the China Academy of Social Sciences. Some provinces are being hit harder than others."[76]

China's future economic growth prospects are robustly debated among scholars, policy and business analysts, and in the mass media given the global implications of the country's success or failure, as noted in the previous section.[77] Paying for a more professional military (including recruiting and retention) plus weapons development and production, in addition to increased healthcare and pensions for a growing elderly population, will certainly be a challenge. However, rising to this challenge will be assisted by robust economic growth predicted by many China watchers—allowing, in principle, for continued increases in defense spending together with more spending on costs related to a rapidly aging population.

Maintaining social stability is another major concern with both domestic and international implications. The growing inequality in Chinese society between urban and rural areas in particular was noted in the previous section. Concerns about youth attitudes and behavior is another aspect of economic and social stability. The so-called lie flat movement among disaffected youth in the 2020s, especially among college graduates, is one such concern.[78] Fed up with a culture of overwork—the so-called 996 life of working 9 A.M. to 9 P.M. six days a week—some have decided not to marry, have children, or strive in an upwardly mobile job, in part because such youth believe that their generation does not have the same prospects for upward mobility as their parents due to China's challenging future demographics.

That said, many of the parents of this new generation of Chinese also made huge sacrifices as workers who built a more powerful China. Though incomes have risen and extreme poverty has been greatly reduced, per capita GDP in China in 2023 of US$12,614 was far lower than in the United States (at US$81,695) or the Northeast Asian democracies.[79] Moreover, China's private consumption rate also trails both developed and many developing countries by double-digits. According to one report: "In 2019, China's private consumption accounted for about 39 percent of GDP, which was about 30 percentage points lower than the US and Europe, according to data from CEIC [a private data firm]. It was also about 20 percentage points lower than developing countries such as India and Brazil."[80]

The previous generation of the larger working-age population saved heavily, financing a wave of investments that created a wide range of world-class infrastructure and boosted productivity. In the 2020s and beyond, China may need to import foreign capital to fund investments, which may or may not materialize as needed. In addition, numerous analysts argue that China needs to use the capital it does have more efficiently, particularly turning away from bloated state-owned industries.[81] More directly related to this study's focus on aging, by the late 2030s, China's median age will be higher than many of its developing-country competitors, reaching levels of highly developed economies despite its much lower per capita income.

And yet, on the demographic front at least, experience with Northeast Asia's rapidly aging democracies suggests a number of options for China to address growing demographic challenges if optimal policies can be implemented, underscoring a broader theoretical point from chapter 1—that how states manage the demographic challenges they face is an important aspect of determining the ultimate effects of population shifts. Raising the retirement age from its current low level (55 for women and 60 for men) is one example of an impactful policy option ahead—and more likely politically than in, say, France in 2023, where large-scale protests resulted when an even less onerous move to raise retirement ages was attempted.

Capitalizing on a healthier and better-educated workforce is another area with substantial economic growth potential. In addition, some studies argue that optimizing labor is not even the most important aspect of China's future growth potential and/or challenge—investment and proper allocation of capital, particularly away from state-owned enterprises, are more important.[82]

Still, even in an autocracy, the ability to implement multiple policies that challenge popular opinion and entrenched interests is not a given. But, as one pair of analysts framed it, "it's still possible for China to be old and rich," citing studies that show that "labor is now only a tiny contributor to China's GDP growth, with much more coming from investment and improvements in total factor productivity (TFP)."[83] Thus, as seen with Northeast Asia's aging democracies as well, these analysts conclude: "It's far less important that China's population is shrinking than it finds a way to more efficiently allocate capital and raise the productivity of the workers that it does have"—noting, for example, the currently low retirement ages plus the potential for artificial intelligence and other new technologies.

The "demographic cliff" that China will face beginning around 2030 may, however, constrain its ability to further grow its military and economy. This possible scenario then creates an incentive for China to achieve regional security objectives in the shorter term, before demographic challenges become more severe. That principal U.S. adversaries also face similar demographic challenges as well as key U.S. allies will further push all major regional states to employ new technologies to offset the effect of shrinking and aging populations. This aging security dilemma may result in a new sort of regional arms race that also raises concerns.

The more youthful demographics of the United States and other allies and potential partners in the region considered in the next chapter offer numerous advantages in the medium term vis-à-vis Northeast Asia's autocracies, in particular China and Russia. Illustrating many of the demographic and strategic advantages of security partnerships with other states in the broader Indo-Pacific—as well as some important challenges—is the focus of the final set of case studies presented in chapter 5. Although beyond the time frame of this study, one report notably calculated that "by 2080,

China could actually have *fewer* men of fighting age than the United States' Pacific alliance network."[84] Similarly, as Chinese defense spending increases may slow as its economic growth slows, increases in defense spending by both the United States and its many allies and partners in the Indo-Pacific may add up to a significant balancing force.

Most directly, as one considers the "China challenge" vis-à-vis the main competitor China envisions globally and regionally, the United States, the contrast in demographics and its related security implications is striking. As expressed by Yoshihara and Bianchi: "The contrasts with China's future predicament could not be sharper. Beyond mere numbers, the United States also enjoys qualitative demographic advantages. The American workforce is among the most highly educated in the world. The U.S. population has generated far more private wealth than its Chinese counterpart while its innovativeness remains unmatched globally. And, as a Chinese academic study acknowledges, the United States is in a far better fiscal position to deal with its aging population than China."[85] Thus, while the effects of demographic change on China's security policies may be delayed, they are nearly certain to exert more influence on China's security-related policy-making in the coming years, underscoring the importance of further study of this unprecedented development in human history, our rapidly aging societies.

CONCLUSIONS FROM THE LEADING EDGE OF ASIA'S RAPID AGING: WHAT MAKES A STRONG MILITARY FORCE?

A close examination of the recent past, present, and predicted futures of Northeast Asia's security policy evolution in the midst of rapid aging shows the complexity of integrating this variable into security policy analysis, but also the new importance of the variable of rapid aging in the security planning of these aging states. The variable of aging also interacts with new and rising security concerns, in particular the proliferation of gray-zone challenges. In summary, and in transition to considering the effect of slower aging—and, in many cases, continued population growth—on the broader security dynamics of the Indo-Pacific, this chapter concludes by linking rapid aging and population size with other components of a strong military force. Five areas should be considered vis-à-vis the six cases examined in this and the previous chapter: personnel, equipment, alliances and partnerships, military strategy and societal will, and the ability to pay for these prior categories.

From the cases of the Northeast Asian 6, we see that the number of military personnel is but one measure of military strength. The level of training of that force, combat experience, and equipment also are important factors. In addition, the pool of potential recruits is important, with Taiwan and South Korea as examples of places where the military is drawing on nearly all available male population resources, Russia approaching this level due to its protracted war with Ukraine, while China has much greater depth due to its much larger total population size. It is also notable that smaller military forces in the region have been effective fighting forces and have managed deterrence successfully for decades. Similarly, merely counting the number of different sorts of military equipment does not offer much insight into military capabilities. Beyond the training of the personnel using the equipment is the level of technology and capabilities of the equipment itself. In many militaries, equipment is showing its age even more than personnel.

Utilizing formal military alliances as well as other security partnerships also can enhance military power, as starkly illustrated in post–World War II East Asia, where U.S. alliances helped to maintain a delicate peace between bitter rivals, often benefitting the side with fewer personnel resources—and, in the case of the Korean War, restoring the independence of South Korea after it was invaded by the North. In this new era of differential demographic change within the Indo-Pacific region, alliances and partnerships are playing a growing role.

Finally, effective and responsive military strategies and planning also are important components of military power, which in these aging states now also includes the need to recognize new demographic challenges and willingness and ability to adapt. Using a limited budget wisely to procure equipment and train personnel will result in a more effective force. Modifying conscription systems, developing flexible recruiting and retention strategies, and/or establishing well-trained reserve forces could prove to be among the most important components for the strategic future of the region's rapidly aging states. In addition, capitalizing on resources beyond the total number of military forces can be important areas for security partnerships, whether this be joint technological development, coordinated diplomacy, or partnerships related to shared facilities and other services. Political leadership skill, in both war and peace, also undergirds a robust military capability.

A common thread among all these components is the ability to pay for these resources. There is a widespread (and largely mistaken) assumption that rapidly aging and/or shrinking populations will be able to afford less, but the reality is more complicated. The total GDPs of Asia's rapidly aging powers are expected to grow through 2050 and beyond, even in the most severely aging and population-shrinking states. A second-order concern is whether, especially in democracies, a population is willing to pay for robust military forces when an aging society may wish to prioritize other needs (like eldercare, pensions, or childcare to promote a higher birth rate in the longer term). Evidence to date suggests that even aging societies respond to perceptions of a growing security threat. Beyond these components of an effective military force, broader determinants of security policy include geography—for military strategy and regarding the threat environment (e.g., neighboring states)—and a strategy for managing threats apart from military solutions (e.g., diplomatic skill).

In conclusion, and as seen in the cases discussed in this and the previous chapter, technological change will mitigate the effects of rapid aging in four primary ways, as initially outlined in chapter 1. The militaries of each of Northeast Asia's aging democracies have employed enhanced civilian technologies to improve efficiencies in their military operations. In terms of military-specific technologies, each is developing new capabilities to address both new security concerns—traditional and gray-zone—and to seek to use technology to address concerns about labor shortfalls in critical areas. Still, each military is facing a need for new personnel to design, build, and operate such new technologies, often experiencing shortfalls in these areas. Growing use of international partnerships is one solution to this challenge being widely employed.

In sum, there are both pros and cons of this new technology ecosystem for rapidly aging states: On the positive side, rapidly aging states do not necessarily face inevitable decline as major security actors. Across Northeast Asia, military power and capabilities are rising together with societal aging. On the negative side, rapidly aging states also do not seem likely to be poised to enjoy the "demographic peace" predicted by studies based on twentieth-century conflicts, in part due to new technologies that have contributed to a proliferation of security concerns. Aging powers are proving to be formidable despite facing a wider range of security concerns and rising tensions. Moreover, as will be discussed in the next chapter, these aging powers face new security challenges from growing states in the Indo-Pacific, as well as potential new and/or enhanced partnerships and offsets for their shrinking populations from this wider demographic range of regional states.

Chapter Five

OPPORTUNITIES AND CAUTIONS FROM THE DEMOGRAPHIC DIVERSITY OF THE BROADER INDO-PACIFIC

WITH KEI KOGA, ASSOCIATE PROFESSOR, NANYANG TECHNOLOGICAL UNIVERSITY, SINGAPORE

The continent of Asia is a vast region with great diversity in many ways, including its population demographics. Northeast Asia, the focus of chapters 3 and 4, largely shares a similar demographic trajectory of rapid aging to the point of super-aged status in the near term as well as projected population shrinkage, with the exception of Mongolia. The southern part of Asia—and more broadly what increasingly is referred to as the "Indo-Pacific"—illustrates much greater demographic diversity that presents both opportunities for and potential challenges to the regional and global security order.[1] Moreover, geopolitically this region has become a focal point for U.S.-China strategic rivalry and the next iteration of international norms and international order broadly conceived.

This chapter contrasts the national security implications of the similar demographic challenges of rapid aging and population shrinkage of the six Northeast Asian cases previously examined with nine southern Indo-Pacific states that especially contribute to the regional security landscape and where changing internal demographics will create new opportunities and pressures in their future roles. The nine countries that are the focus of this chapter—completing the sixteen Indo-Pacific (IP16) territories that are the focus of this book—illustrate the nexus of favorable demographic projections and regional security contribution potential. These nine states vary widely in levels of economic development and military capabilities and postures. They also vary tremendously in population size as well as other internal population characteristics. Six are large-population states with projected population growth through 2050 (and likely beyond) and at least some outward-facing military security posture at present: Australia, India, Indonesia, Malaysia, the Philippines, and Vietnam. The one other large-population state with an outward-facing security posture, U.S. ally Thailand, has population demographics more like Northeast Asian states, including a high median age, projected population shrinkage in 2025, and super-aged status expected in 2031. It also should be noted that six of these nine states are part of the ten-state ASEAN regional institution, which adds an additional element to consider related to the regional security roles of these states.

One theme developed in this chapter relates to the "demographic dividends" that may be enjoyed by several growing, large-population states in this southern region, in particular in India, Indonesia, the Philippines, and to a lesser extent in Vietnam as well as medium-population-sized Malaysia.[2] Another theme is the potentially expanded roles of current U.S. allies Australia, New Zealand, and the Philippines, whose populations are also growing. A third theme is that even smaller-population states and those facing challenging demographic shifts also can play an important role in the expanding regional geostrategic competition, as Singapore and strategically located Pacific islands have shown.

As discussed in previous chapters, only Asia and Africa are projected to see substantial population growth in the rest of the twenty-first century, and even that growth is projected only in parts of each of these two regions. This more limited population growth projection reverses a major trend of the twentieth century where populations ballooned nearly everywhere in the world. Several middle-power states in the Indo-Pacific are projected to see their populations grow and to age much more slowly—and thus are poised to benefit from a demographic dividend that Northeast Asian states experienced decades ago.

A number of population-growing states—India, Indonesia, the Philippines, and Vietnam among them—also have become more enmeshed in the regional security discourse and have begun to deepen security partnerships with the aging powers of Northeast Asia and beyond. India, for example, is a member of the Quadrilateral Security Dialogue (the Quad), and the Philippines has deepened security cooperation both within the Philippines-U.S. alliance framework as well as with Japan and other regional states, including at a historic trilateral summit with the United States and Japan in Washington in 2024. Such contributions to cooperative security arrangements are not just about people (capitalizing on these growing states' growing demographics), but also about land (for training or establishment of military bases), facilities (such as commercial ports and maintenance facilities), equipment, and even diplomatic support—roles that were central to U.S. alliances with Japan, the Philippines, and Thailand in the twentieth century and similarly can be seen in new security partnerships forming across the region in the twenty-first century.

Although the populations of this southern region are not yet as "gray" as those in Northeast Asia, they still are aging, just at a later pace, with an average of a nearly 11 percentage point increase in their aged 65+ populations projected from 2020 to 2050 (see table 5.1.) The median age of these nine states also is projected to increase by over 30 percent, from 31.8 to 41.4, from 2020 to 2050. (Table 2.3 lists the median ages for each of these

TABLE 5.1
Differential demographics of Northern v. Southern IP16 and United States, 2020–2050

Country/ group	TFR, 2024	Total population (millions)		% Change in total population (2020 vs. 2050)	% Change in population 65+ (2020 vs. 2050)	Median age		Increase 2020 v. 2050
		2020	2050			2020	2050	
United States	1.62	339.14	379.16	11.8%	7.1	37.2	42.0	12.9%
Northeast Asian 6	1.30	1,800.18	1,564.65	−12.5%	15.5	40.6	50.9	25.2%
Southern IP-9	1.82	2,020.48	2,440.67	16.5%	10.9	31.8	41.4	30.3%

Source: UN Population Division, 2024 Revision

Notes: Countries with below 2.0 TFR projected with Constant TFR; those above 2.0 (Indonesia) use UN "Medium Variant."

Data on China excludes Hong Kong, Macao, and Taiwan—which are listed separately in UN demographic projections. Northeast Asian 6: China, Japan, North Korea, Russia, South Korea, Taiwan; Chinese territories Hong Kong and Macao are included only in total population columns. Southern IP-9: Australia, India, Indonesia, Malaysia, New Zealand, Philippines, Singapore, Thailand, Vietnam.

states in 2020 and 2050 as well as 2005 and 2035.) Security challenges are graying in this subregion as well, particularly around the contested territories of the South China Sea and growing cyber concerns. The southern Indo-Pacific is very much experiencing the dual graying of its northern neighbors.

As the world enters its third decade of super-aged states, there is a growing diversity as well as number of rapidly aging and super-aged states, as noted in previous chapters. A first wave were nearly all highly developed democracies, whereas the second wave includes several less-developed states as well as nondemocracies like China. Thailand is part of this second wave in Southeast Asia, along with Australia and New Zealand, all of which are projected to reach super-aged status in 2031. Later, a third wave of rapid aging is projected to result in additional states in the Indo-Pacific becoming super-aged, beginning with Vietnam in 2051. Even still comparatively youthful states will see a rapid rise in the proportion of their populations aged 65+. For example, the percentage will more than double in the Philippines from 2020 to 2050, though still not even reaching the aged threshold of 12 percent aged 65+.

States where population growth continues and, as a result, populations remain relatively youthful face different demographics-related challenges compared to the Northeast Asian 6—concerns more in line with population growth fears commonly heard in the twentieth century (as discussed in chapter 1), such as about having too many mouths to feed with not enough employment options and the political instability that can result from that. This issue, the corollary to rapid aging, is examined further in what follows.

"Demographic dividend" is a term typically used to describe economic gains enabled by a well-utilized youth bulge, but the aging powers of Asia also are looking to states with growing populations as prospective security partners. As noted in chapter 2, from 2010 to 2020 the countries of Southeast and South Asia increased defense spending 29 percent and 27.8 percent, respectively, though generally from a much lower starting point than the Northeast Asian states discussed in chapters 3 and 4. A challenge to expanded and deepened security cooperation, however, is that these more youthful and population-growing states often conceptualize national security differently and prioritize different issues as a result. Still, numerous states in the Indo-Pacific will likely play increased regional—and even global—security roles as a result of their growing populations and expected economic growth in the coming decades. At the same time, some of these states may pose new security challenges for Asia's aging powers and existing security architecture, including the ASEAN regional organization.

Although the population demographics of Indo-Pacific states and territories are projected to diverge in important ways, paradoxically the result of this demographic divergence may be to further bind the Indo-Pacific region together economically, even while new economic relationships also are shaped by broader strategic rivalries and concerns. Rapidly aging manufacturing superpowers Japan and South Korea today largely produce their products in other Asian states with more youthful populations. Over one-quarter of Vietnamese GDP was generated by one just South Korean firm, Samsung, in 2018.[3] Importantly, this positive synergy was not one-way, with Samsung's Vietnam operations constituting 30 percent of the company's global sales that year. Still, as in the military-security arena, there is fierce competition among the Northeast Asian aging powers—and the United States—over investment partnerships with growing states as well as among firms from those states to create production networks.

Thus, apart from considering each states' demographics and security policy orientation individually, it also is important to consider potential synergies with the aging powers of Northeast Asia that offer capital investments and improved technologies to enhance labor productivity in their more slowly aging southern neighbors. If Northeast Asian states coordinate their economic policies and facilitate regional integration through such means as the Regional Comprehensive Economic Partnership (RCEP), regional economic integration in East Asia could be further promoted. However, as the current trend of strategic rivalry continues, each of the Northeast Asian states is also creating its own economic connections with other regional states. Given their technological capabilities, they may use their strategic power (including investment and technology transfer "carrots") to drive wedges between these states. As seen in different ways in earlier chapters, this underscores the importance of considering the relational aspect of demographic change on regional relations, including on military security—not just considering demographic change as an issue internal to each state.

Immigration also is an important demographic factor both internally and among regional states. Three states examined in this chapter—Australia, New Zealand, and Singapore—are maintaining population growth and slowing societal aging through robust acceptance of immigrants. By contrast, two other states examined in this chapter are major producers of immigrants to other countries—India and the Philippines. Although in the Northeast Asian 6 there also are two states that are big producers of immigrants, China and Russia, in those states the emigration of younger citizens exacerbates their trend toward rapid aging and shrinking total population size. In the case of the southern part of Indo-Pacific, emigration from India and the Philippines arguably enhances their demographic profiles (apart from concern about so-called brain drain).

ASEAN's Demographic Divergence and Growing Geostrategic Competition in Southeast Asia

Southeast Asia is central to great power competition in the Indo-Pacific, with the ten-state institution of ASEAN playing an important role. ASEAN faces numerous challenges in this era of intensifying strategic competition between China and the United States. The demographic range among its ten members has long been a challenge—from population giant Indonesia to resource-rich but small-population Brunei—and will continue to be one facet of its struggle for unity, with the diverging rates of aging adding complexity.

Five ASEAN states are projected to reach super-aged status by 2051 (with Singapore and Thailand approaching 30 percent of their populations aged 65+ by then), as seen in tables 2.1 and 2.2. Median ages also will diverge further than the present situation. For example, the median age gap between the Philippines and Singapore is projected to widen from 10.4 years in 2020 to 16.2 years in 2050. (Table 2.3 lists median ages for the IP16 minus Mongolia.)

The Southeast Asian subregion is located in the geographic center of the Indo-Pacific, at the confluence of the Indian and Pacific Oceans, with vital sea lines of communication (SLOC), including in the South China Sea, which is estimated to see about one-quarter of global trade transit.[4] Northeast Asian powers Japan, China, and South Korea rely on the Straits of Malacca and Singapore as well as SLOCs in the South China Sea, while the United States and other powers also transit and patrol the area militarily.

Southeast Asia is not new to great power competition. Japan during the Second World War attempted to control the region for its natural resources and geostrategic importance. The United States during the Cold War attempted to prevent communist expansion in the region. China currently is trying to dominate the South China Sea in accordance with its recently deemed "10 Dash Line" expansionary policies. Furthermore, the geographical position of continental Southeast Asia, especially Cambodia, Laos, and Myanmar, has become increasingly important because it can politically and economically connect—or disconnect—China with South and Southeast Asia.

Given this geopolitical and geo-economic attractiveness, Southeast Asian states are sensitive to possibilities of great power intervention. To lessen this potential, as well as to bind in behemoth Indonesia, five Southeast Asian states formed the Association of Southeast Asian Nations in 1967 after several gained independence.[5] A shared anticommunist agenda among the original ASEAN-5 was another early factor. While ASEAN is a multipurpose institution that is now concerned about not only economic and social cooperation but also security and political issues within the region and beyond, the association continues as a useful tool to unite the diplomatic voice of these states and advocate for their national and regional autonomy.[6]

The diplomatic utility of ASEAN continues despite new challenges in an era of deepened U.S.-China strategic rivalry. Southeast Asian states remain unable to fully defend themselves militarily because of their limited resources and need to rely on great powers for regional stability. For many, the U.S. military presence has been explicitly and/or implicitly appreciated as a check on other great powers' interference in the region. That said, given its emphasis on regional autonomy, Southeast Asia has been careful about excessive U.S. security and political commitment to the region. In short, delicate diplomatic tensions exist between regional great powers and Southeast Asian states.

Southeast Asia's importance will likely increase within the Indo-Pacific area, particularly if population-growing states are able to successfully harness their potential demographic dividends. Another question, however, is whether the region can maintain its diplomatic unity and its political will to protect regional autonomy. The Myanmar coup in 2021 already has created a diplomatic schism among ASEAN member states. Moreover, the long-term demographic trends of ASEAN states show growing gaps among them, with implications for future military and economic power, as illustrated later in this chapter. As these states' power resources evolve, their strategic outlook also may evolve, as well as and their alignment strategies— whether they would maintain ASEAN or closely align with particular great powers. In this context, projected demographic change in Southeast Asia needs to be considered in relation to the future of the Indo-Pacific security.

Regional Demographics–National Security Concerns Beyond Rapid Aging

Prior research on the demographics–national security nexus has shown that states with high fertility and/or low median ages are more prone to conflict. As discussed in earlier chapters, Brooks et al. find that "the likelihood of interstate conflict drops sharply (to around one-quarter or one-third below the peak values) once countries reach the following four demographic milestones: (1) a median age above 30 years, (2) a youth-bulge ratio below 20 percent of the adult population, (3) a fertility level below two births per woman, and (4) a life expectancy above 75 years."[7] In 2024 all IP16 states except India and the Philippines had median ages above 30 and, apart from North Korea and also Russia, life expectancies above 75. The remaining twelve all had a TFR below 2.0 in 2024.

By these measures, that would make the four states that have not yet reached the four demographic milestones indicative of later-stage rapid aging more likely to go to war than the other twelve states of the IP16. As discussed in chapter 4, Russia already is at war, and concerns about North Korean belligerence are high. In the southern Indo-Pacific, as noted in chapter 2, India engaged in border skirmishes with China that resulted in (modest) casualties in this decade and continues to be on high alert related to its territorial dispute with Pakistan. This leaves the Philippines to consider further in relation to its projected youth bulge and resulting proneness to future conflict, a topic further examined in the next section of this chapter.

A related concern apparent across more youthful states in the region is internal criticism of "gerontocracies" in states with youth bulges—and even in some states without youth bulges. Generational politics are especially apparent in newly and rapidly developing states (though they have been a facet of U.S. politics of late and have been a critical thread in South Korean and Japanese politics as well). Outside of the region, a wave of protests in Iran in 2022–2023 sparked by the arrest and mistreatment of a young woman for not respecting conservative dress codes shows how important generational politics can be for state security. Numerous states in the southern Indo-Pacific show signs of generational politics playing a role in domestic political instability, a theme noted in case sections that follow.

Finally, shifting ethnic and religious composition within states as well as artificial gender imbalances—as discussed with China in chapter 4—also are demographic concerns in some southern Indo-Pacific states. Specific conflict fault lines vary by country, as detailed in the following sections, but several states face religiously derived identity challenges exacerbated by differential demographic change. In addition, in several others, concerns about Chinese ethnic minorities (including their ratio in the total population mix) continue to generate concern. Potential demographic changes related to these fault lines may affect both characteristics of a state's diplomacy and security conduct as well as their internal stability. In the next section, the Philippines is a good example of a state that faces several challenges related to these internal shifts of its more youthful and ethnically and religiously diverse population.

As emphasized throughout this volume, however, population size and age profiles are only two variables in a diverse strategic calculus that also includes such factors as geographic location and other aspects of geostrategy as well as political foresight, will, and skill. Moreover, demographics are far from the only factor determining the level of future economic growth, with others, including investments in human capital and technological advancement as well as, again, political will and skill, especially important.[8] Still, the differential aging of Asia remains a major factor to consider in the broader Indo-Pacific's emerging future.

Having examined the relational aspects of the region's projected demographic shifts ahead, the remainder of this chapter examines the demographics–national security dynamics of specific states and territories. First, three long-time U.S. allies and security partners of other regional states with more youthful and growing populations—the Philippines, Australia, and New Zealand—are contrasted with the more rapidly aging and population-shrinking Northeast Asian U.S. allies and partners examined in chapter 3. Next, four large, population-growing states that are increasingly enmeshed in the regional security landscape—India, Indonesia, Malaysia, and Vietnam—are evaluated for how their different demographics may contribute to an evolving region militarily. Then, the chapter returns to the book's focus on rapid aging by considering the effect of impending super-aged status and population shrinkage of U.S. ally Thailand on the regional security landscape. Finally, the chapter discusses unique challenges and potential security contributions of small-population states (both rapidly aging and not) on deepening geostrategic competition within the region. A short conclusion then precedes broader conclusions and a summary provided in the final chapter.

TWO U.S. ALLIANCES ON GROWTH TRAJECTORIES: THE PHILIPPINES AND AUSTRALIA/NEW ZEALAND

The U.S.-Philippines and ANZUS alliances are growing in terms population sizes as well as expanded and deepened regional security cooperation. The nature of this security cooperation varies greatly, however, as do the specific demographic trends within these three population-growing states. Australia and New Zealand are projected to reach super-aged status in 2031, and their projected population growth is entirely due to robust immigration. In terms of military-security planning, therefore, Australia and New Zealand also face some challenges similar to the Northeast Asian democracies, while the Philippines (with its more youthful profile) faces challenges more similar to other growing large-population states discussed in the next section. This contrast underscores the difference between population growth or shrinkage and the effects of rapid aging—a contrast elaborated on in this section.

The nature of the alliance relationships with the United States also has differed greatly among these three states, as introduced in chapter 2. The early 2020s, however, have seen movement toward more shared security concerns among these states and the United States, and greater formalized alliance cooperation with the United States as a result. Still, many differences and challenges remain, some of which are accentuated by increasing demographic divergence projected in the coming decades, as illustrated in table 5.2.

U.S. embrace of the concept of the Indo-Pacific region includes a strategic goal to weave the five regional alliances together, going beyond the

TABLE 5.2
Three U.S. allies on growth trajectories, 2023/2024 v. 2050

	Philippines	Australia	New Zealand
TFR 2024	1.92	1.64	1.67
Defense spending 2023 (billions) (% of GDP)	$6.18 (1.43%)	$34.42 (2.04%)	$3.74 (1.5%)
Military personnel 2023	146,000	58,000	9,000
Population 2024 (millions)	115.37	26.6	5.19
Population 2050 (millions)	137.36	32.4	5.79
% 65+ 2024	5.5	17.7	17.2
% 65+ 2050	10.9	23.9	23.9

Population data: UN Population Division (2024), constant fertility projection. Defense data: IISS, *Military Balance 2024.*

traditional "hub-and-spoke" system that predominated in the previous conception of the region as the Far East or even the Asia-Pacific.[9] In the context of the assertive resurgence of China, the Philippines and Australia/New Zealand also have become more concerned about China's influence in the region through coercive diplomacy. To check China's behavior, the Philippines and Australia have tightened their strategic ties with the United States.

At the same time, however, it is uncertain if the Philippines, Australia, and New Zealand will develop over time more significant similarities in their security outlooks. Absent a growing similarity, enhanced security cooperation among these states and the United States could prove challenging. While Australia has become more concerned about China's growing assertiveness and influence, New Zealand does not seem to share as much concern. Moreover, New Zealand holds its firm position on nuclear nonproliferation, which limits its deeper cooperation within the AUKUS framework. Meanwhile, the Philippines's foreign policy is significantly influenced by its president. While the Ferdinand "Bongbong" Marcos administration (2022–) has more tightly aligned with the United States in order to counter China's intrusion in the South China Sea, the previous Duterte administration (2016–2022) attempted a rapprochement with China by drawing in China's cooperation over the infrastructure development. As of 2024, the Philippines is attempting to strike a delicate balance between China and the United States, making sure not to abandon its legal justification to reduce China's maritime presence in the South China Sea through the 2016 Arbitral Tribunal.

Differing demographic trends among these three states—despite all being projected to grow their populations through 2050 (and likely beyond)—also may contribute to different security priorities looking forward. The Philippines is projected to continue to experience a youth bulge with the concomitant need for job creation to accommodate a growing workforce. Moreover, even after nearly three more decades of aging, it is still not projected to enter even "aged" status (where 14 percent or more of the population is aged 65+), much less "super-aged" status by 2050. The Philippines also is projected to continue to provide large numbers of immigrants to other states and yet still become the fourth-largest population state in the IP16 by 2050. By contrast, Australia and New Zealand will face challenges generated by their impending super-aged status despite projected high levels of immigration.

The Philippines: Projected Rise in Population and Power

The Philippines's projected population growth from 2020 to 2050 of almost 26 million to over 137 million (over 23 percent growth) will lead to it displace Russia and Japan to become the fourth-largest-population state in the IP16 after India, China, and Indonesia. Moreover, the Philippines will continue to have the lowest median age of the IP16 and of U.S. allies—only 24.1 in 2020, projected to rise to a comparatively youthful 35.2 in 2050—with an aged 65+ population still under 11 percent in 2050.

The Philippines is projected to continue to see a youth bulge in its population based on a past TFR well above replacement level, even though its 2024 TFR dropped below the 2.1 replacement threshold. For example, even following the UN Population Division's "median variant" scenario, which assumes a gradual decline in TFR in the Philippines over the course of this century, the number of Filipinos in the 15–64-year-old range is projected to continue to grow through 2059, adding over twenty million to that age group from 2024 to 2059. Thus, if the government and private sector can find meaningful work for this growing workforce—and this should not be taken as a given—the Philippines is poised to enjoy the sort of demographic dividend in economic growth that Japan, South Korea, China, and others did in the twentieth century, perhaps with these countries investing their resources for this dividend given their own shrinking populations (in addition to likely continuing to draw Filipino labor into their countries through immigration).

This growing labor pool as well as increasing need for infrastructure and goods and services for a rising middle class and growing population makes the Philippines an attractive economic partner especially to Northeast Asia's aging powers as well as the United States. The Philippines was the second-fastest-growing economy in the Indo-Pacific after China in the decade prior to the Covid-19 pandemic in 2020. Growth rebounded at 7.2 percent in 2022 and is expected to continue at an average of over 6.2 percent through 2028.[10]

In addition, for the United States and its allies, the Philippines has risen in geographical importance due to its location along the strategic First Island Chain that constrains China's naval forces as well as provides proximity to Taiwan. Furthermore, the Philippines faces two important waterways to the Pacific Ocean, the Bashi Channel and the Celebes Sea, which has important implications for China's nuclear strategy: Chinese nuclear submarines have been long interested in passing through these waterways, as China wants to ensure its second-strike capabilities vis-à-vis the United States. As China tilts the military balance vis- à-vis Taiwan in its favor, the Philippines's diplomatic position and willingness to monitor China's naval activities in Philippines-adjacent waters and to provide logistical support to the United States in the event of a military conflict over Taiwan could prove crucial for the success of defending Taiwan. Though this support should by no means be taken for granted given tense periods in alliance relations with the United States, especially in the immediate post–Cold War period but also under President Duterte, 2023 and 2024 saw significant deepening of U.S.-Philippines military cooperation and public statements.

In the post–Cold War era, the Philippines's security challenges were both external and internal. Notably, the South China Sea disputes where the Philippines has territorial disputes with neighboring states, including China, have risen as one of the most important security concerns for the Philippines. In 1995 the Philippines uncovered China's newly installed facilities in the Mischief Reef, which led the Philippines and ASEAN to protest such behavior. Yet, as China began to conduct fait accompli tactics to increase its maritime presence, ASEAN was not unified enough to strongly respond.[11] This is well illustrated by the nonissuance of a joint communique by ASEAN foreign ministers after the 2012 Scarborough Shoal Incident, where China and the Philippines faced a maritime standoff and China began to control the shoal.[12] Since then, relations with China over the South China Sea have become one of the most vital security issues for the Philippines.

At the same time, however, other perceived threats came from the domestic arena in the recent past, particularly on the issue of fighting against separatists such as the Molo Islamic Liberation Front. The Philippines militarily and diplomatically collaborated with international partners, including the United States, Japan, and even China, to respond to the threats coming from separatists. Much of the military forces of the Philippines also were focused internally rather than externally, as with several other large-population states discussed in this chapter. These internal struggles have been gradually mitigated by peace talks and the resulting 2012 Framework Agreement on the Bangsamoro. Although internal insurgencies and terrorist groups, such as ISIS, still exist, internal security issues have recently become less problematic.

The Philippines's external security challenges are likely to remain focused on the South China Sea in the coming decade. Given China's growing naval capabilities, it is difficult for the Philippines to balance against China alone. Its defense capabilities have been improving but are insufficient to manage its vast maritime environment, particularly with its defense spending well below 2 percent of its GDP. Therefore, the Philippines has strategic incentives to have allies and partners to ensure its territorial claims. At the same time, given the intensification of U.S.-China strategic competition, the Philippines's relations with China have become one of its most vital security issues. Although the Philippines tends to balance against China, leadership change may cause an abrupt policy shift, as illustrated by the populist Duterte administration from 2016 to 2022, which attempted to accommodate China while diplomatically distancing the Philippines from the United States.[13]

As with other states examined later in this chapter, a challenge related to the Philippines is the degree to which its allies and partners can assist to balance against China since external powers tend to take a neutral stance over third-country territorial disputes. This question is closely related to the Philippines's future national security posture, which may be affected by its population's youthfulness and substantial growth projected over the next thirty years. If the youth bulge associated with its economic rise propels the Philippines to take a more aggressive stance, as some theories of youth bulges predict, there may be more intensive skirmishes and conflicts over the South China Sea as it assumes a more active regional security role related to its potentially rising economic status.

Australia and New Zealand: One Security Treaty, Differing Security Postures

Australia's and New Zealand's smaller population sizes in relation to most of their northern neighbors, apart from Mongolia and the East Asian portion of Russia, together with their more isolated physical location and large territories in relation to their populations in the southeast corner of the Indo-Pacific region, place them in a different security situation from the other states in the IP16. Their unique demographic profiles combining rapid aging with robustly growing populations due to large numbers of immigrants also distinguish them from other rapidly aging states in the IP16. Both states have traditionally rooted their security in military alliance with the United States (and with each other) but otherwise have pursued distinctive approaches to their military security in the postwar era and continue to pursue different strategies in the 2020s.

Strategically, both countries cooperate in the important Five Eyes intelligence-sharing institution together with the United States, the United Kingdom, and Canada, with Australia's Pine Gap Joint Defence Facility an especially valuable contribution. Geographically, though somewhat isolated from principal regional security concerns, they nonetheless are situated between India and the geopolitically important Straits of Malacca and thus could be seen as an extension of the First Island Chain that constrains China's naval actions. Australia's goal of acquiring nuclear submarines through the AUKUS partnership also would greatly enhance its power-projection capacity, allowing for sustained naval operations in the South China Sea and beyond—assuming that it is able to address current recruiting shortfalls in its military despite its growing youth population.

As indicated in table 5.2, Australia's population of 26.6 million in 2024 is projected to grow to 32.4 million by 2050 despite a TFR of only 1.64. Like many U.S. allies in Europe and in Northeast Asia, it has been increasing its defense spending as a proportion of its GDP in recent years, narrowly surpassing 2 percent of GDP at US$34.42 billion in 2023. It maintains fifty-eight thousand members in its armed forces, a slight decrease recently despite defense spending increases. Although its total population is rapidly aging, with almost 24 percent projected to be aged 65+ by 2050 and projected entrance into super-aged status in 2031, it does not face a shrinking number of military service–age residents due to its robust immigration policies— unlike U.S. security partners in Northeast Asia.

The total number of Australia's working-age population aged 20 to 64 is projected to increase steadily through 2050 (and beyond), even while the percentage of the population aged 65+ also increases—from roughly 15.6 million in 2024 to just under 18 million in 2050. The narrower band of the number of new 20-year-olds each year also is projected to increase by about 20 percent from 2024 to 2050.

Thus, Australia's rapid aging looks quite different from its fellow U.S. allies in Northeast Asia. While it is likely to face a number of military recruiting challenges seen across advanced industrial states, including in the population-growing United States, it does not face the severe demographic pressures seen in Japan, South Korea, and Taiwan. Moreover, a growing working-age population can be expected to contribute to continued economic growth to fund military spending—though increased costs related to an aging population are a concern, as with the aging states of Northeast Asia, where the proportion of elderly in the population will rise.

Similar to U.S. ally Japan, Australia's contributions to regional military security in partnership with the United States are wide-ranging. While Australia does not host large numbers of forward-deployed U.S. troops like Japan and South Korea do, it does offer regular access to strategic ports and training facilities and regularly participates in bilateral and multilateral military exercises with U.S. and related militaries regionally. Australia's recent strategic vision, expressed in *Defense Plan 2020*, shows many similarities to Japan's *2022 National Security Strategy* in its increased defense spending, planned purchase of additional ships, planes, and other military hardware, and additional attention to growing grayzone concerns through enhanced cyber, reconnaissance, and intelligence capabilities.[14] Also like Japan, the new Australian defense plan seeks more durable supply chains and strengthened domestic industrial capabilities to enhance self-reliance.

Australia also has expanded the depth and breadth of its security partnerships with other like-minded states as it eyes an increasingly challenging security environment and experiences the next stage of its demographic aging. As noted in earlier sections, Australia is a founding member of the Quad, a participant in the trilateral AUKUS framework, and has greatly deepened its bilateral security cooperation with Japan and with the United States and Japan in a trilateral framework. Moreover, as discussed in a later section of this chapter, Australia has worked with the United States and Japan to leverage its long-standing relationships with many Pacific islands in an effort to counter growing Chinese influence. These newly emerging strategic coalitions aim to flexibly coordinate security policies to efficiently and effectively achieve their strategic objectives through such means as the expansion of agendas and membership in particular issue areas.[15] While this process often takes time, as shown in AUKUS, which plans to deliver the first nuclear-powered AUKUS-class submarine (SNN-AUKUS) in the late 2030s, Australia's continued demographic dividend enhances the country's ability to plan such a security commitment.

By contrast, New Zealand's security posture has not been evolving to a similar degree, following a pattern of less military security engagement with the region that has characterized its approach for decades. New Zealand's total military force numbers only around nine thousand members, supplemented by a modest reserve force. This is less than one-fifth the size of Singapore's force of fifty-one thousand and less than half Singapore's military spending despite a similar total population size. New Zealand's isolated geography likely plays a role in these decisions, which have been reinforced by multiple political administrations over the years that have distanced themselves from closer integration into the U.S. alliance network, in contrast to neighboring Australia. As noted in chapter 2, however, despite less working-level closeness within the shared ANZUS treaty framework, the United States and New Zealand continue to cooperate militarily, and in 1997 New Zealand was designated as a "major non-NATO ally" (MNNA) by the United States, a status conferred on eighteen non-NATO allies as of June 2021.[16] Despite its projected population growth of nearly 20 percent by 2050, though, this demographic trend—combined with rapid aging—does not seem likely to be a driver of deepened security engagement with the United States or other regional partners. In terms of other nonmilitary aspects of foreign policy, however, New Zealand continues to be active as a smaller-population state—as discussed further later in this chapter.

OPPORTUNITIES AND CHALLENGES OF YOUTH: FOUR LARGE, POPULATION-GROWING STATES ENMESHED IN THE REGIONAL SECURITY LANDSCAPE

Four large-population states in the Indo-Pacific that have been increasing contributions to the regional security landscape are projected to grow in population size and maintain relatively youthful populations through 2050. In population-size order, they are India, Indonesia, Vietnam, and Malaysia (see table 5.3). India became the world's largest population state in 2023 and is a member of numerous regional security organizations. Indonesia and Vietnam also stand out as growing large-population states with important regional security profiles, though Vietnam's population growth phase is projected to end around 2054. These three states also have large standing military forces of over 400,000 troops, with India's standing forces exceeding 1.4 million. Malaysia, though a smaller-population state compared to the other three, has a fast-growing population and also has been playing a growing regional security role while maintaining a standing military force above 100,000. Indonesia, Vietnam, and Malaysia also are all members of ASEAN.

In all four of these states, population growth should ensure that they could maintain or even expand their number of military forces well beyond midcentury if they were so inclined, in contrast to the challenges facing the Northeast Asian 6 to staff their militaries to varying degrees. Due to these differential demographic factors as well as their military-security profiles to date, these four states should be of special interest to those considering the demographic–national security nexus in the region, supplementing the discussion of population-growing U.S. allies Australia, New Zealand, and the Philippines in the previous section.

Not only do these four states have more youthful populations than those of the Northeast Asian 6, they also are fairly young as independent, sovereign states and have spent much of their time since independence engaged in internal nation-building and focused on economic development, but less on regional security concerns. Indonesia declared independence in 1945 and thus reached 80 years old in 2025. India was born as an independent state in 1947; Malaya in 1957 (Malaysia in 1963); and a unified Vietnam only officially in 1976, thus reaching only 49 years old in 2025. The relative newness of these states has contributed to their internal security focus to date, but

TABLE 5.3

Four growing Indo-Pacific states with regional defense roles, 2023/2024 v. 2050

	India	Indonesia	Vietnam	Malaysia
TFR 2024	1.98	2.13	1.91	1.55
Defense spending 2023 (% of GDP)	$73.58b (1.97%)	$8.78b (0.62%)	$7.39b* (1.71%)	$4.01b (0.93%)
Military personnel 2023	1.476m	405k	450k	113k
Population 2024	1.44b	282.4m	100.7m	35.3m
Population 2050	1.72b	320.5m	112.2m	44.4m
% 65+ 2024	7.1	7.3	9.0	7.7
% 65+ 2050	14.3	15.1	19.6	16.7

Source for population data: UN Population Division, 2024 revision

Note: Countries with below 2.0 TFR projected with Constant TFR; those above 2.0 use UN "Medium Variant." Defense data are from IISS, *Military Balance 2024*.

*estimate. b=billion; m=million; k=thousand.

this is beginning to change as these states codify internal practices, further develop economically, and create more capable militaries with greater external security roles. The increased multipolarity of the Indo-Pacific region together with shared concerns about China's role in the region also have contributed to their greater regional security engagement.

The main characteristic of these four states' foreign policy is their quest for strategic autonomy. To date, they have not been willing to relinquish their options to be autonomous—preventing great powers from compelling them to make particular decisions in their favor and maintaining independent decision-making procedures. Even within the ASEAN institutional framework (of which three are members), the principles of unanimity and consensus help to maintain each states' autonomy. Moreover, each also faces a number of internal security concerns that may be exacerbated by population growth and other shifts in their internal demographics that may limit a growing outward security focus. At the same time, this does not mean that these states always refrain from creating coalitions with great powers—as seen with India's membership in the Quad (among other institutions). Looking forward, where there is an opportunity to achieve their policy goals, there may be a greater willingness to cooperate with the United States or China on at least an ad hoc basis.

That said, none of these states looks likely to be a new U.S. treaty ally or substantial external security partner with other regional states in the short term (apart from partnerships with bordering states), but as major demographic changes begin to come to fruition by the mid-2030s (including potentially continued robust economic growth as a result of population growth), the emerging security landscape may be sufficiently different to merit renewed consideration of new institutional arrangements that include some or all of these four states as growing external security providers. A growing population of younger workers will likely (though not necessarily) contribute to demographic dividends in these four countries, particularly in synergy with economic partnerships with Northeast Asia's aging powers that already have been intensifying as the working-age populations of the Northeast Asian 6 shrink, creating further ties between these population-growing states and the super-aged, population-shrinking states in the north.

Beyond the IP16, there are several other large-population states with growing populations that are focused internally on domestic security challenges and economic development, in particular Bangladesh and Myanmar—as well as Pakistan, if one extends the scope of the Indo-Pacific beyond the boundaries established for this book. These additional states' security concerns are beyond the scope of this book, but more likely these would be states requiring security assistance rather than emerging as contributors to regional security coordination and public goods—with, again, Pakistan as a potential exception due to its deep strategic rivalry with India as well as security ties with China. Thus, Pakistan's role should be considered important but not in terms of likely emerging as an Indo-Pacific security actor beyond its immediate borders, as further noted in the following section.

India: A Growing Regional and Global Power

India is a country with tremendous opportunities as well as a number of long-standing and new challenges in the coming decades.[17] It is the rare country with the potential to rise in great power status within the time-frame of this book (though 2050), with its quite different demographics compared to Asia's other great powers making it of special interest. Already India is a major player in regional and world politics as the world's fifth-largest economy with one of the world's largest (and nuclear-armed) militaries while maintaining a recognized global brand as a leader of the so-called Global South. It is poised to play an even larger role in regional and global affairs in the coming decades if it is able to realize its potential demographic dividend in the economic growth realm in the way that Japan, South Korea, China, and others did in the twentieth century while also managing its complex internal diversity within its governing structures as the world's largest democracy. These potentialities are far from certain, but even if they are only partly realized, India still will likely become a more powerful regional and global actor that is sought after as a military-security partner in the coming decades.

Since its independence in 1947, India has pursued an independent foreign policy without formally aligning with other major powers, a practice likely to continue in the coming years. This will not necessarily preclude increased regional and global security cooperation, however, particularly given India's many concerns about regional rival and border-state China.[18] The shrinking workforces of the Northeast Asian powers together with concerns among many investors in China about overreliance on Chinese labor stand to favor India (and other states discussed in this section) in the coming decades, also creating incentives for it to work with other states to guard against an overreliance on China and to counter negative aspects of that country's growing regional influence.

With a 2024 TFR of 1.98—dropping below replacement level in 2020—India's demographic dividend potential will peak in the period of this study, through 2050. From 2024 to 2050, India's total population is projected to grow by 276 million, accentuating further India's position as the world's largest-population country and totaling more than the combined equivalent of the Japanese, Korean, and Taiwanese *total* populations, despite India's declining birth rate. With 2023 defense spending of over US$73.5 billion, India is the third-largest defense spender in the IP16 after China and Russia. This level of spending is about 2 percent of GDP, funding 1.476 million members of the armed forces, making the size of its military forces also second only to China within the IP16. Despite a growing population, India also will experience rapid aging during this period, but from a low base: from under 7 percent of its total population aged 65+ in 2020 to a projected 14.3 percent by 2050. Thus, India will enter the "aged" category during this period but still will rank quite young within the IP16 as the second-youngest in terms of aged 65+ population (after the Philippines) and with the third-lowest median age among the IP16 after the Philippines and Indonesia in 2050.

Headlines about India's pressing security challenges typically empha-size tensions with Pakistan, border friction with China, and domestic interethnic violence, which contrast with core security concerns of the United States and its allies in terms of regional priorities except in their shared concerns about China. In India's case, beyond territorial disputes over Aksai Chin (administered by China) and Arunachal Pradesh (administered by India), China's strategic partnership with India's arch-rival Pakistan is of special concern to India. China's influence with neighboring Nepal and potential stranglehold over water resources (par-ticularly given India's struggles to adapt to the increasingly disruptive effects of climate change) are additional major security concerns related to China which contrast with major concerns of the United States and other Indo-Pacific partners.[19] Still, there also are shared concerns related to China's nuclear arsenal and especially to its growing naval presence in the Indian Ocean region, the so-called string of pearls strategy that India views as encirclement.[20]

India's projected demographic changes will likely exacerbate its internal security challenges—including interethnic violence—that may reinforce an inward focus on its security concerns. Economic development and the effects of climate change both have contributed to increased population movement within India's borders, which have intensified these tensions and likely will continue to do so, as further discussed shortly. India's indepen-dent strategic position related to the Russia-Ukraine war underscores its focus on domestic concerns, such as ensuring an adequate supply of inex-pensive food for its large poor population as well as the hard security con-cern about maintaining strong relations with its largest weapons supplier, Russia.

To date, India has not aligned with the West to directly condemn Rus-sia or to impose sanctions on Russia related to its actions against Ukraine, underscoring India's tradition of nonalignment, including closeness with the Soviet Union during the Cold War. Indeed, in July 2024 President Nar-endra Modi traveled to Moscow to meet President Vladimir Putin for the first time since Russia's full-scale invasion of Ukraine in 2022, describing India's relationship with Russia as a "special and privileged strategic rela-tionship" and alluding to the long-standing close ties between the two coun-tries with the following statement: "Any mention of Russia reminds every Indian of an ally that has been with us through good times and bad, as a trusted friend of India."[21] The fact that this trip to Moscow overlapped with a NATO summit meeting in Washington further sent a signal of India's unwillingness to deepen its security partnership with the United States and its allies at the expense of other strategic options. Still, as India's population grows, and especially if its economy continues to grow with it, the United States and its security partners likely will redouble efforts at external military-security cooperation with India despite challenges to manage and achieve this.

A different sort of demographics-related security issue India faces relates to religion—a factor in India-Pakistan relations and internally in India under the Modi regime (2014–) in particular. In India's domestic politics, the ruling Bharatiya Janata Party (BJP)'s Hindutva ideology focuses popular attention on the internal demographic balance between Hindus and Muslims in ways that have stoked interreligious violence; parties to the right of the BJP advocate even harsher calls to deal with non-Hindu religions in India, particularly Islam. India's 2011 census showed that the proportion of Hindus had slightly shrunk in relation to Muslims, falling from 80.5 percent of the total population in the 2001 census to 79.7 percent in the 2011 census, while Muslims increased from 13.4 percent to 14.2 percent of India's total population.[22] The 2021 census was delayed by the Covid-19 pandemic and subsequent 2024 general elections, with plans to conduct it in 2025, so updated figures were not available at the time of publication of this book, but a concern remains among some partisans that the Hindu proportion of the population is further declining.

One example of Hindutva-motivated concerns is the proliferation in subscribers to the conspiracy theory that Muslim men are engaging in a "love jihad" to covert Hindu women to Islam, which some argue violates Indian law on "unlawful" religious conversion.[23] Although the BJP lost seats in the 2024 parliamentary elections, which forced it to rule together with a coalition partner, there were no signs in the months following these losses that the BJP's ideology in this area would be moderated. Moreover, with Modi subsequently sworn in as prime minister for a third five-year term in June 2024 (only the second prime minister in India's history to enter a third consecutive term), he stands to build on his agenda of the previous ten years to further pursue a Hindu-nationalist agenda that will continue then to draw attention to India's shifting internal demographics, including a shift across India's regions.

Also in the internal security realm, and like China and Vietnam, India has experienced a growing imbalance in its male:female sex ratio, indicating a troubling level of "missing girls" and, conversely, a growing number of men unable to find a marriage partner. An imbalance in India's sex ratio at birth (SRB) emerged at a modest level around 1980 when it rose above the natural level of 105 boys to 100 girls, climbing to beyond 109 in 2000 to a peak of 109.6 for boys in 2010 before modestly declining to 107.9 in 2020.[24] As such, the imbalance was nowhere near as extreme as in China during its One-Child Policy years (as discussed in previous chapters) but still can be expected to lead to social dislocations as this imbalance rises through India's growing population. For example, there were an estimated 151 million 12- to 17-year-olds in India in 2022, those born in the years of the highest imbalance in sex ratio (2004–2010), with an estimated 79.2 million of them boys. Thus, there were roughly 7.5 million "missing girls" in that six-year cohort alone, meaning that young men of that age group will face a substantial shortage of women of their age group as potential marriage partners. Apart from potential domestic instability that may result from this imbalance, some scholars have argued that so-called bare branches (young, unmarried men) could contribute to a more belligerent foreign policy.[25] This is one thread of scholarly literature that examines why growing, youthful populations are statistically more prone to interstate conflict, as discussed in chapter 1.

Climate change is yet another serious security concern for India that has demographic elements.[26] The mounting effects of India's projected population growth exacerbate the challenges of combatting climate change. In contrast to other large, high-carbon-emitting countries like the United States, China, and Japan, India's population is largely rural, rapidly growing, and disproportionately impoverished. India's continued population growth, though slowing, exacerbates its climate challenges in multiple ways. In addition, resource constraints—such as water scarcity and agricultural shortages—will hit India especially hard, a marked difference from the aging powers of Northeast Asia, where declining population size may ease many resource constraints in the coming decades. Because its population is growing, India must increase total consumption in the medium term or face increased poverty. While many activists in the developed world promote global consumption reduction,[27] India's high rate of poverty and comparatively low level of economic development makes consumption reduction highly unlikely. Indeed, the Modi government has consistently placed economic development and reform at the forefront of its agenda, even at the expense of progress on climate change.[28] Coal fulfilled 70 percent of Indian energy demand in 2020, further complicating efforts to address climate change and its detrimental effects on India.[29]

In sum, demographic change will exacerbate a range of security concerns and approaches for India, largely related to its more youthful and growing population profile but also related to issues more common in Northeast Asia, such as how to manage a growing elderly population. The aging of Asia is not the only demographics-related security concern, though it is the primary one in the northern part of the Indo-Pacific. The divergent demographic trajectories of India and U.S. allies South Korea and Japan may create some complementarity between these states—especially economically but also perhaps militarily in the future. These trends make India potentially a more attractive regional (and global) security partner in the coming decades, but states seeking deepened security cooperation with India will likely need also to engage with its divergent security concerns as well to deepen broader security cooperation, as seen recently in India's deepening of cooperation with Russia.

Indonesia: A Growing, Top-Four World Population with Continued Internal Focus

Indonesia, like India, also is projected to see a growing labor force and continued youthful population over the next several decades. Its population is projected to grow by over 38 million from 2024 to 2050, growth exceeding the total population size of neighboring Malaysia in 2024. Indonesia's population of young people aged 15 to 24 has been rising annually for decades and is expected to continue to rise to a peak number in that age-group of just under 47.5 million in 2031. The size of an expanded working-age population 15 to 64 is projected to rise annually through 2050 (and likely well beyond), from just over 193 million in 2024 to just over 213 million in 2050, an increase of 20 million potential workers. Even with this projected population growth, however, Indonesia is projected to slip to sixth place in population size globally by 2050 after Pakistan (the new number four) and Nigeria.

And yet, Indonesia's 2023 defense spending was only US$8.78 billion—substantially less than tiny Singapore—due to spending well under 1 percent of its GDP on defense (only 0.62%). Still, this level of spending funds 405,000 members of the armed forces, though most are focused more on internal security challenges. Like India, Indonesia is projected to experience rapid aging during this period, but from a low base: from 7.3 percent of its population aged 65+ in 2024 to 15.1 percent by 2050. Even with that more than doubling of the aged 65+ population, Indonesia will still have the IP16's third-lowest aged 65+ population (after the Philippines and India) and second-lowest median age (after the Philippines).

Indonesia faces numerous internal security challenges from religious extremists and terrorist groups. In the early 2000s, Jemaah Islamiyah, the Islamist religious group, conducted a series of terrorist attacks within the country, such as the 2002 Bali bombing, the 2004 Australian Embassy bombing in Jakarta, the 2005 Bali bombing, and the 2009 Jakarta bombings of the JW Marriott and Ritz-Carlton Hotels. Although terrorist attacks subsided in the 2010s and 2020s to date, there remains active concern over future attacks, as indicated by Indonesian ministers' and senior government officials' speeches.[30] In 2017, for instance, Jemaah Ansharut Daulah conducted suicide bombings against a Catholic church and a police headquarters in Surabaya. To prevent and mitigate religious radicalism, the government has facilitated deradicalization programs since 2012, through means such as establishing educational institutions including the Indonesian International Islamic University in 2022, organizing theological seminars, and employing social media to explain the benefits of religious pluralism.[31] Yet, in part because of the abundant information for radicalization existing online, the problem persists. This domestic precarious factor related to terrorism and more radical interpretations of Islam may affect Indonesia's political stability—particularly if the government fails to accommodate political demands of the growing younger generations or take measures to manage the effects of natural disasters, and/or leaves ethnic minorities behind in economic development and political inclusiveness. Each of these goals has demographic elements.

Variation in population growth rates of different ethnic and religious groups and in different island locations are thus internal demographic factors with security implications for Indonesia. Such concerns lead it to focus more on domestic security, with security partnerships with external actors often concentrating on supplementing its efforts at domestic security. Indonesia has a vast diversity of ethnic groups, consisting of 1,331 categories for ethnic, subethnic, and sub-subethnic groups.[32] Among them, ethnic Chinese Indonesians have traditionally played a significant economic role, even though they constitute only 1.2 percent of the total population, ranking fifteenth out of over six hundred ethnic groups, according to the 2010 census.[33] From 1965 to 1998, however, when Suharto held political power, Chinese Indonesians' political and social rights were severely restricted—for instance, the government banned Chinese mass media, schools, and organizations—due to strong suspicion about Chinese communist insurgencies and their involvement in the 1965 coup attempt.[34] After Indonesia's democratization process post-1998, the discriminatory laws against Chinese Indonesians were abolished. Yet, it will take more time for ethnic Chinese Indonesians to gain full civil liberties.[35] Although it is not yet statistically well-researched whether the population of Chinese Indonesians is rising, their political influence is likely to increase as civil liberties improve.

Externally, Indonesia has been seen as a leader of the Southeast Asian region, playing an important role in regional unity and collective action. Given it has the largest population size in the region, Indonesia has long been considered Southeast Asia's potential regional hegemon. Indeed, to consolidate its strategic position, it has frequently attempted to prevent external powers from intervening in regional affairs. Sukarno's "Konfrontasi" policy in the 1960s is a case in point. President Sukarno conducted a militarily and politically confrontational policy toward the Federation of Malaysia because he considered it to be under the control of the United Kingdom, preventing Southeast Asia from being free from exploitation by foreign powers. Subsequently, it was Suharto, who gained power after the 30 September Movement in 1965, who brought the end of Konfrontasi and drew Southeast Asian states together by assisting the establishment of ASEAN, aiming to collectively ensure regional autonomy.[36]

Indonesia's political leadership in Southeast Asia notwithstanding, its military capabilities are not sufficient to cover its exclusive economic zone as well as extensive land area, approximately 6.2 million and 2 million square kilometers, respectively.[37] Given the traditionally army-oriented force structure of the Indonesian military, Indonesia's navy has yet to be fully modernized, and its capability for maritime domain awareness is still under development.[38] This creates a barrier to enhanced security cooperation with this demographically rising power, but also a potential area for enhanced cooperation through capacity building.[39]

An additional challenge to enhanced security cooperation with Indonesia is that, as in the Philippines, depending on political leadership, Indonesia's diplomatic priorities frequently change. For example, while the Yudhoyono administration from 2004 to 2014 conducted notably proactive diplomacy in Southeast Asia and beyond, the Jokowi administration from 2014 to 2024 focused on domestic development, maintaining a low-key foreign policy.[40] Thus, Indonesia's foreign policy is characterized as pursuant of regional and national autonomy and being dependent on the leadership style of the day. In February 2024 the general election resulted in the victory of Prabowo Subianto, the minister of defense under the Jokowi administration, assuming the presidency in October 2024. Prabowo's strong partnership with Jokowi during the election campaign indicated that Indonesia's foreign policy was likely to remain on a similar path, and his military background indicated his inclination to strengthen Indonesia's military capabilities to ensure state sovereignty, including the exclusive economic zones encompassing the Natuna Islands in the South China Sea. However, Indonesia's political trajectory remains uncertain, as former President Jokowi's influence may diminish.

Indonesia's past challenge was nation-building through the creation of "national resilience" and "regional resilience" to fend off external interference in Indonesia and Southeast Asia.[41] The solution was to establish and consolidate ASEAN, which saw relative success in and at the end of the Cold War. However, as the geopolitical environment changes in Southeast Asia, mainly caused by growing U.S.-China strategic competition, it has become quite difficult for ASEAN to be united diplomatically. Also, Indonesia has changed its political characteristics from an economically oriented autocratic state to a more democratized state since the Asian Financial Crisis of 1997, which collapsed the Suharto regime. Currently, the country is a member of the G20 and has more opportunities to play an active diplomatic role beyond its own region, although whether it actively pursues this opportunity will depend on the foreign policy orientation of its president.

In this context, with Indonesia's population-growing demographic trend that includes a more youthful population than many of its neighbors, Indonesia likely will become a more attractive country to the existing great powers economically, diplomatically, and geostrategically (in part due to its geographic centrality between the Indian and Pacific Oceans). This means that Indonesia should endeavor to make the most of its growing human resources and allocate them to achieve its economic potential to the fullest extent. If successful, it will have more foreign policy choices that may enable it not only to revitalize its leadership in Southeast Asia and beyond but also to conduct a multidimensional diplomacy through the enhancement of ties with regional major powers, particularly the United States and China.[42]

That said, Indonesia will not likely nurture an alliance with a particular major power. If there were a considerable change in the regional strategic environment, it may temporarily align with a certain major power to ensure its own security. However, its basic principle would essentially remain the same (and similar to India's): to preserve its national and regional autonomy because of the path-dependence of its national interest.[43] As its power increases, rather than aligning with other major powers, Indonesia will likely pursue a regional and global role while ensuring its autonomy.

Malaysia: Growing in Population Size and Roles as a Middle Power

Malaysia can be expected to be increasingly viewed as a middle power given its projected population growth and expected continued economic rise. This demographic trend is unlikely, however, to push Malaysia to shift its security policy immediately. Rather, like Indonesia, Malaysia remains a Southeast Asian country that aims to maintain regional autonomy while increasing diplomatic influence in the region and beyond. Also like Indonesia, Malaysian leaders watch carefully Malaysia's internal ethnic population balance, particularly the role of ethnic Chinese Malaysians.

Chinese Malaysians are Malaysia's largest minority, constituting 22.6 percent of total population, with Malays and Indians at 70.1 percent and 6.6 percent, respectively, in 2023.[44] Playing a significant role in business sector, Chinese Malaysians have been economically wealthier than other ethnic groups.[45] At the same time, as a minority in the Malay-dominant society, they are politically marginalized in general while holding strong economic and social linkages with China. Although their cultural identity rests on Malaysia, their economic and international roles have certain political implications, which Malaysian political leaders monitor carefully.[46] Notably, the rate of aging in Malaysia differs by ethnicity, with Chinese Malaysians rapidly aging more than other ethnicities because of lower fertility, longer life expectancy, and emigration, while Malays and Indians are relatively stable.[47] As a result, the future role of Chinese Malaysians in Malaysia's economic and social settings might shift in the long term.

While Malaysia's TFR of 1.55 in 2024 is now well below replacement level, its 2024 population of 35.3 million still is projected to grow due to earlier higher fertility, up to 44.4 million in 2050. And yet, similar to neighboring Indonesia, Malaysia's defense spending in 2023 was comparatively quite low, just 0.93 percent of GDP, or US$4.01 billion. Given lower costs there, however, this does fund 113,000 members of its armed forces. Malaysia also is projected to experience rapid aging during this period: from 7.7 percent of its aged 65+ population in 2024 to 16.7 percent by 2050. (All these figures are presented in comparative perspective in table 5.3.)

Malaysia's strategic posture is very similar to that of Indonesia: seeking to maintain national and regional autonomy. In the past, it was Malaysia in the late 1960s that proposed the idea of regional neutrality through which Southeast Asia would prevent great power interventions in the region, although it was diluted to a more abstract proposal to create a "Zone of Peace, Freedom and Neutrality" in 1971.[48] Also, it was Malaysia in the post–Cold War era that attempted to reduce U.S. political influence over East Asian countries by proposing the idea of an "East Asian Economic Group," resulting in the establishment of ASEAN+3 in 1997 when East Asia faced the Asian Financial Crisis and received no bailout from the United States (due, in part, to Malaysia's decision to impose capital controls rather than submit to IMF conditions). In this connection, Malaysia (with the support of China) attempted to establish the "East Asian Summit" by elevating ASEAN+3 in the early 2000s, but such an initiative faced disagreement from some ASEAN+3 member states, such as Indonesia, Singapore, and Japan, and the East Asia Summit was eventually created independently from ASEAN+3.[49] However, Malaysia does not aim to ensure regional autonomy by itself given its limited material capabilities. Rather, it aims to act collectively while conducting a hedging strategy against the risk of entrapment and abandonment by great powers. This tendency continues even under the current era of U.S.-China strategic competition.[50]

At the same time, hedging behavior does not mean that a country attempts to behave the same to every great power. There are variations. In the early 2000s, for instance, Malaysia implicitly advocated for the exclusion of the United States from the original idea of the East Asia Summit. Although it attempted to reduce overdependence on or avoid being vulnerable to a single great power, Malaysia did not aim to cut ties with the United States or its Western counterparts. As such, Malaysia has been more diplomatically aligned with China in the 2000s and 2010s to maintain regional autonomy. In this context, even a potential increase in Malaysia's power due to optimal utilization of its population growth and relative youth in the foreseeable future is unlikely shift its foreign policy orientation unless there is a significant external event, such as a regional military contingency.

Vietnam: Adjusting to Final Decades of Population Growth

Vietnam's demographic future differs from the others discussed in this section. It will face challenges to maintain a stable population size without immigration, while also facing challenges of rapid aging and numerous internal demographic shifts like the other states discussed in this section. Vietnam's TFR of 1.91 has been slightly below replacement level since 1999, yet its 2024 population of 100.7 million still is projected to grow due to earlier higher fertility, up to 112.21 million in 2050, with the total population projected to begin to shrink in 2055. Vietnam also is projected to experience rapid aging over the next several decades: from 7.6 percent of its population aged 65+ in 2020 to hit 20 percent (super-aged status) by 2051. Its total defense spending is an estimated US$7.39 billion in 2023, about 1.71 percent of GDP. Still, this level of spending funds 450,000 members of the armed forces, a significant force on China's southern border and in a strategic region broadly (though a reduction of 32,000 from the previous year).

Near the end of the Cold War, Vietnam shifted its economic policy and liberalized its economic structure under the Doi Moi policy in 1986.[51] Vietnam's foreign policy change aimed to strengthen its relations with regional states through such means as gaining membership in ASEAN and conducting multidimensional diplomacy to create a favorable environment for its economic development. This is mainly because the Soviet Union was reorienting its foreign policy by attempting rapprochement with the United States, and thus it was not likely for Vietnam to sustain its Soviet-sided foreign policy. This foreign policy reorientation has largely worked, successfully internationalizing Vietnam as a member of multiple international organizations and cooperative frameworks, including ASEAN in 1995, Asia-Pacific Economic Cooperation (APEC) in 1998, and the World Trade

Organization (WTO) in 2007. Vietnam then overcame economic difficulties to become one of the fastest-growing economies in the region.

Vietnam's population shift from rural to urban areas has been a driver of a robust urban labor market that has fueled the country's export-driven growth. At the same time, adult children moving from rural areas often leave their parents and other siblings behind, creating a lifestyle challenge to balance work and family obligations, similar to Vietnam's northern neighbor, China. Much concern also is apparent in the media and in private conversations about increasing numbers of young Vietnamese workers moving to foreign countries to contribute to those labor markets rather than Vietnam's. At the same time, the growing symbiosis between South Korea and Vietnam—a rapidly aging state with a shrinking working-age population and one with a still-growing labor market—is an excellent example of Asia's demographic interconnectedness, as South Korea continues to locate its lower-cost manufacturing operations outside of Korea (in part due to labor shortages in Korea and also due to cost) and seeks an alternative to locating production in China, a state that South Korea increasingly feels threatened by.

Given its growing population and workforce, Vietnam will likely attract more investment from the world in the future and have more opportunities to host manufacturing and assembly facilities because of U.S. and European attempts to diversify their supply chains given an intensified U.S.-China strategic rivalry. At the same time, however, Vietnam continues to pursue its own political autonomy under Communist Party rule.[52] This is partly why Vietnam maintains economic and security cooperation with India and still has strategic ties with China and Russia, which are now openly considered strategic competitors of the United States and its allies and partners. If the world is going to be further divided and great powers force regional states to choose sides, Vietnam will face a very difficult situation in steering economic cooperation with the West while preventing China and Russia from becoming its strategic rivals.

Nevertheless, as U.S.-China strategic competition continues, Vietnam will likely gain economically because of the de-risking movement between these great powers. Vietnam has become an alternative for region's manufacturing factories due to its relatively large population. This trend to diversify supply chains and Vietnam's cautious posture toward China have attracted the United States and U.S. allies as they are willing to strengthen economic, diplomatic, and defense ties with Vietnam.[53] For example, Vietnam attended the "Quad-Plus" meeting in March 2020 when the Quad members and other regional states discussed how to counter Covid-19. President Biden's visit to Hanoi in September 2023 to announce an upgrade of the U.S.-Vietnam security partnership is another example of this notable expansion of Vietnam's regional security role.[54]

Given the projection of a growing population, Vietnam can situate itself by leveraging its economic strength to manage great power relations. Still, as long as the Communist Party controls Vietnamese politics, Vietnam is likely to conduct hedging behavior in the medium term without concretely aligning with particular great powers.

THAILAND'S MOVE TOWARD SUPER-AGED STATUS YET CONTINUED STRATEGIC POSITION

In contrast to the seven states discussed on the previous two sections, Thailand's demographic direction is more similar to the Northeast Asian 6 examined in chapters 3 and 4. Thailand has a large population of 71.69 million in 2024 but well below replacement-level TFR at 1.21 in 2024. And like the Northeast Asian states, it has resisted large-scale immigration to address its shrinking working-age population and, as a result, is projected to shrink back below seventy million (which it reached in 2015) in 2039—with population shrinkage expected to begin in 2025 and to continue in future decades.

Many Thais have concerns about how to control what is seen as excessive immigration from poorer neighboring countries—though Thailand needs these immigrants to fill lower-wage positions left open because not enough Thais are willing and/or available to do this work (despite continued rural-urban migration within Thailand to partly address such shortfalls). Also like the Northeast Asian states, Thailand is projected to reach super-aged status in the near-term, in 2031; by 2051, 30 percent of the total population is projected to be aged 65+, reaching the next stage of super-aging.

Thailand's defense spending is low by IP16 standards, at US$5.67 billion in 2023, only 1.1 percent of GDP.[55] This is less than Singapore's spending despite Thailand's population being more than tenfold larger, but it nonetheless funds an active military force of 361,000—the second-highest of the Indo-Pacific US allies, after South Korea and twice as large as that of the

Philippines, despite a smaller population. As Thailand's population further ages and population size shrinks, though, it will be challenging to maintain this level of force size—but in terms of regional security contribution, and particularly cooperation within the US alliance framework, it has not been the size or role of Thai military forces but rather Thailand's strategic location and willingness to host US forces that made it a useful ally. The US-Thailand alliance lost prominence at the conclusion of US participation in the war in Vietnam in the early 1970s and further weakened after a military coup in Thailand in 2006, though Thailand and the United States continue to cohost Cobra Gold, the Indo-Pacific region's largest annual multinational military exercise and to cooperate on numerous other fronts.

The case of Thailand helps to underscore the point further developed in the next section of this chapter that population characteristics are only one aspect of a potentially attractive security partner. Location and other geographic as well as geopolitical characteristics can be more important factors than population demographics and indeed often are. Thailand is geopolitically important because of its access to the Indian Ocean and the South China Sea, its continental connection between Myanmar and Indochina countries, and potential establishment of the Kra canal, which would connect the Andaman Sea and Gulf of Thailand if built. Moreover, if Southeast Asia further develops as a theater for great power competition in the Indo-Pacific region, Thailand's strategic value also will increase. Of particular note, if the Kra canal were established, many countries would have an option to no longer solely rely on the Strait of Malacca and Singapore for shipping.

In this context, while the U.S.-Thai alliance has long been on a diminishing trajectory, China's moves to more closely align with Thailand also may have a significant geostrategic impact on future U.S.-China strategic competition. Currently, China has been facing the so-called Malacca Dilemma that its trade and energy supplies rely on the Strait of Malacca and Singapore, making China vulnerable to a sudden disruption. By strengthening strategic ties with Thailand, China would not only potentially mitigate its Malacca Dilemma by facilitating the establishment of the Kra canal but also potentially have access to Thai military bases.[56] If this became the case, the power balance in Southeast Asia would likely change as Malaysia, Indonesia, and Singapore would lose some economic benefits derived from the Malacca Strait. Therefore, although the U.S.-Thailand alliance has been minimized in recent decades, there is an important reason that the United States does not want to abrogate or to allow too much drift in that alliance, which is driven by geopolitics, not demographics.

Thailand attempts to avoid strong alignments with its strategic posture, often referred to as "bamboo diplomacy."[57] Nevertheless, politically the United States and U.S. allies offer diverse means to contribute to the consolidation of democratic governance in Thailand. Although Thailand has experienced multiple military coups, its general tendency to return to democracy remains strong. As such, aging U.S. allies could engage with Thailand to contribute to the fundamentals of democratic governance by experience-sharing. This could facilitate political connections between the United States and U.S. allies and younger generations in Thailand. Also, if this aging ally maintains stability and its present external posture even after the younger generation takes more political power in the coming years, Thailand would likely seek areas of cooperation that are not contentious with external powers.

The general election in 2023 created new political ground where Prayut Chan-o-cha, who conducted the 2014 military coup and led Thailand for almost ten years, was defeated and new political parties, the Move Forward Party and the Phak Thai Party, led by younger politicians Pita Limjaroenrat and Paetongtarn Shinawatra, respectively, gained a majority collectively. However, after they built a political coalition between the two parties, political opposition against Pita becoming prime minister eventually led to different leadership in Srettha Thavisin of the Phak Thai Party—though he was dismissed by the Constitutional Court in August 2024. Paetongtarn subsequently emerged as Thailand's youngest-ever prime minister that month, less than a week short of reaching her thirty-eighth birthday. As such, in some aspects Thailand has undergone a generational change in its political leadership, though Paetongtarn is both the daughter and the niece of former prime ministers and thus does not represent a break from Thailand's longtime political class.

In this context, the areas of cooperation that the United States and U.S. allies might seek to deepen with Thailand are largely in nontraditional security fields, such as counterterrorism, counterpiracy, HA/DR, and peacekeeping operations. This type of cooperation would not only help Thailand avoid being entrapped by great power competition but also contribute to stabilizing the region by facilitating nontraditional security cooperation.

Thus, in relation to the key demographic concern of this study about the security effects of rapid aging, to the central question of whether Thailand's rapid aging is important to its usefulness as a potential enhanced security partner, the answer seems largely to be "no," because Thailand's principal value to the United States and its allies was its provision of bases and non-alignment with U.S. adversaries, not cooperation with its large armed forces. This provides a conceptual segue to the potential contributions of smaller-population states with generally fewer military resources to regional security cooperation to conclude this chapter.

SMALL-STATE DEMOGRAPHIC CHALLENGES AND CONTRIBUTIONS TO THE EVOLVING SECURITY LANDSCAPE

Small states often are neglected in discussions of military security because they are seen to not have substantial material capabilities, particularly militarily. However, as noted in previous sections, small-state Singapore spends more on defense than many large-population states in the region. Moreover, the geographic location of many such states and territories in the Indo-Pacific has led to a new phase of outreach by the United States and its allies and partners as well as by China and others to such states and territories. These smaller-population states and territories have quite diverse demographic profiles, as previously outlined in chapter 2. Depending on their economic capabilities, level of technology, geographical location, and demographic trends, their alignment behavior can enhance or disrupt major powers' foreign policy.

As stressed throughout this volume, security contributions do not come in only one form, such as population size. Logistical hub support and military base access are important. Diplomatic allies matter. These contributions are made by both large- and small-population states. In the growingly tense era of U.S.-China competition, efforts by both powers to deny new partners to the other also have become evident as both powers increase the geographic reach of their regional military strategies. While population demographics do not play a direct role in the attractiveness of small-state security partners, changing demographics of smaller states do pose numerous security concerns, as introduced in chapter 2 and further discussed in this section.

Smaller-population states in the region also have been engaging in their own diplomatic and network-building efforts apart from outreach from the region's larger powers. For example, there has been a rise in quiet diplomacy to formulate minilateral frameworks among smaller states. One notable example is the establishment of the Trans-Pacific Strategic Economic Partnership agreement in 2005, which was concluded by four small states in the Asia-Pacific region: Brunei, Chile, New Zealand, and Singapore. Given their small-scale economies, their free-trade standard was set higher, which eventually attracted regional powers and laid the foundation for the Trans-Pacific Partnership, now the Comprehensive and Progressive Agreement for Trans-Pacific Partnership (CPTPP). In this context, small-state-led minilateral or multilateral arrangements could become a pathway to further cooperation. As another example, the Digital Economy Partnership Agreement (DEPA) concluded by Singapore, New Zealand, and Chile in 2020 has attracted interest from several regional major powers, such as China. Although their arrangements are not necessarily security-oriented, let alone military, those cooperative frameworks can become a tool to closely align with regional states, which may be used to conduct a balancing, bandwagoning, or hedging strategy.

Singapore's Growing Contributions Despite Rapid Aging and Projected Shrinking

Singapore, an important security partner of the United States though not formal ally, is another example (like Australia and New Zealand) of a state with a nonreplacement birth rate and rapidly aging society but where robust immigration is leading to continued population growth and addressing of labor shortfalls. Singapore's population was 5.81 million in 2024, but according to the government of Singapore, only approximately 63 percent of residents are Singaporean—with over half a million permanent residents and an even greater number of temporary foreign workers. Due to continued robust immigration, Singapore's total population size is expected to continue to increase through 2039, to a peak of around 6.14 million, despite its significantly low TFR, which was only 0.94 in 2024. In part to offset this low number, Singapore has robustly pursued immigration and temporary foreign workers. This has not solved another problem, however: rapid aging.

The share of the population aged 65+ is projected to soar from 13.7 percent in 2024 to 27.2 percent in 2050, with the median age rising from 34.5 to 51.4 from 2020 to 2050—similar numbers to the Northeast Asian 6. The year 2050 is also when Singapore's population is projected to have shrunk below six million residents.

At the same time, given its governance structures somewhere between democracy and autocracy, Singapore illustrates how a system that restricts the political role of its citizens can institute tough measures needed to effectively manage population aging. For example, the Singaporean government has made taking care of elderly parents the legal responsibility of children.[58] It also has pursued requiring companies to rehire older workers after the age of 62 to raise worker participation and has instituted other measures to make the labor market more flexible, such as wage reforms to move from seniority-based to job-worth and performance-based compensation.[59]

Singapore also illustrates a demographic concern similar to Indonesia, Malaysia, and others in the region: it is a multiethnic society where there is special attention paid to creating a degree of balance and respect for its three main ethnic groups: Chinese, Indian, and Malaysian Singaporeans. Finding ways to include recent immigrants and their children in military-security matters is another demographics-related challenge the Singaporean leadership faces, particularly for immigrants from China (though, historically, Malaysian Singaporeans also have been viewed with some suspicion in senior the military ranks). These concerns also underscore a related foreign policy priority for Singapore: the attempt to play an intermediary role between the United States and China, despite (or perhaps because of) having very strong ties to both.

Singapore is demographically and geographically small but is situated in a geopolitically critical location and possesses strong military and financial resources. Its Changi Naval Base can accommodate large ships, including the aircraft carriers, which has attracted major powers for port calls—though it has not allowed a large-scale foreign military presence.[60] To avoid an entrapment risk of great power politics, Singapore attempts to project the image of a neutral country even though its security relationships have been much closer to the United States than other major powers, including China.[61]

Singapore's recent defense spending is quite high relative to other regional states. At US$13.4 billion, 2.7 percent of GDP, and 51,000 active armed forces in 2023, it has nearly as many active forces as Australia (7,000 fewer), despite less than one-quarter of the total population size and being a tiny fraction of Australia's territorial size.[62] This level of defense commitment illustrates Singapore's basic security principles to recognize its vulnerability as a small state and to build strong defense capabilities. The founding father of Singapore, Lee Kuan Yew, stated in 1966 that Singapore should become a "poisonous shrimp" that was "small but deadly."[63] However, as with South Korea and Taiwan, Singapore's long practice of universal male conscription to fill its military ranks is challenged by a declining number of Singaporean young men—as opposed to the children of permanent residents and foreign workers, who are not required to serve in the military. This has led to an active debate about national origin and ethnicity within the Singaporean military that demographically speaking will of necessity require changes in longstanding recruiting practices in the coming decades if Singapore is to maintain the size of its military forces.

Historically, Singapore has been strengthening its strategic ties with the United States. It signed a Memorandum of Understanding (MOU) in 1990 that enables the U.S. military to have access to facilities in Singapore, signed the Strategic Framework Agreement in 2005, and signed the Protocol of Amendment to the 1990 MOU in 2019.[64] Given the reality that Singapore is a small country, it needs a strong major power to maintain the regional balance of power in its favor, and the United States, which is geographically distant, has been seen as an ideal partner for that end. However, Singapore has not sought a formal military alliance status with the United States, even rejecting an idea to be named a Major Non-NATO Ally—as the six U.S. treaty allies in the Indo-Pacific are—when the United States proposed this in the early 2000s.[65] This does not mean that Singapore maintains complete nonalignment, however: Depending on the international environment, it has chosen to side with certain states, as illustrated in the case of the Russia-Ukraine war, where Singapore has criticized Russia to a higher degree than most other regional states.

Still, Singapore attempts to nurture friendly relationships with all major powers, particularly those who are closely involved in Southeast Asia. In fact, its relationship with China also has been enhanced as it has strengthened ties with the United States. For example, Singapore and China signed the Agreement on Defence Exchanges and Security Cooperation (ADESC) in 2008 and the Enhanced ADESC in 2019. This strategic posturing is important for Singapore's foreign policy in order to maintain its independence. Thus, and combined with Singapore's demographic struggles in the years ahead, it seems unlikely that Singapore will substantially raise its regional security contribution absent a major regional security disruption to the status quo—but also will likely follow the path of Northeast Asia's aging democracies to find technological offsets to staff its military as its native-born male population continues to shrink in numbers.

Smaller Growing States and Territories with Youthful Populations in a Graying Security Landscape

Population growth is not only projected in large-population states in the Indo-Pacific. In Northeast Asia, Mongolia's population (3.27 million in 2020) is projected to grow by 37 percent from 2020 to 2050 and still not reach an aged 65+ population of 12 percent. In the southern Indo-Pacific, Laos (2020 population: 7.3 million) and Timor-Leste (2020 population: 1.3 million) are each projected to experience population growth over 33 percent from 2020 to 2050, with aged 65+ populations of 9.9 percent and 7 percent, respectively. The island grouping of Melanesia is projected to exceed 51 percent population growth from 2020 to 2050, a particular concern for an area where climate change is projected to reduce space for living and farming. On the positive side demographically, its elderly population (aged 65+) is projected to remain under 8 percent through 2050 (and likely much later). Even with fast-growing populations and relative youth, though, it is not population size that entices greater security cooperation with regional powers, but rather strategic location and the desire to keep these states from closely aligning with China and other states of concern.

A number of Pacific Island states have become a locus for increased U.S.–China competition and rivalry. Given its peripheral diplomacy and diplomatic competition with Taiwan, China has long engaged with the region, providing economic assistance to enhance its diplomatic influence in the region.[66] Australia, a dominant power in the southern Pacific, has been increasingly concerned about China's growing influence. News reports that China and the Solomon Islands would conclude a security agreement in

2022 brought to light the redoubled efforts of the United States to reengage with the region.[67] Although that agreement does not explicitly allow Chinese military to be located in the country, according to the draft agreement, the Solomon Islands now has a right to convene Chinese forces in times of domestic turbulence while China would be able to provide security assistance. This resulted in a relative U.S. increase in its commitment to the region, as indicated by the issuance of the U.S. "Pacific Partnership Strategy" also in 2022.[68]

Additionally, the United States and its allies, particularly Australia, began to increase their collective engagement with other Pacific island states in the early 2020s.[69] Australia and New Zealand have invigorated their policies toward the Pacific islands countries, particularly capacity-building programs regarding climate change, disaster relief, and maritime security, through regional forums such as the Pacific Islands Forum (PIF) and the South Pacific Defense Ministers' Meeting (SPDMM). Japan, which organized the Pacific Islands Leaders Meeting (PALM) in 1997, also has enhanced its engagement in the region, making Fiji one of the four priority countries for its Official Security Assistance (OSA) in 2023.[70] The U.S.-Papua New Guinea defense and maritime cooperation agreement in 2023, Indian prime minister Narendra Modi's visit to Papua New Guinea in 2023, and the 2023 Quad Summit Statement to recommit to the Pacific island countries are all part of the strategy to counter China's influence in the region.[71]

However, even with projected population increases in these states and territories, they are unlikely to develop strong military capabilities on their own because of a lack of economic resources and the existence of other pressing issues, such as climate change. The Pacific islands generally lack natural resources (except through fishing) and require continuous economic assistance. In this sense, those small states' strategic utility is predominantly its geostrategic location for power projection in the southern Pacific region.[72]

CONCLUSION: CHALLENGES AND OPPORTUNITIES IN THE DEMOGRAPHIC DIVERSITY OF THE INDO-PACIFIC

Changes to national populations unfold slowly, across decades and usually across numerous transitions of political power. They are thus often overlooked in favor of seemingly more pressing issues. In numerous aspects of day-to-day policy planning by governments across the Indo-Pacific, however, demographic change is playing a leading role. For example, the population aging and shrinking of Northeast Asia's aging powers contributes to increased investments in population-growing states in the southern Indo-Pacific region, boosting their economic growth and further developing critical infrastructure. As another example, domestic leaders region-wide face mounting political pressures to address inadequate infrastructure in cities growing due to rural-to-urban migration and population increases overall. Thus, in many ways Asia's differential demographic changes underscore the shared challenges states face, despite their different specific demographic paths ahead. Rather than dividing states, Asia's demographic differences have brought many closer together—both economically and in terms of military security—and likely will continue to do so as current demographic trends across the Indo-Pacific intensify in the coming decades.

In the nearer term there does not seem to be a great likelihood for significant change in security policy orientation for any of the states considered in this chapter, but even continued movement in the direction indicated in this and previous chapters would lead to an even more multipolar regional security landscape in the coming decades as numerous regional middle powers gain influence.

Four of the nine states discussed in this chapter offer the best prospects for increased regional security contributions with the United States and its allies: Australia, India, the Philippines, and Singapore—though as India wrestles with its own efforts to develop as a more powerful global actor in its own right, coordination will continue to be a challenge. Indonesia and Vietnam will likely continue more of an independent security posture, despite Vietnam's 2023 enhanced security partnership with the United States; Thailand as well, despite formally being a U.S. ally. Each of these states has worked hard to maintain close relations with China for different reasons, which also will likely limit substantial increased integration into a U.S.-led security architecture.

Of the comparatively smaller-population states, Malaysia and New Zealand also will probably only modestly enhance regional security contributions in the next several decades despite their growing populations. Moreover, if the security postures in regional states continue to revolve around

DEMOGRAPHIC DIVERSITY OF THE BROADER INDO-PACIFIC

great power politics, such as the current trend to counter China, the structural force to divide the Indo-Pacific region may become even stronger in the near future. How the ten-nation regional block of ASEAN will fare in an era of potential greater great-power competition and demographic divergence thus merits special consideration.

Looking to 2050, there is more contingency and thus more possibility of a strategic shift by a demographically shifting state. Demographic factors may be among the variables that could account for such a change in outward security policy, though, as noted throughout this volume, it is not the demographic shifts themselves that create the policy changes within states: Governments and leaders play the determining role in managing a state's demographic transitions.

It is also possible by midcentury that states not discussed in this chapter in detail—particularly larger growing ones like Bangladesh or Myanmar—may play a more outward security role regionally. However, projecting levels of economic and political development several decades out is so full of contingency that it is not something that is considered further this study. The final chapter will offer summary conclusions about the role of the southern Indo-Pacific in the region's diverse security challenges with special attention on the role of this subregion's varied demography on its likely security-policy evolution. It will also pull together major threads of argument from previous chapters and consider numerous wildcards in the future demographic and political development of the Indo-Pacific region.

CONCLUSION

Addressing the Security Implications of Rapid Aging in the Indo-Pacific

Forecasts don't predict the future—they drive investments in the present. In other words, considering a range of demographic forecasts points you toward the investments you need to make today to shape the future you want tomorrow.

—JENNIFER SCIUBBA, *8 BILLION AND COUNTING*

Rapid aging—and even super-aging—in the Indo-Pacific, first seen in Japan at the start of this century and now spreading through the region, has begun to shift regional security dynamics in ways that will intensify as demographic shifts ripple across the region through 2050 and beyond. The resultant population changes will further contribute to a shifting regional balance of power toward a greater number of states and institutions contributing to regional security. The "aging security dilemma" discussed in earlier chapters will intensify, with broad effects on security planning and practices. Moreover, expected demographic change will further encourage development and adoption of new technologies to address existing and future security challenges.

Still, given current regional power asymmetries, the region's aging powers are likely to continue to be its dominant powers for decades to come. As highlighted at the start of this volume, however, even a close grouping of aging states has not been shown to lead to lessened tensions or fewer perceived threats. The idea of a "geriatric peace" has proven to be more aspirational than an expected result of rapid aging, at least to date.[1]

Previous scholarship on the impact of twenty-first century demographic trends on global security has stressed the impact of youth bulges and differential demographic growth across regions. To the extent that the new demographic trend of rapid aging has been considered vis-à-vis military security, most scholarship has been based on logical deduction rather than empirical case studies of rapidly aging states or on just one country case. This study has focused on multiple states in one region, and especially on the effect of rapid aging on the evolving security landscape. It has found that rapidly aging states have many ways to address the challenges posed by their aging—and often shrinking—populations and that they are employing these tools to plan for a future of smaller working-age populations and older societies that still possess a robust military posture. Total population size also has been shown to be an important factor: States with larger populations have more options to redeploy workers to address perceived security concerns.

In short, many existing studies on the demography–national security linkage paint with too broad a brush by not considering specific security contingencies faced by aging states, nor the cultural and political context that demographic pressures are filtered through. By examining sixteen territories facing differing security concerns—protecting a land border vs. the maritime domain, offensive vs. defensive operations, peacetime vs. wartime as well as gray-zone situations—the diverse challenges of rapid aging and population shrinkage become apparent. The differing roles new technologies can play to offset demographic challenges also have been shown to vary greatly based on specific security scenarios.

U.S. security strategy for the Indo-Pacific relies on two rapidly aging and population-shrinking states that are experiencing serious demographic challenges—Japan and South Korea. Both states, however, have expanded their security roles in the region and within the U.S. alliance network as they have rapidly aged, with consistent U.S. calls for even further increases. Meanwhile, Taiwan's future defense also is complicated by its rapid aging and shrinking population. Each of these democracies has begun to address its demographic challenges based on their different threat perceptions and political realities, looking both to new technologies and to new approaches to fill growing gaps in their defensive needs. In addition, each is seeking to work more closely with the United States—including related to development of innovative new technologies—to address challenges posed by changing demographics as well as the changing security landscape due to technological innovation and a shifting regional balance of power.

Rapidly aging and shrinking populations present special challenges for core U.S. allies Japan and South Korea to enhance capabilities to respond to growing security concerns, but nonetheless, both have risen to this challenge and appear committed to continue down this path despite concerns of some—in both the policy and scholarly realms—that aging populations would not support increasing military capabilities. The surprising and strategically important moves by these two allies in 2023 toward greater trilateral security cooperation together with their shared ally, the United States, also indicates how aging powers increasingly are expanding security partnerships to help offset challenges posed by shrinking numbers of young people available to enter military service domestically. Other examples of such growing minilateral security cooperation among rapidly aging (and other) states include the Quad and AUKUS frameworks, in addition to deepening trilateral cooperation among numerous regional states. The less-rapidly-aging United States has introduced new uncertainties to this approach, however, with the return of Donald Trump to the presidency in January 2025. In addition, the United States itself may face a future of more rapid aging if stated plans to reduce immigration as well as the migrant population currently residing in the United States are enacted.

Population aging also has incentivized innovation in numerous sectors of the economy to address challenges faced by aging workers and fewer workers. In countless areas, technology has at least partly filled a gap created by a shrinking working-age population, but with the projected intensified shrinking of workforces in Northeast Asia, it is not clear that technological solutions alone will suffice. Further off-shoring of production as well as increased use of immigrant or guest workers also may be needed, posing new or intensified challenges in the coming years.

To date, all the rapidly aging states examined in this study are increasing their security preparedness and contributions despite their challenging demographics, contrary to what many predicted. In the medium term, however, many still question whether this approach is sustainable, both financially and in terms of mass political support, particularly within Asia's rapidly aging democracies. As seen in preceding chapters, the cultural and political dimensions of demographic change vary widely across countries, and some effects cannot yet be predicted with confidence, such as the potential for growing casualty aversion among shrinking and aging populations and economic trade-offs that may limit future defense budgets.

Beyond Northeast Asia, and important for Indo-Pacific security dynamics and the U.S. security posture in the region, the demographic story of the broader Indo-Pacific is much more varied. Numerous states are projected to grow their populations through 2050 (and beyond), while others will see a declining size of their total populations. As discussed in chapter 5, population-growing states face different challenges more similar to those most countries faced in the twentieth century, including how to realize the gains from a potential demographic dividend and how to obtain additional resources to satisfy a growing population. If the more youthful and population-growing states of the Indo-Pacific can successfully achieve a demographic dividend as Northeast Asian states did during their high-growth phases, the region would experience a further shift in attention away from the traditional powers located in Northeast Asia toward a multipolar security (and economic) environment. Such a development depends on many factors other than population shifts, however—including the ability to maintain the largely peaceful relations among regional states that has characterized the past several decades.

India is projected to see its population grow by the largest total number in the world despite now experiencing a population-shrinking fertility rate and will remain quite youthful in relation to other long-standing U.S. allies and partners through 2050 (and likely beyond). If harnessed successfully, these demographics will boost its economic growth and provide an ample supply of men and women to serve in its increasingly capable military and to take over factory work that China's shrinking working-age population may no longer be able to handle. Other large-population states—Vietnam, Indonesia, and the Philippines—also are projected to experience population growth and relatively young populations over the next several decades (and, for some, way beyond that). The once largest-population state in the world, China, by contrast, will soon enter a new demographic status of super-aging and experience a dramatic reduction in the size of its working-age population over the next several decades and likely beyond.

Beyond the demographics transition underway in the Indo-Pacific, there are simultaneous political and social developments in each country and in military affairs broadly that partly overlap with and partly offset challenges from demographic change, as introduced in earlier chapters. For example, despite the surprising outbreak of protracted kinetic conflict between Russia and Ukraine, there is a counter-trend away from planning for large-scale, protracted military fighting—the million-person armies fighting head-to-head scenarios—toward increased attention to gray-zone conflict and cyber conflict. In addition, there is a growing integration or overlap between civilian and military technologies, including increasing human–technology integration among both civilians (e.g., smartphones and wearable technology) and military personnel.

Beyond changing demographics and new technologies, there also will be numerous other changes over the course of the twenty-first century that will affect a state's approach to its security. Two in particular should be noted in conclusion. There is growing talk of "deglobalization" character-izing the coming decades of this century due to a combination of supply chain and disease vector issues exposed by the Covid-19 pandemic as well as evolving geopolitics that also has put the West on the defensive.[2] These trends could lead to a significant reframing of existing regional alliances and partnerships, particularly those anchored around the United States, and particularly after the return of Donald Trump to the presidency in the United States in 2025. Moreover, despite the high degree of confidence in demographic forecasts, particularly to 2035 but also out to 2050, several demographic wildcards also should be considered, such as the possibility of an even more serious global pandemic than the Covid-19 crisis or a dif-ferent major population disruption, such as through a nuclear, biological, or chemical incident. Longer-term technologies that may affect both fer-tility and the productivity of an aged society as well as military-security dynamics also should be kept in mind as possible disrupters of expected implications of demographic shifts in the medium term.

This book will conclude by considering further such "wild card" possi-bilities and then summarizing some of the major findings from earlier chapters related to the impact of demographic change on the security land-scape of the Indo-Pacific and on the U.S. military security role within that evolving landscape.

AN UNCERTAIN REGIONAL FUTURE DUE TO DEMOGRAPHIC, TECHNOLOGICAL, AND OTHER CHANGES

Despite strong confidence in projections of demographic change in the region in the coming decades, in particular projections through 2035, this book has sought to illustrate the high degree of uncertainty about other factors that will exert countervailing pressures on the security future of the Indo-Pacific. Demographic pressures are filtered through political and social systems. Growing authoritarianism in some states examined in this book suggests that some demographic pressures may be handled (or not) without securing public buy-in. In more democratic states, social pressures may hinder effective government responses to demographic pressures—as widely seen in policies related to immigration and greater gender equality.

Similarly, technological change can both mitigate and complicate how societies will respond to demographic change. There are a surprising number of non-high-tech potential solutions to shrinking workforces and aging that also could be employed by military forces, such as outsourcing and enhancing efficiencies that cases examined in this volume show being more actively considered and implemented as demographic pressures intensify. The growth of gray-zone conflicts and other new military concerns also already can be seen to mitigate the effects of rapid aging and population shrinking among Northeast Asia's aging military powers, shifting the nature of warfare in ways that affect the sorts of human labor required for military security.

National security has never meant only military security, but in an era of proliferating gray-zone security challenges it is even more important to examine the many ways states define and pursue their own security. The Covid-19 global pandemic naturally directed attention to health aspects of national security but also has drawn greater attention to areas such as supply chain resilience and broader notions of economic security. Climate change also has attracted greater attention as a national security imperative for many states that have begun to experience a growing impact from climate change–induced weather events, some of this related to changing internal demographics of those places.

As seen in chapter 5's discussion of India and the Pacific islands, the effects of climate change can be exacerbated by growing populations as well as intensified resource use due to industrialization and economic growth.[3] India's growing use of coal to power electrification of developing areas within the country is just one example. Sciubba also stresses this linkage in her global study of challenges of a world population reaching eight billion in 2022, observing: "Continued population growth and rising incomes will mean continued rises in greenhouse gas emissions barring radical change with clear leadership from the US and China, in particular."[4]

Even though global population growth is projected to end around midcentury—only a few decades from now—concerns about potentially rising consumption patterns of both the current world population as well as the next several billion inhabitants of the planet threaten the limited progress to date in meeting global emission-reduction targets to address climate change concerns. Moreover, and related to global security challenges shown to have resulted from population growth in the past, consumption patterns of the growing number of inhabitants in the Indo-Pacific lead to fears about potentially rising interstate violence as a result of more competition for resources and/or increased instability due to lack of sufficient resources that could lead to state failure. Asia's aging—and population-shrinking—powers may be called on to contribute to regional security in these areas in addition to addressing their own adjustment challenges related to their rapid aging.

In sum, changing regional demographics are likely to further alter the way that regional states—and the United States—define national security imperatives. For many inhabitants of the Indo-Pacific, access to clean water, adequate housing, or protection from persecution based on ethnicity or religious beliefs—all rising challenges in population-growing states—are more urgent security imperatives than the concerns about interstate conflict their governments may prioritize. As a result, leading powers such as the United States and Japan may need to engage in a greater number of tradeoffs with potential security partners about which issues to prioritize. Challenges of coordinating action within the new Quad framework are an example where such tradeoffs already are apparent.[5]

China has shown an astuteness in some cases to aid regional states in areas of those states' priorities in exchange for concessions or cooperation related to China's military-security ambitions. China's expanded access to port facilities and potential locations for future military forces are two examples. Linked to the changing demographics focus of this volume, many regional states with growing populations have substantial infrastructure needs that they cannot meet on their own. All of the current major powers of the region are assisting in infrastructure development in ways that often also advance their military security interests.

Yet another significant challenge to Indo-Pacific security in the coming decades is the potential for global political and economic forces that question the current extent of economic globalization to crest to a degree that the United States disengages with the Indo-Pacific region. Fear of such evolving domestic politics in the United States is widely apparent in the region, particularly after the re-election of Trump to the presidency in November 2024, despite a rising number of regional partnerships with which the United States is engaged. Indeed, this rise in partnerships in advance of Trump's return to office may be the result of lingering fears of future U.S. disengagement.

A growth in nativism domestically also links to possible declining immigration in the United States and across the region, which could lead to more rapid aging and accelerated population-shrinkage in some states. A recent trend of more rapid aging is visible in the United States from 2020 to 2024, but at present it is unclear to what extent this is a temporary blip due to the Covid-19 pandemic or the start of a longer-term trend toward the end of U.S. demographic exceptionalism. In this context, it is notable that several countries within this study have projected population increases entirely due to inward migration, namely, Australia, New Zealand, and Singapore. In numerous other states, inward migration is at least slowing the rate of aging and workforce shrinkage.

As noted in the introduction to this book, looking back to the twentieth century there were numerous mistaken assumptions related to expected demographic trends. Major world wars were not anticipated, which led to tens of millions of deaths and unexpected migration worldwide. Decolonization and the proliferation in the number of independent states also led to substantial global population shifts. The successful harnessing of the unprecedented population boom of the twentieth century led to spectacular economic development in some countries, notably China and elsewhere in Asia. New technologies directly contributed to the fast-growing population sizes. The coming decades also surely will see similar large-scale unanticipated developments that will affect the way that demographic projections for the Indo-Pacific region will shape the regional security landscape.

Demographers and other social scientists understand much more about demographic trends after a half-century of sustained study and lessons learned from mistakes in previous projections. For example, many studies and datasets provide a range of possible demographic futures with probability likelihoods for different scenarios, offering greater transparency as well as options for considering and planning for different futures. This study, for example, was based on the view that the standard "medium variant" scenario in the 2019 and 2022 UN population projections for low-fertility Indo-Pacific states were overly optimistic, resulting in likely a large underestimation of the scale of rapid aging and population shrinkage in Northeast Asia by 2050. The 2024 revised UN population projections continue to base the medium-variant estimate on an expectation of rising birth rates in especially low-birth-rate countries despite having adjusted the TFR downward from earlier projections—for example, the 2024 revision projects TFR in South Korea to rise from 0.73 in 2024 to 1.0 by 2047. These projections for future increases in fertility and resultant population growth should be considered with skepticism based on recent experience.

It can be expected that scientific advances and research will reveal new factors that will affect our shared demographic future, such as recent findings of declining sperm counts among men across the world that may be linked to greater human exposure to chemicals. Technologies not yet developed or even imagined also may affect fertility rates either up or down as well as the productivity of an aging workforce.

It is possible that life expectancy will dramatically change globally or in specific countries by 2050—either in the life-extending direction due to advances in medical technology or in the life-shortening direction due to the spread of illness, a major war, or chemical/nuclear/biological accident. This does not seem especially likely by 2050—considering that even the Covid-19 global pandemic only modestly affected life expectancies—but it is a possibility.

More likely, perhaps, is that the productive age of workers will increase in a significant way due to technological advances, especially in states with rapidly aging populations. Moreover, in the political arena—as opposed to or in conjunction with technological innovation—it seems likely that numerous advanced industrial states will implement policy change to incentivize or compel citizens to remain in the workforce at older ages, despite the notable challenges to implementing such changes apparent in the early 2020s. Relatedly, technological innovation may reduce costs of caring for an aged population, but conversely, new technologies also may increase lifetime costs of caring for an elderly population by extending lifespans without concurrently improving quality of life. In short, technology introduces uncertainty about the future.

The potential divergence across states in development and adoption of such technologies could exacerbate security tensions as well as states' ability to manage their aging populations. For example, drawing on data presented in chapter 4, one effect of Russia's unusually low life expectancy is to lessen the burden of caring for a more elderly population, while, conversely, improvements in life expectancy due to technological innovation could greatly increase costs if life expectancy were to dramatically increase as a result. Similarly, as India develops economically, further improvements in its current life expectancy of 72 years could lead over time to tens of millions of additional elderly citizens requiring care—already it is projected that India's population aged 65+ will rise from 6.4 percent to 14.3 percent in 2050 under current life-expectancy scenarios.

Beyond such expected advances in our knowledge, there are also potential game-changers that could greatly affect the security future of the Indo-Pacific. Development of new military technologies in the longer term—such as advances in AI, quantum computing, robotics, and synthetic biology—may make current demographic concerns less salient. And, of course, there is always potential for a major war—such as one sparked by escalation of the Taiwan standoff or miscalculation from North Korea's nuclear brinksmanship—that could quickly change the security calculus (as well as population demographics) for states region-wide.

From 2050 to 2100 it is much more probable that there will be an unexpected demographic disruption due to future possible technological advances and other uncertainties about the world in general (including growing concerns about the effects of climate change), which, in part, is why the core analysis of this study concludes at 2050. In that context, the following two sections summarize the core implications of predicted demographic change through 2050 for the regional security environment and the U.S. relationship with it.

IMPLICATIONS OF DEMOGRAPHIC CHANGE IN THE INDO-PACIFIC FOR REGIONAL SECURITY

A core argument of this book is that the effects of demographic change on national security are both internal to each country as well as relational among states facing or instigating a security concern. As a result, changing population demographics such as the coming proliferation of super-aged states and still-growing populations of other rising middle powers in the Indo-Pacific have implications beyond the borders of each of these states.

Several important regional implications of the demographic changes that already have taken place and the increasing intensity of projected change have been discussed in earlier chapters. A primary takeaway is a caution about taking for granted the "long peace" most of the Indo-Pacific region has enjoyed for many decades as the region's rapidly aging powers develop new military capabilities as well as engage in a growing range of gray-zone conflict. Evidence from the first decades of rapid aging in Asia leads to less confidence in a "demographic peace" to come and, conversely, more concerns about the negative effects of the aging security dilemma that has emerged as states develop new strategies to adjust to their rapid aging.

Increased military spending region-wide and a growing number of perceived security challenges have led to a renewed focus on what is maintaining the long peace most of the Indo-Pacific has enjoyed for two generations, including through a reimagining of the U.S. alliance system as well as other multilateral and minilateral institutions. Intensifying and expanding security concerns have created a sense of urgency to adapt regional security architecture and strategies for maintaining peace and stability. Moreover, the proliferation of gray-zone concerns has led to renewed attention to challenges and disruptions of new technology already introduced and under development.

While long-standing conflict flashpoints of the traditional "East Asia" or "Asia-Pacific" regions continue as principal security concerns of the United States and its core allies in the Indo-Pacific today—including the growth of China's military ambitions and capabilities, the divided Korean peninsula and North Korea's nuclear ambitions, and the status of Taiwan—new security concerns, emerging technologies, and emergent networks with new security partners have contributed to a growing focus on ways to adapt U.S. strategies for peace and stability in the region. The need for such new approaches is not rooted solely—or even primarily—in demographic change, but such change is an important factor for both U.S. and regional policymakers to consider as they conceptualize the region's security approach and architecture. Demographic pressures of America's aging allies reinforce a trend toward deepening alliances and partnerships with other like-minded states, a strategy that President Trump has called into question.

The China Challenge is a common concern for all U.S. allies and partners as well as for other states seeking to maintain positive relations with both sides of this growing strategic rivalry. Thus, understanding how China's changing demographics will intersect with demographic change elsewhere in the region is of universal interest. There are many unknowns about China's future policy directions unrelated to demographic change, but it is clear is that China's changing demographics will exert a greater effect on its policy choices in the coming decades due to the intensifying rapid aging projected.

To date, however, China's military does not appear to be directly hampered by a shrinking number of younger men of military age, unlike China's democratic neighbors. Indeed, in 2023 and 2024, following the first years of China's overall population shrinkage, China's leaders faced a crisis of unknown proportion about how to successfully utilize even their shrinking number of younger workers.

Looking to the 2030s, China's aging demographics likely will create economic opportunities for population-growing states in the region and lessen the relative power decline of other states that will experience a demographic future similar to that of China (such as South Korea and Japan). Already there has been a substantial shift in production away from China as labor costs there rise, but to date this is only partly due to demographic shifts.

For America's five rapidly aging and population-shrinking allies and partners in the Indo-Pacific—Japan, South Korea, Taiwan, Singapore, and Thailand—this book has shown that the effects of their predicted population transitions will be more nuanced than earlier thought based on straightline demographic projections. Northeast Asian U.S. allies Japan and South Korea are at present increasing defense spending substantially to adjust their militaries to new demographic realities as well as to respond to growing threats and to hedge against a potential U.S. military pullback from the region. Both also are redoubling their alliance partnerships with the United States as well as taking the next tentative steps toward coordinating with each other more in the military-security area. Both face a future of significant further population aging and shrinkage, however, with it unclear that steps taken to date will be sufficient to maintain a robust defense posture and deterrence.

Taiwan also is increasing its military spending to develop new capabilities and to address the personnel shortfalls that are projected for its conscription-based military—but, again, it is unclear if there is political will to take further steps as demographic pressures intensify. Singapore and Thailand, two states with projected shrinking populations in the coming decades in addition to rapid aging, illustrate how alliance partnerships are not always based on deep cooperation among large numbers of military personnel but can also be about access to facilities and broader diplomatic coordination—illustrating in a different way how super-aged, population-shrinking states can be important security partners.

In a similar vein, expanded U.S. coordination with population-growing US allies the Philippines and Australia/New Zealand also illustrates how alliances are not just about soldiers fighting together but about access to facilities, broader diplomatic coordination, and—especially in the case of Australia—partnerships to develop new military technologies. Such opportunities are also being pursued by the United States and others to varying degrees with four more-youthful and population-growing states in the region, India, Indonesia, Vietnam, and Malaysia. While each continues to avoid deep alliance entanglements, new forms of security cooperation are emerging, with the demographic opportunities each of these states may realize being another reason to consider deepened engagement.

These demographic trends have important yet diverging implications for ASEAN's role in Indo-Pacific security. Six of the nine states argued in chapter 5 to play an important and growing regional security role in the coming decades are ASEAN members. Whether those six member states remain willing to act collectively within the ASEAN framework or move toward more independent action will affect the future regional security landscape—and likely will be linked to demographic change underway within these states, especially whether they can achieve a significant demographic dividend in their current window of opportunity. As some gain economic power, they may shift their focus from regional to global concerns, trying to shape the global international order in addition to the regional order. If so, they may de-emphasize the importance of ASEAN, particularly when the institution already faces many difficulties—e.g., a different strategic posture toward great powers and internal problems such as the Myanmar coup and integrating new additional member Timor-Leste. Any of these challenges potentially could change internal political dynamics within ASEAN that may have broader regional security implications.

By contrast, if ASEAN unity can be maintained through defense and economic cooperation, ASEAN could become an even more pivotal player in the Indo-Pacific region because of its likely future trajectory of increasing military and economic capabilities of some ASEAN member states relative to other regional states due to population growth well-harnessed. With expanded material capabilities and their advantageous geopolitical locations, these member states may gain diplomatic power to negotiate with external great powers, including the United States and China, and may become more capable to collectively ensure regional autonomy in Southeast Asia. By contrast, if ASEAN fails to maintain its unity and the member states pursue their own political, economic, and security interests without deep coordination, it could become much weaker, assuming only a role of intraregional economic cooperation while the region becomes more divided by great power strategic competition.

Beyond the varying challenges and opportunities posed by regional demographic change for individual states, this change also contributes to security governance challenges in an increasingly multipolar region with a greater number of security actors developing advanced military capabilities. As yet, there is no single institution that maps onto the newer Indo-Pacific regional concept; instead, there is a mix of overlapping institutions. Demographic change over the next several decades will further alter the regional balance of power, likely toward even greater multipolarity. Economic growth, military spending, and number of soldiers able to be mobilized are all population-growth-related factors of relevance for the Indo-Pacific's security future, as introduced in chapter 1's discussion of existing scholarship on the linkage between population size and national power.

IMPLICATIONS OF DEMOGRAPHIC CHANGE IN THE INDO-PACIFIC FOR THE UNITED STATES

The creation of the U.S. alliance "spokes" of seven states—Japan, South Korea, Taiwan (now not a formal ally), the Philippines, Thailand, Australia, and New Zealand—took place within the contexts of growing populations and the Cold War, evolving over the years into the current era of strategic competition with China and different demographic challenges, though with several important Cold War–era legacies remaining—such as the divided Korean peninsula and standoff over China-Taiwan. The rapid aging of populations of most U.S. allies presents challenges for the United States and these allies as well as incentives to cooperate with a greater number of regional states, especially those with more favorable demographics. Moreover, the proliferation of gray-zone and other new security challenges also has forced the United States and its allies to adapt their cooperative security approaches. These two trends also arguably are related: As some aging states experience declining power resources, they seek to accomplish their aims using less resource-intensive objectives.

There are multiple, overlapping logics for why the United States should reinvigorate and reimagine its network of allies and partners in the Indo-Pacific. Several recent studies have made this case cogently.[6] Each of these studies, however, ignores another important justification for expanding and reimagining roles in the U.S. network of allies and partners: Not only is the system itself showing its age, but many of America's allies and partners themselves are rapidly aging, in some cases leading to a relative decline in their regional power and to competing future priorities in a broadening conception of their national security. For example, in her otherwise excellent study of the unique nature of America's alliances, Rapp-Hooper envisions a future where "allies increase their spending in defense and non-defense areas to make their contributions more symmetric"—ignoring that the gap between the United States and many of its allies will almost certainly *grow* in coming decades due to the different population demographics of these states.[7] Granted, in the *short term* we are in fact seeing even Asia's aging powers increase their defense spending as they transition into super-aged states, but this trajectory will become more difficult to sustain in the medium term. This demographic reality could prove challenging to the new Trump administration's desire to see allies contribute more resources to alliance roles.

Since the beginning of the post–Cold War period, and especially more recently in the context of China's resurgence regionally and globally, the United States and its now six regional treaty allies have come to recognize that the U.S. regional alliance system itself is showing its age—having been born into a regional environment over a half-century ago, when most regional states were poor and lacked regional security engagement. Despite that many of the principal security challenges from that time continue to be the security challenges of the region today, these challenges need to be approached differently due to the different regional balance of power, which in part is due to changed demographics. Moreover, U.S.-led security architecture—as well as supplemental institutions organized by U.S. allies and partners—needs to respond effectively to a much wider range of security concerns, particularly growing gray-zone challenges and new, disruptive military and civilian technologies.

There already had been some early post–Cold War shift to new partners and more networking among allies and partners, largely due to new geopolitical and security concerns, but also drawing on the relational demographic strengths of these new security partners. Although the choice of new partners may not initially have been demographically motivated, in fact all of them are states that have more youthful demographic futures than most current U.S. treaty allies. By 2000, the only exception to the below-replacement-level birth rate among the United States and its regional treaty allies was the Philippines, though even the Philippines's TFR was at a below-replacement-level of 1.92 in 2024. Conversely, the nontreaty ally U.S. security partners within the IP16 focus of this study continued to enjoy replacement fertility rates through 2000 (and in many cases beyond that), with the exception of Singapore (which offset below-replacement fertility with robust immigration).[8] As a result, the total populations of most of these states (apart from Singapore) are projected to grow through 2050.

By contrast, looking to 2050, only the Philippines among U.S. treaty allies is projected to continue to see robust population growth *and* a youthful population, while Australia and New Zealand are expected also to see robust population growth (26.2 percent and 14.9 percent, respectively) due to immigration, but also to see their aged 65+ populations exceed 20 percent of their total populations in 2031, bringing them into the super-aged category. Some U.S. allies and partners already struggle to fill military personnel quotas and to pay for new weapons systems as demand for greater spending on the elderly grows. This struggle will surely intensify in the late 2020s for important U.S. allies Japan and South Korea, and for security partner Taiwan—as discussed in chapter 3. In short, demographic shifts already underway—which will intensify—add urgency to revitalize the U.S. alliance and partner network in order to address strategic *and* demographic shifts washing across the region.

While the United States is expected to continue to be the world's pre-eminent military power for decades to come, its population size relative to the total world population (already quite small) and economic size relative to the total world economy are expected to continue to decline through 2050 (and beyond). Regionally in the Indo-Pacific, this is also the case. In addition, and to exacerbate the challenge, a similar trend is apparent with its core regional ally, Japan. At the same time, the numerous population-growing states of the region and continued projected economic growth even among rapidly aging states should make the Indo-Pacific a region of great possibilities and not a small amount of danger in the coming decades—a place where the United States will want to continue to exert influence to shape a future that will benefit its own national interests as well as the security of the region and the world. Thus, projected regional demographic shifts should incentivize deeper and broader cooperation with like-minded regional security partners, as already seen in the initial years of the trend toward super-aging of traditional U.S. allies and population growth among numerous middle powers in the region.

Future potential conflict among the most advanced states in the Indo-Pacific looks likely to employ fewer of the declining number of human beings available, relying more on autonomous systems, robotics, and artificial intelligence to counter threats. This shift is due more to technological change than demographics but also serves to underscore that security alliances and partnerships are not just about people but also about potential military bases and logistical outposts as well as diplomatic allies and technology co-innovators and developers. In addition, while human beings are still needed to design, produce, operate, and pay for even technologically advanced military systems, the challenge of paying for new weapons systems and technological alternatives to human labor is more complex than often simplistically framed in previous studies. As illuminated in earlier chapters, many rapidly aging states with shrinking workforces are expected to grow economically in the coming decades, often substantially, due to better utilization of existing workforces, including previously underutilized labor in the workforce, and to the development and adoption of labor-saving technologies. As one example from chapter 3, in Japan's first decade of total population shrinkage, the size of its workforce actually grew and overall productivity increased. Such continued economic growth may help to mitigate the effects of expected demands for greater spending on services related to older people in the future.

In contrast to the focus in the earlier post–Cold War period on the creation of larger-scale, institutionalized security architecture, more recently the United States and its major security allies and partners have focused on smaller, minilateral forms of cooperation to supplement the long-standing hub-and-spoke alliance network, such as institutionalized trilaterals (United States–Japan–Australia, United States–Japan–South Korea, the AUKUS grouping of Australia–United Kingdom–United States, etc.) as well as one prominent quadrilateral grouping, the Quad of Australia, India, Japan, and the United States. What characterize this more recent round of institutionalized cooperation are its ad hoc nature, breadth of issues, and smaller number of actors. This sort of minilateral cooperation also can be networked into cooperation among a larger number of actors over a specific issue area, such as supply chain resilience or cybersecurity. Notably, this is a strategy being employed not only by the United States but by U.S. allies and partners as well, who create their own minilateral groupings. Australia, Japan, and South Korea all have pursued such supplements to their core alliance with the United States.[9]

The growing diversity of demographic pathways for states in the Indo-Pacific with growing security concerns and priorities is likely to continue the recent trend toward minilateral approaches to security cooperation. While acknowledging that the system of U.S. alliances and partners is showing signs of its age, new regional security architecture is apparent, as well as new agendas for these aging allies to work together on developing the technology of the future.

New agreements with and among existing treaty allies not only have strengthened the core bilateral alliances but have facilitated greater regional security networking.[10] The United States has deepened its alliance cooperation with all five of its regional treaty allies apart from Thailand, which experienced a military coup in 2006 that has inhibited deepening military-to-military issues in particular. (Still, Thailand remains the cohost of the region's largest annual multilateral military exercise, Cobra Gold.)

Beyond deepening of relations with existing allies and promoting new relationships among existing allies, several additional regional states have emerged as especially important security partners for the United States and its regional allies. Five states in particular—India, Indonesia, Malaysia, Singapore, and Vietnam—have deepened their security partnerships not just with the United States but also with other U.S. allies in the region, as discussed in chapter 5.

The Biden administration (2021–2024) sought to build on efforts of its predecessors to better network formal treaty allies to develop greater efficiencies. This strategy, however, faced many practical political challenges at the outset, such as extremely tense Japan–South Korea relations and a legacy of former Philippine president Rodrigo Duterte's equivocations about U.S.-Philippines alliance cooperation. Japan-Australia security cooperation was an early bright spot, together with the expanded Quad conception that includes nontreaty ally India together with the United States. By 2023, additional efforts at expanded minilateral security cooperation among U.S. allies had begun to bear fruit, seeing an historic trilateral U.S.–Japan–South Korea summit outside Washington, DC, in August 2023 and increased security cooperation with the Philippines under President Ferdinand "Bongbong" Marcos Jr., culminating in a U.S.-Philippines-Japan trilateral meeting in Washington in April 2024.

In addition, cross-regional ally cooperation began to deepen among NATO and its four Indo-Pacific security partners, all U.S. treaty allies: Australia, Japan, New Zealand, and South Korea. AUKUS also networked U.S. allies cross-regionally. Building on experiences through the Covid-19 pandemic and increasing U.S.-China tensions, the Biden administration greatly expanded security cooperation into new areas not traditionally considered within the alliance frameworks, such as supply chain resiliency, protection of critical infrastructure and technologies, and enhanced cyberspace security in the commercial realm. Much of this cooperation could deepen further even with aging societies and shrinking populations, should there remain political will to do so.

This book concludes at a time of future political uncertainty in the United States, with the closely contested presidential election in November 2024 only beginning to take shape in a second Trump administration that began on January 20, 2025. Despite Trump's avowed goals of securing more contributions from U.S. allies and partners in both the economic and security realms, close relations with regional allies and partners in the Indo-Pacific will continue to be critical to the U.S. successfully managing this period of rapid aging and population shrinkage of both its traditional regional allies and its adversaries. Regional partners are hoping for increased constructive engagement but also fearful of a future U.S. disengagement with the region and are developing further hedging strategies as a result, illustrating once again that Asia's aging powers continue to be robust and powerful international actors despite their demographic challenges.

FINAL THOUGHTS: PREPARING FOR OUR SHARED DEMOGRAPHIC FUTURE

The conduct of Asia's aging powers will affect security developments globally, setting precedents for how conflict is addressed in this aging century. Future conflicts among the most advanced states in the Indo-Pacific are on track to employ fewer of the declining number of human beings available in those states, relying more on autonomous systems, robotics, and artificial intelligence to counter threats. This shift is due to technological innovation as well as demographics, but nevertheless, since human beings still need to design, produce, operate, and pay for such systems, demographic change itself is closely linked to new technological development and adoption.

To be clear, the nature of war is changing—posing significant challenges and dangers. The world's most advanced militaries are spending significant resources to be prepared, either to maintain their current strategic advantage or to use this next upcoming revolution in warfare to gain the upper hand. This book has described how the most advanced militaries of the Indo-Pacific are planning for this transition, showing where changing population demographics—in particular rapid aging that is leading to personnel shortages in some cases—are adding pressures for successful development and adoption of such technologies, and where, by contrast, this evolution in warfare is taking place on a parallel but separate track to demographic change.

Demography is not destiny, but it matters more to the security environment in the Indo-Pacific than most scholars and practitioners have considered to date. Some recall past instances in the twentieth century where demographic trends led to substantial attention to concerns that did not materialize. The demographic trends presented in this book are not contingencies but near-certain developments in the short-term futures of numerous regional states critical to the existing security landscape of the

Indo-Pacific. Demographic change has become an important *variable* in the Indo-Pacific security landscape that must be more systematically considered for effective policy planning and for more accurate scholarly conceptualizations and predictions.

Will the coming demographic change threaten the so-called Asian century? Will "Cool Japan" seem as cool or K-pop seem as youthful when a third of the respective populations of those states are over 65? Will China be seen as posing as much of a threat—economically and militarily—when its workforce is no longer hegemonic in global production networks and its retired citizens are clamoring for more social and economic support? Such matters call into question important writing from the previous decade that touted the coming "Asian century" or argued against it.[11] This study has sought to illustrate that answers to the implications of Asia's rapid aging are not as straightforward as they appear on the surface and have often been presented by the media and in some scholarly literature.

Rapid aging and population shrinking of Asia's current major powers is unlikely to shift the economic locus of the world away from the Indo-Pacific, but especially considering the likely growth of other Indo-Pacific states like India, Indonesia, and the Philippines, there is likely to be a change in the balance of power *within* the Indo-Pacific. The unprecedented demographic shifts underway—the fifth stage of worldwide demographic transition discussed in chapter 1—will undoubtedly help to shape the nature of Asia's future, including its future international interactions across the Indo-Pacific and with other states globally.

As seen throughout this volume, the role of government in managing demographic transitions is a critical factor, the variable of political capacity. Related to political capacity also is the issue of cultural or societal willingness to adopt new norms based on shifting demographic pressures. Previous chapters have illustrated areas where change is apparent (especially institutional innovation and technological development and adoption) and where societal willingness to change generally has lagged (especially related to immigration and the underutilization of women in the labor force and in the military). Intensifying demographic change also has been seen to create new domestic political dynamics as well as to challenge existing cultural norms. Looking ahead, demographic change in some states will soon lead to a shift of political power to new generations that espouse a different mix of political beliefs and worldviews, contributing both new opportunities and new challenges for future regional security cooperation and conflict management.

The rapid aging of Asia's existing great powers and differential growth and aging of other regional states will further intersect with the graying of conflict itself in Asia's security future. Asia's aging security trend therefore should be brought to the forefront when designing new security architecture and strategies for regional and global peace in the coming decades.

NOTES

INTRODUCTION

1. By default, all population statistics in this book are drawn from the United Nations Population Division's *World Population Prospects, 2024 Revision*, https://population .un.org/wpp/, using the "constant fertility" projection for states with total fertility rates of 2.0 or lower and the "medium variant" projection for states with total fertility rates over 2.0. Where other statistics are used, such as those from national governments or other international organizations, it will be noted.

2. On the concept of a "security dilemma," see Robert Jervis, "Cooperation Under the Security Dilemma," *World Politics* 30 (1978): 167–214. For an early post–Cold War application of this concept to East Asia, see Thomas J. Christensen, "China, the U.S.-Japan Alliance, and the Security Dilemma in East Asia," *International Security* 23, no. 4 (Spring 1999): 49–80. For a more recent application, see Stephen M. Walt, "Does Anyone Still Understand the 'Security Dilemma'?," *Foreign Policy* (July 26, 2022).

3. The idea of "dual graying" in the Indo-Pacific was first presented in article form in Andrew L. Oros, "The Rising Security Challenge of East Asia's 'Dual Graying': Implications for U.S.-led Security Architecture in the Indo-Pacific," *Asia Policy* (April 2023): 75–100.

4. For a recent and sophisticated examination of the linkage of aging and the likelihood interstate war, together with references to important past literature, see Deborah Jordan Brooks et al., "The Demographic Transition Theory of War: Why Young Societies Are Conflict Prone and Old Societies Are the Most Peaceful," *International Security* 43, no. 3 (Winter 2018/19): 53–95, examined in depth in chapter 1 of this book.

5. See chapter 1 for discussion of the stages of demographic change seen worldwide over time. Most of the states of Northeast Asia have entered the "late-stage rapid

aging" phase caused by below-replacement fertility rates and longer life expectancies.

6. Chapter 1 provides an overview of the stages of demographic transitions, drawing on work by Robert Lee, "The Demographic Transition: Three Centuries of Fundamental Change," *Journal of Economic Perspectives* 17, no. 4 (Fall 2003): 167–90.

7. OECD, *Health at a Glance: Asia/Pacific 2020*, p. 66, https://doi.org/10.1787/23054964. Note that for publications that use the spelling "ageing," it is maintained in this book in quotations and in publication titles.

8. These figures draw on a 2023 baseline. Detailed figures are presented in chapter 2, which also discusses the different conceptualizations of "Indo-Pacific" put forth by different states.

9. This lesson is in contrast to earlier predictions by Mark L. Haas, "A Geriatric Peace? The Future of U.S. Power in a World of Aging Populations," *International Security* 32, no. 1 (Summer 2007): 112–47; and Seongho Sheen, "Northeast Asia's Aging Population and Regional Security: 'Demographic Peace'?" *Asian Survey* 53, no. 2 (March/April 2013): 292–318.

10. A noncomprehensive list includes Abraham M. Denmark, *U.S. Strategy in the Asian Century: Empowering Allies and Partners* (New York: Columbia University Press, 2020); Mira Rapp-Hooper, *Shields of the Republic: The Triumph and Peril of America's Alliances* (Cambridge, MA: Harvard University Press, 2020); Andrew Yeo, *Asia's Regional Architecture: Alliances and Institutions in the Pacific Century* (Stanford, CA: Stanford University Press, 2019); Michael J. Green, ed, *Ironclad: Forging a New Future for America's Alliances* (Boulder, CO: Rowman & Littlefield, 2019); Scott W. Harold et al., *The Thickening Web of Asian Security Cooperation: Deepening Defense Ties Among U.S. Allies and Partners in the Indo-Pacific* (Santa Monica, CA: RAND, 2019); and Michael J. Green et al., *Federated Defense in Asia* (Washington, DC: Center for Strategic and International Studies, 2014).

11. They were Greece, Italy, Poland, Portugal, Romania, and Ukraine. "Countries Where Population Is Declining," *Euronews*, January 20, 2023, https://www.euronews.com/2023/01/17/the-countries-where-population-is-declining.

12. Jennifer D. Sciubba, *8 Billion and Counting: How Sex, Death, and Migration Shape Our World* (New York: Norton, 2022), 3, based on the UN's *World Population Prospects 2019*.

13. Brooks et al., "The Demographic Transition Theory of War," 83, citing *UN Population Prospects 2017*.

14. Brooks et al., 91.

15. Brooks et al., 41.

16. David Adam, "How Far Will Global Population Rise? Researchers Can't Agree," *Nature*, September 21, 2021.

17. Adam.

18. Darrell Bricker and John Ibbitson, *Empty Planet: The Shock of Global Population Decline* (New York: Broadway Books, 2019), 2.

19. Amitav Acharya, *ASEAN and Regional Order: Revisiting Security Community in Southeast Asia* (New York: Routledge, 2021), 116.

20. Russian opposition to the reframing is explained in Neil Melvin, "Russia and the Indo-Pacific Security Concept," *Emerging Insights* (London: Royal United Services Institute for Defense and Strategic Studies, May 2021).

21. I refer to these forty-six separate states and territories as the "IP28" due to the way that the United Nations Population Division groups smaller states and territories, which compresses the forty-six into twenty-eight sets of demographic data. A list of these states and territories, with important demographic data on each, is provided in chapter 2.

22. Nicholas Eberstadt, "With Great Demographics Comes Great Power: Why Population Will Drive Geopolitics," *Foreign Affairs* 98, no. 4 (July/August 2019): 146–57.

23. For a set of interactive maps that both illustrate visually and have pop-up boxes with detailed demographic data for thirty Indo-Pacific states/island groupings from 2020 to 2050, see Andrew L. Oros and Bailey Brya, "New Census Results Underscore Security Challenges of Aging in the Indo-Pacific," *Asia Dispatches*, June 3, 2021, https://www.wilsoncenter.org/blog-post/new-census-results-underscore-security-challenges-aging-indo-pacific.

24. Recent popular books include Bricker and Ibbitson, *Empty Planet*; Stephen Emmott, *Ten Billion* (New York: Vintage Books/Random House, 2013); Stuart Gietel-Basten, *The "Population Problem" in Pacific Asia* (Oxford: Oxford University Press, 2019); and Paul Morland, *The Human Tide: How Population Shaped the Modern World* (New York: Hachette Book Group, 2019).

25. For example, Daniel Susskind, *A World Without Work: Technology, Automation, and How We Should Respond* (New York: Metropolitan Books, 2020); McKinsey Global Institute, "AI, Automation, and the Future of Work: Ten Things to Solve For," *Briefing Note*, June 2018.

26. One of many advocacy books on the concept is Annie Lowrey, *Give People Money: How a Universal Basic Income Would End Poverty, Revolutionize Work, and Remake the World* (New York: Crown, 2018). For a shorter analysis, see Sita Nataraj Slavov, "A Framework for Understanding Universal Basic Income," *Tax Notes Federal* 170 (February 22, 2021), http://www.taxnotes.com.

27. James Feyrer, "Demographics and Productivity in Asia," in *Demographics and Innovation in the Asia-Pacific*, ed. Karen Eggleston, Joon-Shik Park, and Gi-Wook Shin (Stanford, CA: Walter H. Shorenstein Asia-Pacific Research Center, 2021), 36.

28. Feyrer, 37–38.

29. Two recent volumes are Hyun-Hoon Lee and Donghyun Park, *Post-Covid Asia: Deglobalization, Fourth Industrial Revolution, and Sustainable Development* (Singapore: World Scientific, 2021); and Mauro F. Guillen, *2030: How Today's Biggest Trends Will Collide and Reshape the Future of Everything* (New York: St. Martin's Press, 2020).

30. Joseph Grieco is among the prominent realists who advocate this position in "Anarchy and the Limits of Cooperation: A Realist Critique of the Newest Liberal Institutionalism," *International Organization* 42, no. 3 (Summer 1998): 485–507. For a robust exchange of different perspectives on this question, see Joseph Grieco, Robert Powell, and Duncan Snidal, "The Relative-Gains Problem for International Cooperation," *American Political Science Review* 87, no. 3 (September 1993): 727–43.

31. The literature on how shifts in power and/or persuasion among domestic actors can lead to different international priorities is vast. From a constructivist/securitization perspective, the so-called Copenhagen School is a good starting point, e.g., Barry Buzan, Ole Waever, and Jaap de Wilde, *Security: A New*

Framework for Analysis (London: Lynne Rienner, 1998); and Michael C. Williams, "Words, Images, Enemies: Securitization and International Politics," *International Studies Quarterly* 47 (December 2003): 511–31. From a liberal theory perspective, see Andrew Moravcsik, "Taking Preferences Seriously: A Liberal Theory of International Politics," *International Organization* 51, no. 4 (Autumn 1997): 513–53; and Robert O. Keohane and Helen V. Milner, eds., *Internationalization and Domestic Politics* (Cambridge: Cambridge University Press, 1996).

32. Sciubba, *8 Billion and Counting*, 76.

33. A summary of demographic data for 2022 presented by the UN Population division finds "global life expectancy at birth fell to 71.0 years in 2021, down from 72.8 in 2019, due mostly to the impact of the coronavirus disease (COVID-19) pandemic." However, "the impact on life expectancy has varied across regions and countries." For example, "the combined population of Australia and New Zealand gained 1.2 years due to lower mortality risks during the pandemic for some causes of death." United Nations Population Division, *World Population Prospects 2022: Summary of Results*, p. iii, https://www.un.org/development/desa/pd/sites/www.un.org.development.desa.pd/files/wpp2022_summary_of_results.pdf.

34. I would like to acknowledge and thank Dr. Keisuke Nakajima from Kobe University of Foreign Studies for codeveloping the initial dataset for our shared use in related projects based on the 2019 revision of *World Population Prospects*.

35. Sciubba, *8 Billion and Counting*, 205. Note that Sciubba's work is based on 2019 UN data, not the more recent 2022 revision utilized in this study.

36. Renata Kaczmarska and Masumi Ono, "Migration Trends and Families," *Policy Brief* 133 (May 2022), United Nations Department of Economic and Social Affairs, https://www.un-ilibrary.org/content/papers/10.18356/27081990-133.

37. United Nations, "The Number of International Migrants Reaches 272 Million, Continuing Upward Trend in All Regions of the World, Says UN," news release, September 17, 2019, https://www.un.org/tr/desa/number-international-migrants-reaches-272-million-continuing-upward-trend-all.

38. Sciubba, *8 Billion and Counting*, 21.

39. Pew Research Center, *Europe's Growing Muslim Population*, November 29, 2017, 7, quoted by Sciubba, 134.

40. Pew Research Center, 7.

41. United Nations Population Division, *World Urbanization Prospects: The 2018 Revision Key Facts*, 2, https://population.un.org/wup/.

42. As Jennifer Dabbs Sciubba summarizes in *Future Faces of War: Population and National Security* (Santa Barbara, CA: Praeger, 2011): "In practice, the belief that population equals power has led a wide range of states to institute pronatalist policies specifically to increase their standing in the international system, including Hitler, Mussolini, Stalin, and Ceausescu, and more recently Russia's Vladimir Putin and Iran's Mahmoud Ahmadinejad," 45.

43. Sciubba, 163.

44. Note, however, that some studies have argued that the number of "missing girls" in China may be much lower than indicated on census figures due to intentional nonreporting of female births that contravened the One-Child Policy. Simon Denyer, "Researchers May Have 'Found' Many of China's 30 Million Missing Girls," *Washington Post*, November 30, 2016.

45. Sharada Srinivasan and Shuzhou Li, "Unifying Perspectives on Scarce Women and Surplus Men," in *Scarce Women and Surplus Men in China and India: Macro Demographics Versus Local Dynamics*, ed. Sharada Srinivasan and Shuzhou Li (New York: Springer, 2018), 2.
46. Sciubba, *8 Billion and Counting*, 43, citing Quanbao Jiang et al., "Changes in Sex Ratio at Birth in China: A Decomposition by Birth Order," *Journal of Biosocial Science* 49, no. 6 (2017): 826–41.
47. Andrea Den Boer and Valerie Hudson. "Patrilineality, Son Preference, and Sex Selection in South Korea and Vietnam," *Population and Development Review* 43, no. 1 (March 2017): 119–47.
48. The World Health Organization maintains an interactive database of SRB at https://www.who.int/data/gho/indicator-metadata-registry/imr-details/sex-ratio-at-birth-(male-births-per-female-births).

1. RECONSIDERING THE DEMOGRAPHICS-NATIONAL SECURITY NEXUS THROUGH A TWENTY-FIRST-CENTURY INDO-PACIFIC LENS

1. Richard Jackson and Neil Howe, *The Graying of the Great Powers: Demography and Geopolitics in the 21st Century* (Washington, DC: Center for Strategic and International Studies, 2008), was one early and prominent such study. Others are introduced and discussed later in this chapter.
2. Brendan Taylor, *The Four Flashpoints: How Asia Goes to War* (Carlton, Australia: La Trobe University Press, 2018), summarizes four of these long-standing flashpoints.
3. Deborah Jordan Brooks et al., "The Demographic Transition Theory of War: Why Young Societies Are Conflict Prone and Old Societies Are the Most Peaceful," *International Security* 43, no. 3 (Winter 2018/19): 94.
4. One of many possible examples is Paul R. Ehrlich, *The Population Bomb* (New York: Ballentine Books, 1968).
5. Ronald Lee, "The Demographic Transition: Three Centuries of Fundamental Change," *Journal of Economic Perspectives* 17, no. 4 (Fall 2003): 167–90.
6. Brooks et al., "The Demographic Transition Theory of War," 56.
7. United Nations Population Division, *World Population Prospects 2024: Summary of Results*, 1.
8. As Goldstone writes in his demographically centered history of interstate conflict: "Throughout history, competition among leading nations has been affected by the relative size of national populations, and their rate of growth. ... Larger populations ... have often been credited with giving countries major advantages in international competition." Jack A. Goldstone, "Politics and Demography: A Summary of Critical Relationships," in *Political Demography: How Population Changes Are Reshaping International Security and National Politics*, ed. Jack A. Goldstone et al. (New York: Oxford University Press, 2012), 269.
9. Goldstone, 269, referring to Nazli Choucri and Robert North, *Nations in Conflict: National Growth and Industrial Violence* (San Francisco: Freeman, 1975).

10. Thomas Malthus, *An Essay on the Principle of Population* (London: Reeves and Turner, 1888).
11. A number of books have been written based on this theory related to rising U.S.–China strategic competition, such as Graham Allison, *Destined for War: Can America and China Escape Thucydides's Trap?* (Boston: Houghton Mifflin Harcourt, 2017). A more general work from this school of thought is John Mearsheimer, *The Tragedy of Great Power Politics* (New York: Norton, 2001).
12. Jennifer Dabbs Sciubba, *Future Faces of War: Population and National Security* (Santa Barbara, CA: Praeger, 2011), 7.
13. Sciubba writes in 2012: "Russia's demographic decline may drive the leadership to more aggressive behavior over the coming decade." Jennifer Dabbs Sciubba, "A New Framework for Aging and Security," in *Population Demography: How Population Changes Are Reshaping International Security and National Politics*, ed. Jack A. Goldstone et al. (New York: Oxford University Press, 2012), 76. Sciubba also quotes Dale Copeland's earlier work on Russia that argued that "the probability of major war increases when decline is seen as both deep and inevitable." Dale C. Copeland, *The Origins of Major War* (Ithaca, NY: Cornell University Press, 2000), 15.
14. Early work in this area was A.F.K. Organski et al., *Births, Deaths, and Taxes: The Demographic and Political Transitions* (Chicago: University of Chicago Press, 1984). These core ideas are further developed and adapted in Ronald L. Tammen et al., *Power Transitions: Strategies for the Twenty-First Century* (New York: Chatham House, 2000).
15. Timothy Beardson, *Ageing Giant: China's Looming Population Collapse* (Oxford: Signal Books, 2021), 211.
16. Sciubba, "A New Framework for Aging and Security," 70–71.
17. Sciubba, 71.
18. Sciubba, 71.
19. Jennifer D. Sciubba, *8 Billion and Counting: How Sex, Death, and Migration Shape Our World* (New York: Norton, 2022), 75, fig. 14, illustrates this variation.
20. Three important examples are Jackson and Howe, *The Graying of the Great Powers*; Goldstone et al., *Political Demography*; and Martin C. Libicki, Howard J. Shatz, and Julie E. Taylor, *Global Demographic Change and Its Implications for Military Power* (Santa Monica, CA: Rand Corporation, 2011).
21. Haas, "A Geriatric Peace?," 112–47.
22. Sciubba, *Future Faces of War*.
23. An early example is Nicholas Eberstadt, "Asia-Pacific Demographics in 2010–2040: Implications for Strategic Balance," in *Strategic Asia, 2010–11: Asian's Rising Power and America's Continued Purpose*, ed. Ashley J. Tellis et al. (Seattle: National Bureau of Asian Research, 2010).
24. Seongho Sheen, "Northeast Asia's Aging Population and Regional Security: 'Demographic Peace?'," *Asian Survey* 53, no. 2 (March/April 2013): 292–318.
25. Susan Yoshihara and Douglas Sylva, eds., *Population Decline and the Remaking of Great Power Politics* (Washington, DC: Potomac Books, 2011).
26. Brad Glosserman, *Peak Japan: The End of Great Ambitions* (Washington, DC: Georgetown University Press, 2019); Tom Phuong Le, *Japan's Aging Peace: Pacifism and Militarism in the 21st Century* (New York: Columbia University Press, 2021).

27. Five scholars provide a wide-ranging critique and praise of Le's work in a "book review roundtable" that appeared in *Asia Policy* (April 2023), 166–89.

28. Brooks et al., "The Demographic Transition Theory of War," 94.

29. North Korean life expectancy at birth, 73.6 in 2023, is projected to reach 75 in 2034. Russian life expectancy at birth, 73.2 in 2023, was projected to reach 75 in 2026 in 2022 UN Population Division data, but this milestone is not projected to be reached until 2033 in 2024 UN Population Division data, two years after the full-scale war with Ukraine commenced.

30. Brooks et al., "The Demographic Transition Theory of War," 68, 70.

31. Brooks et al., 62, 62 n. 12.

32. Brooks et al., 63.

33. Brooks et al., 71.

2. INDO-PACIFIC SECURITY CHALLENGES AND RAPID AGING

1. In addition to the 2022 *Indo-Pacific Strategy of the United States* (Washington, DC: The White House, 2022), see U.S. Department of Defense, "Indo-Pacific Strategy Report: Preparedness, Partnerships, and Promoting a Networked Region," June 1, 2019; and *National Security Strategy of the United States of America* (Washington, DC: The White House, 2017).

2. One estimate of U.S. war deaths from the Pacific Theater of World War II is 111, 606; from the Korean War, 36,574; and from the Vietnam War, 58,209. "Pacific War Encyclopedia Online," http://pwencycl.kgbudge.com/C/a/Casualties.html; and John W. Chambers, II, ed., *The Oxford Companion to American Military History* (Oxford: Oxford University Press, 1999), 849.

3. Like China, Russia actively opposes the reframing of the region as the "Indo-Pacific," as explained in Neil Melvin, "Russia and the Indo-Pacific Security Concept," in *Emerging Insights* (London: Royal United Services Institute for Defense and Strategic Studies, May 2021).

4. Many scholars have examined the introduction and nuances of the term "Indo-Pacific," including Akiko Fukushima, "From the Asia-Pacific to the Indo-Pacific: Drivers and Hurdles," *Policy Perspective*, Canada Global Affairs Institute (March 2021); and Timothy Doyle and Dennis Rumley, *The Rise and Return of the Indo-Pacific* (Oxford: Oxford University Press, 2019).

5. "Far East" was the regional term typically used to describe the region in U.S. government planning documents from the Second World War era through the early Cold War era, when East Asia became more routinely used until the end of the Cold War. In the post–Cold War era, "Asia-Pacific" become the most oft-used term—until the mid-2010s, when U.S. allies Japan and Australia introduced the term "Indo-Pacific" into their regional strategy documents.

6. "History of the United States Indo-Pacific Command," https://www.pacom.mil /About-USINDOPACOM/History/ (accessed July 8, 2021).

7. These figures are calculated from SIPRI (2021) data in local currency. Table 3.2 in chapter 3 also provides the figures in constant 2019 U.S. dollars (USD), which show a smaller percentage increase.

8. Figures calculated from SIPRI (2021) data in constant 2019 USD.

9. Figures calculated from SIPRI (2021) data in local currency. Table 3.2 also provides the figures in constant 2019 USD, which show a smaller percentage increase. China's estimated defense spending is adjusted by SIPRI researchers.

10. Abraham M. Denmark, *U.S. Strategy in the Asian Century: Empowering Allies and Partners* (New York: Columbia University Press, 2020), 92.

11. The nine countries, in descending order of the projected population increase, are India, Nigeria, Pakistan, the Democratic Republic of the Congo, Ethiopia, Tanzania, Indonesia, Egypt, and the United States. "Growing at a slower pace, world population is expected to reach 9.7 billion in 2050 and could peak at nearly 11 billion around 2100." United Nations Department of Economic and Social Affairs News, June 17, 2019, https://www.un.org/development/desa/en/news/population/world-population-prospects-2019.html.

12. Five Pacific islands have entered into so-called free association agreements with the United States or New Zealand to provide for their external security; another seven are territories of the United States, New Zealand, or France.

13. The UN Population Bureau includes the following twenty-one states and territories within three island groupings: Melanesia (five): Fiji, New Caledonia, Papua New Guinea, Solomon Islands, Vanuatu; Micronesia (seven): Guam, Kiribati, Marshall Islands, Fed. States of Micronesia, Nauru, Northern Mariana Islands, Palau; and Polynesia (nine): American Samoa, Cook Islands, French Polynesia, Niue, Samoa, Tokelau, Tonga, Tuvalu, Wallis, and Futuna Islands.

14. In addition to the six showing a reduced population size from 2020 versus 2050 in table 2.1, North Korea and Singapore also are projected to be experiencing total population size shrinkage by 2050, though their 2050 total number is projected to be larger than their 2020 population.

15. Indian Ocean Rim Association members, with states not included in this study in italics: Australia, Bangladesh, *Union of Comoros (French Republic)*, India, Indonesia, *Iran, Kenya, Madagascar*, Malaysia, *Maldives, Mauritius, Mozambique, Oman, Seychelles*, Singapore, *Somalia, South Africa*, Sri Lanka, *Tanzania*, Thailand, *United Arab Emirates*, and *Yemen*. https://www.iora.int/en.

16. For a set of interactive maps that both illustrate visually and provide detailed data in pop-up boxes on projected changes in population sizes in each of the IP16 and OIP12 territories from 2020 to 2050, see Andrew L. Oros and Bailey Brya, "New Census Results Underscore Security Challenges of Aging in the Indo-Pacific," *Asia Dispatches*, June 3, 2021, https://www.wilsoncenter.org/blog-post/new-census-results-underscore-security-challenges-aging-indo-pacific.

17. Derek Grossman et al., *America's Pacific Island Allies: The Freely Associated States and Chinese Influence* (Santa Monica, CA: RAND, 2019).

18. On the growing urgency of this concern, see Oriana Skylar Mastro, "The Taiwan Temptation: Why Beijing Might Resort to Force," *Foreign Affairs* 100, no. 4 (July/August 2021): 58–67. Russia's invasion of Ukraine in early 2022 has increased concern in many quarters about a possible invasion of Taiwan by China.

19. "CIA Estimates Taiwan's Fertility Rate to Be World's Lowest," *Kyodo News*, April 21, 2021.

20. Twenty Indian soldiers were reported to have died. In addition, the deaths of four Chinese soldiers were acknowledged only eight months after the incident.

Archana Chaudhury, "Why Chinese and Indian Troops Clash in the Himalayas," *Washington Post*, July 2, 2021.

21. The Center for Strategic and International Studies (CSIS) in Washington, DC, has an innovative program, the Asia Maritime Transparency Initiative, that tracks China's expanding territorial claims in the region. It includes many interactive maps, available at https://amti.csis.org/.

22. On the former, so-called bare branches phenomenon, see Valerie Hudson and Andrea Den Boer, *Bare Branches: The Security Implications of Asia's Surplus Male Population* (Cambridge, MA: MIT Press, 2004). On the declining Uyghur birth rate, see "China's Repression of Uyghurs Is Not Only Cultural, but Also Physical, a New Report Shows," *Washington Post*, May 16, 2021.

23. Eleanor Albert, "North Korea's Military Capabilities," *CFR Backgrounder* (New York: Council on Foreign Relations), November 16, 2020, https://www.cfr.org/backgrounder/north-koreas-military-capabilities.

24. Albert.

25. It should be emphasized, though, that there are more concerns about the reliability of population data on North Korea than on other countries in this region, though the UN Population Division and other demographic entities attempt to correct data for apparent reporting anomalies.

26. For an overview of the regional piracy issue, see the collection of essays in Ted Biggs and Carolin Liss, eds., *Piracy in Southeast Asia: Trends, Hot Spots and Responses* (New York: Routledge, 2016).

27. Michael Green provides a detailed account of the U.S. approach in *By More than Providence: Grand Strategy and American Power in the Asia Pacific Since 1783* (New York: Columbia University Press, 2017).

28. The Inter-American Treaty of Reciprocal Assistance (Rio Treaty, first signed in 1947) and the North Atlantic Treaty Organization (NATO, first signed in 1949) are the other two. https://www.defenseone.com/ideas/2017/02/mapped-americas-collective-defense-agreements/135114/.

29. Victor Cha, among others, examines the origins of this system in *Powerplay: The Origins of the American Alliance System in Asia* (Princeton, NJ: Princeton University Press, 2016).

30. Mira Rapp-Hooper, *Shields of the Republic: The Triumph and Peril of America's Alliances* (Cambridge, MA: Harvard University Press, 2020), 5.

31. Denmark, *U.S. Strategy in the Asian Century*, 87.

32. U.S. Department of State, "Fact Sheet: Major Non-NATO Ally Status," January 20, 2021, https://www.state.gov/major-non-nato-ally-status/.

33. For a broad overview of this deepening over time, see James L. Schoff, *Uncommon Alliance for the Common Good: The United States and Japan After the Cold War* (Washington, DC: Carnegie Endowment for International Peace, 2017). For an authoritative report on an ambitious future agenda for the alliance, see "The US-Japan Alliance in 2020: An Equal Alliance with a Global Agenda" (Washington, DC: Center for Strategic and International Studies, December 2020).

34. For an overview, see Scott A. Snyder, *South Korea at the Crossroads: Autonomy and Alliance in an Era of Rival Powers* (New York: Columbia University Press, 2018). For a provocative view of potential deepening in an era of political polarization

in South Korea, see "The Future of the US-ROK Alliance" (Washington, DC: Atlantic Council, February 2021).

35. Rapp-Hooper, *Shields of the Republic*, 6.
36. Andrew Yeo, *Asia's Regional Architecture: Alliances and Institutions in the Pacific Century* (Stanford, CA: Stanford University Press, 2019), chaps. 3 and 4, provides a contemporary overview of this early period.
37. Yeo offers an excellent overview of this evolution up through 2019 in *Asia's Regional Architecture*. Substantial media reporting has been devoted to recent developments with AUKUS and the Quad.
38. Richard Fontaine, "Networking Alliances and Deepening Minilateral Security Cooperation in the Indo-Pacific," in *Ironclad: Forging a New Future for America's Alliances*, ed. Michael J. Green (Boulder, CO: Rowman & Littlefield, 2019), 156.
39. For a discussion of the Australian and Japanese cases, see Fontaine. For the South Korea case, see Andrew Yeo, "South Korea's New Southern Policy and the United States Indo-Pacific Strategy: Implications for the U.S.-ROK Alliance," Mansfield Foundation Working Paper, July 2021.
40. Nicholas Eberstadt, ed., *China's Changing Family Structure: Dimensions and Implications* (Washington, D.C.: American Enterprise Institute, 2019).

3. NORTHEAST ASIA'S RAPIDLY AGING DEMOCRACIES

1. Ronald L. Tammen et al., *Power Transitions: Strategies for the Twenty-First Century* (New York: Chatham House, 2000).
2. I expand on these changes and broader argument in Oros, *Japan's Security Renaissance: New Policies and Politics for the 21st Century* (New York: Columbia University Press, 2017), chaps. 4 and 5.
3. Tom Le develops this imagery related to aging in his introduction to *Japan's Aging Peace: Pacifism and Militarism in the 21st Century* (New York: Columbia University Press, 2021).
4. CNS North Korea Missile Test Database, https://www.nti.org/analysis/articles/cns -north-korea-missile-test-database/. The database records flight tests of all missiles launched by North Korea capable of delivering a payload of at least 500 kilograms (1102.31 pounds) a distance of at least 300 kilometers (186.4 miles). 2024 data is through November 4.
5. Japan Cabinet Secretariat, National Security Strategy (December 2022), provisional English translation, p. 35, http://www.cas.go.jp/jp/siryou/131217anzenhoshou/nss -e.pdf.
6. Deborah Jordan Brooks et al., "The Demographic Transition Theory of War: Why Young Societies Are Conflict Prone and Old Societies Are the Most Peaceful," *International Security* 43, no. 3 (Winter 2018/19): 53–95.
7. Japan Cabinet Secretariat, *National Security Strategy*, December 2022, 2.
8. World Bank data (2023) as summarized at https://www.theglobaleconomy.com /Japan/gdp_share/.
9. Yusuke Ishihara, "Japan's Grand Strategy as a Declining Power," *East Asia Forum*, June 18, 2023, https://www.eastasiaforum.org/2023/06/18/japans-grand-strategy-as -a-declining-power/.

10. Jennifer Dabbs Sciubba was an exception in expressing optimism about Japan's ability to adapt despite challenges of aging, illustrating the adage that necessity is the mother of invention thusly: "Long aware that they would face a shortage of care workers for their burgeoning elderly population, Japan's government and industry have teamed to develop a line of robots that provide nursing and other health care services. They have washing machines to bathe the elderly, robotic cats that monitor vital signs as the owner 'pets' them, and even robotic nurses with videoconferencing capabilities so that family members can 'drop in.' ... Japan has turned a population trend that most term an economic disaster into an economic opportunity, demonstrating that aging brings both challenges and opportunities." Sciubba, "A New Framework for Aging and Security," in *Political Demography: How Population Changes Are Reshaping International Security and National Politics*, ed. Jack A. Goldstone et al. (New York: Oxford University Press, 2012), 63–64.
11. Brad Glosserman, *Peak Japan: The End of Great Ambitions* (Washington, DC: Georgetown University Press, 2019), 216.
12. Oros, *Japan's Security Renaissance*.
13. Japan Cabinet Secretariat, *National Security Strategy*, December 17, 2013, http://www.cas.go.jp/jp/siryou/131217anzenhoshou/nss-e.pdf.
14. Glosserman, *Peak Japan*, 2.
15. SIPRI (2023), based on spending in Japanese yen.
16. Tom Phuong Le, *Japan's Aging Peace: Pacifism and Militarism in the Twenty-First Century* (New York: Columbia University Press, 2021), 207–14.
17. Le, 4.
18. Although widely repeated, technically the rise in spending is not "double" because some prior spending is recategorized to count toward the new 2 percent target. Adam Liff explains this accounting plan in "No, Japan Is Not Planning to 'Double Its Defense budget,'" May 22, 2023, https://www.brookings.edu/articles/no-japan-is-not-planning-to-double-its-defense-budget/.
19. SIPRI (2023); by this measure, calculated in current USD, Japan's defense spending peaked in 2011.
20. Le, *Japan's Aging Peace*, 127, fig. 4.6, illustrates that around 44 percent of Japan's expenditures on defense were on "personnel and provisions expenses."
21. Tomoyuki Sasaki, *Japan's Postwar Military and Civil Society* (London: Bloomsbury Academic, 2017).
22. Le, *Japan's Aging Peace*, 82.
23. Corey John Wallace, "The Evolution of the Japanese Strategic Imagination and Generation Change: A Generationally-Focused Analysis of Public and Elite Attitudes towards War and Peace in Japan," PhD diss., University of Auckland, 2014.
24. Japan Cabinet Office, "Public Opinion Survey on Self-Defense Forces and Defense Issues" (in Japanese), November 2022, https://survey.gov-online.go.jp/r04/r04-bouei/2.html#midashi16.
25. *Sankei Shimbun*, "39.6% 'Yes' to Defense Tax Increase, Up 10 Points from the Previous Month" (in Japanese), February 20, 2023.
26. In one poll, conducted in January 2023 by the right-of-center *Yomiuri* newspaper, 43 percent agreed with the plan to increase defense spending, with 49 percent opposed and 8 percent not answering; when asked if they would support a tax

increase for this additional spending, however, support plummeted to just 28 percent, with 63 percent opposed and 8 percent not answering. *Yomiuri Shimbun*, "January 2023 Telephone Nationwide Poll Questions and Answers" (in Japanese), January 1, 2023.

27. Prime Minister's Office of Japan, "Policy Speech by Prime Minister KISHIDA Fumio to the 211th Session of the Diet," January 23, 2023, https://japan.kantei.go.jp/101_kishida/statement/202301/_00012.html.

28. *Defense of Japan* (2023), 236, https://www.mod.go.jp/j/press/wp/wp2023/pdf/R05shiryo.pdf.

29. Data from FY2019 to FY2023 were provided to the author via email communication from Japan's Ministry of Defense, July 31, 2024. As communicated, the recruiting target for FY2022 was 17,846, while 11,758 were recruited (65.9 percent of the target); for FY2023, the target was 19,598, while 9,959 were recruited (50.8 percent of the target).

30. Japan Ministry of Defense, *National Defense Strategy*, December 28, 2022, 36, https://www.mod.go.jp/j/approach/agenda/guideline/strategy/pdf/strategy_en.pdf.

31. Le, *Japan's Aging Peace*, 96; NATO, "Annual Summary of the National Reports 2020," https://www.nato.int/nato_static_fl2014/assets/pdf/2023/6/pdf/2020-summary-national-reports.pdf; Le, *Japan's Aging Peace*, 96. Data from FY2022 and FY2023 were provided via email communication from Japan's Ministry of Defense, July 31, 2024.

32. U.S. Department of Defense, "Department of Defense Releases Annual Demographics Report—Upward Trend in Number of Women Serving Continues," December 14, 2022, https://www.defense.gov/News/Releases/Release/Article/3246268/department-of-defense-releases-annual-demographics-report-upward-trend-in-numbe/.

33. Japan Ministry of Defense, *Defense Buildup Program*, December 16, 2022, 41–45.

34. Le, *Japan's Aging Peace*, 10.

35. Le, 109, explains the latter challenges.

36. Statistics Bureau of Japan, "Unemployment Rate [by age group]," October 1, 2024, https://www.stat.go.jp/english/data/roudou/lngindex.html.

37. Japan Ministry of Defense, *National Defense Strategy*, December 28, 2022, 33–35. In addition, the May/June 2023 issue of *Japan Spotlight* includes several articles that describe challenges in Japan's labor market with relevance to defense production. https://www.jef.or.jp/jspotlight/backnumber/detail/249/.

38. Ministry of Internal Affairs and Communications (Japan), *Statistical Handbook of Japan 2022*, 125, https://www.stat.go.jp/english/data/handbook/pdf/2022all.pdf.

39. E-Stat Japan, "Statistics on Foreign Residents for December 2022" (in Japanese), July 7, 2023, https://www.e-stat.go.jp/.

40. Toshihiro Menju, "Japan's Sharply Declining Population and Immigration Policy," *Japan Spotlight* (May/June 2023), https://www.jef.or.jp/journal/pdf/249th_Cover_Story_04.pdf.

41. Institute of Energy Economics Japan, *IIEJ Outlook 2023*, https://eneken.ieej.or.jp/data/10974.pdf.

42. International Monetary Fund, *World Economic Outlook Database*, April 2023, http://www.imf.org.

43. Japan Cabinet Secretariat, *National Security Strategy*, December 2022, 2.

44. Yamaguchi Shinji et al., eds., "NIDS China Security Report 2023: China's Quest for Control of the Cognitive Domain and Gray Zone Situations," National Institute for Defense Studies, 2022.

45. Japan Cabinet Secretariat, *National Security Strategy*, 2.

46. Paul Midford emphasizes Japan's increased need for resources for territorial defense in *The Senkaku Island Confrontation and the Transformation of Japan's Defense* (New York: Palgrave Pivot, 2025). Ishihara writes in "Japan's Grand Strategy as a Declining Power": "Unlike during Japan's economic ascent, no members of the Japanese government are entertaining departing from the defence treaty with the United States. Instead they emphasize how Japan's eroding self-restraints will bring Tokyo and Washington even closer together as military allies. A weakened Japan cannot imagine any other option but to embrace the United States, especially in dealing with China's rising power."

47. See, for example, Scott W. Harold et al., "U.S.-Japan Alliance Conference: Meeting the Challenge of Amphibious Operations," RAND Corporation, 2018, https://doi.org/10.7249/CF387.

48. For an overview of the deepened integration into shared roles and missions between Japanese and U.S. military forces, see Sheila Smith, *Japan Rearmed: The Politics of Military Power* (Cambridge, MA: Harvard University Press, 2019).

49. Japan Cabinet Secretariat, *National Security Strategy*, December 2022, 13.

50. Le, in *Japan's Aging Peace*, stresses the continued resilience of Japan's antimilitarist culture, as does Oros in *Japan's Security Renaissance*. Midford, in *The Senkaku Island Confrontation and the Transformation of Japan's Defense*, argues forcefully that Japan's recent defense enhancements are motivated by concerns about territorial defense. Adam P. Liff warns about Japan's ambivalence over participating in a Taiwan contingency in "Beyond Territorial Defense? The U.S.-Japan and U.S.-ROK Alliances and a 'Taiwan Strait Contingency,'" *Pacific Review* (2024): 1–30, https://doi.org/10.1080/09512748.2024.2400277.

51. Paul Midford and Wilhelm Vosse, eds., *New Directions in Japan's Security* (London: Routledge, 2020), includes several chapters that describe this expanded cooperation on a country-by-country basis.

52. Jeffrey W. Hornung, *Allies Growing Closer: Japan-Europe Security Ties in the Age of Strategic Competition* (Santa Monica, CA: RAND, 2020); and Elena Atanassova-Cornelis et al., eds., *Alliances in Asia and Europe: The Evolving Indo-Pacific Strategic Context and Inter-Regional Alignments* (London: Routledge, 2024).

53. Louisa Brooke-Holland, "UK-Japan Defence Agreement 2023," *Research Briefing #9704*, January 13, 2023 (House of Commons Library), https://researchbriefings.files.parliament.uk/documents/CBP-9704/CBP-9704.pdf; Mari Yamaguchi, "Japan, UK, Italy Push Joint Fighter Jet Development by 2035," March 16, 2023, https://apnews.com/article/japan-uk-italy-fighter-jet-2035-3ed647eee772fa1e622479fffda49801.

54. NATO, "Individually Tailored Partnership Programme Between NATO and Japan for 2023–2026," July 12, 2023, https://www.nato.int/cps/en/natohq/official_texts_217797.htm.

55. "The Sun Sets Over the NATO Liaison Office in the Land of the Rising Sun," August 3, 2023, https://europeanvalues.cz/en/the-sun-sets-over-the-nato-liaison-office-in-the-land-of-the-rising-sun/.

56. Bruce W. Bennett, "South Korea: Capable Now, Questions for the Future," in *A Look at Hard Power: Assessing the Defense Capabilities of Key US Allies and Security Partners, Second Edition*, ed. Gary J. Schmitt (Carlisle, PA: US Army War College, 2020), 290.

57. Joori Roh, "With Plans to Show Women More Respect, South Korea Tries to Fix Its Demographic Crisis," *Japan Times*, January 4, 2019.

58. Korean Institute of Child Care and Education, "President Yoon's Government Policies for Enhancing Child-Rearing," *KICCE Policy Brief 23* (October 2022), https://kicce.re.kr; "Yoon Declares 'Demographic National Emergency,' Vows All-Out Efforts to Tackle Low Birthrate," *Korea Times*, June 19, 2024.

59. OECD, "Poverty Rate," https://www.oecd.org/en/data/indicators/poverty-rate.html.

60. Sook Jong Lee, "Generational Divides and the Future of South Korean Democracy," Carnegie Endowment for International Peace, June 29, 2021.

61. Elizabeth Hervey Stephen, *South Korea's Demographic Dividends* (Washington, DC: Center for Strategic and International Studies), 67.

62. Stephen, 79.

63. Katrin Park, "South Korea Is No Country for Young People," *Foreign Policy*, November 2, 2021.

64. Chang May Choon, "36-year-old Elected Youngest Leader of South Korea's Main Opposition Party in Sign of Generational Shift," *Straits Times*, June 12, 2021.

65. Erin Aeran Chung, "How South Korean Demographics Are Affecting Immigration and Social Change," Carnegie Endowment for International Peace, June 29, 2021; Stephen, *South Korea's Demographic Dividend*, 50–51.

66. Erin Aeran Chung, *Immigrant Incorporation in East Asian Democracies* (Cambridge: Cambridge University Press, 2020).

67. Katharine H. S. Moon, "South Korea's Demographic Changes and Their Political Impact," *East Asia Policy Paper 6* (October) (Washington, DC: Brookings Institution, 2015), 5.

68. Bennett, "South Korea," 255.

69. Bennett, 258–62.

70. Yonhap News Agency, "N. Korea Likely Hacked S. Korea Cyber Command: Military," December 6, 2016, https://en.yna.co.kr/view/AEN20161205010451315.

71. Alex Catellier and Markus Garlauskas, "Debunking the Korean Peninsula 'Arms Race': What's Behind South Korea's Military Force Development," *On Korea* 16 (2023): 15; Bennett, "South Korea," 263–64.

72. For a detailed discussion of weaknesses in South Korea defense capabilities, see Bennett, "South Korea," 267–84.

73. Under the Moon administration, increases in military personnel compensation also was one of the largest budget items. Specific figures are provided in Si-young Choi, "Korea Urged to Pay Conscripts Better," *Korea Herald*, January 12, 2020.

74. David Shin and Young-Gon Kim, "Military Recruitment Issues in the ROK Armed Forces and Policy Alternatives: Focusing on the Army Non-Commissioned Officer," *Korean Journal of Defense Analysis* 31, no. 3 (September 2019): 458.

75. SIPRI (2023).

76. Ministry of National Defense (Korea), *2018 Defense White Paper*, 94.

77. Troy Strangarone, "South Korea's Demographic Decline and National Security," ms., October 27, 2021, 11.
78. Kathryn Botto, "How Unification Would Affect the Demographics of the Korean Peninsula," Carnegie Endowment for International Peace, June 29, 2021.
79. Catellier and Garlauskas, "Debunking the Korean Peninsula 'Arms Race,'" provide a broader overview, including making the point that "decrease manpower required to operate key military assets without reducing deterrence or capabilities" is one of these goals (p. 11).
80. See, for example, Brendan Balestrieri and Won-Geun Koo, "South Korea Needs a Wake-Up Call on Its Reserve Forces," *War on the Rocks*, July 26, 2022, for the opportunities and challenges in this area.
81. Yonhap News Agency, "Army Chief Stresses Drive for Tech-Based Innovation," April 3, 2019. The *2018 Defense White Paper*, 50–51, 147, also sets out these goals.
82. Kyle Ferrier, "Can Emerging Technologies Cushion South Korea's Demographic Downturn?," Carnegie Endowment for International Peace, June 29, 2021.
83. Institute of Energy Economics Japan, *IIEJ Outlook 2023*, https://eneken.ieej.or.jp/data/10974.pdf.
84. OECD, "Pension Spending," https://www.oecd.org/en/data/indicators/pension-spending.html.
85. Stephen, *South Korea's Demographic Dividend*, 71.
86. Ronald Lee and Andrew Mason, "What Is the Demographic Dividend?," *Finance and Development* 43, no. 3 (September 2006): 16–17, https://www.imf.org/external/pubs/ft/fandd/2006/09/basics.htm.
87. Lee and Mason, 17.
88. Stephen examines these arguments in greater depth in *South Korea's Demographic Dividends*, 12–16.
89. Stephen, 92.
90. Work discussed by Stephen, 15, includes William Scarth, "Population Aging, Productivity and Living Standards," in *The Review of Economic Performance and Social Progress: Towards a Social Understanding of Productivity*, ed. Andrew Sharpe et al. (Montreal, Institute for Research on Public Policy, 2002); and David M. Cutler et al., "An Aging Society: Opportunity or Challenge?," *Brookings Papers on Economic Activity* (Washington, DC: Brookings Institution, 1990).
91. International Monetary Fund, World Economic Outlook Database (April 2023).
92. Institute of Energy Economics Japan, *IIEJ Outlook 2023*, https://eneken.ieej.or.jp/data/10974.pdf.
93. Institute of Energy Economics Japan.
94. Moon, "South Korea's Demographic Changes."
95. Chung Min Lee, "South Korea's Military Needs Bold Reforms to Overcome a Shrinking Population," Carnegie Endowment for International Peace, June 29, 2021.
96. Lee.
97. Kijeong Nam, "Aging Population, Decreasing Birthrate and National Security: Searching for the Possibility of Cooperation Between Japan and Korea," in *Japan Study as a Public Good in Asia*, ed. L. Huang et al., 17–27 (Singapore: Springer Nature Singapore Pte, 2019).

98. As just one of many possible examples: "On January 2, 2019, Chairman Xi declared on Chinese state television that the annexation of Taiwan was necessary for the fulfillment of China's 'great rejuvenation.' He stated that he would not renounce the use of force and said that 'Taiwan independence will lead to a dead end.'" Ian Easton et al., *Watching Over the Taiwan Strait: The Role of Unmanned Aerial Vehicles in Taiwan's Defense Strategy* (Washington, DC: Project 2049 Institute, 2020).
99. U.S. Congress, Taiwan Relations Act, January 1, 1979, https://www.ait.org.tw/taiwan-relations-act-public-law-96-8-22-u-s-c-3301-et-seq/.
100. Kari Lindberg and Cindy Wang, "A Far-Flung Taiwan Island Risks Triggering a US-China Clash," *Bloomberg*, June 16, 2021.
101. Ministry of National Defense (ROC), *2019 National Defense Report*, 46, http://www.ustaiwandefense.com/tdnswp/wp-content/uploads/2020/02/Taiwan-National-Defense-Report-2019.pdf.
102. Ministry of National Defense (ROC), *2017 Quadrennial Defense Review*, 9–10.
103. The Legislative Yuan passed an amendment to the Act of Military Service System on December 13, 2011, stipulating that males of conscription age must still undergo a mandatory four-month military training even after the country's military switches to full voluntary enlistment. John Pike, "Military Personnel," Global Security.org. December 27, 2018, https://www.globalsecurity.org/military/world/taiwan/personnel.htm.
104. SIPRI (2024).
105. Sherry Hsiao, "KMT Suggests Agency to Tackle Birthrate," *Taipei Times*, April 2, 2021.
106. Flor Wang and Tzi-yu Pan, "Taiwan Set to Become Super-Aged by 2025: NDC," *Focus Taiwan*, August 18, 2020, https://focustaiwan.tw/society/202008180025.
107. IISS, *Military Balance 2023*, 291.
108. John Dotson, "Taiwan Initiates Its New One-Year Military Conscription Program," *Global Taiwan Brief* 9, no. 3 (February 7, 2024), https://globaltaiwan.org/2024/02/taiwan-initiates-its-new-one-year-military-conscription-program/.
109. Whitney McNamara, *Perspectives on Taiwan: Insights from the 2017 Taiwan-U.S. Policy Program*, ed. Bonnie S. Glaser and Matthew P. Funaiole (Center for Strategic and International Studies, 2018), 48, https://doi.org/10.2307/resrep22433.13.
110. David Pierson and Ralph Jennings, "To Stop a Chinese Invasion, Taiwan Needs a Stronger Armyk" *Los Angeles Times*, October 6, 2020, https://www.latimes.com/world-nation/story/2020-10-06/china-taiwan-military-service.
111. Drew Thompson, "Winning the Fight Taiwan Cannot Afford to Lose," *Strategic Forum*, no. 310 (October 2021) (Washington, DC: Institute for National Strategic Studies, National Defense University), 9.
112. Dee Wu, "Taiwan's All-Volunteer Force and Military Transformation" (Arlington, VA: Project 2049 Institute, December 2017), 2–3, https://www.ciaonet.org/record/54842.
113. Ministry of National Defense (ROC), *2019 National Defense Report*, 120.
114. McNamara, *Perspectives on Taiwan*, 49.
115. Vanessa Molter provides further detail on the costs involved in the transition to an all-volunteer force, writing that "to achieve a successful transition to the All-Volunteer Force (AVF), Taiwan's Military National Defense (MND) has raised

salaries for military personnel, through both an increase in base pay as well as the introduction of a system with attractive bonuses and benefits. … For example, the base salary for a voluntary enlisted Private 1 (requires secondary education degree) is now NT $34,340, exceeding salary expectations of even new university graduates at NT $33,053." Vanessa Molter, "Taiwan's Transition to All-Volunteer Force—a Policy Assessment," *Defense Security Brief 8*, no. 3 (October 2019): 48–49, https://indsr.org.tw/en.

116. John Pike, "Military Personnel," Global Security.org, December 27, 2018, https://www.globalsecurity.org/military/world/taiwan/personnel.htm.

117. As McNamara explains: "The MND has tried to glamorize the profession through unorthodox means, currently supporting the drama series *The Best Choice*, a military-themed romance drama, in an effort to energize young people about the military." McNamara, *Perspectives on Taiwan*, 50.

118. Ministry of National Defense (ROC), *2017 Quadrennial Defense Review* (Taipei: Ministry of National Defense, 2017), 60.

119. Ian Easton et al., *Transformation of Taiwan's Reserve Force* (Santa Monica: RAND, 2017). www.rand.org/pubs/research_reports/RR1757.html.

120. Thompson, "Winning the Fight," 1.

121. IISS, *Military Balance 2023*, 291.

122. Ministry of National Defense (ROC), *2021 Quadrennial Defense Review* (Taipei: Ministry of National Defense, 2021), 54.

123. The conclusion states: "In the face of future challenges, the key points of the ROC national defense and force buildup endeavors are: (1) accelerating the development of asymmetric capabilities to deter the enemy from invading Taiwan, maintain the peace and stability in Taiwan Strait and the region, and counter the gray zone threats imposed by the PRC, so as to protect the precious democratic system." Ministry of National Defense, 68.

124. Ministry of National Defense (ROC), *2023 National Defense Report*, 41.

125. Drew Thompson, "Hope on the Horizon: Taiwan's Radical New Defense Concept," *War on the Rocks*, October 2, 2018, https://warontherocks.com/2018/10/hope-on-the-horizon-taiwans-radical-new-defense-concept/.

126. Thompson, "Winning the Fight," 3.

127. Easton et al., *Watching Over the Taiwan Strait*, 19.

128. Thompson, "Winning the Fight," 4.

129. Josh Rogin, "The U.S. Military Plans a 'Hellscape' to Deter China from Attacking Taiwan," *Washington Post*, June 10, 2024.

130. Sam LaGrone, "Pentagon Will Spend $1B on First Round of Replicator Drones," *US Naval Institute News*, March 11, 2024, https://news.usni.org/2024/03/11/pentagon-will-spend-1b-on-first-round-of-replicator-drones.

131. Rogin, "The U.S. Military Plans a 'Hellscape.'"

132. Kari Lindberg and Cindy Wang, "A Far-Flung Taiwan Island Risks Triggering a US-China Clash," *Bloomberg*, June 16, 2021.

133. Thompson, "Winning the Fight," 5, 6.

134. As Thompson notes, "The US decision in October 2020 to sell HIMARS gives the Taiwan army a defensive long-range strike capability that can reach portions of China's coastline, potentially placing embarkation points for a PLA invasion force at risk" ("Winning the Fight," 11).

135. "Biden Signs $858bn Defense Bill Including Funds for Taiwan, Allies," *Nikkei Asia*, December 24, 2022.

136. Caitlin Campbell, "Taiwan: Defense and Military Issues" (Washington, DC: Congressional Research Service, August 15, 2024.)

137. Noah Robertson, "US Close to Sending $567 Million in Immediate Security Aid to Taiwan," September 20, 2024, https://www.defensenews.com/pentagon/2024/09/20/us-close-to-sending-567-million-in-immediate-security-aid-to-taiwan/.

138. Thompson, "Winning the Fight," 8.

139. Jonathan Harman, "Taiwan's Missile Production Program: A Success Two Years Ahead of Schedule," *Global Taiwan Brief* 9, no. 20 (October 30, 2024), https://globaltaiwan.org/2024/10/taiwans-missile-programs/.

140. The Taiwanese Ministry of Foreign Affairs has created a web portal to facilitate this concept: https://nspp.mofa.gov.tw/nsppe/.

141. John Feng, "Taiwan and Japan Track China Warship Together in Apparent Team-Up at Sea," *Newsweek*, May 4, 2021.

142. Greg Torode and Jess Macy Yu, "Taiwan Courts Security Ties with Bigger Friends as Beijing Snatches Allies," Reuters, September 13, 2018.

143. John Dotson, "Taiwan's Indigenous Submarine Program Announces Milestone Goals for 2023," *Global Taiwan Brief* 8, no. 12 (June 14, 2023).

144. Wu, "Taiwan's All-Volunteer Force and Military Transformation," 5.

145. Thompson, "Winning the Fight," 12.

146. The World Values Survey included the "concern for war" question only in the most recent two rounds (waves 6 and 7) indicated in figure 3.1. R. Inglehart et al., eds., *World Values Survey: Round Six—Country-Pooled Datafile Version* (Madrid: JD Systems Institute, 2014), www.worldvaluessurvey.org/WVSDocumentationWV6.jsp; and C. Haerpfer et al., eds., *World Values Survey: Round Seven—Country-Pooled Datafile Version 6.0* (Madrid: JD Systems Institute, and Vienna: WVSA Secretariat, 2022), https://doi.org/10.14281/18241.24.

147. In this April 2022 survey, Japanese "willingness to fight" was reported as 19 percent across all age-groups. https://www.datum.com.pe/new_web_files/files/pdf/WWS%20WAR%20FINAL_220530105639.pdf.

148. Chapter 1 refers in particular to work in this area by A.F.K. Organski et al., Ronald L. Tammen et al., and Jennifer Sciubba.

4. NORTHEAST ASIA'S RAPIDLY AGING AUTOCRACIES

1. According to Russian government population data, as of January 2023 there were approximately 36.8 million people living in the Asian federal districts of the Russian Federation (Ural, Siberian, and Far Eastern). https://rosstat.gov.ru/storage/mediabank/OkPopul_Comp_2023_Site.xlsx. The Rondeli Foundation of Georgia maintains an interactive map of Russian units. https://gfsis.org.ge/maps/russian-military-forces.

2. John Bacon and Jorge L. Ortiz, "'Massive Cyberattack' Disrupts Russian Airports; Moscow's Economy Struggles," *USA Today*, September 28, 2023.

3. Deborah Jordan Brooks et al., "The Demographic Transition Theory of War: Why Young Societies Are Conflict Prone and Old Societies Are the Most Peaceful," *International Security* 43, no. 3 (Winter 2018/19): 89.

4. Such studies include Nicholas Eberstadt, *Russia's Peacetime Demographic Crisis: Dimensions, Causes, Implications* (Seattle: National Bureau of Asian Research, 2010); Keir Giles, "Where Have All the Soldiers Gone? Russia's Military Plans Versus Demographic Reality," *Russian Series* 6, no. 47 (Shrivenham, UK: Conflict Studies Research Centre, Defence Academy of the United Kingdom, 2006); and Jennifer Dabbs Sciubba, "Coffins Versus Cradles: Russian Population, Foreign Policy, and Power Transition Theory," *International Area Studies Review* 17, no. 2 (June 2014): 205–21.

5. Sim Tack, "An Aging Workforce Dims Russia's Economic Forecast," Stratfor, January 23, 2020, https://worldview.stratfor.com/article/aging-workforce-dims-russia-s-economic-forecast-population-demographic-decline-labor.

6. Michael Khodarkovsky, "Playing with Fear: Russia's War Card," *New York Times*, October 26, 2016. https://www.nytimes.com/2016/10/27/opinion/playing-with-fear-russias-war-card.html.

7. One example from recent media reporting: The probability that a Russian man would die before he turned 55 years old in 2020 was 25 percent, versus a one in eleven chance in the United States and even less in Northeast Asia's democracies. Rachel Nuwer, "Why Russian Men Don't Live as Long," *New York Times*, February 17, 2014, https://www.nytimes.com/2014/02/18/science/why-russian-men-dont-live-as-long.html.

8. Tatiana Kossova, Elena Kossova, and Maria Sheluntcova, "Gender Gap in Life Expectancy in Russia: The Role of Alcohol Consumption," *Social Policy and Society* 19, no. 1 (January 2020): 37–53, https://doi.org/10.1017/S1474746419000058.

9. Paul Globe, "2018 Spring Draft Highlights Russia's Demographic Decline," *Eurasia Daily Monitor*, April 10, 2018, https://jamestown.org/program/2018-spring-draft-highlights-russias-demographic-decline/.

10. Paul Globe, "Upcoming Spring Draft Set to Be Most Difficult in Russia's Recent History," *Eurasia Daily Monitor*, January 20, 2023, https://jamestown.org/program/upcoming-spring-draft-set-to-be-most-difficult-in-russias-recent-history/.

11. Globe, "Upcoming Spring Draft," explains additional strategies that the government might employ to achieve a higher number of soldiers.

12. Paul Globe, "Moscow May Not Be Able to Count on North Caucasians Any Longer to Fill Draft," *Eurasia Daily Monitor*, April 19, 2022, https://jamestown.org/program/moscow-may-not-be-able-to-count-on-north-caucasians-any-longer-to-fill-draft/.

13. Andrew S. Bowen, "Russian Armed Forces: Military Modernization and Reforms," *In Focus* (Washington, DC: Congressional Research Service, July 20, 2020), https://sgp.fas.org/crs/row/IF11603.pdf.

14. "Putin Announces End of Compulsory Military Service in Russia," *Russia Monitor*, May 19, 2019, https://warsawinstitute.org/putin-announces-end-compulsory-military-service-russia/.

15. According to *Russia Monitor*, May 19, 2019, an average Russian draftee at the time was paid an equivalent of US$30 per month, while a professional soldier earned between US$400 and US$600 per month. https://warsawinstitute.org/putin-announces-end-compulsory-military-service-russia/.

16. International Institute for Strategic Studies (IISS), "An Introduction to Russia's Military Modernisation," September 30, 2020, https://www.iiss.org/blogs/analysis/2020/09/rmm-introduction.

17. Yu Koizumi, "Russian Military Modernization in the Northern Territories and Its Implications for Japanese Foreign Policy," *Dispatch from Japan*, May 31, 2021, Sasakawa Peace Foundation, https://www.spf.org/iina/en/articles/koizumi_01 .html.

18. Japan's annual defense white paper, *Defense of Japan 2022*, 4, states that Japan scrambled planes to respond to Russian aircraft 226 times in FY2021, twice the number as in FY2001.

19. The year 2022 saw the highest number of such exercises, at six, in the past two decades—two-thirds of China's total number of joint military exercises. Kari Lindberg, "China Intensifies Military Drills with Russia Amid US Sanctions," *Bloomberg*, July 16, 2023.

20. Reuters, "Japan Says Russian Warships Spotted Near Taiwan, Okinawa Islands," July 1, 2023, https://www.reuters.com/world/asia-pacific/japan-says-russian-war ships-spotted-near-taiwan-okinawa-islands-2023-07-01/.

21. Chris Miller, *We Shall Be Masters: Russian Pivots to East Asia from Peter the Great to Putin* (Cambridge, MA: Harvard University Press, 2021).

22. Andrew Yeo provides a concise overview of North Korea's extreme measures of controlling its population in *State, Society, and Markets in North Korea* (Cambridge: Cambridge University Press, 2021), especially 11–28. For a broader overview of North Korean governance and the centrality of the military in it, see Kongdan Oh and Ralph Hassig, *North Korea in a Nutshell: A Contemporary Overview* (Lanham, MD: Rowman & Littlefield, 2021), especially 87–114.

23. Daniel Goodkind, Loraine West, and Peter Johnson, "A Reassessment of Mortality in North Korea, 1993–2008," paper presented at the Annual Meeting of the Population Association of America, Washington, DC, March 28, 2011, 3.

24. Office of the Secretary of Defense (United States), *Annual Report to Congress: Military and Security Developments Involving the People's Republic of China 2020*, 138, 140.

25. Michael S. Chase et al., *China's Incomplete Military Transformation: Assessing the Weaknesses of the People's Liberation Army (PLA)* (Santa Monica, CA: RAND Corporation, 2015), 53–54, https://www.rand.org/pubs/research_reports/RR893 .html.

26. Lindsay Maizland, "China's Modernizing Military," *Backgrounder* (New York: Council on Foreign Relations, February 5, 2020), https://www.cfr.org/backgrounder /chinas-modernizing-military.

27. Timothy Beardson, *Ageing Giant: China's Looming Population Collapse* (Oxford: Signal Books, 2021), 9–11.

28. Further discussion of the details and implications of the OCP are provided in Nicholas Eberstadt, ed., *China's Changing Family Structure: Dimensions and Implications* (Washington, DC: American Enterprise Institute, 2019). For a more extended discussion of China's population size and efforts to manage it, see Beardson, *Ageing Giant*.

29. For example, the 2021 report warns of "severe difficulties recruiting volunteers" to Taiwan's military. Office of the Secretary of Defense (United States), *Annual Report to Congress: Military and Security Developments Involving the People's Republic of China 2021* (Washington, DC: U.S. Department of Defense, 2021), 122, https://media.defense.gov/2021/Nov/03/2002885874/-1/-1/0/2021-CMPR-FINAL

.PDF. The 2023 report includes a special section on "PLA Recruitment and Personnel Management Situation" (pp. 182–83). https://media.defense.gov/2023/Oct/19/2003323409/-1/-1/1/2023-MILITARY-AND-SECURITY-DEVELOPMENTS-INVOLVING-THE-PEOPLES-REPUBLIC-OF-CHINA.PDF.

30. Office of the Secretary of Defense (United States), *Annual Report to Congress: Military and Security Developments Involving the People's Republic of China 2024*, (Washington, DC: U.S. Department of Defense, 2024), 148.

31. SIPRI, *SIPRI Military Expenditure Database 2023*, https://www.sipri.org/databases/milex.

32. Bonnie Glaser et al., "Breaking Down China's 2020 Defense Budget" (Washington, DC: Center for Strategic and International Studies), October 25, 2020, https://www.csis.org/analysis/breaking-down-chinas-2020-defense-budget.

33. GDP growth predictions from Institute of Energy Economics Japan, *IIEJ Outlook 2023*, https://eneken.ieej.or.jp/data/10974.pdf. Michael Beckley and Hal Brands' use of the term "Peak China" in "The End of China's Rise: Beijing Is Running Out of Time to Remake the World," *Foreign Affairs Snapshot*, October 1, 2021, created a tsunami of related articles in popular and scholarly venues. A recent iteration of this thesis, more closely focused on the demographic element, is Nicholas Eberstadt, "East Asia's Coming Population Collapse: And How It Will Reshape World Politics," *Foreign Affairs Snapshot*, May 8, 2024. For a forceful reply to this thesis from a U.S. perspective, see Evan S. Medeiros, "The Delusion of Peak China: America Can't Wish Away Its Toughest Challenger," *Foreign Affairs* (May/June 2024). For a Chinese perspective, see "Busting 6 'Peak China' Myths," *Diplomat*, March 9, 2024.

34. Cissy Zhou, "China's GDP 'Paradox': Why Young Chinese Despair About Future Prospects Despite Rapid Economic Growth," *South China Morning Post*, accessed February 16, 2021.

35. Edward Wong, Jane Perlez, and Chris Buckley, "China Announces Cuts of 300,000 Troops at Military Parade Showing Its Might," *New York Times*, September 2, 2015).

36. Ian E. Rinehart, "The Chinese Military: Overview and Issues for Congress" (Washington, DC: Congressional Research Service, 2016), ii, https://fas.org/sgp/crs/row/R44196.pdf.

37. Chase et al., *China's Incomplete Military Transformation*, 22.

38. Maizland, "China's Modernizing Military."

39. Brooks et al., "The Demographic Transition Theory of War," 87, referencing, for example, Graham Allison, *Destined for War: Can America and China Escape Thucydides's Trap?* (Boston: Houghton Mifflin Harcourt, 2017).

40. Brooks et al., 87.

41. John Pike, "Military: Recruitment and Conscription" (2020), Global Security.org. https://www.globalsecurity.org/military/world/china/pla-conscription.htm.

42. Chase et al., *China's Incomplete Military Transformation*, 59.

43. Marcus Clay and Dennis J. Blasko, "People Win Wars: The PLA Enlisted Force, and Other Related Matters," *War on the Rocks*, August 1, 2020, https://warontherocks.com/2020/07/people-win-wars-the-pla-enlisted-force-and-other-related-matters/.

44. Moore and Barreda, "China's PLA Gets Smarter." Moreover, Moore and Barreda report, a wide range of incentives similar to those offered in the United States were

put into place to encourage college students and graduates to enlist, such as tuition aid and student loan write-offs. One unique-to-China incentive was the ability to change the location of one's *hukou*, the registration status linked to a particular province that all Chinese must maintain. Increased pay is another factor, cited by Melissa Hellman, "China's Military Reduces Requirements to Allow Shorter, Wider Recruits" *Time*, June 17, 2014, https://time.com/2889121/chinas-military -reduces-requirements-to-allow-shorter-wider-recruits/.

45. Office of the Secretary of Defense (United States), *Annual Report to Congress: Military and Security Developments Involving the People's Republic of China 2023*, (Washington, DC: U.S. Department of Defense, 2023), 182.

46. Office of the Secretary of Defense, *Annual Report to Congress 2020*, 147; Office of the Secretary of Defense, *Annual Report to Congress: Military and Security Developments Involving the People's Republic of China 2024*, 149.

47. Elsa B. Kania, "AI Weapons," in *China's Military Innovation* (Washington, DC: Brookings Institution, April 2020), https://www.brookings.edu/wp-content /uploads/2020/04/ FP_20200427_ai_weapons_kania_v2.pdf. Kania provides several specific examples of such technologies being pursued by the PLA, PLAN, and PLAAF (pp. 2–3).

48. Office of the Secretary of Defense, *Annual Report to Congress 2020*, 143; *Annual Report to Congress 2024*, 152.

49. As Kania writes in her 2020 report: "Chinese military initiatives in AI are motivated by an acute awareness of global trends in military technology and operations; concerns about falling behind the U.S. military" (p. 2).

50. Avi Goldfarb and Jon R. Lindsay, "Prediction and Judgment: Why Artificial Intelligence Increases the Importance of Humans in War," *International Security* 46, no. 3 (Winter 2021/22): 7–50, https://doi.org/10.1162/isec_a_00425.

51. Chase et al., *China's Incomplete Military Transformation*, 93–94.

52. Peter E. Robinson, "Cost Disease in China's Military: The Headline Figures Showing China's Growing Military Spending Are Misleading," *Diplomat*, May 13, 2015, https://thediplomat.com/2015/05/chinas-miliary-and-cost-disease/.

53. Oh and Hassig, *North Korea in a Nutshell*, 87–114.

54. Toshi Yoshihara and Jack Bianchi, *Seizing on Weakness: Allied Strategy for Competing with China's Globalizing Military* (Washington, DC: Center for Strategic and Budgetary Assessment, 2021), 29.

55. In addition to substantial media reporting on this issue, see Alec Ash, *China's New Youth: How The Young Generation Is Shaping China's Future* (New York: Arcade, 2020).

56. Bernard Nauck, "Value of Children and the Framing of Fertility: Results from a Cross-Cultural Comparative Survey in 10 Societies," *European Sociological Review* 23, no. 5 (December 2007): 615–29 (especially 624–25), https://doi.org/10.1093/esr /jcm028.

57. Xiaobing Li, "The Impact of Social Changes in the PLA," in *Civil-Military Relations in Today's China: Swimming in a New Sea*, ed., David Michael Finkelstein and Kristen Gunness (Armonk, NY: Sharpe, 2007), 28–29.

58. National Bureau of Statistics of China, "Main Data of the Seventh National Population Census," May 11, 2021, http://www.stats.gov.cn/english/PressRelease/202105 /t20210510_1817185.html.

59. Charlie Campbell, "China's Aging Population Is a Major Threat to Its Future," *Time*, February 7, 2019, https://time.com/5523805/china-aging-population-working -age/. Beardson, *Ageing Giant*, 51–62, summarizes fourteen studies of this issue from both Chinese and international research teams, offering additional nuances to this complex measurement issue.

60. Campbell, "China's Aging Population."

61. Valerie Hudson and Andrea Den Boer, *Bare Branches: The Security Implications of Asia's Surplus Male Population* (Cambridge, MA: MIT Press, 2004).

62. Beardson, *Ageing Giant*, 13–14.

63. Eva Dou, "China Seeks to Reduce Abortions, as Beijing Pushes for More Children," *New York Times*, September 27, 2021.

64. Campbell, "China's Aging Population."

65. National Bureau of Statistics of China, "Main Data of the Seventh National Population Census," May 11, 2021, http://www.stats.gov.cn/english/PressRelease/202105 /t20210510_1817185.html.

66. *BBC News*, "China Policy 'Could Cut Millions of Uyghur Births,'" June 7, 2021.

67. *BBC News*. The BBC report notes that "the Chinese government denies making any attempt to reduce the Uyghur population specifically, arguing that the decline in minority birth rates in Xinjiang is due to the implementation of general birth quotas in the region as well as increases in income and better access to family planning."

68. National Bureau of Statistics of China, "Main Data of the Seventh National Population Census," May 11, 2021, http://www.stats.gov.cn/english/PressRelease/202105 /t20210510_1817185.html.

69. Scott Kennedy and Mingda Qui, "Surprises from China's Latest Census," in *Trustee China Hand* (Washington, DC: Center for Strategic and international Studies, May 14, 2021), csis.org/blogs/trustee-china-hand.

70. Scott Rozelle and Natalie Hell, *Invisible China: How the Urban-Rural Divide Threatens China's Rise* (Chicago: University of Chicago Press, 2020).

71. Chase et al., *China's Incomplete Military Transformation*, 54–55.

72. Viola Rothschild, "China's Pension System Is Not Aging Well," *Diplomat*, March 7, 2019, https://thediplomat.com/2019/03/chinas-pension-system-is-not-aging-well/.

73. Graham Allison has framed this challenge as "the Thucydides trap" in *Destined for War: Can America and China Escape Thucydides's Trap?* (Boston: Houghton Mifflin Harcourt, 2017).

74. Rothschild, "China's Pension System Is Not Aging Well"; China Power Team, "Does China Have an Aging Problem?" (Washington, DC: Center for Strategic and International Studies, March 19, 2020), https://chinapower.csis.org/aging -problem/.

75. Beardson, *Ageing Giant*, 26–31, offers a summary of several Chinese studies of this issue.

76. Rothschild, "China's Pension System Is Not Aging Well."

77. Beardson, *Ageing Giant*, 162–205, offers a summary of many of the different lines of argument about the economic challenges China faces related to rapid aging and population shrinkage.

78. Kelly Tang and Lin Yang, "China Youth 'Lie Flat' as Good Life Seems Unattainable," *Voice of America*, June 15, 2021.

79. World Bank, https://data.worldbank.org/indicator/NY.GDP.PCAP.CD?locations =CN.
80. Zhou, "China's GDP 'Paradox.'"
81. Nathaniel Taplin, "China Begins Feeling Its Age," *Wall Street Journal*, May 22, 2019.
82. Kennedy and Qui, "Surprises from China's Latest Census."
83. Kennedy and Qui.
84. Lyman Stone, "The Chinese Communist Party Wants a Han Baby Boom That Isn't Coming," *Foreign Policy*, June 30, 2020, https://foreignpolicy.com/2020/06/30 /chinese-communist-party-han-baby-boom-sterilization-ethnic-minorities/.
85. Yoshihara and Bianchi, *Seizing on Weakness*, 27.

5. OPPORTUNITIES AND CAUTIONS FROM THE DEMOGRAPHIC DIVERSITY OF THE BROADER INDO-PACIFIC

1. The introduction and chapter 2 of this book discuss the emergence and different conceptions of the Indo-Pacific as a region.
2. The importance and scholarly lineage of the term "demographic dividend" for understanding demographic dimensions of economic growth potential are discussed in the introduction and chapter 2.
3. Eun-Jin Kim, "Samsung Electronics Accounts for 28% of Vietnam's GDP," *Business Korea*, March 19, 2019, http://www.businesskorea.co.kr/news/articleView.html ?idxno=29966.
4. The China Power Project of the Center for Strategic and International Studies explains this calculation for 2016. https://chinapower.csis.org/much-trade-transits -south-china-sea/.
5. Alice Ba offers an excellent summary of ASEAN's origin in *(Re)Negotiating East and Southeast Asia: Region, Regionalism, and the Association of Southeast Asian Nations* (Stanford, CA: Stanford University Press, 2009).
6. Kei Koga, *Reinventing Regional Security Institutions in Asia and Africa: Power Shifts, Ideas, and Institutional Change* (London: Routledge, 2017).
7. Deborah Jordan Brooks et al., "The Demographic Transition Theory of War: Why Young Societies Are Conflict Prone and Old Societies Are the Most Peaceful," *International Security* 43, no. 3 (Winter 2018/19): 94; they define "youth-bulge ratio" as the ratio of people aged 15–24 to the total adult population (p. 75).
8. Jong-Wha Lee and Eunbi Song, "Demographic Change and the Long-Term Economic Growth Path in Asia," Working Paper, Korea University, September 2023.
9. This goal is discussed in Abraham M. Denmark, *U.S. Strategy in the Asian Century: Empowering Allies and Partners* (New York: Columbia University Press, 2020); Scott W. Harold et al., *The Thickening Web of Asian Security Cooperation: Deepening Defense Ties Among U.S. Allies and Partners in the Indo-Pacific* (Santa Monica, CA: RAND, 2019); and Michael Green, *Ironclad: Forging a New Future for America's Alliances* (Boulder, CO: Rowman & Littlefield, 2019), among others.
10. IMF, World Economic Outlook Database, April 2023.
11. For further explication of this point, see Bill Hayton, *The South China Sea: The Struggle for Power in Asia* (New Haven, CT: Yale University Press, 2014); and Kei

Koga, *Managing Great Power Politics: ASEAN, Institutional Strategy, and the South China Sea* (Singapore: Palgrave Macmillan, 2022).

12. See Michael Green et al., *Countering Coercion in Maritime Asia: The Theory and Practice of Gray Zone Deterrence* (Washington, DC: CSIS, 2017).

13. Richard Heydarian, *The Rise of Duterte: A Populist Revolt Against Elite Democracy* (Singapore: Palgrave Macmillan, 2017); Weiqing Song and Joseph Ching Velasco, "Selling 'Independent Foreign Policy' amid the US-China Rivalry: Populism and Philippine Foreign Policy Under the Duterte Government," *Pacific Review* (2022), https://doi.org/10.1080/09512748.2022.2137227.

14. Australian Government Defence, *2020 Force Structure Plan*, July 2020, https://www.defence.gov.au/about/strategic-planning/

15. Kei Koga, "Tactical Hedging as Coalition-Building Signal: The Evolution of Quad and AUKUS in the Indo-Pacific," *British Journal of Politics and International Relations* (2024), https://doi.org/10.1177/13691481241227840.

16. U.S. Department of State, "Fact Sheet: Major Non-NATO Ally Status," January 20, 2021, https://www.state.gov/major-non-nato-ally-status/.

17. Shivshankar Menon, a former Indian foreign minister and national security advisor, offers a contemporary overview of both present and past challenges in *India and Asian Geopolitics: The Past, Present* (Washington, DC: Brookings Institution Press, 2021).

18. S. Jaishankar, India's foreign minister (2019–), advances a similar argument in *The India Way: Strategies for an Uncertain World* (New York: HarperCollins, 2022).

19. Brahma Chellaney, *Water, Peace, and War: Confronting the Global Water Crisis* (Lanham, MD: Rowman & Littlefield, 2015), refers to China as a "water hegemon with no modern historical parallel" (p. 229) in his important study that dovetails with the demographic focus of this book.

20. Dhiraj Kumar notes recent developments related to the "string of pearls" concern in connection with India's deteriorating relationship with the Maldives as well as China's port-related developments with Myanmar, Sri Lanka, and Pakistan. Kumar, "India vs China: The String of Pearls and Belt & Road," *Times of India*, January 27, 2024.

21. Gerry Shih et al., "Modi Bear Hugs Putin in Moscow, Marking Deep Ties Between Russia and India," *Washington Post*, July 9, 2024.

22. Jennifer D. Sciubba, *8 Billion and Counting: How Sex, Death, and Migration Shape Our World* (New York: Norton, 2022), 161.

23. Lauren Frayer, "In India, Boy Meets Girl, Proposes—and Gets Accused of Jihad," National Public Radio, October 20, 2021.

24. The World Health Organization maintains an interactive database of SRB at https://www.who.int/data/gho/indicator-metadata-registry/imr-details/sex-ratio-at-birth-(male-births-per-female-births).

25. Valerie Hudson and Andrea Den Boer, *Bare Branches: The Security Implications of Asia's Surplus Male Population* (Cambridge, MA: MIT Press, 2004).

26. Some of the ideas and examples expressed in this paragraph are drawn from Andrew Oros and Andrew Gordan, "The Quad Should Help India Address Its Most Pressing Security Challenge: Climate Change," December 7, 2021, https://www.newsecuritybeat.org/2021/12/quad-india-address-pressing-security-challenge-climate-change/.

27. See, for example, Homi Kharas, "Missing from COP26: Lifestyle Choices of Middle-class and Rich Consumers," November 23, 2021, https://www.brookings.edu/articles/missing-from-cop26-lifestyle-choices-of-middle-class-and-rich-consumers/.

28. *Financial Express*, "Modi 2.0: Here Are Top Priorities for BJP-led NDA Government," May 23, 2019, https://www.financialexpress.com/economy/modi-2-0-heres-are-top-priorities-for-bjp-led-nda-government/1587153/.

29. Stuti Mishra, "Cop26: Why Modi's Climate Pledges Have Sparked Confusion in India," *Independent*, November 4, 2021, https://www.independent.co.uk/climate-change/news/india-cop26-modi-speech-pledges-b1951200.html.

30. For example, Irine Hiraswari Gayatri, "Australia and Indonesia's Cooperative Relationship on Terrorism," *Australian Outlook*, November 4, 2022, https://www.internationalaffairs.org.au/ australianoutlook/australia-and-indonesias-cooperative-relationship-on-terrorism/; "Indonesia Eyes Strengthened Cooperation in Tackling Terrorism at AMMTC," *ANTARA*, August 22, 2023, https://en.antaranews.com/news/291684/indonesia-eyes-strengthened-cooperation-in-tackling-terrorism-at-ammtc.

31. A'an Suryana and Nur Syafiqah Mohd Taufek, "Indonesian Islam Beyond Habib Rizieq Shihab: Deconstructing Islamism and Populism," *Fulcrum*, April 27, 2021, https://fulcrum.sg/indonesian-islam-beyond-habib-rizieq-shihab-deconstructing-islamism-and-populism/; William Frangia, "Has Indonesia's Deradicalization Program Done Enough to Combat Terrorism?," *Strategist*, June 14, 2023, https://www.aspistrategist.org.au/has-indonesias-deradicalisation-program-done-enough-to-combat-terrorism/.

32. Aris Ananta et al.,"Changing Ethnic Composition: Indonesia, 2000–2010," International Union for the Scientific Study of Population (IUSSP) Working Paper (2013), http://iussp.org/sites/default/files/event_call_for_papers/ IUSSP%20Ethnicity%20Indonesia%20Poster%20Section%20G%202708%202013%20revised.pdf.

33. E. N. Arifin et al., "Chinese Indonesians: How Many, Who and Where?," *Asian Ethnicity* 18, no. 3 (2016): 310–29, https://doi.org/10.1080/14631369.2016.1227236.

34. Leo Suryadinata, "Chinese Indonesians in an Era of Globalization: Some Major Characteristics," in *Ethnic Chinese in Contemporary Indonesia*, ed. Leo Suryadinata (Singapore: ISEAS-Yusof Ishak Institute, 2008).

35. Jonathan Chen, "Representing Chinese Indonesians: Pribumi Discourse and Regional Elections in Post-Reform Indonesia," *Journal of Current Southeast Asian Affairs* 41, no. 1 (2022): 59–87, https://doi.org/10.1177/18681034211036716.

36. Alice Ba, *(Re)Negotiating East and Southeast Asia* (Stanford, CA: Stanford University Press, 2009), provides greater depth of analysis on this founding period.

37. International Institute for Law of the Sea Studies, "Exclusive Economic Zone (EEZ) Map of the World," May 23, 2021, https://iilss.net/exclusive-economic-zoneeez-map-of-the-world/.

38. See, for example, Koh Collin, "What Next for the Indonesian Navy? Challenges and Prospects for Attaining the Minimum Essential Force by 2024," *Contemporary Southeast Asia* 37, no. 3 (2015): 432–62; and Iis Gindarsah and Adhi Priamarizki, "Explaining Indonesia's Under-balancing: The Case of the Modernisation of the Air Force and the Navy," *Journal Asian Security and International Affairs* 8, no. 3(2021): 391–412.

39. Sean Quirk and John Bradford, "Maritime Fulcrum: A New U.S. Opportunity to Engage Indonesia," *Issues and Insights* 15, no. 9 (October 2015), Honolulu: Pacific Forum.
40. Moch Faisal Karim, "Role Legitimation in Foreign Policy: The Case of Indonesia as an Emerging Power Under Yudhoyono's Presidency (2004–2014)," *Foreign Policy Analysis* 17, no. 3 (2021); Dewi Fortuna Anwar, "Indonesia's Regional Foreign Policy After the 2019 Election," *Asia Policy* 14, no. 4 (2019): 72–8; I Gede Wahyu Wicaksana, "Indonesia's Foreign Policy: The Need for a New Approach," *Southeast Asian Affairs* (2023): 136–46.
41. Ba, *(Re)Negotiating East and Southeast Asia*; Koga, *Reinventing Regional Security Institutions*.
42. This would be similar to a hedging strategy, as discussed in Dewi Fortuna Anwar, "Indonesia's Hedging Plus Policy in the Face of China's Rise and the US-China Rivalry in the Indo-Pacific Region," *Pacific Review* 36, no. 2 (2022): 351–77.
43. For example, Rizal Sukma, "Indonesia, ASEAN, and Shaping the Indo-Pacific Idea," *East Asia Forum Quarterly* (October–December 2019): 11–12, https://search.informit.org/doi/epdf/10.3316/INFORMIT.281227453826465.
44. *Statista*, "Share of Population in Malayisa from 2019 to 2023, by Ethnicity," September 13, 2023, https://www.statista.com/statistics/1017372/malaysia-breakdown-of-population-by-ethnicity/.
45. Muhammed Abdul Khalid and Li Yang, "Income Inequality and Ethnic Cleavages in Malaysia: Evidence from Distributional National Accounts (1984–2014)," April 2019, WID.world Working Paper, https://wid.world/document/9231/.
46. Peter T. C. Chang, "Chinese in Malaysia: Proud of China's Rise, Yet Fiercely Malaysian," *Fulcrum*, June 12, 2024, https://fulcrum.sg/chinese-in-malaysia-proud-of-chinas-rise-yet-fiercely-malaysian/.
47. Sen Tyng Chai and Tengku Aizan Hamid, "Population Ageing and the Malaysian Chinese: Issues and Challenges," *Malaysian Journal of Chinese Studies* 4, no. 1 (2015): 1–13.
48. Heiner Hanggi, *ASEAN and the ZOPFAN Concept* (Singapore: Institute of Southeast Asian Studies, 1991).
49. Kei Koga, "Wedge Strategies, Japan-ASEAN Cooperation, and the Making of EAS: Implications for Indo-Pacific Institutionalization," in *The Courteous Power: Japan and Southeast Asia in the Indo-Pacific Era*, ed. John D. Ciorciari and Kiyoteru Tsutsui, 73–96 (Ann Arbor: University of Michigan Press, 2021).
50. Cheng-Chwee Kuik, "Malaysia Between the United States and China: What Do Weaker States Hedge Against?" *Asian Politics and Policy* 8, no. 1 (2016): 155–77; John Ciorciari, "The Variable Effectiveness of Hedging Strategies," *International Relations of the Asia-Pacific* 19, no. 3 (2019): 523–55.
51. See Le Hong Hiep and Anton Tsvetov, eds., *Vietnam's Foreign Policy Under Doi Moi* (Singapore: ISEAS Publishing, 2018).
52. Huong Le Thu, "Vietnam's Persistent Foreign Policy Dilemma: Caught Between Self-Reliance and Proactive Integration," *Asia Policy* 13, no. 4 (2018): 123–44.
53. For example, see Orla Ryan, "Vietnam Becomes Vital Link in Supply Chain as Business Pivots from China," *Financial Times*, July 3, 2023, https://www.ft.com/content/29070eda-3a0c-4034-827e-0b31a0f3ef11; Le Nguyen and An Hai, "Experts: Vietnam May Benefit as US Companies De-risk Supply Chains in China," *Voice*

of America, July 27, 2023, https://www.voanews.com/a/experts-vietnam-may-benefit-as-us-companies-de-risk-supply-chains-now-in-china/7201579.html.

54. The White House, "Readout of President Biden's Meeting with Prime Minister Pham Minh Chinh of Vietnam," September 11, 2023, https://www.whitehouse.gov/briefing-room/statements-releases/2023/09/11/readout-of-president-bidens-meeting-with-prime-minister-pham-minh-chinh-of-vietnam/.

55. IISS, *Military Balance 2024*.

56. For example, see Shaun Cameron, "By Land or Sea: Thailand Perspectives with the Kra Canal," *Interpreter*, September 22, 2021, https://www.lowyinstitute.org/the-interpreter/land-or-sea-thailand-perseveres-kra-canal.

57. Chanintira na Thalang, "Unpacking Thailand's Conceptions of and Position Within the Liberal International Order," *International Affairs* 99, no. 4 (2023): 1519–36; Ryan Ashley and Apichai Shipper, "The Art of Thai Diplomacy: Parables of Alliance," *Pacific Affairs* 95, no. 2 (2022): 227–63.

58. Jayant Menon and Anna Melendez-Nakamura, "Aging in Asia: Trends, Impacts and Responses," Asian Development Bank, February 2009, 5, https://www.adb.org/publications/aging-asia-trends-impacts-and-responses.

59. George Magnus, *The Age of Aging: How Demographics Are Changing the Global Economy and Our World* (Singapore: Wiley, 2009).

60. Kei Koga, "Singapore's Distinctive 'Quasi-bases,'" in *Exploring Base Politics: How Host Countries Shape the Network of U.S. Overseas Bases*, ed. Shinjia Kawana and Minori Takahashi (New York: Routledge, 2020).

61. Yuen Foong Khong, "Singapore and the Great Powers," in Ang Guan Teo and Kei Koga, "Conceptualizing Equidistant Diplomacy in International Relations: The Case of Singapore," *International Relations of the Asia-Pacific* 22, no. 3 (2022): 375–409.

62. IISS, *Military Balance 2024*.

63. "LKY's 1966 Poisonous Shrimp Analogy & How It Laid the Foundation of Today's SAF," *Petir*, February 27, 2022, https://petir.sg/2022/02/27/lkys-1966-poisonous-shrimp-analogy-how-it-laid-the-foundation-of-todays-saf-1/.

64. U.S. Department of State, "Singapore (05–712)-Strategic Framework Agreement for a Closer Cooperation Partnership in Defense and Security," July 12, 2005, https://www.state.gov/05-712; Ministry of Defence, Singapore, "Fact Sheet: 2019 Protocol of Amendment to the 1990 Memorandum of Understanding," September 24, 2019, https://www.mindef.gov.sg/web/portal/mindef/news-and-events/latest-releases/article-detail/2019/September/24sep19_fs.

65. Tim Huxley, "Singapore and the US: Not Quite Allies," *Strategist*, July 30, 2012, https://www.aspistrategist.org.au/singapore-and-the-us-not-quite-allies/.

66. For example, see Joel Atkinson, "China-Taiwan Diplomatic Competition and the Pacific Islands," *Pacific Review* 23, no. 4 (2010): 407–27; Euan Graham, "Assessing the Solomon Islands' New Security Agreement with China," *IISS Online Analysis*, May 5, 2022, https://www.iiss.org/online-analysis/online-analysis//2022/05/china-solomon-islands.

67. Zongyuan Zoe Liu, "What the China-Solomon Islands Pact Means for the U.S. and South Pacific," *In Brief* (Council on Foreign Relations), May 4, 2022, https://www.cfr.org/in-brief/china-solomon-islands-security-pact-us-south-pacific.

68. The White House, "Pacific Partnership Strategy of the United States," September 2022, https://www.whitehouse.gov/wp-content/uploads/2022/09/Pacific-Partnership-Strategy.pdf.

69. Peter Layton, "Fixing Australia's Failing Pacific Step-Up Strategy," *Interpreter*, April 26, 2022, https://www.lowyinstitute.org/the-interpreter/fixing-australia-s-failing-pacific-step-strategy; The White House, "Pacific Partnership Strategy."

70. Kei Koga, "Japan's Strategic Approach Toward Island States: Case of the Pacific Islands," *Journal of Indo-Pacific Affairs* 5, no. 7 (2022): 62–83, https://media.defense.gov/2022/Dec/06/2003126852/-1/-1/1/JIPA%20-%20KOGA.PDF; Anri Takahashi, "Japan Eyes 6 Nations to Receive Security Aid in Fiscal 2024," *Asahi Shimbun*, August 28, 2023, https://www.asahi.com/ajw/articles/14991342.

71. Ryo Nakamura and Rurika Imahashi, "U.S. Military to Use Papua New Guinea Naval Base for 15 Years," *Nikkei Asia*, July 19, 2023, https://asia.nikkei.com/Politics/Defense/U.S.-military-to-use-Papua-New-Guinea-naval-base-for-15-years; Michael Kugelman, "Modi Visits Papua New Guinea as Biden Skips," *Foreign Policy*, May 24, 2023, https://foreignpolicy.com/2023/05/24/modi-papua-new-guinea-diplomacy-biden-indo-pacific/; The White House, "Quad Leaders' Joint Statement," May 20, 2023, https://www.whitehouse.gov/briefing-room/statements-releases/2023/05/20/quad-leaders-joint-statement/.

72. Derek Grossman et al., *America's Pacific Island Allies: The Freely Associated States and Chinese Influence* (Santa Monica, CA: RAND, 2019).

CONCLUSION

1. As noted in earlier chapters, this finding contrasts with earlier predictions by Mark L. Haas, "A Geriatric Peace? The Future of U.S. Power in a World of Aging Populations," *International Security* 32, no. 1 (Summer 2007): 112–47; and Seongho Sheen, "Northeast Asia's Aging Population and Regional Security: 'Demographic Peace?,'" *Asian Survey* 53, no. 2 (March/April 2013): 292–318.

2. Two studies that discuss these trends are Hyun-Hoon Lee and Donghyun Park, *Post-Covid Asia: Deglobalization, Fourth Industrial Revolution, and Sustainable Development* (Singapore: World Scientific, 2021); and Mauro F. Guillen, *2030: How Today's Biggest Trends Will Collide and Reshape the Future of Everything* (New York: St. Martin's Press, 2020).

3. Lee and Park, *Post-COVID Asia*, further develop the linkages between the climate crisis and population challenges in some parts of growing Asia.

4. Jennifer D. Sciubba, *8 Billion and Counting: How Sex, Death, and Migration Shape Our World* (New York: Norton, 2022), 209.

5. This argument is developed further in Andrew L. Oros and Andrew Gordan, "The Quad Should Help India Address Its Most Pressing Security Challenge: Climate Change," New Security Beat, December 7, 2021, https://www.newsecuritybeat.org/2021/12/quad-india-address-pressing-security-challenge-climate-change/.

6. A noncomprehensive list includes Rapp-Hooper, *Shields of the Republic*; Abraham M. Denmark, *U.S. Strategy in the Asian Century: Empowering Allies and Partners* (New York: Columbia University Press, 2020); Andrew Yeo, *Asia's*

Regional Architecture: Alliances and Institutions in the Pacific Century (Stanford, CA: Stanford University Press, 2019); Michael J. Green, ed, *Ironclad: Forging a New Future for America's Alliances* (Boulder, CO: Rowman & Littlefield, 2019); Scott W. Harold et al., *The Thickening Web of Asian Security Cooperation: Deepening Defense Ties Among U.S. Allies and Partners in the Indo-Pacific* (Santa Monica, CA: RAND, 2019); and Michael J. Green et al., *Federated Defense in Asia* (Washington, DC: Center for Strategic and International Studies, 2014).

7. Mira Rapp-Hooper, *Shields of the Republic: The Triumph and Peril of America's Alliances* (Cambridge, MA: Harvard University Press, 2020), 195.

8. The average TFR for the five security partners in 2000 was 2.6, and individually as follows (highest to lowest): India, 3.48; Malaysia, 3.13; Indonesia, 2.55; Vietnam, 2.25; and Singapore, 1.57.

9. Harold et al., *The Thickening Web.*

10. Several detailed studies have illustrated this broad point for allies and partners across the region, which were discussed in the country-specific chapters of this volume, including Denmark, *U.S. Strategy in the Asian Century*; Harold et al., *The Thickening Web*; Green, *Ironclad*; and Green et al., *Federated Defense in Asia.*

11. Parag Khanna, *The Future Is Asian* (New York: Simon & Schuster, 2019); Kishore Mahbubani, *The New Asian Hemisphere: The Shift of Global Power to the East* (New York: Public Affairs, 2008); cf. Michael Auslin, *The End of the Asian Century* (New Haven, CT: Yale University Press, 2017).

BIBLIOGRAPHY

SELECTED PRIMARY SOURCES

International Institute for Strategic Studies. *The Military Balance* (annual). https://www
.iiss.org.
International Monetary Fund. *World Economic Outlook Database*. http://www.imf
.org.
Japan Cabinet Secretariat. *National Security Strategy*, December 17, 2013. http://www
.cas.go.jp/jp/siryou/131217anzenhoshou/nss-e.pdf.
——. *National Security Strategy*, December 16, 2022. https://www.cas.go.jp/jp/siryou
/221216anzenhoshou/nss-e.pdf.
Japan Ministry of Defense. *Defense of Japan* (annual). https://www.mod.go.jp
——. *National Defense Strategy*, December 28, 2022. https://www.mod.go.jp/j/approach
/agenda/guideline/strategy/pdf/strategy_en.pdf.
National Security Strategy of the United States of America. Washington, DC: The White
House, 2017.
Organisation for Economic Co-operation and Development. *Health at a Glance: Asia/
Pacific 2020*. https://doi.org/10.1787/23054964.
People's Republic of China Ministry of National Defense. *China's National Defense in
the New Era*, July 24, 2019. https://eng.mod.gov.cn.
Republic of China Ministry of National Defense. *2017 Quadrennial Defense Review*.
https://www.mnd.gov.tw.
——. *2021 Quadrennial Defense Review*. https://www.mnd.gov.tw.
Republic of Korea Ministry of National Defense. *Defense White Paper* (bi-annual).
https://www.mnd.go.kr.
Stockholm International Peace Research Institute (SIPRI). *SIPRI Military Expenditure
Database*. https://www.sipri.org/databases/milex.

United Nations. "The Number of International Migrants Reaches 272 Million, Continuing Upward Trend in All Regions of the World, Says UN." News Release, September 17, 2019. https://www.un.org/.

United Nations Population Division. *World Urbanization Prospects: The 2018 Revision Key Facts*. https://population.un.org/wup/.

——. *World Population Prospects 2019*. https://population.un.org/wpp/.

——. *World Population Prospects 2022*. https://population.un.org/wpp/.

——. *World Population Prospects 2022: Summary of Results*. https://population.un.org /wpp/.

——. *World Population Prospects 2024*. https://population.un.org/wpp/.

——. *World Population Prospects 2024: Summary of Results*. https://population.un.org /wpp/.

United States Census Bureau. International Data Base (IDB).

United States Department of Defense. "Indo-Pacific Strategy Report: Preparedness, Partnerships, and Promoting a Networked Region," June 1, 2019. https://dod.defense .gov/.

——. "Summary of the 2018 National Defense Strategy: Sharpening the American Military's Competitive Edge." https://dod.defense.gov/.

United States National Intelligence Council. *Global Trends 2030: Alternative Worlds* (2012).

——. *Global Trends 2035: Paradox of Progress* (2017).

——. *Global Trends 2040: A More Contested World* (2021).

United States National Security Commission on Artificial Intelligence. *Final Report* (2021).

United States Office of the Secretary of Defense. *Annual Report to Congress: Military and Security Developments Involving the People's Republic of China* (annual).

United States White House. *National Security Strategy of the United States of America*. 2017.

——. *2022 Indo-Pacific Strategy of the United States*. 2022.

World Bank. *World Development Indicators*. http://datatopics.worldbank.org/world -development-indicators/.

BOOKS, REPORTS, AND JOURNAL ARTICLES

Acharya, Amitav. *ASEAN and Regional Order: Revisiting Security Community in Southeast Asia*. New York: Routledge, 2021.

Albert, Eleanor. "North Korea's Military Capabilities." *CFR Backgrounder*. New York: Council on Foreign Relations, November 16, 2020. https://www.cfr.org/back grounder/north-koreas-military-capabilities.

Allison, Graham. *Destined for War: Can America and China Escape Thucydides's Trap?* Boston: Houghton Mifflin Harcourt, 2017.

Anwar, Dewi Fortuna. "Indonesia's Regional Foreign Policy After the 2019 Election." *Asia Policy* 14, no. 4 (2019): 72–78.

Ash, Alec. *China's New Youth: How The Young Generation Is Shaping China's Future*. New York: Arcade, 2020.

Ashley, Ryan and Apichai Shipper, "The Art of Thai Diplomacy: Parables of Alliance." *Pacific Affairs* 95, no. 2 (2022): 227–63.

Atanassova-Cornelis, Elena, Yoichiro Sato, and Tom Sauer, eds. *Alliances in Asia and Europe: The Evolving Indo-Pacific Strategic Context and Inter-Regional Alignments.* London: Routledge, 2024.

Atkinson, Joel. "China-Taiwan Diplomatic Competition and the Pacific Islands." *Pacific Review* 23, no. 4 (2010): 407–27.

Auslin, Michael R. *The End of the Asian Century: War, Stagnation, and the Risks to the World's Most Dynamic Region.* New Haven, CT: Yale University Press, 2017.

Ba, Alice. *(Re)Negotiating East and Southeast Asia: Region, Regionalism, and the Association of Southeast Asian Nations.* Stanford, CA: Stanford University Press, 2009.

Beardson, Timothy. *Ageing Giant: China's Looming Population Collapse.* Oxford: Signal Books, 2021.

Bennett, Bruce W. "South Korea: Capable Now, Questions for the Future." In *A Look at Hard Power: Assessing the Defense Capabilities of Key US Allies and Security Partners, Second Edition*, ed. Gary J. Schmitt. Carlisle, PA: US Army War College Press, 2020.

Bensahel, Nora. "Darker Shades of Gray: Why Gray Zone Conflicts Will Become More Frequent and Complex." *E-Notes*, Foreign Policy Research Institute, February 13, 2017.

Biggs, Ted, and Carolin Liss, eds. *Piracy in Southeast Asia: Trends, Hot Spots and Responses.* New York: Routledge, 2016.

Bjarnegard, Elin, and Joakim Kreutz. *Debating the East Asian Peace: What Is It. How It Came About. Will It Last?* Copenhagen: NIAS Press, 2017.

Botto, Kathryn. "How Unification Would Affect the Demographics of the Korean Peninsula." Carnegie Endowment for International Peace, June 29, 2021.

Bricker, Darrell, and John Ibbitson. *Empty Planet: The Shock of Global Population Decline.* New York: Broadway Books, 2019.

Brooks, Deborah Jordan, Stephen G. Brooks, Brian D. Greenhill, and Mark L. Haas. "The Demographic Transition Theory of War: Why Young Societies Are Conflict Prone and Old Societies Are the Most Peaceful." *International Security* 43, no. 3 (Winter 2018/19): 53–95.

Brose, Christian. "The New Revolution in Military Affairs: War's Sci-Fi Future," *Foreign Affairs* 98, no. 3 (May/June 2019), online edition.

Buzan, Barry, Ole Waever, and Jaap de Wilde, *Security: A New Framework for Analysis.* London: Lynne Rienner, 1998.

Caldwell, John C. *Demographic Transition Theory.* Leiden: Springer, 2006.

Campbell, Kurt. *The Pivot: The Future of American Statecraft in Asia.* New York: Twelve, 2016.

Catellier, Alex, and Markus Garlauskas. "Debunking the Korean Peninsula 'Arms Race': What's Behind South Korea's Military Force Development." *On Korea*, an academic paper series by the Korea Economic Institute of America (2022): 3–20. https:// keia.org/publication/defying-united-nations-sanctions-three-reasons-for-african -engagement-with-north-korea/.

Ceccorulli, Michela, Enrico Fassi, and Sonia Lucarelli. "NATO's Demographic Paradox." *Global Change, Peace and Security* 29, no. 3 (2017): 249–71. https://doi.org/10 .1080/14781158.2017.1361392.

Cha, Victor. *Powerplay: The Origins of the American Alliance System in Asia*. Princeton, NJ: Princeton University Press, 2016.

Chase, Michael S., Jeffrey Engstrom, Tai Ming Cheung et al. *China's Incomplete Military Transformation: Assessing the Weaknesses of the People's Liberation Army (PLA)*. Santa Monica, CA: RAND Corporation, 2015. https://www.rand.org/pubs/research_reports/RR893.html.

Chin, Warren. "Technology, War and the State." *International Affairs* 95, no. 4 (July 2019): 765–83.

Choucri, Nazli. *CyberPolitics in International Relations*. Cambridge, MA: MIT Press, 2012.

Choucri, Nazli, and Robert C. North. *Nations in Conflict: National Growth and International Violence*. San Francisco: Freeman, 1975.

Christensen, Thomas J. "China, the U.S.-Japan Alliance, and the Security Dilemma in East Asia." *International Security* 23, no. 4 (Spring 1999): 49–80.

Chung, Erin Aeran. "How South Korean Demographics Are Affecting Immigration and Social Change." Carnegie Endowment for International Peace, June 29, 2021.

——. *Immigrant Incorporation in East Asian Democracies*. New York: Cambridge University Press, 2020.

Chung, Min Lee. "South Korea's Grand Strategy in Transition: Coping with Existential Threats and New Political Forces." In *Strategic Asia 2017–18: Power, Ideas, and Military Strategy in the Asia-Pacific*, ed. Ashley J. Tellis, Alison Szalwinski, and Michael Wills, 107–39. Seattle: National Bureau of Asian Research, 2017.

Chung, Min Lee, and Kathryn Botto, eds. *Demographics and the Future of South Korea*. Washington, DC: Carnegie Endowment for International Peace, 2021.

Ciorciari, John. "The Variable Effectiveness of Hedging Strategies." *International Relations of the Asia-Pacific* 19, no. 3 (2019): 523–55.

Cliff, Roger. "A New U.S. Strategy for the Indo-Pacific." *NBR Special Report #86* (June). Seattle: National Bureau of Asian Research, 2020.

Copeland, Dale C. *The Origins of Major War*. Ithaca, NY: Cornell University Press, 2000.

Cronin, Patrick, Richard Fontaine, Zachary M. Hosford, Ely Ratner, and Alexander Sullivan. *The Emerging Asia Power Web*. Washington, DC: Center for a New American Security, June 2013.

Cutler, David M., James M. Poterba, Louise M. Sheiner, and Lawrence H. Summers. "An Aging Society: Opportunity or Challenge?" *Brookings Papers on Economic Activity*. Washington, DC: Brookings Institution.

Den Boer, Andrea, and Valerie Hudson. "Patrilineality, Son Preference, and Sex Selection in South Korea and Vietnam." *Population and Development Review* 43, no. 1 (March 2017): 119–47.

Denmark, Abraham M. *U.S. Strategy in the Asian Century: Empowering Allies and Partners*. New York: Columbia University Press, 2020.

Doyle, Timothy, and Dennis Rumley. *The Rise and Return of the Indo-Pacific*. Oxford: Oxford University Press, 2019.

Easton, Ian, Mark Stokes, Cortez A. Cooper III, and Arthur Chan. *Transformation of Taiwan's Reserve Force*. Santa Monica, CA: RAND, 2017. https://www.rand.org/pubs/research_reports/RR1757.html.

Easton, Ian, Mark Stokes, Yang Kuang-shun, Eric Lee, and Colby Ferland. *Watching Over the Taiwan Strait: The Role of Unmanned Aerial Vehicles in Taiwan's Defense Strategy*. Washington, DC: Project 2049 Institute, 2020.

Eberstadt, Nicholas. "Asia-Pacific Demographics in 2010–40: Implications for Strategic Balance." In *Strategic Asia, 2010–11: Asia's Rising Power and America's Continued Purpose*, ed. Ashley J. Tellis, Andrew Marble, and Travis Tanner, 237–78. Seattle: National Bureau of Asian Research, 2010.

——, ed. *China's Changing Family Structure: Dimensions and Implications*. Washington, DC: American Enterprise Institute, 2019.

——. "East Asia's Coming Population Collapse: And How It Will Reshape World Politics." *Foreign Affairs*, May 8, 2024.

——. "Russia's Peacetime Demographic Crisis: Dimensions, Causes, and Implications." *NBR Project Report* (May). Seattle: National Bureau of Asian Research, 2010.

——. "With Great Demographics Comes Great Power: Why Population Will Drive Geopolitics." *Foreign Affairs* 98, no. 4 (July/August 2019): 146–57.

Eggleston, Karen, Joon-Shik Park, and Gi-Wook Shin. *Demographics and Innovation in the Asia-Pacific*. Stanford: Walter H. Shorenstein Asia-Pacific Research Center, 2021.

Ehrlich, Paul R. *The Population Bomb*. New York: Ballentine Books, 1968.

Eldridge, Robert. "Japan's Changing Demographics and the Impact on Its Military." *Education About Asia* 22, no. 3 (Winter 2017): 27–30.

——. *Population Decline and the Self-Defense Forces* (in Japanese). Tokyo: Ikuhosha, 2019.

Emmerson, Donald K., ed. *The Deer and the Dragon: Southeast Asia and China in the 21st Century*. Stanford, CA: Walter H. Shorenstein Asia-Pacific Research Center, 2020.

Emmott, Stephen. *Ten Billion*. New York: Vintage Books/Random House, 2013.

Feyrer, James. "Demographics and Productivity in Asia." In *Demographics and Innovation in the Asia-Pacific*, ed. Karen Eggleston, Joon-Shik Park, and Gi-Wook Shin, 17–40. Stanford, CA: Walter H. Shorenstein Asia-Pacific Research Center, 2021.

Freedman, Lawrence. *The Future of War: A History*. New York: PublicAffairs, 2017.

Fukushima, Akiko. "From the Asia-Pacific to the Indo-Pacific: Drivers and Hurdles." *Policy Perspective*. Canada Global Affairs Institute, March 2021.

Gietel-Basten, Stuart. *The "Population Problem" in Pacific Asia*. Oxford: Oxford University Press, 2019.

Gindarsah, Iis, and Adhi Priamarizki. "Explaining Indonesia's Under-balancing: The Case of the Modernisation of the Air Force and the Navy." *Journal Asian Security and International Affairs* 8, no. 3 (2021): 391–412.

Glosserman, Brad. *Peak Japan: The End of Great Ambitions*. Washington, DC: Georgetown University Press, 2019.

Glosserman, Brad, and Tomoko Tsunoda. "The Guillotine: Demographics and Japan's Security Options." *PacNet* 45 (June 17, 2009). http://csis.org/files/publication/paco945.pdf.

Goldfarb, Avi, and Jon R. Lindsay. "Prediction and Judgment: Why Artificial Intelligence Increases the Importance of Humans in War." *International Security* 46, no. 3 (Winter 2021/22): 7–50. https://doi.org/10.1162/isec_a_00425.

Goldstone, Jack A., Eric P. Kaufmann, and Monica Duffy Toft, eds. *Political Demography: How Population Changes Are Reshaping International Security and National Politics*. New York: Oxford University Press, 2012.

Goodhart, Charles, and Manoj Pradhan. *The Great Demographic Reversal: Ageing Societies, Waning Inequality, and an Inflation Revival*. Cham, Switzerland: Palgrave Macmillian, 2020.

Goodkind, Daniel, Loraine West, and Peter Johnson. "A Reassessment of Mortality in North Korea, 1993–2008." Annual Meeting of the Population Association of America, Washington, DC, March 28, 2011.

Green, Michael J. *By More than Providence: Grand Strategy and American Power in the Asia Pacific Since 1783*. New York: Columbia University Press, 2017.

——. *Ironclad: Forging a New Future for America's Alliances*. Boulder, CO: Rowman & Littlefield, 2019.

Green, Michael J., Kathleen J. Hicks, and Zack Cooper. *Federated Defense in Asia*. Washington, D.C.: Center for Strategic and International Studies, 2014.

Grieco, Joseph. "Anarchy and the Limits of Cooperation: A Realist Critique of the Newest Liberal Institutionalism." *International Organization* 42, no. 3 (Summer 1998): 485–507.

Grieco, Joseph, Robert Powell, and Duncan Snidal. "The Relative-Gains Problem for International Cooperation." *American Political Science Review* 87, no. 3 (September 1993): 727–43.

Grossman, Derek, Michael S. Chase, Gerard Finin et al. *America's Pacific Island Allies: The Freely Associated States and Chinese Influence*. Santa Monica, CA: RAND, 2019.

Guillen, Mauro F. *2030: How Today's Biggest Trends Will Collide and Reshape the Future of Everything*. New York: St. Martin's Press, 2020.

Haas, Mark L. "A Geriatric Peace? The Future of U.S. Power in a World of Aging Populations." *International Security* 32, no. 1 (Summer 2007): 112–47.

Haerpfer, C., R. Inglehart, A. Moreno et al., eds. *World Values Survey: Round Seven—Country-Pooled Datafile Version 6.0*. Madrid and Vienna: JD Systems Institute and WVSA Secretariat, 2022. https://doi.org/10.14281/18241.24.

Hanggi, Heiner. *ASEAN and The ZOPFAN Concept*. Singapore: Institute of Southeast Asian Studies, 1991.

Harold, Scott W., Derek Grossman, Brian Harding et al. *The Thickening Web of Asian Security Cooperation: Deepening Defense Ties Among U.S. Allies and Partners in the Indo-Pacific*. Santa Monica, CA: RAND, 2019.

Harold, Scott W., Yoshiaki Nakagawa, Junichi Fukuda et al. *The U.S.–Japan Alliance and Deterring Gray Zone Coercion in the Maritime, Cyber, and Space Domains*. Santa Monica, CA: RAND, 2017.

Hayton, Bill. *The South China Sea: The Struggle for Power in Asia*. New Haven, CT: Yale University Press, 2014.

Heydarian, Richard. *The Rise of Duterte: A Populist Revolt Against Elite Democracy*. Singapore: Palgrave Macmillan, 2017.

Hicks, Kathleen, Zack Cooper, John Schaus, and Jake Douglas. *Countering Coercion in Maritime Asia: The Theory and Practice of Gray Zone Deterrence*. Washington, DC: Center for Strategic and International Studies, 2017.

Hiebert, Murray. *Under Beijing's Shadow: Southeast Asia's China Challenge*. Lanham, MD: Rowman and Littlefield, 2020.

Hiep, See Le Hong, and Anton Tsvetov, eds. *Vietnam's Foreign Policy Under Doi Moi.* Singapore: ISEAS Publishing, 2018.

Hornung, Jeffrey W. *Allies Growing Closer: Japan-Europe Security Ties in the Age of Strategic Competition.* Santa Monica, CA: RAND, 2020.

——. "Japan's Growing Hard Hedge Against China," *Asian Security* 10, no. 2 (2014): 97–122. https://doi.org/10.1080/14799855.2014.914497.

Hornung, Jeffrey W., Scott Savitz, Jonathan Balk, Samantha McBirney, Liam McClane, and Victoria M. Smith. "Preparing Japan's Multi-Domain Defense Force for the Future Battlespace Using Emerging Technologies." *Perspective* (July). Santa Monica, CA: RAND, 2021.

Hudson, Valerie, and Andrea Den Boer. "A Surplus of Men, a Deficit of Peace: Security and Sex Ratios in Asia's Largest States." *International Security* 26, no. 4 (Spring 2002): 5–38.

——. *Bare Branches: The Security Implications of Asia's Surplus Male Population.* Cambridge, MA: MIT Press, 2004.

Hughes, Christopher. *Japan's Security Agenda: Military, Economic, and Environmental Dimensions.* Boulder, CO: Lynne Rienner, 2004.

Inglehart, R., C. Haerpfer, A. Moreno et al., eds. *World Values Survey: Round Six—Country-Pooled Datafile Version.* Madrid: JD Systems Institute, 2014. https://www.worldvaluessurvey.org/WVSDocumentationWV6.jsp.

Ishihara, Yusuke. "Japan's Grand Strategy as a Declining Power." East Asia Forum. June 18, 2023. https://www.eastasiaforum.org/2023/06/18/japans-grand-strategy-as-a-declining-power/.

Izumikawa, Yasuhiro. "Network Connections and the Emergence of the Hub-and-Spokes Alliance System in East Asia." *International Security* 45, no. 2 (Fall 2020): 7–50.

Jackson, Richard, and Neil Howe. *The Graying of the Great Powers: Demography and Geopolitics in the 21st Century.* Washington, DC: Center for Strategic and International Studies, 2008.

Jervis, Robert. "Cooperation Under the Security Dilemma." *World Politics* 30 (1978): 167–214.

Jiang, Quanbao, Qun Yu, Shucai Yang, and Jesus J. Sanchez-Barricarte. "Changes in Sex Ratio at Birth in China: A Decomposition by Birth Order," *Journal of Biosocial Science* 49, no. 6 (2017): 826–41.

Jung, Joo-Sung, and Mye Sohn. "Korea's Military Service Policy Issues and Directions for Mid- and Long-term Development." *Korean Journal of Defense Analysis* 23, no. 4 (December 2011): 473–88.

Kaczmarska, Renata, and Masumi Ono. "Migration Trends and Families." *Policy Brief* 133 (May 2022). United Nations Department of Economic and Social Affairs.

Kania, Elsa B. *Battlefield Singularity: Artificial Intelligence, Military Revolution, and China's Future Military Power.* Washington, DC: Center for a New American Security, 2017.

Karim, Moch Faisal. "Role Legitimation in Foreign Policy: The Case of Indonesia as an Emerging Power Under Yudhoyono's Presidency (2004–2014)." *Foreign Policy Analysis* 17, no. 3 (2021).

Keohane, Robert O., and Helen V. Milner, eds. *Internationalization and Domestic Politics.* Cambridge: Cambridge University Press, 1996.

Khana, Parag. *The Future Is Asian*. New York: Simon & Shuster, 2019.

Khong, Yuen Foong. "Singapore and the Great Powers." In *Perspectives on the Security of* Singapore, ed. Barry Desker and Cheng Guan Ang. World Scientific, 2015. https://doi.org/10.1142/9632.

Koga, Kei. "Japan's Strategic Approach Toward Island States: Case of the Pacific Islands." *Journal of Indo-Pacific Affairs* 5, no. 7 (2022): 62–83.

——. *Managing Great Power Politics: ASEAN, Institutional Strategy, and the South China Sea*. Singapore: Palgrave Macmillan, 2022.

——. *Reinventing Regional Security Institutions in Asia and Africa: Power Shifts, Ideas, and Institutional Change*. London: Routledge, 2017.

——. "Singapore's Distinctive 'Quasi-Bases.'" In *Exploring Base Politics: How Host Countries Shape the Network of U.S. Overseas Bases*, ed. Shinjia Kawana and Minori Takahashi. New York: Routledge, 2020.

——. "Wedge Strategies, Japan-ASEAN Cooperation, and the Making of EAS: Implications for Indo-Pacific Institutionalization." In *The Courteous Power: Japan and Southeast Asia in the Indo-Pacific Era*, ed. John D. Ciorciari and Kiyoteru Tsutsui, 73–96. Ann Arbor: University of Michigan Press, 2021.

Koh, Collin Swee Lean. "What Next for the Indonesian Navy? Challenges and Prospects for Attaining the Minimum Essential Force by 2024." *Contemporary Southeast Asia* 37, no. 3 (2015): 432–62.

Korean Institute of Child Care and Education. "President Yoon's Government Policies for Enhancing Child-Rearing." *KICCE Policy Brief* 23 (October 2022). https://kicce.re.kr.

Kossova, Tatiana, Elena Kossova, and Maria Sheluntcova. "Gender Gap in Life Expectancy in Russia: The Role of Alcohol Consumption." *Social Policy and Society* 19, no. 1 (January 2020): 37–53. https://doi.org/10.1017/S1474746419000058.

Kuik, Cheng-Chwee. "Malaysia Between the United States and China: What Do Weaker States Hedge Against?" *Asian Politics and Policy* 8, no. 1 (2016): 155–77.

Le, Tom Phuong. "Japan and the Revolution in Military Affairs. *Journal of Asian Security and International Affairs* 5, no. 2 (2018): 172–96. https://doi.org/10.1177/2347797018783112.

——. *Japan's Aging Peace: Pacifism and Militarism in the Twenty-First Century*. New York: Columbia University Press, 2021.

Lee, Chung Min. "South Korea's Military Needs Bold Reforms to Overcome a Shrinking Population." Carnegie Endowment for International Peace, June 29, 2021.

Lee, Chung Min, and Kathryn Botto. *Demographics and the Future of South Korea*. Washington, DC: Carnegie Endowment for International Peace, 2021.

Lee, Hyun-Hoon, and Donghyun Park. *Post-COVID Asia: Deglobalization, Fourth Industrial Revolution, and Sustainable Development*. Singapore: World Scientific, 2021.

Lee, Kai-fu. *AI Superpowers: China, Silicon Valley, and the New World Order*. New York: Houghton Mifflin, 2018.

Lee, Ronald. "The Demographic Transition: Three Centuries of Fundamental Change." *Journal of Economic Perspectives* 17, no. 4 (Fall 2003): 167–90.

Lee, Sook Jong. "Generational Divides and the Future of South Korean Democracy." Carnegie Endowment for International Peace, June 29, 2021.

Libicki, Martin C., Howard J. Shatz, and Julie E. Taylor. *Global Demographic Change and Its Implications for Military Power*, Santa Monica, CA: Rand Corporation, 2011.

Liff, Adam P. "Beyond Territorial Defense? The U.S.-Japan and U.S.-ROK Alliances and a 'Taiwan Strait Contingency.'" *Pacific Review* (2024): 1–30. https://doi.org/10.1080/09512748.2024.2400277.

Lowrey, Annie. *Give People Money: How a Universal Basic Income Would End Poverty, Revolutionize Work, and Remake the World*. New York: Crown, 2018.

Mahbubani, Kishore. *The New Asian Hemisphere: The Shift of Global Power to the East*. New York: Public Affairs, 2008.

Malthus, Thomas. *An Essay on the Principle of Population*. London: Reeves and Turner, 1888.

Magnus, George. *The Age of Aging: How Demographics Are Changing the Global Economy and Our World*. Singapore: Wiley, 2009.

Mastro, Oriana Skylar. "The Taiwan Temptation: Why Beijing Might Resort to Force." *Foreign Affairs* 100, no. 4 (July/August 2021): 58–67.

McKinsey Global Institute. "AI, Automation, and the Future of Work: Ten Things to Solve For." *Briefing Note*, June 2018.

McNamara, Whitney. *Perspectives on Taiwan: Insights from the 2017 Taiwan-U.S. Policy Program*, ed. Bonnie S. Glaser and Matthew P. Funaiole. Center for Strategic and International Studies, 2018. https://doi.org/10.2307/resrep22433.13.

Mearsheimer, John. *The Tragedy of Great Power Politics*. New York: Norton, 2001.

Melvin, Neil. "Russia and the Indo-Pacific Security Concept." In *Emerging Insights*. London: Royal United Services Institute for Defense and Strategic Studies, May 2021.

Menon, Jayant, and Anna Melendez-Nakamura. "Aging in Asia: Trends, Impacts and Responses." Asian Development Bank, February 2009.

Midford, Paul. *The Senkaku Islands Confrontation and the Transformation of Japan's Defense*. New York: Palgrave Macmillan, 2025.

Midford, Paul, and Wilhelm Vosse, eds. *New Directions in Japan's Security*. London: Routledge, 2020.

Miller, Chris. *We Shall Be Masters: Russian Pivots to East Asia from Peter the Great to Putin*. Cambridge, MA: Harvard University Press, 2021.

Molter, Vanessa. "Taiwan's Transition to All-Volunteer Force—a Policy Assessment." *Defense Security Brief 8*, no. 3 (October 2019): 48–49. https://indsr.org.tw/en.

Moravcsik, Andrew. "Taking Preferences Seriously: A Liberal Theory of international Politics." *International Organization* 51, no. 4 (Autumn 1997): 513–53.

Morland, Paul. *The Human Tide: How Population Shaped the Modern World*. New York: Hachette Book Group, 2019.

Moon, Katharine H. S. "South Korea's Demographic Changes and Their Political Impact." *East Asia Policy Paper* 6 (October). Washington, DC: Brookings Institution, 2015.

Nam, Kijeong. "Aging Population, Decreasing Birthrate and National Security: Searching for the Possibility of Cooperation Between Japan and Korea." In *Japan Study as a Public Good in Asia*, ed. L. Huang et al., 17–27. Singapore: Springer Nature Singapore Pte, 2019.

Nauck, Bernard. "Value of Children and the Framing of Fertility: Results from a Cross-Cultural Comparative Survey in 10 Societies." *European Sociological Review* 23, no. 5 (December 2007): 615–29. https://doi.org/10.1093/esr/jcm028.

Oh, Kongdan and Ralph Hassig. *North Korea in a Nutshell: A Contemporary Overview.* Lanham, MD: Rowman & Littlefield, 2021.

Oizumi, Keiichiro. *Aging in Asia: When the Structure of Prosperity Changes.* Tokyo: Oriental Life Insurance Cultural Development Center, 2013.

Ono, Keishi. "Demographics and Security: Defense Capabilities Building and Economic Hegemony Towards the 22nd Century." *NIDS Journal of Defense and Security* 18 (December 2017): 33–57.

Organski, A.F.K., Jacek Kugler, J. Timothy Johnson, and Youssef Cohen. *Births, Deaths, and Taxes: The Demographic and Political Transitions.* Chicago: University of Chicago Press, 1984.

Oros, Andrew L. "Addressing America's Aging Allies in Asia." *Global Asia* (June 2021): 76–84.

——. *Japan's Security Renaissance: New Policies and Politics for the Twenty-First Century.* New York: Columbia University Press, 2017.

——. "The Rising Security Challenge of East Asia's 'Dual Graying': Implications for U.S.-Led Security Architecture in the Indo-Pacific." *Asia Policy* (April 2023): 75–100.

Oros, Andrew L., and Bailey Brya. "New Census Results Underscore Security Challenges of Aging in the Indo-Pacific." *Asia Dispatches*, June 3, 2021. https://www .wilsoncenter.org/blog-post/new-census-results-underscore-security-challenges -aging-indo-pacific.

Oros, Andrew L., and Andrew Gordan. "The Quad Should Help India Address Its Most Pressing Security Challenge: Climate Change." *New Security Beat*, December 7, 2021. Woodrow Wilson International Center for Scholars, Washington, DC. https://www .newsecuritybeat.org/2021/12/quad-india-address-pressing-security-challenge -climate-change/.

Patierno, Kaitlyn, Elizabeth Leahy Madsen, and Smita Gaith. "The Demographic Dividend: Positive Prospects, Unclear Path." In *A Research Agenda for Political Demography*, ed. Jennifer D. Sciubba, 199–214. Northampton, MA: Edward Elgar, 2021.

Payne, Kenneth. "Artificial Intelligence: A Revolution in Strategic Affairs?" *Survival* 60, no. 5 (2018): 7–32. https://doi.org/10.1080/00396338.2018.1518374.

Quirk, Sean, and John Bradford. "Maritime Fulcrum: A New U.S. Opportunity to Engage Indonesia." *Issues and Insights* 15, no. 9 (October 2015), Pacific Forum.

Rapp-Hooper, Mira. *Shields of the Republic: The Triumph and Peril of America's Alliances.* Cambridge, MA: Harvard University Press, 2020.

Ratner, Ely. *Resident Power: Building a Politically Sustainable U.S. Military Presence in Southeast Asia and Australia.* Washington, DC: Center for a New American Security, 2013.

Roy, Denny. "Prospects for Taiwan Maintaining Its Autonomy Under Chinese Pressure." *Asian Survey* 57, no. 6 (2017): 1135–58.

Rozelle, Scott, and Natalie Hell. *Invisible China: How the Urban-Rural Divide Threatens China's Rise.* Chicago: University of Chicago Press, 2020.

Sasaki, Tomoyuki. *Japan's Postwar Military and Civil Society.* London: Bloomsbury Academic, 2017.

Scarth, William. "Population Aging, Productivity and Living Standards." In *The Review of Economic Performance and Social Progress: Towards a Social Understanding of*

Productivity, ed. Andrew Sharpe, France St-Hilaire, and Keith Banting. Montreal: Institute for Research on Public Policy, 2002.

Scharre, Paul. *Army of None: Autonomous Weapons and the Future of War*. New York: Norton, 2019.

Schmitt, Gary J., ed. *A Look at Hard Power: Assessing the Defense Capabilities of Key US Allies and Security Partners, Second Edition*. Carlisle, PA: US Army War College, 2020.

Schoff, James L. *Uncommon Alliance for the Common Good: The United States and Japan After the Cold War*. Washington, DC: Carnegie Endowment for International Peace, 2017.

Sciubba, Jennifer Dabbs. "Coffins Versus Cradles: Russian Population, Foreign Policy, and Power Transition Theory." *International Area Studies Review* 17, no. 2 (June 2014): 205–21.

——. *Eight Billion and Counting: How Sex, Death, and Migration Shape Our World*. New York: Norton, 2022.

——. *The Future Faces of War: Population and National Security*. Santa Barbara, CA: Praeger, 2011.

——. "A New Framework for Aging and Security." In *Political Demography: How Population Changes Are Reshaping International Security and National Politics*, ed. Jack A. Goldstone, Eric P. Kaufmann, and Monica Duffy Toft. New York: Oxford University Press, 2012.

Sciubba, Jennifer Dabbs, and Chien-Kai Chen. "The Politics of Population Aging in Singapore and Taiwan: A Comparison." *Asian Survey* 57, no. 4: 641–64.

Shambaugh, David. *Where Great Powers Meet: America and China in Southeast Asia*. New York: Oxford University Press, 2021.

Sheen, Seongho. "Northeast Asia's Aging Population and Regional Security: 'Demographic Peace?'" *Asian Survey* 53, no. 2 (March/April 2013): 292–318.

Shin, David, and Young-Gon Kim, "Military Recruitment Issues in the ROK Armed Forces and Policy Alternatives: Focusing on the Army Non-Commissioned Officer." *Korean Journal of Defense Analysis* 31, no. 3 (September 2019): 457–75. https://www.kida.re.kr.

Singer, P. W. *Wired for War: The Robotics Revolution and Conflict in the 21st Century*. New York: Penguin Books, 2009

Singer, P. W., and August Cole. *Ghost Fleet: A Novel of the Next World War*. New York: Mariner Books, 2016.

Singer, P. W., and Allan Friedman. *Cybersecurity and Cyberwar: What Everyone Needs to Know*. Oxford: Oxford University Press, 2014.

Slavov, Sita Nataraj. "A Framework for Understanding Universal Basic Income." *Tax Notes Federal* 170 (February 22, 2021). http://www.taxnotes.com.

Smith, Sheila. *Japan Rearmed: The Politics of Military Power*. Cambridge, MA: Harvard University Press, 2019.

Snyder, Scott A. *South Korea at the Crossroads: Autonomy and Alliance in an Era of Rival Powers*. New York: Columbia University Press, 2018.

Song, Weiqing, and Joseph Ching Velasco. "Selling 'Independent Foreign Policy' amid the US-China Rivalry: Populism and Philippine Foreign Policy Under the Duterte Government." *Pacific Review* (2022). https://doi.org/10.1080/09512748.2022.2137227.

Srinivasan, Sharada, and Shuzhou Li. "Unifying Perspectives on Scarce Women and Surplus Men." In *Scarce Women and Surplus Men in China and India: Macro Demographics Versus Local Dynamics*, ed. Sharada Srinivasan and Shuzhou Li. New York: Springer, 2018.

Stephen, Elizabeth Hervey. "Policy Concerns of Low Fertility for Military Planning in South Korea." *Asia-Pacific Issues*, no. 102 (November). Washington, DC: East-West Center, 2011.

——. *South Korea's Demographic Dividend: Echoes of the Past or Prologue to the Future?* Washington, DC: Center for Strategic and International Studies, 2019.

Strangarone, Troy. "South Korea's Demographic Decline and National Security." Ms., October 27, 2021.

Strangio, Sebastian. *In the Dragon's Shadow: Southeast Asia in the Chinese Century*. New Haven, CT: Yale University Press, 2020.

Sukma, Rizal. "Indonesia, ASEAN, and Shaping the Indo-Pacific Idea." *East Asia Forum Quarterly* (October–December 2019): 11–12. https://search.informit.org/doi/epdf/10 .3316/INFORMIT.281227453826465.

Susskind, Daniel. *A World Without Work: Technology, Automation, and How We Should Respond*. New York: Metropolitan Books, 2020.

Tammen, Ronald L., Jacek Kugler, Douglas Lemke et al. *Power Transitions: Strategies for the Twenty-First Century*. New York: Chatham House, 2000.

Taylor, Brendan. *The Four Flashpoints: How Asia Goes to War*. Carlton, Australia: La Trobe University Press, 2018.

Teo, Ang Guan, and Kei Koga "Conceptualizing Equidistant Diplomacy in International Relations: The Case of Singapore." *International Relations of the Asia-Pacific* 22, no. 3 (2022): 375–409.

Thalang, Chanintira na. "Unpacking Thailand's Conceptions of and Position Within the Liberal International Order." *International Affairs* 99, no. 4 (2023): 1519–36.

Thompson, Drew. "Winning the Fight Taiwan Cannot Afford to Lose." *Strategic Forum*, no. 310 (October 2021). Washington, DC: Institute for National Strategic Studies, National Defense University.

Thu, Huong Le. "Vietnam's Persistent Foreign Policy Dilemma: Caught Between Self-Reliance and Proactive Integration." *Asia Policy* 13, no. 4 (2018): 123–44.

Wallace, Corey John. "The Evolution of the Japanese Strategic Imagination and Generation Change: A Generationally Focused Analysis of Public and Elite Attitudes Towards War and Peace in Japan." PhD diss., University of Auckland, 2014.

Walt, Stephen M. "Does Anyone Still Understand the 'Security Dilemma'?" *Foreign Policy* (July 26, 2022).

Weiner, Myron, and Sharon Stanton Russell, eds. *Demography and National Security*. New York: Berghahn Books, 2001.

Wicaksana, I Gede Wahyu. "Indonesia's Foreign Policy: The Need for a New Approach." *Southeast Asian Affairs* (2023): 136–46.

Williams, Michael C. "Words, Images, Enemies: Securitization and International Politics." *International Studies Quarterly* 47 (December 2003): 511–31.

Yamaguchi Shinji, Yatsuzuka Masaaki, and Momma Rira, eds. "NIDS China Security Report 2023: China's Quest for Control of the Cognitive Domain and Gray Zone Situations." National Institute for Defense Studies, 2022.

Yeo, Andrew. *Asia's Regional Architecture: Alliance and Institutions in the Pacific Century.* Stanford, CA: Stanford University Press, 2019.

——. "South Korea's New Southern Policy and the United States Indo-Pacific Strategy: Implications for the U.S.-ROK Alliance." *Mansfield Foundation Working Paper,* July 2021.

——. *State, Society, and Markets in North Korea.* Cambridge: Cambridge University Press, 2021.

Yoshihara, Susan, and Douglas Sylva, eds. *Population Decline and the Remaking of Great Power Politics.* Washington, DC: Potomac Books, 2011.

Yoshihara, Toshi, and Jack Bianchi. *Seizing on Weakness: Allied Strategy for Competing with China's Globalizing Military.* Washington, DC: Center for Strategic and Budgetary Assessments, 2021.

INDEX

Muslims, 24, 25, 199

Myanmar, 58, 62, 196, 210, 219, 267n20; coup, 183, 232–33; Rohingya Muslims in, 25

National Defense Authorization, U.S., 133

National Defense Report, Taiwan, 123, 128, 130–31

National Development Council, Taiwan, 126

National Institute for Defense Studies (2023), Japan, 102

national security: demographic change and, 28–30, 64–65; demographic measures relevant to, 24; documents, 52, 88; early twenty-first century studies on demographic change impacting, 40–44; five stages of global demographic transition, 31–33; hypothesized effects of late-stage rapid aging on military security, 38–39, *39*, 45; international relations theory with demographics and, 30–40; oppression with demography as threat to, 25; population variables influencing military security, *36*; rapid aging influencing, 45–49; rapid aging with demographics and, 184–86; second-order effects of late-stage rapid aging on military security, 45–47, *46*; strategies, 4, 86, 88, 92, 94, 95, 100, 102–6, 136, 192

nativism, 23, 227

NATO. *See* North Atlantic Treaty Organization

Natuna Islands, 204

Nauru, 250n13

navies, 132, 135, 151, 203

Nepal, 58, 198

net migration, 19, 22–23

New Caledonia, 250n13

New Southbound Policy, Taiwan, 134

New Zealand, 9, 52, 58, 213, 217, 238; ANZUS treaty, 76, 186, 193; China and, 187; immigration, 61, 182, 188,

227; life expectancy, 246n33; military, 43, 73, 76, 78, 191, 193, 194, 233; populations, 61, 178, 185, 227, 232, 235; security partnerships, 191, 193, 218, 250n12; as super-aged by 2031, 180, 186; TFRs, 75; U.S. and, 73, 76, 78, 186, 191, 193, 233

NIDS. *See* National Institute for Defense Studies

Nigeria, 201, 250n11

Niue, 250n13

non-Han population, 168

non-NATO allies, 76, 193, 215

North Atlantic Treaty Organization (NATO), 43, 95, 105, 199, 238, 251n28; female troops, 100, 114; non allies, 76, 193, 215

Northeast Asia. *See* autocracies; democracies

Northeast Asian 6, 144, 180, 194, 209, 214; "aging" status, 147, 170; immigrants, 182; life expectancy, 149; military, 156, 164–65, 174; population shrinkage, 153, 196. *See also* China; Japan; North Korea; Russia; South Korea; Taiwan

Northern Mariana Islands, 250n13

Northern Territories, disputed, 145, 152

North Korea, 3, 36, 41, 83, 89, 144, 147; birth rate, 154; demographics–security nexus, *153*; life expectancy, 149, 184, 249n29; median age, 70; military, 44, 52–53, 69–70, 86, 90, 107–8, 153–54, 156, 164–65; Northeast Asian 6, 149, 153, 156, 164–65; nuclear weapons, 53, 69, 87–88, 112, 120, 154–55, 229–30, 252n4; populations, 61, 70, 115, 153–55, 250n14, 251n25, 262n22; South Korea and, 1, 69, 70, 73, 88, 108, 110–12, 117, 120–21, 154, 155, 234; as super-aged by 2040, 80, 153; as threat, 12, 65, 69–70, 78, 95, 102, 108, 112, 115, 116, 154, 184

nuclear accident, 20, 224, 228

"nuclear free zone," 76

nuclear submarines, 135, 189, 191, 193

GPSR Authorized Representative: Easy Access System Europe, Mustamäe tee
50, 10621 Tallinn, Estonia, gpsr.requests@easproject.com